Backcountry Democracy
and the Whiskey Insurrection

Backcountry Democracy and the Whiskey Insurrection

The Legal Culture and Trials, 1794–1795

LINDA MYRSIADES

The University of Georgia Press
ATHENS

© 2024 by the University of Georgia Press
Athens, Georgia 30602
www.ugapress.org
All rights reserved
Set in 10.5/13.5 Adobe Caslon Pro Regular by Kaelin Chappell Broaddus

Most University of Georgia Press titles are
available from popular e-book vendors.

Printed digitally

Library of Congress Cataloging-in-Publication Data

Names: Myrsiades, Linda, 1941– author.
Title: Backcountry democracy and the whiskey insurrection :
the legal culture and trials, 1794–1795 / Linda Myrsiades.
Description: Athens : The University of Georgia Press, 2024. |
Includes bibliographical references and index.
Identifiers: LCCN 2023038217 | ISBN 9780820366265 (hardback) | ISBN 9780820366241
(paperback) | ISBN 9780820366258 (epub) | ISBN 9780820366272 (pdf)
Subjects: LCSH: Whiskey Rebellion, Pa., 1794. | Tax protests and appeals—Pennsylvania. |
Government, Resistance to—Pennsylvania—History. | Alcoholic beverages—Taxation—
Law and legislation—United States—States—History. | United States—Politics and
government—History. | Pennsylvania—Politics and government—History.
Classification: LCC KFP471.5 .M97 2024 | DDC 973.4/3—dc23/eng/20230929
LC record available at https://lccn.loc.gov/2023038217

*For Nathan,
who
taught me to Build-A-Bear
so I could
build-a-book*

CONTENTS

ACKNOWLEDGMENTS ix

INTRODUCTION 1

PART I

CHAPTER 1
The Government Narrative and Its Western "Experiment"
21

CHAPTER 2
Federal, State, and Popular Law in the Western Country
59

CHAPTER 3
The Culture of Resistance and Its Agitation-Propaganda
98

PART II

CHAPTER 4
Judges and Grand Jury Charges
129

CHAPTER 5
The Trials, 1795
161

CHAPTER 6
A Rebel Defense
207

CONCLUSION
An Afterword
237

APPENDIX A
Trial Research Sources
251

APPENDIX B
Trial Records
254

NOTES 257

BIBLIOGRAPHY 305

INDEX 331

ACKNOWLEDGMENTS

I would like to thank first and foremost West Chester University for making this research possible. Their staff and services were indispensable to locating and accessing documents, maps, and rare primary materials in manuscript. In particular, Ron McColl's excellence and expertise and his ability to find the unfindable deserves high praise; Jennifer O'Leary's ability and willingness to provide speedy turnaround from interlibrary sources has over the years made my work much easier. The Historical Society of Pennsylvania deserves special mention as an incredible resource for this study. I thank the anonymous readers from University of Georgia, whose detailed readings allowed me to make much-needed emendations to the draft of this book. Gautham Rao has been especially supportive on historical matters in offering his time to read an unknown colleague's work and for helpful comments to keep the work going. To Richard Newman, Esq., I extend my gratitude for being available on legal questions, and for being a willing reader of my work in legal history. I am particularly appreciative of the kindness of Wythe Holt, a scholar of long standing in this field, who has graciously provided an unpublished manuscript to assist me in my work. And I readily share my gratitude to my editor, Nate Holly at University of Georgia Press, who is far and away the best editor I have had the good fortune to work with. I appreciate the permissions granted for reprinting images by the Library Company of Philadelphia and Bridgeman Images. I would like to acknowledge especially the *Pennsylvania Magazine of History and Biography*, in whose pages parts of chapter 4 of the present work were originally published, in a different form, for permission to use that material. Finally, I would be remiss if I did not share my affection and deepest gratitude to the person who kept me going and inputted my computer changes while I struggled through a crushed wrist and broken shoulder that left me feeling like a turtle turned on its back—thank you Kostas.

Backcountry Democracy
and the Whiskey Insurrection

INTRODUCTION

[Hamilton]: Sir, is this about the Whiskey Rebellion?
[Washington]: You could've given me a word of warning.
—LIN-MANUEL MIRANDA, "One Last Ride," *Hamilton*

Lin-Manuel Miranda's musical *Hamilton* opened on Broadway in 2015 and proceeded to win eight Drama Critics' Awards, eleven Tony awards, a Pulitzer Prize for drama, and a Grammy for best musical theater album. Had the world seen an earlier draft, it would have heard a different version of the song "One Last Ride," a late twentieth-century take on the Whiskey Rebellion.[1] In this variation, George Washington expresses his impatience with Alexander Hamilton when he hears about the rebellion, as if to suggest that it was an event that would have pleased his secretary of the treasury who at the very least "could've given me a word of warning." For his part, Hamilton shifts the blame to Thomas Jefferson, whom he depicts as an agitator with an interest in creating discontent, even though Jefferson had already resigned his position of secretary of state. Still, Hamilton, obsessed with paying the country's war debt, avows, "The whiskey tax is very unpopular / But necessary, sir."

Like the Roman general Cincinnatus, Washington is distracted by his desire to retire to his country estate, preoccupied with memorializing his run as president, and annoyed with the mess James Madison made of the first draft of his farewell address, which is still two years away. In response to Washington's wish to "teach 'em how to say goodbye," Hamilton asks, "But what about the rebels / Who are mad about this whiskey?" "First," Washington insists, "write my farewell address," playing on Hamilton's reputation as the fixer in his administration and the fact that Hamilton had been drafting the president's proclamations to the nation throughout the rebellion.

Ultimately, Miranda's Washington declares he's ready for "[o]ne last ride" while he's still in his prime. He has a plan to "win this thing!" but needs Hamilton by his side. Assuming his historical role in accompanying Washington to join the federal army sent to quell the rebellion, Hamilton prods Washington to suit up and flatters him that he was "born to lead" and can reign "as long as you're alive." Washington's false modesty makes him appear a reluctant warrior, as he "never wanted a crown [. . .] never wanted to lead." But lead he must as he takes what purports to be his "last ride" against an "outgunned," "outmanned," "outnumbered," "outplanned" bunch of tax dodgers, shouting, "Pay your fucking taxes." Hamilton presents his boss as "the greatest man in all the land" and cries out, "Please rise for your president." "George Washington," the crowd acclaims, to which Hamilton adds—having stage-managed the whole charade—"History has its eyes on you!"

Intentionally or not, Miranda touches on central themes in our changing understanding of an event in early American history that served as a stress test for the new country's experiment in democracy, primarily the conflict between Republican and Federalist partisan interests; Hamilton's overweening ambition in pursuing and enforcing a federal excise tax; and Washington's preoccupation with his reputation and his public image. But it was also a question of who controlled the government's position (the solitary Hamilton or the more collaborative Washington) and why the rebels were constructed not as citizens participating in democracy but as rabble undermining the development of a nation. More consequentially, it was a test of whether the events of 1794 were merely a question of a tax on whiskey or a struggle between competing visions for the United States—localism and democratic rights as opposed to centralized power and federal control over the states.

Views of the rebellion have continued to shift over time because historians failed to take on the challenge of dealing seriously with the rebel perspective. To what extent was popular resistance a question of the First Amendment rights of petitioning, assembly, speech, association, and the right to bear arms? How invested were the people in representative democracy and constitutional rule? Who were these rebels, what were their views, and how did they express them?

Once one begins to probe popular assemblies and examine popular culture, it becomes clear that their struggle was more than a riot over paying a whiskey tax. It extended to whether frontier settlers' homesteads would be foreclosed and families ejected, as well as to the unavailability of currency and a punishing debt crisis. The government's failure to protect westerners from Indians, war debt, land speculation, and a lack of public loans; to remove British forts; and to gain access to the Mississippi River were all part of the rebels' grievances, leading to violence and threats of secession from the union of states.

The disrespect for convention that *Hamilton* displays gives us permission to see the Whiskey Rebellion through different lenses. For the present study, the reader should take away a new perspective that understands the rebel world as the rebels saw it—apart from the framing given them by their powerful opponent—not merely what they revealed about themselves or their view of the federal government, but also what the government revealed about its predispositions and needs in opposing them. What the reader takes away is more than the tale of struggle between participatory democracy and centralized government power. It is the story of a struggle for liberty transformed into the paranoia and delusion of anarchy as told by Hamilton and Washington. It is the story of a founding document that enabled continuing revolution as much as it controlled democratic impulses. It is a tale of choice in one's allegiance turning into a movement for secession that could dissolve a government or undermine the unity of states.

What the study offers is a picture of Anti-Federalist rebels continuing the Revolution and an antidemocratic government having settled into a counterrevolutionary stance. The allegiance demanded of the rebels was no more than the old Blackstonian trade of obedience for protection, except that protection was hardly in evidence for the western country, whereas Washington's model for governance was uncomfortably close to what he knew, had experience of, and understood—English-style rule. The conditions under which the new government operated were striking. Washington had an intense fear of rebel assemblies, Anti-Federalist societies, and the worst excesses of the French Revolution. But the same attributes that had won Americans their freedom were inherent in the entities he feared. The assemblies were representative entities and exhibited organizational skills that recalled the committees of correspondence and the self-governance of the Continental Congress. The democratic-republican clubs exemplified the principled pragmatism of grounded political theory and debate. And the French Revolution expressed the combination of excessive democracy, localism, and self-organizing military force. Similarly, the justification that colonists had brought with them to America—the legitimate rights of Englishmen—was mimicked by the whiskey rebels, whose legitimate rights appeared in the bills of rights in state constitutions and the U.S. Constitution.

Whatever the commonalities of the Whiskey Rebellion and the American Revolution, from the perspective of Washington's government the Revolutionary War was a "natural" response to unlawful rule, not disobedience or rebellion, whereas the Whiskey Rebellion was a delusional and deceptive reaction to legitimate government. The Declaration of Independence was regarded as nation building, not government destroying, while the petitions, resolutions, and grievances of the whiskey rebels were considered perverse and imagined. In the government's reading, the Constitution was intended to discipline democracy, which the whiskey rebels countered with "constitutional resistance"—the mantra under which they fought to regulate government and control its abuse of its citizens' liberties. Thus, in the hands of the new government, the Constitution justified state violence in opposition to popular violence that supported self-governance, personal liberties, and antistatism. In his address to Congress, Washington himself celebrated citizens who joined the federal army that would tame the rebels, declaiming that they understood the "true principles of Government and liberty"—that they were an "army of the constitution."[2]

What the reader takes away from this study, in sum, is a fuller understanding of the importance, and the limitations, of participatory democracy by factoring in what has been left out—the role the rebel perspective played in balancing centralized government power in America's first opportunity to face what democracy meant, for all its fears and faults.

Rebellion

To understand the role of the rebels, we need first to lay out a picture of the context in which the rebellion festered and then broke out into violence. From 1791 to 1793, a series of local meetings and county assemblies in the western counties greeted the imposition of the 1791 federal excise tax on whiskey. In addition, inhabitants of Fayette, Washington, Westmoreland, and Alleghany counties attacked tax collectors; officials were variously kidnapped, tarred and feathered, ridden on a rail, or left tied to a tree in the forest; liberty poles were mounted and excise officers hung in effigy; and distillers and officials alike were harassed by bands of disguised figures. The most serious violence, however, broke out in 1794 when U.S. marshal David

Lenox and inspector of the survey general John Neville began serving writs on noncompliant distillers. On July 16–17, 1794, two attacks against Neville's house at Bower Hill and a turbulent meeting at Couch's Fort left Neville's home destroyed and rebel Oliver Miller and rebel militia leader James McFarlane dead. Those involved in the violence demanded the support of their confederates, which moved events to a new stage in which a radical mob controlled events.

An ad hoc assembly of several rebel factions convened at Mingo Creek (July 23) to address the mob's demands. That assembly resolved to hold a representative, elected assembly at Parkinson's Ferry (August 14) where delegates from the four western counties could consult on a common course of action. The consensus reached at Mingo Creek was breached by a small group of radicals led by David Bradford, who decided to rob the U.S. Mail (July 26). The group immediately called local militias to an interim rendezvous at Braddock's Field on August 1. There, they revealed letters that had been written in opposition to the excise tax and demanded the writers be exiled. The highly charged crowd armed itself and marched on Pittsburgh. With the assistance of moderate rebels who provisioned the marchers with drink, inhabitants invited the rebels into the city and the march was transformed into a drunken revel.

The 1794 developments effaced ground gained from 1791 to 1793 in meetings that had argued broadly for protection of constitutional liberties, equal treatment within the Union, and redress of the people's economic grievances. With the rebels split, the radical faction now argued for a plan that included armed response and secession; moderates argued for a more temperate rights-based approach. The Washington administration objected to the erratic attacks on officials and the political organizing that took place in assemblies, which in Washington and Hamilton's minds appeared to compete with legitimate institutions.[3] Washington convened a conference of his cabinet and top Pennsylvania officials on August 2 that questioned whether treason had been committed and the need for a federal militia to quell the rebellion. The prospect of public protests, political resistance, and difficulty in recruiting volunteers for a national army persuaded Washington to appoint a U.S. Commission to meet with the rebels in concert with a Pennsylvania Commission.

In the meantime, moderates in the August 4 Parkinson's Ferry assembly had successfully generated a common position based on constitutional resistance. This proved to be a turning point for the rebellion and the basis for sending a rebel delegation to confer with the U.S. Commission on August 21. Negotiations with the commission appeared to legitimize the political authority of the assemblies, despite the instructions under which the commission operated and the administration's preparations to mount a federal militia. With Washington and Hamilton determined to put an end to the assembly experiment, a subsequent assembly in Brownsville (August 28) produced some of the most powerful speeches of the rebellion in defense of the western position. A final U.S. Commission report followed advising the president on September 24 that it could not fulfill its mission of dictating terms of submission in exchange for an offer of amnesty. Washington then deployed the federal militia, which he met at its staging point in Carlisle on October 4. Having reviewed the troops and provided orders to its commander, General Henry Lee, he returned to Philadelphia on October 20. On November 13, in the dead of night, the federal militia rounded up some 150 rebels, many barefoot or half-naked, prodded them along for seven miles on muddy roads to Pittsburgh and housed them in pens and stables. The captured rebels were then turned over for interrogation and eighteen of them were charged by the U.S. district judge and the U.S. attorney for Pennsylvania, who had accompanied the army. They were marched over the mountains three hundred miles to Philadelphia, none among them leaders of the violence. Together with other rebels gathered in the city, and including rebels who had fled, twenty-four were indicted for treason by the Eastern Pennsylvania Circuit Court. Ten were tried; two were convicted and subsequently pardoned.

Background

Far from occurring in isolation, the tax revolt erupted in concert with significant resistance to the tax in Kentucky, North and South Carolina, and Virginia.[4] Even more widely, it was part of a larger swath of disunion from West to East and from North to South, linking to a deep history of popular "regulations" of government that ran from the 1760s (in North Carolina) to the 1780s (in Shays's Rebellion in Massachusetts) and resurged in the late 1790s (with the Whiskey Rebellion and Fries's Rebellion).[5] One argument has it that the disturbances reflected continued tests of the U.S. government from the failure in the 1780s of the Continental Congress to the constitutional convention of 1787 and thereafter to a contentious ratification process and continuing challenges to the new U.S. Constitution till the end of the century.[6]

Instability was hardly new to the state of Pennsylvania, despite the order maintained within the commonwealth under the Penn Proprietorship, which had preserved order and trade with the Indians from 1681 through the 1750s.[7] The struggle for land between speculators, homesteaders, and Indian tribes from the Shawnee and the Delaware Indians to the Six Nations of the Iroquois ensured that Penn's peace would not last. Nor would border conflicts in the 1760s and 1770s involving Maryland (to the south), Virginia (to the west), and Connecticut (to the north) bring stability to Pennsylvania. Because large parts of what now constitutes the state were contested, the commonwealth was contained to east of the Shenandoah River. It would only secure its borders with the end of the American Revolution in 1783 and the treaty purchase of 1784, which created nine new counties.[8] A land purchase in 1792 in the Lake Erie area produced the state's final boundaries and facilitated the prospect of an East-West highway, preparing the state for commerce and the nation for a farther westward push.[9] Then the Whiskey Rebellion broke out. The rebellion would have to be suppressed and the Indians finally quelled before western Pennsylvania and the federal government would be secure.

With expansionist pressures weighing on the national government and local demands for land tearing apart the state, the Whiskey Rebellion was more than a mere nuisance. It was equally apparent that the Washington administration's choice of Pennsylvania for its test case in enforcing the federal whiskey tax had a personal element to it. The president had for decades surveyed and soldiered on the frontier to good effect, leading to a personal investment of forty thousand acres of western land that made him one of the largest landholders in the nation.[10] His holdings also led to disputed land claims and involvement in a high-profile Pennsylvania Supreme Court case, *George Washington v. James Scott, et al.* (1786), against settlers whom he ejected from his land.[11] Ironically, many of those implicated in the case—settlers, jurors, militia officers, justices of the peace—later became involved in the rebellion.[12] Beyond Washington's local affairs, Pennsylvania's geographic centrality and its economic potential made cries for secession from radical leaders among the whiskey rebels a national concern. There was no question that the volatility of the rebellion had put Pennsylvania at the top of Washington's agenda for preserving the Union. The Pennsylvania frontier was thus a crucial test case for a country poised to assert itself as a nation and to seek its own empire.

To understand further the nature of this test case, we need to turn to templates that explain the backcountry in terms of several key aspects: legal primitivism, colonization in a postcolonial context, and the backcountry as a foil for the city. Primitive law establishes a baseline of sorts as a public and customary means of sustaining backcountry community. The conditions of life on the frontier required settlers and tribes alike to maintain communal harmony through local traditions of self-help and cooperation, and retribution and direct redress.[13] There was no required formal code of law,[14] no citizens' rights or protection as a group. Rather, local militias imposed their own form of summary justice by means of posse comitatus (community self-defense call-ups), justifying hostilities as acts of war against an alien culture in their midst.[15]

A second frame construes both Indians and settlers as colonized and disparaged minorities. This frame proposes a dichotomy between friends of empire and friends of settlement,[16] where settlers practiced a democratizing localism that elite eastern empire builders found destabilizing. In a revealing transitional moment, post-Revolutionary Federalists tried to instantiate nationalism and eliminate the leftovers of local self-determination. Settlers were caught in the paradoxical position of subjugating the Indians to claim their land and yet being subjugated themselves; in this sense, both Indians and settlers were victimized by a process of erasing disobedience by domesticating it.[17]

A third, integrative frame links frontier primitivism and postcoloniality to rebellion in defining the backcountry. Here, rebellion is a revealing manifestation of resistance to the frontier under erasure, that is, as both marginal and disposable.[18] As primitives, westerners were represented by the figure of the Hydra—the many-headed monstrous mass which the ruling elite must disperse.[19] The backcountry ("back" is both "beyond" coastal authority and a perspective from below) responded by combining to embody a law that denied existing laws and opposed the city and its elites.[20] Here, the power of the militia bound the debtor class and settlers together despite their dispersal, so that the "hue and cry" of alarm held the frontier together. As postcolonials, collective resistance constituted backcountry individuation, while reciprocity yielded a form of judicial order.[21] What we find, in sum, is a distinctive western sociology with its own identity.

Framing allows us to capture the parameters of the backcountry environment and furnishes a floor for the events that would play out in 1794. But it does not excavate beneath the broader picture. It does not locate the particulars of a legal discourse or an ideological position within the subject of rebellion. In this regard, existing studies of the Whiskey Rebellion also prove discouraging. Without examining the positions of rebel factions, the nature of assembly discourse, the message of agitation-propaganda and popular culture, connections to the Anti-Federalists, and rebel trial arguments, studies have concluded that the rebels were hapless, confused, and incoherent; that their leaders were delusional, disorganized, and wavering.[22] Discounting the possibility that it was not a popular movement but rather a contest over political resources between groups of elites or a hybrid of backwater violence mixed with a degree of organization does not do justice to the complexity of the rebellion's vernacular legal culture, however untidy it might be, much less the possibilities inherent in its more formal legal arguments.[23] Nor does conceding the ground to the moral certainty of governmental discourse demonstrate an understanding of the proliferation of perspectives within a volatile and unpredictable dispute.[24] More importantly, it is insufficient to conclude that the Whiskey Rebellion was a test for understanding something not itself—the legacy of the America Revolution as an unambiguous victory.[25]

Not only do we lack studies that find rebel dissent worthy of study, but the law and the trials of the Whiskey Rebellion have yet to be fully studied. Some studies provide critical context; for example, that the trials were part of the transformation occurring in the aftermath of ratification of the Constitution or that the trials can be viewed through the lens of the tension between state and federal courts and Federalism.[26] Others provide essential political content and outline critical judicial issues in early American treason law, while my own study of judges' grand jury charges sets the stage for the trials.[27] A notable exception to this bleak picture, Wythe Holt's work on trial records, unfortunately, remains unpublished.[28] The picture as a whole, nonetheless, points to the need for a full examination of the law, the trials, and the legal culture of the Whiskey Rebellion.

The present study takes on the whole picture of Whiskey Rebellion legal culture, which it studies through the grand juries and the trials, courts and cases leading to the trials, the state of western courts, popular interaction with the courts, popular justice, and the development of popular courts and assemblies. The more common focus on violent events and democratic societies has eclipsed such study, thereby sidetracking thoughtful dissent or meaningful discourse on issues of governance as well as the ideology of popular constitutionalism, the rights of assembly and petition, and the right to bear arms in the militia, considerations that are central to the rebel assemblies, grand jury charges, and the trials. The rebellion's ties to the constitutional ratification debate and Anti-Federalism's effect on popular discontent with courts, together with the demand for popular participation in making the law and conducting court proceedings, have gone largely untouched.

Consequently, we lack a full understanding of the law, courts, and trials of the rebellion and how they shaped and were shaped by legal culture, how they created meaning and exercised power in the years of rebellion, and how legal discourse constructed communities. The point of this study is to rectify these omissions.

The Argument

The conflict of legal cultures that characterized the Whiskey Rebellion trials, I argue, embodied the antithesis of the government and the rebel narratives that arose over the four years that resistance to the excise tax festered in the western counties. In prosecuting the rebel trials, the government defended national unity while it undermined collective and individual liberties. The rebellion, meanwhile, defended the authority of states, popular governance, free speech and assembly rights, and reliance on the communal right to a militia while it threatened the security of national government.[29] On one side, a Federalist legal culture adopted a constructivist reading of constitutional and common law treason that its courts secured as part of a formal legal culture. This contrasted with an informal legal culture rooted in local custom and in a popular sovereignty that gave the people authority over the Constitution. In this sense, the contest between the government and the rebels went well beyond the violent resistance to the whiskey tax that has so taken up the interest of historians of the rebellion.[30] Instead, I argue that a general view of the rebel cause as badly managed, absent leadership, without justification, and so disorganized that it cannot be taken seriously is profoundly wrong.[31]

Where previous works tend to focus on the social history of the rebellion and its challenge to fledgling democracy, this book focuses specifically on the law and legal culture of the rebellion. The study's use of a variety of previously unexamined materials makes it possible to explore aspects of law and legal culture that have long been disregarded. It analyzes for the first time accounts of the rebel assemblies, documentation of their proceedings, and propaganda related to the rebellion. It examines unstudied law reports for western Pennsylvania riot trials and grand jury charges by federal judges as well as the jury statements responding to them. The defense position is reconstructed from a "dissertation" on treason law based on notes taken during the rebel trials. And recovery of the judge's bench notes for four unstudied trials, representing the only surviving trial transcripts, doubles the number of trials now open to our examination while it allows us to study trial practice and the pragmatics of judicial decision-making.

Not only does this study break new ground, but it broadens our understanding of U.S. law. It moves beyond Federalist judges' unbridled use of legal discretion by considering constitutional law in relation to both English common law and popular sovereignty. In tracing the uneven application of treason law, it notes earlier expansive conceptions but also locates opportunities that ease the law into more stable constructions. It provides insights into the operation of a new national court system struggling with preexisting local legal practices and a popular system of frontier justice. The story does not simply trace Alexander Hamilton's construction of an indiscriminate mob run riot; it does not merely observe the federal government manipulate its taxing power and apply its military power. Rather, it reflects the complex alliances of conflicting legal cultures that contributed to the rebellion. It is a story that incorporates competing positions within the rebellion as well as the desires of those who sided with the government or joined the federal army to pressure judges such as Richard Peters to imprison and punish insurgent westerners.

Reexamining the rebellion by combing through its legal culture, I argue, reveals something that has gone unrecognized: the rebellion had a developed popular understanding of the law, and its political and judicial stances competed effectively with the government position. Whereas, for example, its ideology was rooted in popular culture, its trial defense constituted a justifiable baseline for later treason law. The Whiskey Rebellion, in sum, makes a decided contribution to our understanding of late eighteenth-century popular dissent in Pennsylvania as well as its diverse inputs into American law.

In what is certainly more than a sidenote, the book responds to a renewed interest in our times to the challenges democracy faces and the prospect for its survival. This provides an impetus to reconsider the Whiskey Rebellion and the period of the 1790s as a "critical juncture" in the history of the United States. Creating a new government inevitably leads to conflict and resistance both through local action and deliberative processes,[32] making the crisis provoked by the Whiskey Rebellion an exemplary case for illustrating the competing visions of direct local community control by an active citizenry and of national power exerted by a distant representative government.

To be clear, the main conflict studied is between the power of government and the rights of its subjects, particularly the circumstances in which political stakes incite extraconstitutional actions and the suppression of individual liberties while testing the legal order. In the 1790s, the government's legitimacy depended on its ability to maintain stability while navigating the conflict between citizens' rights and the limits of government. But democracy also required that citizens defend against transgressions of government while the success of the new government depended on order supported by the people. So long as the people had no incentive to cooperate in crises and so long as federal force was unable to contain emerging threats, the legitimacy of national government was under assault.[33] Re-establishing government authority would require bringing participants in the rebellion back within the law, which meant, in the end, asserting the federal courts, which constitutes an essential aspect of this story.

Legal Culture

To facilitate our study of legal culture, we need to set parameters for what it means. In the context of the early republic legal system, legal culture has been studied through subjects as diverse as legal libraries, legal texts, legal education, the role of lawyers, and equity, oratory, and adversarial law.[34] It includes children's legal identity, "legalities" that define subjects differently, racial difference in the law, and gender and transgression in the law.[35] New studies have pluralized our understanding of what makes up legal culture to insist on the social, intellectual, and political and to emphasize that social experience operates as the venue in which the detailing of legal culture takes place. Studies have pointed the field in a direction that privileges voices left out of the democratic conversation—women, Blacks, Indians, children, immigrants—to underline the importance of a more accessible, customary law that reflects the experience of farmers, the urban and rural poor, and servants, among others. Material culture and voice become as central to our understanding of the law as lawyers and juries in the courtroom. New studies have enhanced our appreciation for how democracy struggled through a series of legal crises to fulfill its promise; and they have helped us to recognize epistemological changes in early America that included a revolution in authority, hardened gender categories, and "raced" narratives.

Legal culture is thus many things, which is its strength and potentially its weakness. In other words, displacing the focus from a narrow, ontological view allows us to view the law situated in the interactivity of society and culture. Fundamentally, law and culture operate as a system in which they are mutually constitutive and where law functions as an organism created, defined, and sustained as a living thing. Legal culture contextualizes practice as a way of being and seeing, and inscribes itself discursively through written, oral, and gestural language. It can thus be narratively constructed to operate as a culture of argument through conflict analysis, thick description, and rhetorical study, and it can be read as a text, as Clifford Geertz suggests, to draw "explanatory conclusions" out of the flow of discourse.[36] Tongue in check or not, Peter Fitzpatrick reminds us of two incommensurate ideas: that law and culture are essentially (in)compatible and that culture is now one of the things on which law relies.[37] Elsewhere, we are brought face to face with counterfactual textual readings to assist in understanding those who were historically present as well as to enable those who study the past to read the landscape where actors contested meaning and made history.[38] What we are looking for, in a related reading, is the interface between law and culture where they intervene with each other.[39] Yet one is hard put to say what exactly legal culture excludes or what distinguishes different approaches to it.[40]

Within this messy bag of tendencies and issues, the approach taken in the present study imposes certain limits on the study of legal culture to make it more intelligible while still harnessing its explanatory power. It reads closely the language and texts of official and unofficial legal culture with the goal of discovering the lessons of conflict between, and within, hegemony and resistance, and stability and instability. The study thus traces conflict between and within the heterogeneous rebel narrative, the singular government narrative, and the authoritative judicial narrative. The study can be seen as a set of cross-talking narratives, each its own small story and each in conflict with the others, in the spirit of Jean-Françoise Lyotard and Antonio Gramsci. Lyotard conceives of a field of heterogeneous games (*petits récits*) whose pragmatic positions resist the imposition of the rules of other games or of master narratives. The field encourages dissensus and accepts the richness and the incommensurability of language games. In a Gramscian universe, the interdependence of the hegemonic and that which resists it become apparent only when the world as hegemonically constituted comes into conflict with the world as experienced. Within these terms, the present study adopts the view that conflicting narratives seek to define the world of which they are a part and to control that world in small or large measure. In doing so, they reveal their conflicting, interactive, and mutually reinforcing nature.[41]

One way of squaring the circle in dealing with complex discourse and conflicting narratives (including gestures and rituals) provides a powerful example for us: examining how texts respond to other texts to resolve tensions, how they reveal unstable meanings and silences and read others' arguments.[42] Herein lies the benefit of the present study. While historical, sociological, and economic studies of the Whiskey Rebellion might reconstitute events and forces by narrativizing them, the conflict of discursive cultures is not their focus. The present study, by contrast, engages resistance narratives, and the discourse they resist, to determine their goals, perceived stakes, and effects. It speaks to the discursive culture of the Whiskey Rebellion across the various domains through whose spaces legal culture operates: the popular rituals and traditions, assemblies, and formal political and legal systems. Rebellion framed in these terms narrates itself into existence through the fungible discursive capital (the gestures, rituals, identity themes, rhetoric, storylines, and arguments) that defines it and its process of meaning-making. We are thus able to read the motifs and themes that characterize the discursive community ensconced on the frontier.[43] Their rhetoric gives texture to rebel self-expression and shape to historical and ideological struggle to render rebel self-presentation a testable proposition.

This reading complements existing scholarship grounded in the historical events of the rebellion to reveal how resistance constitutes itself from the perspective of the culture, language, and law of backcountry democracy. It fills in a gaping hole in Whiskey Rebellion studies by targeting critical popular elements that have been elided or glossed over and by turning our attention to law and culture. In reconstructing the rebel perspective, the study elaborates an explanatory framework that shifts our gaze to a new way of thinking about the rebellion. It is striking that the Whiskey Rebellion—a prime instance of the workings of legal culture—has yet to be examined in this light, which should make this study a welcome change of direction.

Storyline

The storyline of the Whiskey Rebellion taken up by this study divides into historical conditions and cultural traditions (the first three chapters) and the legal scene (the last three chapters); each part opens with a dominating government position and then transitions to a statement of the rebel position. The storyline begins with the clash between government and rebel narratives as they delineate the parameters within which official and unofficial legal culture operate. To clarify the dominant position of the government and its oppositional framing of backcountry democrats, the study first explores the contributions of Hamilton's spy network in the western counties and his report to the president, which served as the administration's basic, if incomplete and prejudicial, source of information. This initial misstep will inform Justice Wilson's authorization of the federal militia and establish a precedent for the chaotic collection of depositions and the haphazard interrogations of the rebels in preparation for bringing charges in the treason trials.

But it is fundamentally the creation of a sense of oppositionality in forming the government narrative of the rebellion that will color the trajectory of events leading up to the government's pretense of a peace commission and employment of military force to quell the rebellion. That narrative will deepen the criticality of national military power. Noah Webster might have concluded in 1792 that unjust laws in America could not be enforced by the sword "because the whole body of the people are armed"; nor could a military force execute any law "but such as the people perceive to be just and constitutional."[44] Washington would transform that sentiment in his address to Congress after the invasion, confident that he put into motion an army so great as to render "resistance desperate."[45] The "experiment" inherent in defining the rebellion proved just the opportunity national government required to fully establish its power and authority in the eyes of the nation and European powers (which we see in chapter 1).

The conditions under which Washington's conquest would take place included an unformed legal culture disoriented by a Revolution that left it bereft of functional county courts. The government found itself relying on a new form of law (constitutional and federal) and facing popular forms of justice with longer and deeper indigenous roots than anything a nascent national government had to offer. These conditions were most palpably felt in the frontier lands where inhabitants were adamantly opposed to the government's efforts to establish its power of taxation and to control the power of an armed people. And they were informed by the political thought of a western Anti-Federalism receptive to secessionist attitudes on the periphery of the nation. Popular attitudes were reinforced by the prevalence of extralegal courts, participation in private prosecution and arbitrations, militia courts, and rebel assembly courts that dealt out more local and innovative forms of justice. These circumstances would form the fundaments of the rebel narrative (which we begin examining in chapter 2).

Popular traditions and forms proved even more receptive to the power of localism and Anti-Federalism than the inventions of justices of the peace or the extrajudicial law of pseudo courts. They included hangings in effigy, tarring and feathering, and agitation-propaganda together with community-based liberty pole raisings and the penchant of "white Indians" for "going native." The predisposition for such rough justice turned to support for rogue banditry and the radicalism of armed popular militias. This would soon exhibit demands for shared ownership of acts of violence that led to armed assemblies. But popular traditions would also feed the ideology of popular sovereignty on which the rebellion would feed as it developed more moderate leanings toward petitions, debates, and deliberative assemblies that turned away from militia musters toward direct rather than representative democracy. These were the conditions that gave life to the rebel narrative (the subject of chapter 3).

With these two pieces in place—the establishment of elitist national government and the assertion of the natural force of backcountry democracy—the collision of narratives that would occur in federal treason trials was imminent. Grand juries in newly founded federal circuit courts proved to be the venue where the legal battle between these two entities was first introduced. In the Eastern Pennsylvania Circuit Court in Philadelphia, the site of the treason trials, Federalist judges teased out a judicial narrative in their jury charges that would guide the trials that followed. This narrative represented a politico-legal approach to educating the public on nationhood and treason that grand jury statements largely complemented and reinforced (as we find in chapter 4).

The trials themselves exhibited the clash of government and rebel legal cultures through government prosecution and rebel defense arguments. While the conflict was expressed as much in the pragmatics of dealing with vicinage, procedural, and evidentiary problems as in more substantive adversarial proceedings, it was reflected as well in the judge's notes. In the process, judicial constructions of treason law and the inability of American judges to wean themselves from English law became central issues of the clash. At the same time, it became apparent that American law was moving out of the shadow of British common law practices into the realm of statutory and constitutional law (chapter 5).

The storyline concludes with full focus on the rebel perspective expressed through the trial defense and its subsequent justification in John Marshall's nineteenth-century *Burr* opinion. Having begun with the government's demonization of the rebel cause and ending with Marshall's course correction on constructivist treason, this study completes our journey with a salutary message: times change and the law changes with it. Closing by examining defense treason notes, this study submits, gives the rebels the last and most thoughtful word on how they might be perceived going forward. History has now the opportunity to revisit its verdict on the presumptively rowdy mob of hooligans pictured by the first president and his Federalist cabinet. That verdict must now be considered in light of the contribution popular participation in democracy made when it insisted on balancing state power; when it realigned what allegiance means in reinventing government. In the end, the Whiskey Rebellion checked a counterrevolutionary interpretation of the Constitution with a rights-based vision common citizens chose to embrace because it reflected them. Thomas Jefferson, it seems, was not entirely wrong: some rebellion "now and then" might be good for the country, giving everyone an opportunity to have a "just influence" (chapter 6).[46]

In "Conclusion: An Afterword," the argument of the book is pulled together, with some final thoughts on the nature of the rebel perspective as a narrative. It offers a statement on how legal culture matters together with commentary on the lessons we can learn about democracy for our own time. At the end of the book, appendix A and the bibliography provide trial resources and a comprehensive list of primary and secondary sources, with the hope of opening research to a new generation of students and bringing to light the many voices touched by and shaping study of the rebellion. Appendix B gives us the basic numbers for the circuit court trials. These materials are intended to supplement and update the valuable resource provided by Thomas Slaughter in his 1985 historiographical essay on the rebellion.[47]

As a parting note, I have adopted the term "Whiskey Rebellion" for this study in preference to such terms as insurrection (the term initially used by Treasury Secretary Hamilton and adopted in his period) and regulation (a new usage that ties the rebellion to a larger swatch of popular resistance from 1760 to 1800).[48] The 1795 circuit court trials in Philadelphia used "insurrection" and "rebellion" indiscriminately, as did jury statements attached to various grand jury charges. Histories by participants (William Findley and Hugh Henry Brackenridge) in the uprising used the term "insurrection" in their titles. Nevertheless, studies over time have consistently used the term "Whiskey Rebellion." Reflecting the merit of longevity and familiarity, the term "Whiskey Rebellion" thereby appears throughout the text, while Hamilton's term is retained in the title of the work to remind us of the condescension with which the rebellion was greeted by the Washington administration.

Part I

CHAPTER 1

The Government Narrative and Its Western "Experiment"

We start by reconsidering the government's role in constructing perceptions about the Whiskey Rebellion. How it saw itself and needed to be seen in the public sphere was related to the need to exert control and maintain national unity. These objectives underlay the national narrative it pursued over a critical time of transitioning from a destabilizing revolutionary era to a stable order. During this time, a framing of the rebellion was established that dominated contemporary understanding of the event and has continued to dominate historical perceptions in an ongoing way. To some extent control over public discourse by the leading figures of the Washington administration was the result of a customary pattern whereby gentlemen preserved careful records of their communications. Made up of an elite group, the executive branch's network of private correspondence and exchanges of government communications supplemented printed pamphlets and proclamations as well as routinely printed newspaper accounts of executive, legislative, and judicial activities. Reports that appeared in urban newspapers were regularly recirculated in local papers that allowed for wider dispersion of official perspectives. No such pattern existed on the frontier where record keeping was erratic. The rebels had limited access to the print media and no regular political base on which to rely. Distribution of agitation-propaganda included handwritten notes, circular letters, posted notices and handbills, newspaper accounts and letters to the editor, and was highly dependent on road conditions, weather, and ad hoc networks of communication. The founding of the *Pittsburgh Gazette* in 1786 gave westerners their only public medium for featuring local issues until 1795, while broadsides and intercepted correspondence provided opportunities for exposure and mischief.[1] Together with petitions to the legislature, these efforts maintained popular agency in the struggle for the attention and support of the public in what was a marginally effective, if undervalued, means of keeping its story alive.

The nationalizing force of federal communication overcame a disconnected local and state-based antifederalism and the vernacular culture which supported it; but the presumption that it did so because of the incompleteness or inferiority of vernacular culture is belied by robust localism and self-organizing democratic impulses. In truth, there were two spaces in opposition: the materially rooted plurality of locales and the more homogeneous political space of national scope. The association and self-identity that operated directly at the level of towns and counties were not understood in a uniform way over more disparate space, just as national consensus was undermined at the level of local particulars. "Translocal" community was difficult to imagine, at least in Benedict Anderson's sense of an imagined simultaneity to counter the scattered communities dispersed across the country.[2]

The clash of the local and national pictures has, I argue in this and the following two chapters, been imperfectly understood. How this clash affected perspectives on the western rebellion is reflected in two readings. In one, Hamilton goaded rebel defiance to the whiskey tax, while western elites such as Federalist John Neville and his circle promoted the rebellion to maintain local influence. This influential reading interprets the rebellion as a contest of sources: Alexander Hamilton's report to the president as opposed to William Findley's and Hugh Henry Brackenridge's after-the-fact renderings of events.[3] The narrative imagines the president in control of a conscious plan to manage a volatile situation, unperturbed by the lack of information and the contesting views among his advisers. His popularity surged with the spectacle of a federal militia marching westward, featuring Washington as the very figure of a popular sovereign. Here, the rebels are conceived as hapless and unlikely to have raised much opposition, with moderate rebels intuitively backing off as they saw the writing on the wall. The rebel leaders in this narrative were largely delusional political figures anxious to keep the goodwill of the people.

Relying to a large extent on Hamilton's report to Washington and the president's subsequent proclamation, a second reading argues that the government converted a volatile and unpredictable dispute into a clear, manifest solution to what was a complex ideological struggle.[4] This reading supports the idea that Hamilton was the driving force behind the Washington administration's compelling messaging. Exploiting the authority of the president, grand and historical language assumes a constitutional aura and the sanction of founding figures. The narrative speaks in a voice of unity and "metropolitan" centrality to transform the rebels' geographic isolation into a political periphery. It focuses on a clear danger and foregrounds the use of military force to cut through the uncertainty of a rebel threat before it becomes uncontrollable. The administration's narrative was not better or more truthful than a conflicted, disorganized rebel narrative, but it created a sense of its own inevitability. It plotted events to create an appearance of truthfulness that was predictable and consonant; it was a narrative of necessity driven by repetition, teleology, and seamless simplicity.

Neither of these narratives acknowledges the possibility of a competitive counternarrative or that Hamilton and Washington's insistence on the indispensability of crushing this threat to authority grossly underestimated the nature of their opponent. Neither seriously considers what U.S. attorney general Edmund Randolph and Chief Justice John Jay feared—that such a threat was not ripe for engagement by a democratic government.[5] What they do elicit is the sense of a government well situated to control the flow of information and dominate discourse when disaffected western Pennsylvania farmers, frontiersmen, and their allies posed a serious threat to its tax policy. What we shall discuss in this chapter is the nature of the government's best, and most unassailable, weapon against the rebels: its rhetorical superiority. We shall discover in subsequent chapters that the rebels did not compete for popular support rhetorically. Their medium of communication was oral, not written; their persuasive tools were traditional practices; their statements were political expressions of their collective rights of petition and assembly.

Hamilton's Spies

To trace the beginning of the government narrative, we need to turn to Hamilton's network of informants in the western country who were tasked with reporting on resistance to the excise tax. In a November 17, 1791, letter to supervisor of the revenue for Pennsylvania George Clymer, John Neville established several themes to create a prototype of what would become the government story of the rebellion.[6] Neville was one of the most popular and well-positioned men in the Monongahela region until he became excise inspector. He had served in the Revolution, where he was responsible for occupying Fort Pitt for two years, was taken prisoner in 1780, and ended the war as a brigadier general. A prosperous farmer with a plantation of slaves, he headed a network of wealthy men (the "Neville connection"), which together with his position as inspector for the western district (one of four surveys into which the state had been divided) made him a target of the rebels.[7]

In his letter to Clymer, the tax inspector struck an elitist position, calling the rebels barbarians. The best trope the rebels might hope from him was that of the noble savage, playing on the intimation that they blackened their faces and dressed like Indians. Neville contended that rebel committees assumed a constant communitarian threat, joining together "to oppose [the excise tax] in every stage, and to make a joint expence of any costs or damages that may accrue." Individuals, he reported, feared being subjected to the community's will but were equally indebted to its collective spirit and unwilling to accommodate the distant, "foreign" government of the Washington administration. Neville depicted a territory unreceptive to government agents moving through the countryside to serve process on a larger number of stills and individuals brewing spirits than he had imagined. Compounded by the hapless state of collectors, their number stymied Neville, who had at this point considered serving processes himself until he realized the hazardous nature of such an undertaking. Neville's story of self-organizing alien figures appealed to people in the East with embedded perceptions and little knowledge of the terrain and people of the West. As he wrote to Clymer on November 7, 1792,[8] this was a "multitude" whose class and interests were unlikely to be sympathetic to an eastern audience, particularly the "vain boasts" of secessionists who renounced allegiance to the government and proposed to join British troops who had not yet evacuated their forts in the West.

Hamilton appears to have suspected that Neville's concern was of the "danger to himself,"[9] though Neville's letter of August 23, 1792, to Clymer indicated there was more to it. He had established offices of inspection in two places, Pittsburgh and Washington, thinking it a necessary "Experiment," but complained that no one would attend him at Pittsburgh for fear of arson should they do so.[10] The owner of the house in which the Washington office was located, Captain Faulkner, was met by several people who "threatened to scalp him, tar and feather him" and torch it as well. Neville placed a notice in the *National Gazette* closing that office, and he told Clymer that he would cease "further attempts to fulfill the law." What Neville did not share was his embarrassment at the hostile reception he received from a community that had respected him as the patron of an elite network. Having reversed himself on his initial distaste for the excise law so he could take up the lucrative post of inspector, Neville was now reduced to currying favor with federal authorities to maintain himself and those who depended on his influence. He thus included in his letter the minutes of the August 21–22, 1792, rebel meeting in Pittsburgh in which the question of Neville's resigning his appointment was the subject of debate by those he called "leading men." Published in the *Pittsburgh Gazette*, the minutes included the names of attendees, those who assumed responsibilities, the organization of a committee of correspondence, advertisement of the meeting's activities to comparable committees in other counties, and the meeting's resolutions. Considering that Neville's letter was the first time Hamilton had heard of the August meeting, access to the minutes represented quite a coup and would later figure handily in his case against the rebels.[11]

Hamilton immediately ordered Tench Coxe, commissioner of the revenue, to instruct Clymer to examine the state of all divisions of the survey and to collect evidence on those who attended meetings. Clymer, who had a reputation as a devout Quaker and proud signer of the Declaration of Independence, had not only helped frame the 1776 Pennsylvania Constitution but was also responsible for negotiating a treaty to keep the Delaware Indians neutral during the Revolution. Unfortunately, during his four-month trip to the West, he would develop an antipathy to frontier militia and align himself with Neville, an unreliable, self-interested partner, making Clymer a less-than-neutral observer.

Clymer's instructions were to take depositions on the circumstances of obstructive "language and conduct" from "as many respectable characters" as he could. He was to encourage revenue officers, persuade inhabitants of the counties to come "into the law," and converse "with decent men" to the effect that the government would no longer remain passive in the face of persisting contempt for the law. Hamilton contended it was "absolutely necessary" to use the western country as a test for a legally supported federal revenue system and (reflecting Neville's framing) that "a decided experiment should without delay be made of the energy of the laws, and of the ability of the government to put them in execution."[12] Coxe reported back that while most in the four western counties were generally well disposed to the government, a violent few were almost entirely able to prevent the laws from being executed. The safety of those tasked with performing legal services was everywhere in danger, he represented, while good citizens who wished to obey the courts or comply with the law were considered the enemy; a minority thus posed a universal danger to peace and good order. Coxe's summary of the state of western Pennsylvania would form a baseline for the government narrative developed over the next two years.[13]

It was the tone of Clymer's reports from September through October

1792, however, that was most revealing.[14] Clymer assumed that citizens ought to have gravitated naturally toward the government's position and that it was strange so many were indifferent to it. He blamed their disposition on corruption and disaffection and found it unfortunate that "all their men of distinction" were "sordid shopkeepers, crafty lawyers, or candidates for office" disinclined to respond to the call of truth, honor, and sacrifice. The people of the western country, he claimed, had a poor understanding of citizenship, a condition he attributed to the depravity of morals occasioned "by the intemperate use of the favourite drink." Clymer proceeded to specify county by county those "most repugnant to the law." He regarded the elite professional class (members of the state assembly, lawyers, an attorney general, a county lieutenant, justices of the peace, and clergy) "among the most outrageous," expecting that men of a given class would identify with their betters rather than the rabble.[15] Clymer pointed to David Bradford and James Marshall, in Washington County, and John Smilie and Albert Gallatin, in Fayette County, as the "great" and the "professed" leaders of their county (all but Marshall were members of the Pennsylvania House of Representatives)[16] and he targeted U.S. congressman William Findley as "the father of all the disturbances in the western country." Clymer faulted Findley for trying to save his own reputation by keeping the people of Westmoreland County away from committees and "combinations" and steering them to exercise their right of petition.[17] He blamed the people for being content with a town meeting at Pittsburgh at which "[t]heir deliberations, if I can call them, were open, for nothing was done but the repeated reading of a petition to Congress—agreed to without dissent"; he presumed the petition was "only a device to keep up the mad temper of the people" and that the people knew it would be rejected.[18] When the August Pittsburgh meeting passed an aggressive resolution admonishing the people to have no contact with or aid excisemen, Clymer approached the chair of the meeting, John Cannon, who declined his offer to publicly disavow the meeting and accept immunity from the government. Findley represented that the meeting had "respectfully" petitioned the government, but Clymer expressed his belief that it constituted a "seditious confederacy." Mimicking Hamilton's view of the meeting, Clymer recommended that bringing the participants to justice would make the law easier to execute.[19]

Despite his apparent confidence in reporting to Hamilton, Clymer's trip west was a public relations disaster. First there were letters between him and Judge Alexander Addison in which he expressed the dangers of traveling to the town of Washington to collect depositions and implored the judge to go in his place.[20] He then faced a humorous account of his fear of the inhabitants of Washington published first in the *Pittsburgh Gazette* and then in Philadelphia for all to see in *The Mail; or Claypoole's Daily Advertiser*.[21] Contributing to what turned out to be a press war of sorts, Clymer responded with a straight-faced, unsigned defense of each of the burlesque charges.[22] Finally, he was accosted in the press by "Monongahela," a pseudonym for William Findley, whom Clymer had erroneously outed to Hamilton as the force behind the western outrages. In a longish diatribe, Findley exposed Clymer's unsupported assertion of the "paramount influence ascribed to the Westmorland character" (Findley was from Westmoreland) while proclaiming that Clymer had done more "to irritate the people" against the excise law than any rebel assembly. He pointed out to the public, moreover, the incongruity of Clymer's having signed the Declaration of Independence when he was so willing to "stoop to any *device*, to avert danger to his person."

On the same day, September 1, that Hamilton engaged Coxe to send Clymer to the western counties, Hamilton had written to the president to express the urgency of the situation. He pressed the need to develop information on the violence and to prosecute offenders; he supported indemnifying officials for losses and, indispensably, exerting "the full force of the law," the last resort of a president's power.[23] Within a week, Hamilton urged the expediency of issuing a presidential proclamation. He not only warned the president that discontent had spread to the Carolinas, but without having been instructed to do so he had already written a draft proclamation and begun circulating it among members of the cabinet.[24] He lobbied Chief Justice John Jay "that a high misdemeanor has been committed" at the Pittsburgh meeting as its "avowed objective" was to obstruct the law by legal means. Hamilton proposed that the next circuit court expedite judicial notice of the Pittsburgh proceedings and the president issue a proclamation stating their criminality.[25] Findley, no friend of Hamilton's, thought the offending resolution bad policy and even worse politics, but not "contrary to law," noting that Hamilton was aware "the attorney general did not think it actionable."[26] Hamilton, however, knew his audience: Washington found organized resistance to the government so concerning that he gave Hamilton's recommendations his full "sanction and authority" should the proceedings be found "illegal and the members indictable."[27]

Attorney General Randolph outlined his disagreement the next day.[28] The situation in Pittsburgh did not "warrant a judicial movement in the United States" merely because a few individuals had resolved to obstruct the government's ability to execute the laws. "To assemble to remonstrate, and to invite others to assemble and remonstrate to the Legislature," he held, "are among the rights of Citizens." Moreover, "measured cautious and artfull" language was likely to "disappoint the expectation of public punishment" considering the latitude given to the accused in libel cases. Randolph argued that the meeting resolution Hamilton found so objectionable did not meet the strict standard of criminality, despite its contempt for the law. Indeed, the matter's "more serious complexion" outweighed isolated acts of obstruction of the laws.[29] That is, of the three resolutions delivered at the meeting, two were not censurable, while individual rights of free speech, petition, and assembly were not prosecutable. By contrast, the third resolution, prescribing personal exile and contempt for excise officials, was censurable, but it could be reached by a proclamation. Even that would leave the president in the position of animadverting "upon acts to which no law had prescribed a penalty," that is, acts that were not criminal. In sum, Randolph feared the president's interference "might excite an idea of usurpation," particularly where the acts punished manifested infringements of the peace unlikely to be found worthy of legal censure. Rather, Randolph advised Hamilton, "My maxim is to examine well; to forebear a doubtfull power, and to enforce one, clearly rightfull." Considered the administration's most astute interpreter of federal law,[30] Randolph had reached to the weakest part of the Hamilton narrative: its concerted, persistent attempt to proscribe acts that were fully constitutional.

Despite Randolph's counsel, Hamilton continued to attack the Pittsburgh meeting in his correspondence with Washington.[31] The president's dislike of the more than forty democratic societies (bourgeois, Francophile political clubs) that sprung up in the country in the 1790s and which the president blamed for inciting the insurrection[32] gave Hamilton an advantage. The Pittsburgh meeting minutes had resolved that committees were to "correspond together" and to call general meetings of the people or conferences of the committees, a strategy linked to the American Revolution Committees of Correspondence and Safety which had been adopted by the societies as well. In linking the societies to the rebel meetings, Hamilton's strategy was to deny the rebels the high ground of a revolutionary legacy and undermine their ability to organize and spread resistance throughout the rebellious western counties.

Hamilton discovered even more ammunition in the third resolution that Randolph had found censurable. Indeed, he cited it as a centerpiece of his critical report laying out proof of a rebellion.[33] The minutes of the Pittsburgh meeting, distributed as a broadside,[34] made the military response that Randolph advised against in his opinion more attractive and necessary to both Washington and Hamilton as its call to the people to hold excisemen in contempt affronted federal officials executing constitutional laws. The September 15 proclamation which Hamilton had drafted and circulated without authorization thus directed itself to "certain violent and unwarrantable proceedings"; it ordered the cessation of "all unlawful combinations and proceedings whatsoever" as they subverted good order and contravened the duty citizens owed to their country and its laws.[35] Referring to meetings, the term "unwarrantable proceedings" was repeated as a theme throughout the short statement, indicating not only meetings in Pittsburgh but in Brownsville (Old Redstone Fort), in Fayette County, and in Washington County that were dismissive of the moderation displayed by the legislature and the executive's duty to carry out the laws faithfully. The president conceded to Hamilton's pressure but stopped short of exerting the full power of his office.[36]

The "Experiment"

The government narrative's early themes, it became clear, were established by Hamilton's informants in the West. The rebels were pictured as drunken barbarians. Their assemblies, said to be directed by leading men of the community, promulgated resolutions that were like legislation. And the rebellion obstructed the law by preventing government officials from doing their duty. The second anchor of the government narrative also came from the information Hamilton's spies had provided. The theme of "experiment," like the perceived threat to executing the law, had been put forth by Neville and endorsed by Clymer and Hamilton. Neville's August letter to Clymer sponsored the necessity of an experiment, but it was targeted at establishing revenue offices. Hamilton expanded on the idea, claiming it was "absolutely necessary" to use the western country as a test for a legally supported federal revenue system. The experiment was urgent; it should be decisive; it affected the implementation of the laws in general; and it tested the government's ability to execute the law.[37] Since the twin objectives of the experiment were to test the "energy" of the laws and the competence of the government, it was defined downward in terms of appointing local officials, opening excise offices, and serving writs requiring delinquents to travel to federal courts east of the mountains.

Resistance in Pennsylvania by 1794 served as a synecdoche for dissidence in the nation; Philadelphia was, after all, the seat of national government. Concentrating execution of the excise law in the western counties of Pennsylvania also made the experiment less costly. And as the most vulnerable point of the resistance,[38] Pennsylvania was more likely to be a successful test than the Carolinas or Kentucky. The president had, in any event, requested advisory letters from members of his cabinet, to which Hamilton and Randolph (by this time secretary of state), among others, responded on August 5. Here, Hamilton continued to develop his version of the experiment. He explained that the government's patience had been worn thin by an experiment tried long enough to determine that "the root of the evil lay deep; and required measures of greater efficiency than had been pursued."[39] Hamilton construed the government's efforts as a "proportionable decision" to allow the law to assert itself and the rebels "to yield to reason reflection and experience." As well, it pleased him that the laws had been reaffirmed by the legislature; attempts to repeal them were feeble, and evidence conduced to general support from the community. If there were complaints, he reiterated, it was because the laws had not been executed, so that the government had no choice but to prosecute "with vigour delinquents and Offenders."[40]

Unwilling to embrace Hamilton's aggressive Federalism, Randolph qualified his remarks on application of the term "experiment." He argued that unnecessarily harsh measures (presumably Hamilton's "greater efficiency") should not be exerted before efforts at conciliation or "the people will be estranged from the administration which made the experiment."[41] Their differences centered on Hamilton's contention that the experiment had already failed, whereas Randolph contended it had yet to be tried. With Hamilton arguing that incompetent judicial efforts justified sending the militia, Randolph considered that sending the militia would give the lie to the "overtures of peace" made by a presidential commission and send the message "that the design of sending Commissioners was only to gloss over hostility."[42] Randolph was distressed by the view of "some gentlemen" (the most likely candidates being Hamilton and his handpicked network) "that when reconciliation is offered with one hand, terror should be borne in the other." He appreciated the hypocrisy of offering a false choice: terror lurking behind the public face of peace.

In the end, Hamilton's plan prevailed. Executing the next step in the experiment, he accompanied the militia as it wended west, ensuring no missteps occurred. By his reckoning, the experiment delivered the optimal outcome: military strength, financial stability, and political reputation. As he wrote to his wife's sister, Angelica Church, Hamilton was on his "way to attack and subdue the wicked insurgents of the West."⁴³ He justified his trip (lest she consider him "a Quixote") saying that the army might have "cooled the courage of those madmen," but there must be "no mistake in the management of the affair," an acknowledgment that having proposed the militia he felt himself obligated to participate in its operation.

In one sense, Hamilton had stage-managed the insurrection from the instigating moment of his revenue policy to establishing a network of spies, assigning excise officials, reporting to the president, proselytizing for the use of force, challenging alternative narratives within the administration, and, ultimately, getting the militia authorized. His role extended to judicial oversight of arrests and interrogations and the filing of charges in pursuit of federal trials. He could now pass on his assurance to his sister-in-law that "the insurrection will do us a great deal of good and add to the solidity of every thing in this country"; condescending to denominate the rebellion "the whiskey insurrection," he represented that all was well with his project: "Our insurrection is most happily terminated. Government has gained by its reputation and strength, and our finances are in a most flourishing condition."⁴⁴

Hamilton's Report

Hamilton's advice to the president was not merely an advisory opinion. Unlike his fellow cabinet members, he had devised a catalog of events leading up to the rebellion that he shaped to create the impression of sustained lawlessness and violence. Hamilton pressed for publication, convinced that priming the citizenry would reinforce the government's version of events and generate public support for a federal militia. Washington, in a move that reflected his innate caution, sent the report to Randolph, who advised him to communicate it "to the world in some other manner, than under your auspices" and not to make use of his "name and character, without necessity." Randolph proposed leaving the whole affair to rest "upon the responsibility of the Secretary of the treasury alone."⁴⁵ Following a meticulous review by Randolph, nonetheless, the report was publicly printed in August in *Dunlap and Claypoole's American Daily Advertiser*, and was subsequently used by the president in his address to Congress in November.⁴⁶ Tellingly, the newspaper published it as a Treasury Department report over Hamilton's signature.⁴⁷

The report covered a period from September 1791 to July 1794, citing nineteen acts of violence against excise officers, six meetings, and several "intemperate resolutions."[48] Presented as a litany of isolated violence, the report arranged a stream of attacks over a three-year period to create the impression of coordinated long-term opposition. It concluded in a short paragraph that held there was "just cause to believe" the opposition was connected to a refusal to share the "common burden of the community" and a desire to embarrass the government.[49] Hamilton's report focused on crude acts of violence likely to enrage its eastern readers together with pseudo-facts, prejudices, and grudges. It did not provide proof so much as it endorsed greater federal authority over the states and the supremacy of the federal government over western judiciary and local officials whom he accused of complicity with outlaws and enemies of the people. More specific charges of judicial resistance (against sheriffs, registrars, the attorney general's deputy, justices of the peace, associate judges, and, more directly, President Judge Alexander Addison of the western courts) would appear in a later report to Washington on September 2, 1794.[50]

Hamilton's August report exploited a familiar tradition of riotous behavior connected to banditry that resonated with those familiar with western populism. In the mid-1780s, for example, a report concerning William Graham, an excise collector, declared he was abused by a mob of bandits, a large combination of "a certain class" acting deliberately and not out of passion.[51] According to Hugh Henry Brackenridge, the people "occasionally amused themselves at [Graham's] expence"; they took him hostage, singed his wig, shaved his head, cut off the tail of his horse, and put coal in his boots, before a mob conducted him out of the county.[52] In 1789, "banditti" were referred to as "those disaffected from the state and federal government," while in 1792 "predatory banditti" were described as forming "a powerful confederacy secretly abetted by our natural enemies the British."[53] By the time William Findley applied the term to reflect the mob mentality[54] of the whiskey rebels, the term "banditti" had aggregated to describe a class of people, passionless combinations, spontaneous ruffians, antigovernment dissidents, and a confederacy linked to foreign enemies.

Hamilton's report repeated and varied iterations that implanted the term as a seemingly overdetermined code. He saw western tax resisters as "perpetrators of these excesses," "molesting," "obstructing," "threatening," and "disorderly," and as "rioters" and "insurgents." He foregrounded a tarring and feathering by armed men painted in black, men in disguise who terrorized a collector's family, and audacious bandits who carried off witnesses to prevent their testifying in court.⁵⁵ The president's proclamation of August 7, 1794, drafted by Hamilton, used the term "banditti" to describe men disguised to escape discovery who were employed by the rebels for "unwarrantable purposes."⁵⁶ As Hamilton represented, bandits were "bold enough to encounter the guilt, and the danger" of reducing excisemen to virtual outlaws, an inversion of the order of things and a condition that mirrored their own existence.⁵⁷ In capturing the language and tone of banditry, highwaymen, and outlawry run riot, Hamilton held the attention of both Washington and a gullible eastern public.

Countering the Narrative: Findley and Randolph

Hamilton's narrative was well documented in letters and directives between officials, proclamations, and addresses to Congress. It was an authoritative telling that few were willing to contest. But western representative Albert Gallatin was one of those few. In a speech to the Pennsylvania Assembly in October 1794, he publicly attacked Hamilton's version of the government narrative for "obscuring the truth."⁵⁸ Gallatin contended that it "cannot even claim the feeble and delusive aid of hypothetical conjecture, and doubtful inferences."⁵⁹ Congressman William Findley, who held many of the same moderate views as Gallatin, supported him in a series of public letters in 1794, charging that Hamilton's behind-the-scenes political deceptions isolated the president from all but the heads of departments so that he received no other information than they provided. Hamilton's intention, Findley avowed, was to enrich those of the East at the expense of the impoverished West.⁶⁰ In terms of specific motives, Findley described Hamilton's report as a "narrative [...] calculated to inflame the army in a high degree" and motivated to persuade Justice Wilson to provide "the important certificate" needed to call out the militia against the rebels. Hamilton's motives, according to Findley, evolved ideologically from the principle that "a government could never be considered as established, till its power was put to the test by a trial of its military force." That sentiment illustrated the value of the "experiment" the government conducted in the western country, a scheme the administration never denied. Prosecutions by federal officials far from where rebel crimes occurred and process-serving when court was not in session were "in perfect correspondence," Findley said, with rendering the federal militia "the more necessary and justifiable."⁶¹

Despite the extreme nature of Hamilton's "misrepresentations," Findley conceded he was a credible source for his chosen audiences, coming as he did "from so respectable a quarter." Hamilton's audience included those who could justify the federal militia, a group that included his spies, the president and his cabinet, Justice Wilson, collaborating local officials, and volunteers who supported and served in the government's army. Findley identified a third audience, "the secretary's admirers," an excitable group of easterners opposed in general to "citizens of the western country."[62] Focused on these readers, Hamilton delivered accounts "with the highest colouring they would possibly bear," making untruthful charges and forwarding inaccurate intelligence provided by "vigilant spies."[63] Findley condemned the secretary's failure to consult such truthful sources as official records and the law; he assailed Hamilton's cloaking of lawful rebel conduct in garb that represented it as criminal.[64] Hamilton, he argued, had "[a]nother object in view" in charging the western country "with every description of odium" that was "absolutely void of truth." He pointed to the notorious final paragraph of the report in which, Findley claimed, Hamilton's "information and advice" had left "an impression that there was not a good citizen in the country but the excise officers"; he added the inflammatory accusation that Hamilton's conduct in executing the law was "of a manner that was calculated to promote" the very event, the rebellion, he pretended to despise.[65]

In the final analysis, Hamilton's greatest sin might have been positioning himself as the president's surrogate to gain advantage in shaping discourse about the rebellion. By accompanying the president on his trip west with the militia, the secretary associated himself with Washington to enhance his own authority over the judicial and military authorities who commanded the expedition. Without an official title or role, he created the appearance that he superseded General Henry Lee, commander of the federal militia.[66] His posturing was exposed by Randolph, who claimed Hamilton's continued presence at the commander in chief's side was much "talked of out of doors."[67] Vindicating himself in a scandal related to the French ambassador Jean Antoine Joseph Fauchet, Randolph reported that Hamilton had managed "to acquire in the sight of his enemies a formidable and imposing consideration."[68] Gesturally, the optics and the symbolism for Hamilton were striking, while the effect on Washington's reputation was mixed. Fauchet represented that the press felt Washington's traveling with the militia was an "artful attempt" to present himself commanding an armed force like an English monarch and that the spectacle had the opposite effect, leaving Washington "ridiculed and reduced to an absurdity." His transatlantic perspective supported Findley's domestic analysis in suggesting that the government itself provoked the rebellion or, at best, that it came about by accident, for public notice of the rebel acts and declarations suggested ardency rather than anarchy. Notably, the ambassador concluded that the desire to mount the militia made it "necessary to magnify the danger, to disfigure the views of [the] people" as well as to excite the citizenry about the "the fate of the Constitution" and the design of some to unite with England; in reality, he suggested, the rebellion threatened only the administration.[69]

In the end, the idea persisted in the public sphere that the rebellion was not premeditated and the federal militia was unnecessary. In Findley's reading, the insurrection arose spontaneously; the events that precipitated it were unforeseen, and there was no collusion among the people, those presumed to be its leaders, or state officials. Findley contended that the U.S. Commission gave no indication in its official report that the insurrection had been planned, so that without Hamilton's machinations "the expedition might never have been carried out."[70] Findley, Fauchet, and Randolph were all suspicious of Hamilton's stratagems to advise the president and influence the army, as well as to construct official and public perceptions of the rebellion. Nonetheless, it appears each of them was reluctantly impressed not only by his agility in placing himself indispensably close to the seat of power but also by his ability to massage the facts, draw a persuasive picture, and communicate an effective narrative.

Taking the Narrative Public

Hamilton's ascendency continued apace, this time in the public sphere. By publishing his report to the president with Washington's blessing, Hamilton committed the government publicly to his narrative. Moreover, his draft of Washington's August 7 proclamation worked hand in glove to reify a public sphere narrative. A loyal but moderating voice, Secretary of War Henry Knox had advised Washington that the proclamation should limit itself to the mild measures already taken; it should establish the principles that justified calling the militia and the objective sought in doing so.[71] In fact, the proclamation announced the act of Congress that authorized the militia and, as required by the act, directed the rebels to disperse and peacefully retire.[72] The proclamation thereafter, however, took on a Hamiltonian line to delineate menacing acts against those executing the laws and violations of individual rights that humiliated those who would be friends of order.[73] It railed against "combinations," applying the term indiscriminately to bands of armed men, rebel assemblies, and political organizations. It then impugned the motives of the insurgents in preventing execution of the law by force of arms and resisting "by open violence" the government's lawful authority. The "essential interests of the Union," it proclaimed, thereby demanded that the laws be duly executed and those "combinations" suppressed.

With the parameters for an oppositional narrative set, the proclamation identified the institutional players—the legislature (the source of the excise law), the executive (the executor of tax collection and prosecution), and the Supreme Court (the authorizer of the militia act for the use of force)—giving priority to the supreme executive (the president) and the federal militia (his armed enforcer). The arc of the narrative proceeded from instability to stability, from the expression of irregular popular violence to its suppression through the power of legitimate representative government and constitutional laws. Stakeholders on the rebel side were contrasted in two camps, or "combinations," that the language of the militia act asserted were "too powerful to be oppressed by the judiciary." The first combination ("machinations of persons whose industry [is] to excite resistance") exerted criminal purposes through irregular meetings to influence opposition. The second combination ("many persons [...] hardy enough to perpetrate acts which I [the president] am advised amount to treason") acted in concert with armed bandits to interfere with officials and private citizens. The proclamation slipped seamlessly from "banditti" (the spontaneous actions of bands of men) to "combinations" (organized interference with "the execution of the laws") to "whiskey rebels" (who threatened the treasonable overthrow of the established order), asserting their mutual subversion of the "just authority of government and of the rights of individuals."[74] Confounding spontaneous attacks against federal excise officials with organized meetings, the proclamation expressed its antipathy to democratic societies, a favored theme of Washington's on which he would expand in his November address to Congress. By capitalizing on the exercise of constitutionally protected speech, association, and assembly as communicating groups capable of organized discourse, the societies represented for Washington the most powerful form of "combination" against an established government.

Like banditti, combinations had a history of their own. Writing to Hamilton, Thomas Sim Lee located the danger of combinations in the "licentious and daring" manner of their enmity to the measures of Government.[75] Combinations had not only declared themselves in favor of rebellion but had refused to acknowledge officers "appointed by the Constitutional authority"; they asserted "the right of making such appointments in themselves." Lee's operational definition of "combinations"—their declarations, conduct, and views—clarified Hamilton's contention that they were a "disease," a malignancy "with which we have to contend." Findley argued that the government had accused state officials and even members of Congress of using their influence to promote unlawful combinations, implying that the organization of like-minded parties was itself evidence of criminality and that the corrosive effect of combinations implicated elected officials.[76] A "combination" also implied "a preconcerted plan" by the people so that the insurrection might commence "among the people" as well as within a state "defective in its duty."[77] This prospect might have been suggested in Hamilton's report and in the language of the militia act, but in the proclamation it was openly communicated as an official government narrative for public consumption.

On the day after the proclamation was published, Randolph authored instructions to operationalize it. He communicated the president's sentiments to the U.S. Commission, made up of Senator James Ross, Pennsylvania Supreme Court justice Jasper Yeates, and Attorney General William Bradford. The commission was mandated to pursue a peaceful resolution to the conflict, "confer [with the rebels] in order to quiet and extinguish" the rebellion, and report to the president on the proceedings. In conformity with the proclamation's command that insurgents disband and its warning against aiding and abetting treason, the instructions directed the commission to advise "whomsoever they choose to speak" that "orders have already issued for the proper militia."[78] Whereas the president might have intended "to take measures for calling forth the militia [rather] than immediately to embody them," as Washington clarified in a subsequent proclamation on September 25,[79] the certification was dated just three days after the president's only meeting with federal and state officials, where the idea of a commission was first raised. The president, it was clear, was pursuing a bifurcated course of action, just as Randolph had warned (peace on one hand and terror on the other), weighing more heavily the use of force.[80] Nearing its endgame, the government interpreted events along two parallel but unequal tracks: the overtly peaceful but not publicly proclaimed overtures of the commission and the openly declared shadow force of the federal militia. In this two-pronged approach, the commission's instructions might have appeared to give it discretion amounting to relative autonomy, but the commission clearly considered itself fully constrained by an understanding that only total submission within an impossible deadline was permitted.[81] It delivered its final report to the president on September 24 with the militia already assembled and ready to march.[82]

The President's Part

At this point, a critical question arises: to what extent was Hamilton, and not Washington, running the show? Thus far into the process, documents suggest that Hamilton had taken charge of the government narrative. But despite Hamilton's persistence, Washington was not a passive observer in the decision-making process. Washington had requested opinions from four cabinet members as a follow-up to a crucial state-federal conference on August 2: Secretary of the Treasury Hamilton, Attorney General Bradford, Secretary of State Randolph, and Secretary of War Knox.[83] The president had stated categorically at the conference that the events struck "at the root of all law & order [...] for if such proceedings were tolerated there was an end to our Constitution & laws."[84] And he had clearly laid out the case: if Justice Wilson were to certify that the facts fell under the law, a militia "should be called forth." Hamilton echoed Washington's language referring to executing the law: "the very existence of Government demands the course and that a duty of the highest nature urges" its pursuit. Knox went even further. He argued that the Constitution imposed on the president the duty of enforcing the laws; his "legal authority" did not extend to failing to execute them.

When we get to Bradford's opinion, however, debate began to open up. Bradford supported the view that the offenses in the West were "High Treason by levying war against [the United States]." And he agreed with Hamilton and Knox that the law had given the president the means to call a federal militia if ordinary means were ineffectual; indeed, his duty was to "exert the higher powers which the people [...] have entrusted to him." But Bradford's opinion was nuanced. He was not averse to offering a warning and weighing the prospects of failed militia recruitment and its potential effect on the government. He proposed alternative circumstances whereby the government might exert forbearance: immediate relief might be provided by the governor of Pennsylvania, and the insurgents might be surveilled to feel out their temper. He proposed that the idea of a militia might be agreed to, but a proclamation should be issued to make the government's case, to express its determination, and to command disbandment. If all else failed, then one could use the militia.

Randolph was more direct. He admitted that Wilson "did not yield to my reasoning," indicating that his objections to certification of the militia had not been well received. Supposing the certificate's validity, however, Randolph offered that the president was not compelled to "array the militia." Indeed, "a calm survey [...] *banishes every idea of calling them into immediate ac-*

tion." Whereas Bradford had begun with the proposition that treason had occurred, and the president could not fail to enforce the law, Randolph was opposed from the outset to the idea that the militia was justified. He had thrown down the gauntlet to open an alternative line, whether it was countenanced or not. That line surely challenged the singularity of the narrative. Considering the varying perspectives provided to the president, the government narrative was no longer predictable or incontrovertible; Washington had been provided choices. The president decided for action over delay, removing the narrative's contradictions rather than allowing for ambiguity or conflict. Randolph would once more adopt the president's position, though not without having registered his disagreement.[85]

On September 2, while preparations for the militia went ahead, Hamilton wrote a report that added another critical level to the narrative. The "unwarrantable proceedings" of 1792 had become a fully developed theme over time, exploiting the president's antipathy to resolutions and political action that undermined the Federalist project or embraced ideas of the French Revolution. That term would later be joined to another, "constitutional resistance," signaling Hamilton's aversion to the citizenry's right to engage in all legal and nonviolent opposition in support of popular sovereignty. Here, the term served as an indicator for the democratic-republican societies that were an underlying target of the August 7 proclamation.[86] Democratic societies were more formal, permanent entities than assemblies or the erratic activities of the rebels. The societies, made up of ordinary citizens and the elite alike, took on a more bourgeois appearance in defending communal rights of freedom of association, speech, petition, and assembly.[87] The societies were more respectable, and thereby more persuasive, political adversaries whose pursuit of legitimacy led them to disassociate from the violence of rebel mobs.[88] But in redefining or displacing popular actions, they also reinforced them.[89] Federalist journalist William Cobbett warned that these "back-door Clubs [...] put a Janus's face" on the matter of the western rebellion: the clubs did not approve of the rebels'"*hostile* operations"; at the same time "they would *never cease to oppose the law which had given them umbrage.*" Cobbett taunted the rebels, claiming that the societies would desert them when times got tough "as the devil ever does at a baffled sinner." Thus, he advised, "all you understrappers of Democratic Clubs; leave off your bawling and your toasting, go home and sell your *sugar* and your *snuff*, and leave the care of Posterity to other heads."[90]

In the face of such taunts, the societies continued to benefit from the symbolic power of their association with the Revolution, with which the whiskey rebels liked to compare their own organized efforts.[91] Indeed, aspects of the Revolution that exploited meeting minutes, resolutions, and correspondence committees informed similar activities within both the rebel assemblies and the democratic societies. Writing to Randolph, the president expressed his deep dissatisfaction with such activity by enclosing a "specimen" of a remonstrance by the Democratic Society of Washington[92] that warned the society would never submit to the whiskey tax. Having declared its love of "those states from which we were all congregated," the remonstrance railed against burdens suffered without benefits from the federal government and complained of the wretched condition of a western country sacrificed to "the prosperity of the Atlantic states."[93] Washington warned Randolph, "The first fruit of the Democratic Society [the insurrection] begins, more and more, to unfold itself."[94] The president was adamant that the "societies were instituted by [their] *artful & designing members* [...] primarily to sow the Seeds of Jealousy & distrust among the people, of the government." They were, in Washington's words, diabolical, "under popular and fascinating guises" and thereby connected to and responsible for instigating the rebellion. In a letter to Daniel Morgan (a Virginian and a brigadier general in the American Revolution), Washington expressed perhaps his clearest understanding of the threat to democracy posed by the combination of rebellious mobs and the societies in his statement that if "the daring and factious spirit which has arisen (to overturn the laws, & to subvert the Constitution)" was not subdued, "there is an end of, and we may bid adieu to all government in this Country; except mob, or Club government."[95]

While translating Washington's warning into action seemed implausible, disparaging the societies proved a convenient political tool in the larger Federalist struggle with the Republican party.[96] As James Madison was to write to James Monroe, Washington's "game" (to which he objected) "was to connect the democratic societies with the odium of the insurrection—to connect the Republicans in Congress with those Societies—to put the President ostensibly at the head of the other party, in opposition to both."[97] Madison declared that denouncing the societies "was perhaps the greatest error of [Washington's] political life." It punished that which the law allowed (free speech and association) and that which the government could not legitimately censure, the very posture Randolph had advised against in 1792.[98] Censuring them, Madison warned, would lead to censuring individuals and the press, a prescient warning that would bear fruit in the sedition acts of 1798.[99]

The Duplicity of Constitutional Resistance

Washington's preoccupation with the democratic societies continued through his November 19 address to Congress, where he gave it even greater oxygen. This raises the question whether the clubs were more than merely a sideshow distracting the government from the more immediate physical threat offered by the rebellion or whether the narrative found them a useful meme to take a swipe at Jacobin antagonists across the country who had little to do with the rebellion itself. Hamilton, nonetheless, never missed a step. The 1792 Pittsburgh meeting continued to incense him, which he had called to John Jay's attention at the time as an egregious demonstration of the "spirit of resistance."[100] The published meeting broadside had focused on a "duty to persist in our remonstrances to Congress' (clearly a constitutionally protected right), "until we are able to obtain its total repeal" (referring to similar measures presumed to be lawful).[101] Hamilton attacked the meeting for using "legal measures to obstruct the operation of a law," which he claimed was "a contradiction in terms." Hamilton was laying down another line of attack, which reappeared in a September 2, 1794, report to Washington.[102] There he contended that "[t]he idea of pursuing *legal* measures to *obstruct* the *operation* of a Law needs little comment" as obstructing the execution of a law after its constitutional enactment was an illegal, that is, a criminal, act. Extending the original language to mean that illegal measures were being incited, Hamilton accused the meeting participants of concealing their intention "under forms that may escape the hold of the law." He built on the theme by attaching it to "what has been called legal or constitutional opposition" against excise officers, referencing the censurable language of the 1792 resolution.

Even as he continued to elaborate on themes for the government narrative (he would, for example, expand the theme of concealing intentions under dubious forms to a main line of attack), Hamilton's immediate targets were Judge Addison and the Pennsylvania judiciary; Hamilton was convinced they were undermining prosecution of the federal excise law.[103] Addison, a legal luminary in Washington County, was the first president judge of the fifth judicial district of Pennsylvania. Initially sympathetic to the anti-tax movement, he became a rigid Federalist but was mistrusted by Hamilton who felt the western courts held back in prosecuting violations.[104] In a letter to Governor Mifflin of March 31, 1794, Addison had distinguished riotous behavior "of a criminal nature" from his own principled view of proper, constitutional resistance, which, he asserted, "alone is justifiable in a free people."[105] Quoting only the language that indicated Addison had urged constitutional resistance, Hamilton represented the judge's words as "proof by his own confession" that he had exerted influence against obeying the law. Hamilton cited the Pittsburgh meeting's resolution refusing contact with and assistance to excise collectors and contended that such resistance permitted everything "short of actual violence or breach of the peace" as it countenanced and promoted noncompliance with execution of the law.[106]

Hamilton went public in a contemporaneous series of newspaper pieces under the pseudonym "Tully," ironically adding his voice to a culture of anonymous writers whose ability to conceal their identity undermined deference to authority.[107] As "Tully," he queried whether resistance would be justifiable in a case where "the bounds of the constitution are manifestly transgressed" or constitutional authority produced oppression. He answered that it was not justified where such resistance originated in an "inconsiderable part of a community," where the oppression was not "extraordinary," or where the law was "acquiesced in by the BODY OF THE COMMUNITY."[108] Such resistance was treason, Hamilton reasoned, for once a law was passed, no matter how unconstitutional or illegal it might appear, the people had no right to resist it. In his view, the censurable resolution, actions against officials, and obstruction of the law all qualified as such constitutional opposition.

The government narrative's separation of constitutional laws (legally enacted by the legislature) from constitutional resistance (the expression of individual rights protected by the Constitution) was much like its distinguishing corresponding committees organized by rebel meetings from similar legitimated committees of the American Revolution. The rebels were not to be permitted access to either constitutional cover or the revolutionary aura of 1776. They fell neither within the boundaries of the foundational text of the new nation, nor under the penumbra of the sanctified acts that birthed it. In making his case, Hamilton's intent in his September 2 report to Washington was to cement the narrative's binary friend/enemy construction and disarm the use of the concept "constitutional resistance" in an effort to construe the rebellion in terms of illegal or unconstitutional acts that could only be resolved using military force.[109]

Hamilton's construction of Addison's phrase underlined the narrative's new use of a potent theme, the duplicity of the rebel cause. If constitutional resistance was merely a phrase "used to conceal a disorderly & culpable intention," and if there was no way to obstruct a "constitutionally enacted law, without illegality and crime," recommending constitutional opposition revealed the rebels' disguised and duplicitous aspect.[110] Thus, Hamilton railed, the rebel spirit could not be rendered palpable, specified precisely, or proved; it appeared in other shapes and "in ambiguous hints susceptible of different interpretations." This language was not unique to Hamilton in 1794. He had already tried it out in 1792 to accuse Thomas Jefferson of engaging in politics that tended to "national disunion, insignificance, disorder and discredit" and to denigrate those who persisted in proposing "innovation and change—the tribe of pretended philosophers, but real fabricators of chimeras and paradoxes."[111] Jefferson, like those who headed the rebellion or, like Addison, tried to engage with it, was no more, Hamilton said, than the treacherous leader of a dance "to the tune of liberty without law" seducing and intoxicating his "deluded followers" with "poisonous draughts." This language of enchantment and magical association, of charismatic leadership and delusion pervaded the early republic as a negative definition of irrational power, nowhere more impressively than in the use to which Hamilton put it.[112]

In constructing the rebels in terms of duplicity, the government narrative established their liminality, their ambiguity. Terms such as "masked" and "disguised" placed them on the margins seeking "for the most part to escape discovery";[113] seditious words attacking government were "covered by a measured cautious and artful language" to escape legal penalties; and those who committed outrages were "obstinate from delusion."[114] Proselytizing in the public square while masked in the guise of the pseudonymous "Tully," Hamilton alerted his fellow citizens to the great cunning of a design "artfully calculated to divert your attention" from an "insidious & pernicious" adversary intent on duping the people by artifice.[115] The insurgents, he claimed, distracted the people with cabals and intrigues from addressing the true question: "shall there be government, or no government?"[116] As Hamilton represented to "Franklin," an anonymous respondent, the insurgents were incapable of understanding freedom; rather, as "jinglers," "barkers," "plotters," they merely seduced others into their "dark conspiracy."[117]

Washington Redux: The Endgame

With the "Tully" essays and the decision to send a federal militia, it appeared that Hamilton was very much in control of the government's construction of the narrative. But Hamilton's win was only tactical. The final telling would not, however, occur at the concrete level at which Hamilton operated, but at the more abstract level where Washington weighed in. In a coda to the government narrative—Washington's proclamation in September and his critical address to Congress in November 1794, as well as his farewell address in September 1796—the president coordinated the appeals the government relied on to characterize the rebellion in a way that inscribed them with his imprint. The proclamation, for example, announced that a federal militia was already on its way to contain the disturbance, consistent with the president's constitutional duty to faithfully execute the laws.[118] Washington knew a call-up of troops from four states to assault western citizens would be unpopular; indeed a letter to the president to that effect, appearing in the *General Advertiser* on August 12, 1794, made that clear. The author "Nestor" objected to "savages" being entitled to negotiation while citizens were threatened with civil war and had to arm themselves against their brothers and shed their blood. Was it necessary to turn the country "into a slaughter-house because the dignity of the United States will not admit of conciliatory measures?"[119] Washington met the objections with an appeal to a superior authority. Acting against their own government, the proclamation declared, the people dishonor the "Divine favor" and "perfect freedom" granted to them that they might "elect their own government." Taking a tone distinctive to Washington, it reflected on the gift of American exceptionalism that had blessed the people and for which they had a duty of care, an "inestimable blessing" evidenced in their constitution and laws.

With the proclamation sticking to the government's binary script, the president had concluded that the influence of the "well-disposed" could not "reclaim the wicked from their fury"; "friends of order" had been alienated and enemies had been invited to join in defiance of the government. The country faced the prospect that "a small portion of the United States shall dictate to the whole union," resetting the political equation of majority rule and presenting the country with an "opportunity" to consider the costs "of a treasonable opposition [. . .] propagating principles of anarchy."[120] Like Hamilton's "experiment," Washington's "opportunity" firmly cast the rebellion in the light of a test for democracy whereby the part dictated to the whole.

The President's Address

More personally invested than the proclamation, the president's address to Congress was not only substantively the more crucial of the two documents, but it revealed Washington's deep interest in putting his own stamp on events. Where the proclamation embodied specific public requirements and policy goals, the address represented Washington's private thoughts made public in the hope they would constitute history's final words concerning the insurrection. As he wrote to his ambassador to Great Britain, Chief Justice Jay, he planned to "be more prolix" than usual[121] but had not had time to prepare his communication to Congress, having just returned "from my tour to the westward." Expressing the "imperious necessity" of returning to "the seat of government while Congress is in Session," Washington recognized the importance of owning the narrative and the danger of letting the matter "go naked into the world, to be dressed up according to the fancy or the inclination of the readers, or the policy of our enemies."[122]

Randolph reinforced the president's fears; if he had merely acknowledged the existence of the rebellion and left the public to its own conjectures, Randolph maintained in a public letter, Washington would lose control of the narrative.[123] As Washington explained to Jay, his usual practice was to convey public matters through his secretary of state; in this instance, he felt pressure from speculations abroad to address matters directly. More importantly, he would not have responded but for the prospect that the insurrection would be variously represented "according to the wishes of some, and the prejudices of others, who may exhibit it as an evidence of what has been predicted 'that we are unable to govern ourselves.'" Washington understood that controlling the narrative of the rebellion was critical to the welfare of the state.

In terms of timing, the parameters were clear. First, Washington was caught between the insurrection and finalizing a neutrality treaty with Britain, the Jay Treaty, that would resolve outstanding issues related to the Revolution; he needed to put the domestic rebellion behind him before he could deal with the international turmoil created by the war between France and Britain. Second, he was worried about how the rebellion would be understood both domestically and internationally and wanted to construct his own reading of the rebellion for his two audiences. He was determined to express publicly a version that made him an active player rather than an acolyte in constructing the narrative. If political figures such as Jefferson thought that challenging Hamilton was as good as challenging the president, Washington put them straight. Washington wrote to Jefferson as late as 1796, for example, to address Republican fears that he was a party man and "a person under a dangerous influence," that of Hamilton. He contended, there was "abundant proof [. . .] that truth and right decisions were the *sole* objects of my pursuit."[124] In criticizing Philip Freneau's *National Gazette* for inciting opposition to the government in the matter of the rebellion, Washington took it that he was being attacked directly or he must otherwise "be a fool inde[e]d to swallow the little sugar plumbs here & there thrown out to him." In condemning his administration, they condemned him: "if they thought there were measures pursued contrary to his sentiment, they must conceive him too careless to attend to them or too stupid to understand them. that tho indeed he had signed many acts which he did not approve in all parts, yet he had never put his name to one which he did not think on the whole was eligible."[125]

In his preparations to deliver his address, Washington made it clear that he was not simply a naïf manipulated by Hamilton or that he played a secondary role in crafting the government narrative. Moreover, Hamilton was not the only player in the administrative equation; there were a circle of federal officials (Knox, Randolph, Bradford) who conveyed different perspectives. As well, a body of recalcitrant Republican state leaders (chief justice of the Pennsylvania Supreme Court Thomas McKean, Pennsylvania governor Thomas Mifflin, and secretary of the commonwealth Alexander Dallas) constituted a formidable council of voices challenging him on the issues of state courts, the militia, and the liberties of the people. Washington, in any case, was a man whose vast military experience defined his professional life, so that, however one argues the case, it is a far stretch to presume that Hamilton had to lead the president on a military matter that had the potential to become the defining moment of his presidency: deploying the military against his own countrymen.[126] Speaking in person before Congress, Washington would project himself as the architect behind how Americans and the world saw the new nation. For Washington, the rebellion might have been fortuitous—"having happened at the time it did." But it was also costly, as it allowed his opponents to express their objections to the Constitution and the laws.[127] Conscious of the moment, Washington would not waste the occasion by delegating his understanding of events. In his address to Congress, he would express his most deeply held views himself.

The question of Washington taking charge in his November address had broader meaning than whether he wrote it himself or if it was in his own words. Just as he intimated in his letter to Jay, which set the table for his address, Washington was taking responsibility for his administration. In his statement ending the rebellion, he took ownership of the government narrative. From the government's point of view, Washington's address was the last act of a drama—telling the tale for the historical record so that the Whiskey Rebellion would be perceived in the future through a government lens. As a matter of discourse, the address clearly narrated the cause of the rebellion, the justification for government action, the ordering of events, the principles and criteria for opposing and then ending the rebellion, what was at stake, and the lessons learned. As Washington told the story, the execution of the constitutionally granted authority to tax was the centerpiece of government concern. In the face of "prejudice, fostered and embittered by the artifice of men," Congress's patience was condemned as fear of executing the law. To avoid the perception of impotence, the executive instituted administrative and legal processes that were met by a violent response. The president, weighing his choices, postponed military action and authorized a commission to offer an amnesty to those who would submit to becoming dutiful citizens. The commission's failure to attract rebel support triggered the use of a militia, which followed in due course.

As a narrative statement, the address established at the outset that the failure of all order and the preservation of "that precious depository of American happiness, the constitution" were at stake. Washington predictably reaffirmed his government's position. Its guiding principles were that the laws be secure from obstruction; that the judiciary be able to bring to justice those who rejected amnesty to serve as examples; and that private individuals be secure from abuse as "friends to peace and good government." The fundamental principle had been posited in the proclamation: no small part of the United States could violate the constitutional dictate that "the will of the majority shall prevail." Two lessons were to be taken from the story. The first was a message from the government to citizens that they could expect "real and substantial consolations" for their misfortune from a republican government. The second was a message from citizens to their government. The process of raising a national militia had demonstrated that citizens understood "the true principles of government and liberty," the necessity of an inseparable Union, and the need to defend both their rights and "the authority of the laws against licentious invasions."[128]

These invasions were the work of Washington's most insidious political opponents, the societies, whom the president foregrounded in his letter to Jay.[129] It was a subject with which he had become obsessed. The rebellion might have insulted his leadership, but he regarded the societies as the underlying enemy. His letter to Henry Lee in the midst of the rebellion revealed he had determined in August to first wage an information campaign against the democratic societies for expressing their "enmity to the Constitution" and "to the exercise of the power of a government."[130] Prosecution, he maintained, would have been "the ready way to make them grow stronger," whereas pursuing a public relations war opened the possibility that they would "fall into disesteem from the knowledge of their origins, and the views with which they have been instituted." An information campaign would expose the "artful design" and "diabolical attempts" that constituted the object of the societies: to shake the government by spreading mistrust and discord. Sensing the power of accounts meant to unsettle his political relationships and the trust of the people, Washington understood that should such efforts not be contradicted the insurrection would gain time and thereby "make the evil more extensive—more formidable—and of course more difficult to counteract and subdue." Washington intimated that the most unshakable integrity was no safeguard against these "fomenters of the Western disturbances," for they sowed distrust and jealousy "to effect some revolution in the government." Fortunately, in his view, the societies were unprepared for the crisis they provoked, which Washington trusted would hasten their annihilation.

The opening lines of Washington's address constituted his most damning words on the rebellion and his final blow against the societies. He wanted the country to be fully aware that "some of the citizens of the United States have been found capable of an insurrection."[131] This grave matter drove Washington "to publish the dishonor of such excesses," hoping to be excused for pitting "citizen against citizen." Publicly, Randolph gave Washington an assist in explicating this part of the narrative under the pseudonym "Germanicus." Washington's use of the term "self-created," he clarified, referred to the societies' proceedings as arrogating "the direction of our affairs, without any degree of authority derived from the people."[132] Thus, "Germanicus" related, societies presumed to usurp the representative powers of the elected legislature and executive.[133] Ever the master of nuance, "Germanicus" denied knowing whether members joined the "patriotic army" individually, whether the societies obeyed the dictates of party and foreign influence, or whether "by their combinations [...they] will not usurp the direction of the people" with the tendency to create a revolution. He denied knowing whether the societies engaged in actions that required force; whether they grew in stages of opposition from the one to the other "from heated argument to riot and violence" and thereafter to associations"; or whether they merely steered the rebels by their influence.[134] Despite these reservations, Randolph held that since the efforts of the societies and the insurgents converged in their antiexcise posture, the societies' objectives "were contemplated in the insurrection." The government narrative converged with Randolph's view as it imputed that any separation of insurgents from the societies was inconsequential since the one emerged from the other like a moth from a cocoon.

Importantly, both Randolph and Washington saw in the insurrection a means of incapacitating the societies that "ought not to be lost."¹³⁵ "Germanicus" thereby took up the task of disabling their collective rights as an association, which, Randolph claimed, differed from those vested in individuals; the Constitution was not designed to protect societies, and individual liberties were not "dependent upon such societies," he argued. Indeed, "the general government was ordained" for the benefit and protection of individuals, not the protection of societies.¹³⁶ Because Washington believed that a society-created mistrust of government could end in a new Revolution—however unjustified—he, too, was amenable, as Thomas Jefferson complained, to curtailing constitutional liberties and doing so by arming "one part of the society against another, of declaring a civil war" with no more of a justification in the speech than was to be found in "a parcel of shreds of stuff from Aesop's fables and Tom Thumb."¹³⁷ Randolph's defense, as a result, ironically reinforced the Republican image of Washington as undercutting the sovereignty of the people, silencing his political opponents, and choosing the Union over the collective rights of association, assembly, and speech for which the American Revolution had stood.¹³⁸

The International Theme

At this point, Washington's willingness to be perceived as undermining citizen's rights became an issue. It was a risk he seems to have accepted because of the audiences he wanted to reach, which included in addition to his domestic audience an international one. This became clear in his farewell address of September 19, 1796, which structured the president's leave-taking in terms of two dominating themes. The primary theme was an international one: a warning to his compatriots of foreign entanglements whereby a foreign power might enslave the United States or undermine its independence through foreign meddling.¹³⁹ Second, Washington warned of the domestic threat of "domination of one faction over another; sharpened by the spirit of revenge, natural to party dissention." The twin threats of "inveterate antipathies" and "passionate attachments," he asserted, were equally to be avoided as influences against whose "insidious wiles" and "set of primary interests" the nation must be constantly aware. Washington chose these themes to ensure the viability of the republic beyond his retirement from public life, encapsulating a vision of the republic that defended the rule of law and the integrity of the Union while it protected "against threats to ordered liberty from mob rule, factionalism and sectionalism."¹⁴⁰ Washington did not speak of a democracy but of a republic, not of authority (which can lead to tyranny) nor of freedom (which can lead to anarchy), but of "ordered liberty" and, ultimately, of the need for Union to preserve liberty. And he did so within the same secular theology combining morality with politics[141] that characterized the government narrative of the rebellion.

For the government narrative's ideal reader, the domestic threat was explicit and imminent and the international threat implied and ominous.[142] But the international issues surrounding the Whiskey Rebellion were nothing if not pragmatic. Such international issues arose with Judge Addison's hopes that the Jay Treaty would terminate the Indian wars in the western counties and negotiations with the Spanish would open the Mississippi; and when tax inspector Neville invoked the fearful prospect that the rebels would "renounce their allegiance to the United States and annex themselves to the British at Detroit."[143] Equally, the presence of British forts created a conflict between Governor Mifflin and the Washington administration over Pennsylvania's plan to settle Presqu'Isle on Lake Erie.[144] And Hamilton's agent Coxe was disturbed that the people in the western counties confused "U.S. excises and those of Great Britain" and that they supposed Congress had adopted "the exceptionable parts of those foreign Systems."[145]

While it was clear that the government's first challenge was to vindicate the Revolution by creating constitutional governance, institutionally the president also carried the burden of foreign affairs. He was as responsible to treaty obligations and the law of nations as he was to an act of Congress.[146] The foreign affairs part of the task, with which Americans had little experience, was important for trade and security and for nation building, particularly in the absence of a standing army.[147] Not only would American interdependence with other nations and the exercise of international power enhance Washington's role as chief executive, but it would enable nation building. On the other hand, with the president's domestic and international agendas so clearly intertwined, it would prove problematic for both nationhood and the country's international standing if states did not bend to federal authority on issues of power and social order.[148]

Internal governance was crucial to fostering stable relations abroad, which was illustrated by the government's preoccupation with quelling the rebellion and trying the whiskey rebels at the same time it was negotiating and ratifying the Jay Treaty.[149] For fear of destabilizing U.S. relations abroad, Federalist congressman Fisher Ames, for example, claimed he had grown tired, "if not ashamed," that the House debate over the democratic societies "gave the world but a bad prospect of our conciliation and unanimity."[150] The infamous journalist William Cobbett, British-born publisher of the widely popular *Porcupine's Gazette*, persisted in laying blame on the rebellion for various political sins. He declared the democratic societies and the whiskey rebels agents of Jacobin France wearing "national cockades" and rallying "under the *tree of liberty* mounted with a bloody Parisian cap," justifying Washington's use of the militia.[151] And he considered that those who contested "the President's Proclamation of Neutrality" (the Jay Treaty) would reduce executive authority to that "of nothing but a Democratic or Jacobin Club." Ever content to roil the political waters, Cobbett blamed Anglophobes for fanning the flames of western rebellion in their newspapers to prevent Washington's re-election, and for openly declaring that they "might want [the chief judge] here to—try the President!"[152]

Public anxiety over the international threat offered by the French to the Washington administration was reinforced in public discourse by accusations that Secretary of State Randolph had colluded with French ambassador Fauchet and that members of the government considered the Constitution a "stepping-stone" to monarchy. The ambassador hinted that the insurgents might align with the British for the purposes of protection or secession and that "political divisions in the United States might weaken the government and excite a considerable conflict." Randolph himself allowed, "[I]f the British could once be found to have meddled with the insurrection, the friends of the insurgents would abandon them, and the militia would step forth with alacrity."[153] A critique from "Atticus" emphasized grievances from the western country about the government's submission to Britain's presence in the West,[154] while a response from "Correspondents" blamed "scribblers, like *Atticus*" for adding to the disorder by publishing "poisonous pieces" that incited the hopes of foreign nations "to see us thrown into confusion, and of course weakness, just at this critical state of our national affairs."[155]

Whatever the president might have hoped, the rebellion was indelibly inscribed in the public mind as an event with international implications for the success of the new American democracy. His construction of the government narrative inevitably reflected the tension between domestic and international motives. We find that tension expressed consequentially in the president's pursuit of a standing U.S. army, which he attached as an appeal to his 1794 Address to Congress. Conscious of the importance of suppressing a domestic rebellion, Washington saw an opportunity to enhance his position on the international stage. He offered an argument that Republicans had long feared, appealing to Congress to support a standing army that could, as the Constitution envisioned, "execute the Laws of the Union, suppress Insurrections, and repel Invasions."[156] It would take a year for Congress to act, but the combined domestic and international threats offered by the Whiskey Rebellion, the war between Britain and France, and General Wayne's Indian War would join in gaining from Congress what Washington had been seeking since he accepted command of the Continental army. On February 28, 1795, An Act for Calling Forth the Militia repealed the 1792 Militia Act and gave the president the power Congress itself had previously exercised under Article 2, Section 8 of the Constitution to call forth the militia.[157] The intimation behind the government narrative that the rebellion would ultimately be a good thing, an experiment that would provide an unexampled opportunity for national government, seemed, at least in this sense, to have paid off.

Conclusion

In assessing how the Washington administration told the story of the Whiskey Rebellion, we can draw several conclusions. Taken together, its central themes read like a popular novel with a moral for those who would escape their assigned station in the political hierarchy. The narrative blurred the line between fact and fiction, sensationalized unique events, and created a litany of crimes to constitute an epidemic of lawlessness and disorder. The opportunity presented was multifold. First, in playing against a long tradition of resistance rooted in popular sovereignty, the government exploited language attached to banditry to frame the rebels as outlaws on the fringe of society. A whole range of conduct became fodder for opprobrium: chivarees, hangings in effigy, and raising liberty poles, outright refusal to pay excise taxes, rejecting legal writs, and closing courts and inspectors' offices, as well as such extreme forms of rough justice as abductions, beatings, tarring and feathering, and arson. Second, the government narrative attacked officials sympathetic to the rebels, nonviolent protest, petition, correspondence committees, assemblies, and societies. This part of the narrative focused on resistance most likely to be constitutionally protected. The government's contesting of "constitutional resistance" such as organized gatherings and associations was itself a contradiction in terms. As the term was framed, one could not constitutionally resist a properly constituted government aside from elections. Organized "combinations" were considered such a threat, reaching to the very foundation of constitutional democracy. If banditry consisted of incidental acts of violence against selected targets, combinations represented organized resistance by large numbers of dissidents against legitimate government activity. Organization itself became a high-end enemy whereby speeches and resolutions developed the ideological framework of resistance and disseminated it in handbills, circular letters, and newspaper notices and letters to the editor. As the government discovered, while acts of bandits could be controlled by ensuring the judicial system functioned properly, freedom of speech and association were not so easily contained as they were constitutionally guaranteed rights essential to the foundation of democracy.

One could argue that the abstractness of the government account was key to its appeal.[158] The end-of-game "Tully" and "Germanicus" pieces in the press created the impression of high seriousness like the language that declared the nation's revolution against Britain or made up the constitutional ratification debate. But the critical reports, communications, addresses, and proclamations that contributed to the developing narrative largely tell a different story. Their appeal was cast not in the high rhetoric of principled discourse. Rather, easily massaged messages simplified and reified the factual record. Here, the government discounted legitimate rebel grievances to vilify the rebels. It smoothed the narrative, glossed over events, and conflated parties to the conflict to essentialize the threat of rebellion. When this body of material waxed eloquent, it was to raise the stakes for the nation to a political jeremiad, exploiting biblical tropes of the type used in the yellow fever epidemics of the 1790s; it called on divinity to punish the sins of the metaphorical son who had denied the source of his blessings and risked his own and his country's destruction.

The backstory to the government narrative explains much of the complicated set of economic, political, and military conditions that motivated its construction. For one thing, western Pennsylvania was in many ways a laboratory for the nation. It stood as a new land on the edge of the world, determined to make productive that which was barbaric. Washington speculated in land and ejected western squatters like those who would later take part in the rebellion.[159] Justice Wilson, too, grabbed up land to become, like the president, one of the most substantial landholders in the country. Wilson would certify the use of the federal militia to suppress the rebellion, while Washington would ride into the rebellion with the aura of the American Revolution trailing in his wake.[160] Both men's fortunes were menaced by the rebel threat to lay waste the western country.[161]

The government narrative also revealed less personal motives. The nation needed to pay off debts from the American Revolution and to pursue Indian wars on the frontier.[162] It had paid soldiers with land bounties that led to their selling what they had earned for a pittance to speculators whom the government later reimbursed with full repayment. To complicate matters, the republican spirit of western immigrant Scottish and Irish settlers ran up against the interests of a wealthy elite in the East which saw its fortune in their land. In this unstable terrain, the Whiskey Rebellion became the ultimate experiment for suppressing the obstreperous localism of settlers and reinforcing a national government that favored wealthy eastern land speculators. The government narrative became a tool in the hands of that assertion of state power, allowing an elite to capitalize on the opportunities the narrative promised. The government enhanced its political standing, partisan Federalist interests, Hamilton's economic plan, and the pursuit of a standing army. As a side benefit, the country saw a general gain to the nation's strength, finances, and reputation.

The construction of the narrative included several steps. Initially, it had to establish a floor that would justify the military intervention as a necessity and ensure the persuasiveness of the story it told. This was accomplished by depicting legislative attempts to repeal the excise tax as feeble, the courts as incompetent, and the executive as left without a choice. The narrative emphasized that while the western population desired order, it "unaccountably" worked against its own interests in "unwarrantable" ways. Its eastern audience found government-sponsored themes such as patience, agreement, peace, and common ground more attractive than the fear, hate, conflict, and suspicion that the rebellion evoked. The propensity to hear steadying words favored the government account and undermined a rebel counternarrative, setting a scene where it could easily discount the victimhood of the rebels and their negative message of grievances.

The compositional process was relatively simple. While central thematic refrains reinforced the government version (the patient government, the ungrateful rebel, the story of waste, the story of fulfilling the law), the legitimacy of a rebel narrative was rhetorically disabled. Accusations of deviousness assaulted the credibility of a conflict-ridden rebel camp to inflect any counterargument with a presumed duplicity. Hamilton's chronicle of events established the deep roots and pervasiveness of rebel violence, its predatory nature and mob mentality. It represented the rebellion as an armed force disguised to evade discovery and aimed against private citizens. The narrative created an inverted order in which, perversely, those who were themselves outside the law outlawed officials. It repeated the mantra of rebel bandits having proved "too powerful to be suppressed" by ordinary means. Insurgents were outside ordinary experience, baffling, unreachable by any other means than those exerted by a superior force justified in using excessive power. The government narrative spoke to an essentialized representation that indiscriminately conflated criminal with legal acts. It treated acts at varying expressive, symbolic, and physical levels indistinguishably, so that speech became predetermined acts and those of the moment went undifferentiated. It redefined constitutional expression as treasonous conduct and confused individual acts with organized resistance to create a general impression of resistance against all law. Obfuscating legal, peaceful, and constitutional opposition allowed the government to construe a wide range of activity as rebellion. In an abundance of contradictions, even unconstitutional laws were legal.

The government's cover story for its inconsistent treatment of rebel activity was that rebel acts were hidden, conjectural, or contested and that, once discovered, they were obscurantist, politicized, ambiguous, or hypothetical. Such obfuscations justified claims that the rebels had interfered with data collection, suborned perjury, or otherwise undermined prosecution. The deviousness of the rebels was, moreover, responsible for the oxymoronic nature of their "constitutional resistance." In this reading, any presumably peaceful or constitutional opposition could be redefined as subversive. Much like the "invisible" proceedings of the Salem witch trials, the cunning design and artful language of the rebels made any defense a subterfuge and left any act open to any number of interpretations.[163]

To this depiction of rebel instability and pathological resistance the government narrative opposed the full force of official legitimacy. Disinclined to exercise self-reflection, it assumed the truth of its own interpretive plot. It deleted complications, cut off alternative explanations, and rejected meaningful realignment or mediation. In the same way, the government's preferred ending—amnesty, "perpetual oblivion" for past acts in exchange for total, unconditional submission—expressed the superordinate authority of a hegemonic narrative.[164] The binary nature of the government experiment required not merely a negative force (a violator of the public welfare) and a positive goal (to re-establish the law), but total and absolute differences between the government message and the rebel message, irrespective of the variety of rebel factions and grievances or shared beliefs between the parties. The narrative required an intensity as well in the opposed elements to justify a potent counterforce: the full power of the presidency exhibited in the military option. If the response was not harsh, then the evil was not deep, so that Randolph's theory of the least harsh means necessary to achieve a peaceful end had limited appeal. If the evil was not great, the experiment in which the government was engaged was unworthy and the opportunities created were limited. The smaller goal of returning the western country to order and law thereby paled in comparison with an announced, larger goal (preserving the Union) that required so great an opponent as the federal government.

To be credible, the threat to the Union had to be recognizable to the target group (like something that could happen to its members) and insidious (a rot from within) to be meaningful; but to be feared, it must be outside the group's experience (from beyond the frontier, outlawed). The white man disguised as a savage, masked, having "gone native," was a prototype the narrative could easily capture and exploit to this purpose, a theme to be discussed in chapter 3. To cool the madman, as Hamilton described the process, the narrative must put down the beast internalized from the margins. In an extended sense, the West was the beast on the margin that the East must tame before it inhabited the body politic.

While the government narrowed its view to extreme examples of simplified rebel acts, it excluded a broad range of nonviolent and moderate conduct that cut across classes and occupations. This latter body of rebel activity expressed an ideological content in common with the government and spoke not of physical confrontation but of abstract political values leading to autonomy for rights-bearing subjects. The government thus purposefully elided many who saw themselves not as bad bandits but as democratic actors, good victims denied their autonomy by economic oppression. Redefined in the narrative as a treasonous subject, the rebel produced by the government subverted government by asserting individual rights in the face of an assertion of the power of government that subjugated individual rights. Positioned in an inverted relationship, the rebel's choice was revolt or servitude, a double bind in which rebellion took on opposed, contradictory meanings; it was both treason and an assertion of one's legal rights, transforming the party subject to oppression into a treasonous subject.

The government narrative, in sum, narrowed rebels' rights to just one: the right of total submission. The narrative produced not the rights-bearing citizen typified by the revolutionary legacy but a nonagentive figure antithetical to democratic man. If the rebel were to come within the world of order, it would be through total submission, not as an autonomous agent. The narrative thus emptied the rebel figure of the multiple meanings and heterogeneity by which it was imaginatively recognized at the level of lived experience (the story of economic oppression, diminished political representation, and geographic discrimination told by the rebels). Those issues were concrete and local in a world in which allies and advocates crossed class lines and represented diverse positions. There was little here that was reductionist in the sense that the government represented it. All laws did not reside in one law as the government contended; all factions did not collapse into the rebel imaginary concocted by the government; all grievances did not reduce to lawlessness. The abstract rebel position assumed and imposed by the government was not that of the rebel on the ground. What the government's underdetermined perspective missed was what fed the rebellion, made it persist, and made it so difficult to suppress.

To assess the effect of the government narrative, it helps to understand its source: the revolutionary elite. The salience of the government message depended on the reputation of high officials with historic credentials, those responsible for the sanctity of the state and its survival. Its appeal lay in the East where the class, lineage, and elevated rhetoric of elites supplied its cachet. There, confrontation of the government message only confirmed the oppositional hostility on which the narrative depended; toning down its response would have run the risk of appearing weak or seeming to concede. The government's best bet for its eastern constituency was to remain stubbornly within twin themes: the disloyal child or servant resisting the unappreciated parent or master; the bad neighbor turning away from a common burden and imposing on his neighbor's liberties. Both themes added biblical overtones to the secular political logic that dominated the narrative. Meanwhile, at the base of the narrative sat the theme that had the greatest resonance for an eastern audience: the nation's voracious economic appetite, in the form of the whiskey tax, had to be satiated. To satisfy this appetite, the government had pitted citizen against citizen, risking the dishonor of a nation willing to send an army against its own citizens and the humiliation of a proud administration. But the prize was one for which the government was willing to pay a considerable price. Washington himself had already conceded in 1792 that he would reluctantly stay in office for a second term to ensure that the price was worth the prize: the federal government's right to tax its citizens, access to western land, and, ultimately, an inseparable Union.[165]

With the government narrative established as a tale of existential threat and oppositionality, and with the government having seized on the opportunity offered by the frontier counties to strengthen the powers of centralized government, we can begin the process of identifying the conditions that underlay the rebellion and the context in which it arose. Our storyline thus proceeds in chapter 2 by examining the environment in which popular law thrived and fed into the rebellion. There we will ask what constituted resistance from the rebel perspective and how it contributed to the development of a rebel narrative. Supplying these missing pieces to the history of the rebellion entails understanding how resistance defined itself in opposition to authority, including several critical pieces. First, the court system and the law were caught in the crush between the localism of popular politics and the aspirations of national leadership. Once western Anti-Federalists exposed the fault lines between state and national legal culture, it became clear that the antitax movement would become implicated in the battle over the law and that popular participation in the law was a critical part of what inspired those who joined the Whiskey Rebellion. Popular participation in official courts thus becomes as important as popular court closings if we are to gauge the people's relation to the law and their attempts to engage in forms of popular justice on their own. Second, we need to understand how rebel assemblies operated through the scattered and conflicting agency of popular sovereignty, which displaced and decentralized responsibility across numerous actors. The amorphous, protean mass represented by the collectivity of popular assemblies stood in stark relief to the singular agency of a legitimate government and a charismatic leader identified with the origins of the nation.[166] In political terms, these antithetical frameworks fractured the common community created by the Revolution and accelerated the popular politics of the 1790s as the country began to split into Republican and Federalist parties.[167]

Chapter 2 begins an exploration of western legal practices that will be complemented by chapter 3's examination of traditional and invented forms of resistance. Chapter 2 considers how Pennsylvania Anti-Federalists debated federal-state court jurisdiction and the peoples' access to individual rights in the ratification convention; many would go on to join the rebellion to continue and extend that debate in rebel assemblies. It examines the assertion of federal authority on the frontier and its effect on state courts, including a review of state riot cases during the rebellion. The popularity of arbitration and other forms of participation in the courts provide a background for examination of extralegal popular courts ranging from militia and democratic society courts to courts that arose as an extension of the rebel assembly apparatus. Together, chapters 2 and 3 advance our understanding of the rebel perspective by telling the untold tale of local traditions and inventions, of official and unofficial popular inputs into the rebel understanding of law and justice. They explicate the popular struggle for rights in terms of regional equality and direct participation in democratic governance and law, uncovering a powerful narrative that challenged both the government construction of the rebellion and the country's assumptions about constitutional democracy.

CHAPTER 2

Federal, State, and Popular Law in the Western Country

The sphere of influence dominated by the government narrative did not include the western counties that resisted government control. As we pick up the thread that adds the rebel perspective to the story of the Whiskey Rebellion, we find that resistance to the government narrative lay in a local sense of justice and individual rights and an insistence on grassroots traditions. This expression of backcountry democracy undermined the people's confidence in state and federal government courts and law while it fed a preference for extrajudicial arbitrations, private prosecution, and the localism of justice of the peace courts; it indulged just as readily in extralegal forms of justice that emerged from democratic societies and assemblies. Insofar as ordinary people felt legitimized by a law that gave them respect, how law achieved popular acceptance becomes a critical floor for understanding the rebellion. Here we find that the forces of localism and the conflict between federal, state, and local jurisdiction created the parameters within which the western legal system operated. Local forces served as a base for the rebel movement in its struggle for rights-based subjecthood, including such questions as how the courts and the law worked for those on the frontier. At the same time, the legislated law, judicial proceedings, and enforcement of court verdicts were essential forms of dispute resolution and a necessary platform for government order and legitimacy. As an expression of their agency, common people felt they had a right to participate in processes that made the law, adjudicated it, and enforced it; that participation was informed by local theories of popular sovereignty whereby the people assumed an understood role in governance. When popular participation was abrogated or the people felt disenfranchised of their rights, they raided jails, closed courts and roads, and boycotted debt auctions; officials, for fear of being humiliated, declined to do their jobs. Practices within the legal system that were popular with the people increased their participation in government and acceptance of local authority; equally, customary forms of justice were supported because they were familiar and close to the life of ordinary people. These processes were the subject of popular governance efforts in the assemblies and popular enforcement rituals and traditions and were related to popular forms of law that developed within or were collateral to the courts. Taking up these aspects of the people's relationship to the law, this chapter contends, is indispensable to understanding the nature and function of rebel dissent and the construction of a rebel narrative.

Problems with the law leading up to the Whiskey Rebellion began with the courts in colonial times. In 1766, for example, New Yorkers instituted a popular court to address the fact that common people did poorly in official courts.[1] In North Carolina and South Carolina in the 1760s and 1770s, "regulators" imposed a local form of justice that legitimized vigilante efforts, adopting tactics similar to those of the Sons of Liberty of 1766 and the Tea Act resistance of 1774–1775.[2] Despite its disruptive appeal, popular regulation had its own rules, not entirely the work of a mob as much as citizens establishing agreed-upon measures. Self-governing regulations and local committees were established to discipline those who offended community norms, adjudicate complaints, and reform delinquents.[3]

Western county court systems basically underperformed from the time they were established in the 1780s and early 1790s in cases the people cared greatly about, especially debt cases and conflicting land claims; this stimulated a popular cry for arbitration and extralegal courts and increased the use of private prosecution. Nationalization of the Ohio region under the 1787 Northwest Ordinance further complicated affairs by establishing national authority in law and governance that competed with state authority.[4] Meanwhile, forces sent to the West failed to protect against pervasive Indian attacks, and eastern land speculators successfully accessed state courts to dislodge settlers, a situation assisted by corrupt, unresponsive officials. Initially, traditional popular justice compensated for ineffective courts through customs of physical and symbolic shaming called "rough music" that immigrants had brought with them when they crossed the Atlantic in the 1700s.[5] Such practices addressed domestic discord and property disputes, but with broad social change and the breakdown of hierarchy and domestic order crowds took the law into their own hands.⁶

Western Pennsylvania crowds were led by men of the community, often justices of the peace and militia officers, who generally maintained good relations with elite landholders and office holders.⁷ The crowds themselves were made up largely of homesteaders and townspeople. Squatters and hunters were intermixed, many of whom lived the white Indian life even as they had a stake in the community as intermittent settlers and farmers.⁸ Resolved to agitate for government reform and the rights of the people, crowds constituted a moral economy of a quasi-judicial nature.⁹ Because they acted as an arm of the community, they were granted leeway to control community standards and act unofficially in remonstrating with the state legislature on specific grievances such as land disputes, debts, and official fees.¹⁰ Their political skills were, in any case, underdeveloped,¹¹ which often resulted in a pattern of behavior somewhere between riot and popular assembly.

The isolation of the Pennsylvania frontier led westerners to disregard unfriendly laws and interfere in a legal system that favored creditors and where debtors were forced to choose beggary or resist the legal process.¹² Scarcity of cash and debt-based foreclosures on properties were crucial factors that led many to close courts and obstruct sheriff's auctions;¹³ witnesses refused to testify and juries to indict or convict, while justices of the peace shielded reluctant witnesses. Charges against constables and other officials who declined to do their jobs were overwhelmingly dismissed.¹⁴ The picture was not totally one-sided, however, for the frontier population's contempt for the rule of law met with "an institutional response" in which challenges to the authority of the state saw 100 percent convictions and commanded the stiffest penalties.¹⁵ Prosecution in cases where the elite were victims was favored but not where victims were Indians or members of the working class. Western Pennsylvania was open, as a result, to being made an example by the Washington administration as a warning to frontier areas in Kentucky, Virginia, and the Ohio valley.¹⁶

Pennsylvania Anti-Federalists and the Constitution

The challenge to judicial authority came not only from popular resistance but from political figures who found the federal authority granted by the Constitution oppressive. Ratification of the Constitution brought the conflict to a head, as Anti-Federalists warned of potential conflicts between the state and national judiciaries that would last through the first half of the 1790s. With western Anti-Federalists voting seven to two against ratifying the Constitution and calling for amending it in the failed Harrisburg convention of 1788,[17] the conflict appeared to be resolved by a compromise in the 1789 Judiciary Act that created three levels of federal courts—district, circuit, and supreme courts. Unfortunately, the compromise did little to make the states feel part of national government.[18] Western politicians had not only been excluded from the convention that wrote the federal Constitution, but from 1785–1795 they remained in the minority in the state assembly. Five of the seven westerners who voted against the Constitution (William Findley, Albert Gallatin, John Smilie, John Edgar, and James Marshall) ultimately became involved as leaders of the rebellion and shaped the ideology of the assemblies organized by the four insurgent counties (Washington, Westmoreland, Fayette, and Alleghany).

Unlike the gentlemanly bourgeoisie that met in democratic societies, the insurgents provoked a major challenge to national authority in reopening the debate Anti-Federalists had initiated on how fair and equal representation must be to prove responsive to the people's needs.[19] On a more pragmatic level, western Pennsylvania was a crucible for Anti-Federalist thought on topics that would come up again in the rebel assemblies discussed in the present chapter and in the rebel trials taken up in the next chapter. These included assaulting the competency of state courts to administer the law, undermining the liberty rights of speech, petition, and assembly, and federalizing a militia to enforce execution of federal law. When backcountry democracy erupted in rebellion in 1794, as a result, it was not a unique event but a continuation of Anti-Federalist resistance to the federal Constitution and the rise of popular constitutionalism.[20]

The ratification fight reverberated in the Whiskey Rebellion around the very issues that were the cornerstones of Anti-Federalist participatory democracy and the radical politics of localism and egalitarianism.[21] Of particular importance for the purposes of this chapter, three western delegates (Findley, Smilie, and Edgar) signed an "official" report dissenting from the work of the ratification convention on the issues of federal judicial powers and the rights of the people. Of the fourteen amendments the report proposed, nine related to positive protections for liberty rights, one to reserving power over the militia to the states, one to preserving the independence of the judicial branch, and one to limiting federal judicial power. The remaining two related to power over elections and treaties. The report linked the overarching concern that federal government would "annihilate and absorb" state governments to the fear that only a despotic form of government could rule so extensive a national territory. The Article 1 authority the Constitution granted to the national government to make all laws necessary to executing its powers and Article 6's assertion of the supremacy of federal law alarmed Anti-Federalists, who were convinced the states would be deprived of every means of defense against the larger sovereign. That state judges would be bound to national laws and the U.S. Constitution and would be required to credit the laws and courts of every other state was equally debilitating. Conjoined within one government, the states were thereby to be constrained by the "so various and extensive" judicial powers of Congress.[22]

The Constitution's omission of a bill of rights, which eleven of the thirteen original state constitutions contained, was another matter of distress. As one critic, "Brutus," queried, in a constitution "vested with such extensive and indefinite authority" that did not specify the powers guarded by a bill of rights, how were citizens' rights to be preserved?[23] The dissenting western report argued that the stipulation of those rights in state constitutions were "entirely superseded" in the national constitution, affecting the liberty and welfare of the people in ways that would undermine trials by jury, involve the use of a federal militia against the people, and increase government interference in local affairs, intimating the evils that in fact followed in the insurrection. The report predicted that appellate courts might try both fact and law without a jury; persons tried in federal courts may be removed to courts in a distant vicinage without the benefit of a jury of their neighbors; and federal civil courts would not require trial by jury. It identified the prospect of using a militia to oppress those who resisted despotism and crushing "the last efforts of expiring liberty" and of an ominous process in which the government would multiply its officers—"judges, collectors, tax gatherers, excisemen, and the whole host of revenue officers"—until, like a swarm of locusts, they covered the land.[24] The paranoia attending the threat to liberty rose to such a level that Brackenridge, who supported the Constitution but had lost his election bid for the convention, resorted to a wicked burlesque of the Anti-Federalist position, pointedly on the question of a bill of rights: "There was no occasion for a bill of *wrongs* for there will be wrongs enough. But oh! A *bill of rights*." Without trial by jury, lawyers who harangue and "bend" juries would be demolished. Without a free press, "Not so much as an advertisement for a stray horse, or run away negro, can be put in any of the Gazettes."[25]

For Anti-Federalists, the conflict between the state and federal judiciary was a matter of the gravest judicial concern.[26] "Centinel" argued that "state judiciaries would be wholly superseded" if they were used as federal trial courts and that a clear separation between the two was implausible.[27] Nor should federal courts take on cases that should be tried by the states or be empowered to address conflicts between states and between citizens and foreign states. The scope of the law was also at risk, based on the fear that federal courts might assert "a potentially expansive common-law criminal jurisdiction," unrestricted by positive law.[28] One threat did come to fruition: that the lower federal courts would use the law as a governing instrument. This tendency, as chapter 4 discusses, was clearly visible in the jury charges of federal circuit courts in the 1790s where judges established a nexus between politics and law in the struggle between Federalists and Republicans over the stability of the state. As we shall see in chapter 5, early treason cases such as those of the Whiskey Rebellion constituted a perfect site for the intersection, allowing courts to test the viability of punishing political opponents using common law and presenting an opportunity to protect the administrative state.[29] Throughout the 1790s, this prospect, as Anti-Federalists in the ratification conventions had anticipated, represented a dangerous tendency away from local and state control.

The issue of vicinage proved the point of the spear in demonstrating just how much control state courts would retain.[30] Federal courts could move a federal excise tax case from its local vicinage and a state court's jurisdiction, affecting the understood right to trial in the place where, in the words of "[a] Citizen," "each knows every man by whom he may be judged."[31] Once federal intervention abridges the power of common man jurors and imposes itself on their "share of Judicature," he argued, the soul flees; "only a dead corpse [is] left behind." By implication, federal appeal courts would leave no place for a jury. Further, federal appellate review would have the authority to determine the validity of state laws, influencing local concerns in any matter in which the federal government had an interest.[32] Another complaint assailed appointed federal courts that might enlarge their power over interpreting the Constitution and bind the legislature to adopt its principles as rules.[33] Federal courts might then expand criminal law into all private disturbances and public commotions and might aggregate additional courts to manage trials they appropriated, creating new laws to keep them in business and expand their authority.

If Anti-Federalists distrusted the power of the federal judiciary, Federalists were afraid of local prejudice. Because general and local policies did not subscribe to the same interests, state courts could not be trusted with enforcing national laws. A prime reason to establish federal courts, Federalists held, was to overcome local objections to state courts recovering debts, the influence of debtors, and juries susceptible to local pressures, all of which hampered the ability to collect taxes. Despite being structurally ill-defined, national courts had the ability to overturn state verdicts and override state courts; at the same time, a national court system would serve federal interests.[34] Federal and state jurisdictions would be separated, in the end, but federal power would be enlarged. Where the federal government was the weaker of the two when the 1789 Judiciary Act was passed, it was no longer so by the end of the 1790s.[35]

Pennsylvania Courts

Distrust of courts in Pennsylvania might have infused popular resistance and the ratification debates, but it had roots as well in state history, emanating from changes that occurred when the state replaced its liberal 1776 Constitution with a more conservative one in 1790 and enacted a judicial reform act in 1791. Judicial reform replaced popularly elected local justices of the peace with appointed, salaried judges[36] and gave more power to Pennsylvania Supreme Court circuit courts. In the same way they elevated technical legal forms over oral evidence, these changes nullified local practices in favor of state control and eastern interests.[37] On the critical question of land issues, for example, the state supreme court discounted settlers' claims in favor of land companies with eastern connections. Even with the legislature accommodating western communities, the Supreme Court prevailed on land questions from 1790 to 1806, deploying the same justices who ruled on titles in the circuit courts to preside over appeals to the full court.[38]

State courts were nonetheless obliged to respect federal law and see it was enforced, even as federal encroachment undermined respect for state law[39] and exacerbated popular discontent. The Washington administration accused Pennsylvania's courts of incompetence for their failure to prosecute whiskey tax cases successfully and used the federal Judiciary Act of 1789 to redirect important cases to newly instituted federal courts.[40] The government's excuse that the western counties were in upheaval and the jails in Philadelphia were "more secure than the others" was a palpable insult to state authority.[41]

The story of the state-federal struggle over prosecution for riotous acts and violations of the whiskey tax is best told by tracking western court president judge Alexander Addison's judicial activities from 1792. Even as he transitioned from a backcountry democrat to a Federalist, the judge grew increasingly frustrated over who should try the rebels. Addison advocated for aggressive action by state courts to render the power of federal courts moot and thus nullify the federal assault on state sovereignty.[42] He argued that resort to the federal courts was "impracticable" without sacrificing individual liberty and "the just authority of state courts."[43] All the same, as Congress's laws were "as punishable in the state courts" as state laws, Pennsylvania courts had to assure suppression of the riots and give the federal government no excuse "to take notice of them."[44] It was better, he claimed, to render the federal courts useless than dangerous.[45]

Addison instructed a grand jury in 1792 to examine, try, and punish those who broke the laws of their county like "watchmen sanctioned by the laws."[46] An attack in Washington County on excise inspector William Faulkner, he warned, wounded the dignity of government and endangered the state.[47] The most insidious acts were those of unauthorized private citizens redressing local grievances. Such acts represented "specious pretences of justice" and yet were "boasted of as patriotic labors."[48] Addison appealed to state judges to shore up the courts, but many hesitated, as he informed Governor Thomas Mifflin, thinking "it was not our duty to hunt after prosecutions."[49] Nonetheless, Addison resisted the entreaties of Hamilton's supervisor of collections, George Clymer,[50] to take depositions in 1792 regarding federal enforcement of the excise tax. Clymer, he complained, wanted to farm out his commission to "an inhabitant of this corner, everyday exposed to the passions of the people in it." Like his fellow judges, Addison faced the danger of isolation in the western country, which, coupled with a desire not to stray too far from popular sentiment, led many judges to refuse tasks that would appear coercive to the people. Judges could limit local pressure by circuit riding through the western counties, but it also prevented them from appreciating local conditions. To add another layer of complexity, judges identified with members of the elite and their fellow professionals and maintained career ambitions that would profit from government support. In Addison's case, he concluded that he would do all that was proper "to bring justice in the proper courts of Pennsylvania," but that was all that could be expected until he was convinced of his duty to do any more.[51]

By 1794, Addison's response to Governor Mifflin's appeal to prosecute more cases related to violation of the federal tax was hardly different. In March, he contended that he found little in the way of criminal cases before the court that he could prosecute, other than what he and Mifflin had shared in a private conversation.[52] His claim of limited cognizance was soon enough leaked to Hamilton, who reacted to "the resentment of a subordinate officer of notorious and unfriendly affections."[53] Addison's recourse was to alert Pennsylvania secretary of the commonwealth Alexander Dallas that he had sent urgent instructions to state judges, magistrates, attorneys, and courts "to procure testimony by subpoenaing & recognizing witnesses, etc., & to prefer indictments against those who may be discovered as engaging in the riots."[54] His intent was to convince the government there was a viable judicial alternative to sending a federal militia. Addison's letter was sent on July 14, two days before the defining events precipitated by the armed attacks on Inspector Neville's home. In little more than a week, a broadside appeal was issued in which the governor directed officials "to exert all your influence and authority" within their jurisdictions to "pursue with the utmost vigilance, the lawful steps for bringing the offenders to justice."[55]

By the time state and federal officials joined the president at a crucial conference on August 2,[56] the performance of the state judiciary had become a major point of contention. It was as vital a concern at the conference as the discussion of treason law (treated in chapter 1) and the reliability of Hamilton's evidence of rebellion (to be taken up in chapter 5). The issue here was whether civil authority was incompetent to its task, a sufficient condition for calling out military force. Dallas cited Addison to the effect "that if the business was left to the courts, the rioters might be prosecuted and punished." Chief Justice McKean declared "that the judiciary power was equal to the task of quelling and punishing the riots." And Governor Mifflin, in reprising the conference, told the president "the incompetency of the Judiciary Department of [Pennsylvania] to vindicate the violated laws, has not at this period been made sufficiently apparent"; employing military power should not occur until a fair judicial experiment "has proved incompetent to enforce obedience, or to punish infractions of the law." Like Addison and Dallas, Mifflin clarified that where rioters opposed U.S. laws they had been "indicted, convicted, and punished, before the tribunals of the State" in the same manner as rioters who opposed Pennsylvania laws. He contended, tellingly, that he considered it improper to call out the state militia while judicial authority was "competent to punish the Offenders" and that he had issued instructions to every official from sheriffs and judges to militia inspectors and the state attorney general to investigate the riots and "institute the regular process of the law" to bring offenders to justice.[57]

Chastised two days later by Secretary of State Edmund Randolph, Mifflin responded that under the federal Constitution jurisdictional questions of state and federal authority were confused and overlapping.[58] Mifflin was careful not to undermine federal authority while he still hoped to exert the state's civil authority (its judiciary) and exhort state officers, and he gingerly referred to "the auxiliary intervention of the State Government." He would not condemn the federal government for measures he would have approved if Pennsylvania had undertaken them, but, as governor, it was only proper that he take into consideration both federal and state policy, laws, and authority without being misunderstood. He believed, and contended that the president agreed, that whereas it was untenable to place the state in a "separate and unconnected" position, it was also the case that the general government's powers were insufficiently clear.

The competency of the state courts to which Mifflin adverted had become the linchpin on which authorization of a federal militia would depend. With little in the way of trial records, Addison's law reports and Hugh Henry Brackenridge's accounts of litigation in western county courts provide useful insights into this issue. As early as 1785, Brackenridge represented twelve rioters indicted in criminal court in Westmoreland County on a charge of attacking excise inspector William Graham to protest a despised state excise tax on whiskey. On the back of his argument "that an honest fellow ought not to be severely treated, who had done nothing more, than to shave the under hairs from the head of an excise man, who wore a wig at any rate," the rioters were still convicted and fined.[59] Brackenridge's attack on the excise law in another case that year involving seventy distillers in Alleghany County had political if not legal value. It gained him a reputation of being so "staunch against all excises"[60] that he used his fame to get himself elected to the legislature in 1786.

Regarding the federal whiskey tax, Brackenridge defended in a Washington County district court case (*United States v. Jacob Wolf*, 1796) in which a violation for distilling whiskey eventuated in a promise to pay arrears. This case involved the payment of a duty on a still and the general suspension of that duty from July 1793 to July 1794. Enforcing the payment of arrears was a hardship, Brackenridge argued; there was no office of inspection in Washington County in 1793, so that no arrears were demandable; moreover, a subsequent law in 1794 ought not to be applied as the promise, made "without consideration," was obtained by false pretense.[61] The judge rejected his argument and charged the jury in favor of the government: whether there was an inspection office or not, unpaid duties were due along with a penalty to prevent evasion.[62]

In another riot case (*Pennsylvania v. Charles Craig, Adam Craig, and four others*, 1794), Addison allowed that rules were a condition of government;

while they might not be the best, they "must be presumed the best."[63] As all men were duty bound to preserve the peace and standing by and doing nothing may be considered acquiescence, "a presumption of guilt may be drawn from it." Addison considered the defendants were accomplices, allowing that merely "countenancing" a riot was sufficient for culpability. Incongruently, he also held that to be declared a party to a riot one had to be active.

Brackenridge took on a case directly related to the July 1794 events at Bower Hill in which he hoped to quash federal court writs issued by U.S. marshal David Lenox and excise inspector Neville.[64] In a comment on the case, he remarked that whereas the marshal's oath required the writs be returned, final "judgment could not be taken" on them, on the analogy of a subpoena.[65] With just nine years having passed since he embraced a reputation for supporting the excise, he litigated this case without a fee to signal his presumed neutrality.[66]

In an Alleghany County liberty pole case (*Pennsylvania v. Norris Morrison et al.*, 1795) dealing with an August 1794 riot against the U.S. Commission, the defendants were charged with raising "a pole or standard" (the import of which is discussed in chapter 3) and refusing to sign the government's offer of submission in exchange for amnesty.[67] John Woods (counsel for Neville in other cases)[68] defended in the case and claimed those accused raised the pole under duress. They did not intend to oppose the government or its laws "but to save the town from violence," and they had not signed the amnesty "because they supposed themselves innocent." Judge Addison's charge, however, underlined that peaceful assembly with the possibility of promoting violence (by raising the pole) was likely to produce official violence (on the part of the government). This was sufficient to determine a guilty verdict for unlawful assembly. Rather than illegal conduct and intent, the "probability" of their illegality and disguised designs in opposing the government and pole raising were sufficient in Addison's view to convict six of the eight accused of unlawful assembly, disturbing the peace, and riot. His jurisprudence on liberty poles was elucidated in a grand jury charge in December 1794 where Addison redefined criminal offenses by including among them what were "not *acts* of violence alone," holding that "[o]ffences may be committed by writings, by words, or by other signs of an evil purpose."[69] Addison told the jury that liberty poles were not protected by law. Signifying a liberty to do what one pleased, pole raisings were not speech but "standards of rebellion, and signs of war." Those who raised them were seditious and their "avowed intent [was] to hold under fear" all who were peaceable; they aimed to reduce the community to "riot and confusion" and to prevent submission to the government and a return to duty.

In Westmoreland (*Pennsylvania v. Jacob Cribs, Daniel Harold, and eleven others*, 1795), a riotous assault occurred in September 1794 "with intent to beat, wound, tar and feather, and evilly intreat" the U.S. Commissioners who had demanded submission of the rebels; when the public heard that excise cases would be tried in Carlisle, a riot erupted.[70] The case led to the indictment of thirty-six rioters and the conviction of thirteen for riot, six for assault, and the acquittal of nine.[71] Pennsylvania Supreme Court justices Thomas McKean and Jasper Yeates (the first a member of Governor Mifflin's Pennsylvania Commission and the second a member of the U.S. Commission) ordered the arrest of the rioters, upon which a second mob marched to Carlisle and erected liberty poles with "seditious inscriptions" at the courthouse. The judges having already departed, the crowd of two hundred torched an effigy of McKean,[72] reprising a 1788 Anti-Federalist riot in the same town. In the earlier instance, the chief justice's image was carted through the streets, beaten, hanged, and burned, while an armed militia released the jailed protesters.[73] In his Westmoreland jury charge, Addison defined an unlawful riot as an assembly of several people at night who "by noise or otherwise disturb peaceable citizens." Indeed, "collecting a party, for any purpose or a violent tendency, so directly leads to mischief" that the authors would be guilty of any consequence that could plainly be foreseen. No matter how civil the appearance or reluctant the crime, no matter which individual in the crowd committed a given act, according to Addison, assembling for either a lawful or unlawful purpose and then "proceed[ing] to an unlawful act" was a riot.

Despite the Washington administration's contention that Addison and the state courts under his control were incompetent and refused to convict rioters, the evidence of these cases support Addison's claim that the courts rigorously pursued and regularly punished unlawful acts where there was proof. Rioting, accomplice to riot, attacking excise officers, violations by distillers, raising liberty poles, failing to sign submission statements, failing to abort breaches of the peace, and unlawful assembly were all punished by state courts. Addison's law reports show that state courts held one party guilty for another's acts and found failure to sign the amnesty evidence of ill intent. They considered that a defense of having acted under duress masked one's true motives, and they adjudged that an assembly collected for any purpose, whether it disturbed the peace or had a civil appearance, was responsible for any consequences that might have been foreseen. State courts were not only as likely as federal courts to prosecute riots (common law misdemeanors for breach of the peace), but state prosecutions were more effective.⁷⁴ The federal circuit court in Philadelphia elevated such charges to treason only to prove its own incompetence when the grand jury refused to indict them as treason.⁷⁵

Popular Acceptance

If state courts were more competent than their federal counterparts, they still faced the problem of popular acceptance in the riotous summer of 1794. The status of the courts was certainly at a low-water mark. Brackenridge, for example, mocked popular discontent in telling a client "the government is gone to the devil; the courts are overthrown; all law is at an end; there can be no justice now."⁷⁶ On the way to the Braddock's Field assembly, he reported "a man of some note" waving a tomahawk over his head, complaining, "[I]t is not the excise law only, that must go down; your district and associate judges must go down; your high offices and salaries."⁷⁷ At the assembly, the crowd "rendered [Judge Addison] obnoxious" for allowing writs to be served against noncompliant distillers and deterred him from returning home from Philadelphia.⁷⁸ The state of affairs was such that members of the U.S. and Pennsylvania commissions questioned opening Alleghany County Court at the end of September and debated whether to present the grand jury with the latest offenses.⁷⁹ Brackenridge considered that the court should still sit as "the suspension of justice might strike the public mind, with [a] view of the lurid state of things."⁸⁰ From his contrarian perspective, he imagined such a suspension might be well received, in the same way that "an interdict of the pope" suspending performance of the Catholic rites might be regarded "as a liberation from the restraint of law." The most violent, he offered, might wish it "should always remain so."

The people's resentment against the law had indeed placed judges in the position of "losing their confidence by a compliance with what was desired,"⁸¹ as Secretary of the Treasury Hamilton said of Addison. By catering to the people, Hamilton averred, the judge confessed himself unfit to be a judge. Working behind the scenes, Addison had in fact indicated he was conflicted over how to perform his role. He revealed his discomfort well before the July attack on Inspector Neville's house in providing David Redick (prothonotary of Washington County Courts) with advice on what questions to ask the government: Who should be covered, or not, by a government amnesty? Which offenders would the government require to be tried in state courts? Is it the government's intention they all be tried in federal courts? Or is it "the will of the government that no steps be taken till the army come here" and those entrusted with "the power of coercion & punishment" act based on their "own view and according to the system of government"?[82] Cryptic about his own role, Addison considered his words "but hints" from which Redick might "easily perceive (I hope) what I intend." Without openly interfering with federal authority, he indicated the government ought to admit that "the people of this country can now be trusted as the agents of publick justice." For himself, he displayed little trust in local officers, noting that it will "be attended to that the magistrates here generally can have no knowledge of the offenders nor of what offenders are completely within the amnesty."

In truth, the legal situation on the frontier was unstable. The lack of a western network of county courts until the 1780s meant that the backcountry lacked a floor for self-government where the burdens of harsh local conditions and lack of security were most strongly felt.[83] Even then, the legal culture of the common people was such that westerners found courts alienating as a means of resolving disputes, particularly disputes involving land and debts. Not only did county courts favor those with wealth and influence, but communities had developed norms and customs that were more in line with local magistrates' courts and resolution by arbitration. Lawyers were the products of loosely structured apprenticeships or, like judges, self-taught. Common people found neither trustworthy; they regarded juries more highly as it was the people themselves from among whom jurors were chosen.

A literary figure as well as a lawyer and legal commentator, Hugh Henry Brackenridge penned a fictional account of the western Pennsylvania backcountry, *Modern Chivalry*, which portrayed a blind judge who found the law valuable only as "a substitute for sense if you could cite cases."[84] *Law Miscellanies*, Brackenridge's handbook of Pennsylvania law, cited errors in judges' "contemplation of reason and common sense." Mistrust of the judiciary's influence peddling and legal trickery had contributed to rendering the courts suspect, so that Brackenridge claimed he had "been as much shocked at the decision of a court [...] as I have ever been at the verdict of a jury"; the law was vulnerable to whatever a judge might decide.[85] Nor did it help that the legal system had yet to resolve which English precedents might be applied to American law, leaving westerners to suspect judge-made English common law and to prefer local legal practices rooted in custom and tradition. But if the states were to shrug off common law, precedent went with it, including, critically, the guarantee of the very liberties Americans had fought for.[86]

In a doctrinal sense, the advent of the U.S. Constitution had radically unshackled the country from its past. Post-Revolutionary America had lost its moorings. With citizenship, the people thought they had become creators of their own laws, which they preferred shorn of technicalities and Latinisms.[87] Populists wanted simplified court procedures, along with laymen pleading their own cases, lay justices of the peace, and juries from their own vicinage. In the years after the Revolution, it became clear that the judiciary, the branch of government that affected the lives of people in the most direct way, was the most problematic of the three branches.[88] The rash of court closings that characterized rebellions from 1787 to 1799 sent a clear message: the courts needed to be more responsive to popular influence.[89]

Extralegal Courts and Popular Participation in the Law

There were, however, venues in which the people could participate in making and enforcing the law. Popularly supported justice operated in several spaces, from established courts to popular traditions and rituals, clan customs, peoples' courts, and private courts, that is, as legal, extralegal, and extrajudicial law. Legal fictions were, for example, employed by courts to make their peace with the community. A fiction constructed for "trouver" allowed that goods detained by a defendant might be considered somehow lost by the plaintiff and merely found and converted to the defendant's own use, even if the latter had refused a request to return them. Peace bonds were often resorted to by courts as a means of prior restraint to satisfy community complaints about behavior that could not be successfully punished as criminal conduct. They, too, were fictional in the sense that they publicly displayed the power of the law before any offense had occurred and even after a party had been acquitted.[90]

The greatest concession to popular participation in the court system, of course, resided in the deference given to juries. The importance of common citizens' involvement in, and insertion of, themselves into the legal system became evident when colonial American juries challenged the powers of politically dependent and arbitrarily appointed judges. With judicial independence at risk, ordinary citizens took on greater authority in judging the law.[91] Jurors rejected the theory that the law was a legitimate instrument of state power rather than an expression of customary authority within their common understanding. They challenged the content of law, judicial decisions, and the juror's role in the judicial space, often assuming the right to decide both the law and the facts. Judges responded by awarding a new trial or returning a jury to further deliberation as well as removing cases from jury trials and putting them in the hands of a judge. In some ways, the court was like the public sphere, a place where citizens could directly represent themselves and assert common reason. In that space, colonial juries, unlike judges, were free of political influence and more likely to render innovative judgments.[92]

In periods of great change and instability and in places like colonial America and the frontier, common people turned to alternate legal forms such as local magistrates' courts, private prosecution, and extrajudicial arbitrations for access to the legal system. Agreed-upon private arbitrations and the filing of private criminal complaints were typically activities initiated by common people who by acting on their own felt they had a stake in local justice. With no guarantee of public prosecution or access by the accused to counsel, victims brought forward their own cases and questioned witnesses; the accused defended themselves and judges acted as referees. Although most states established some form of local public prosecution within the first two decades of the nineteenth century, private prosecution was endemic; it proved itself a significant force in displacing private forms of revenge as it allowed common citizens to bring forward cases of larceny, assault, burglary, breaches of the peace, and even domestic issues.[93] On the one hand, private prosecution was a form of extreme localism, making it difficult to determine whether the prosecutor or the prosecuted was to blame in a given case. It was open to dishonesty and local prejudice and was hugely unreliable in finding the truth. On the other hand, common people could participate in defining crime and the law could be brought into the lives of the poorer parts of the population.[94] In this regard, popular culture entered courthouses and linked them to a variety of disputes, crimes, and disorders.[95] The poor, the working class, and Blacks engaged in private prosecution in large numbers and made it a popular legal mechanism that sustained itself over time against considerable official antagonism.

A second popular legal form, arbitration, also developed an extensive following among common people. Founded in concert with justice of the peace courts by the Quaker Proprietorship in Pennsylvania, it represented an informal way to keep cases out of the hands of anonymous parties, that is, lawyers.[96] The arbitration system required the consent of those who participated while it offered inexpensive and simpler choices for resolving conflicts.[97] More equitable than legal judgments, arbitration forewent strictures on evidence and permitted the parties to frame the limits of the case.[98] Unfortunately, its success fostered litigiousness to the point that by the 1790s many legislators and judges pushed for a law to discourage its use.

In the western part of the state, the Pennsylvania General Assembly generally supported alternative means of dispute resolution for the poor to enhance local democracy as well as to minimize the influence of powerful landowners and land companies on the courts.[99] Chief Justice McKean of the Pennsylvania Supreme Court, however, was intent on stemming the growth of extrajudicial practices. In *Williams v. Craig* (1788), he argued that awards had to be approved by a court to be valid under the 1705 Defalcation Statute that authorized them, a view that went well beyond the precedent established in English law where proof of "corruption, or other misbehaviour, in the Arbitrators" had to be provided.[100] Like other sitting judges, McKean found that arbitration competed with the courts. In *Primer v. Kuhn* (1789), for example, he complained that whereby the 1705 statute only allowed arbitration in "the case of accounts," the "right and benefit" of arbitrations had been extended to every kind of action.[101] Brackenridge, too, decried excessive use of the practice; he preferred expanding the jurisdiction of justices over "unmanageable, and desultory arbitrations."[102] By the end of the eighteenth century, arbitration in Pennsylvania had become so common, however, that Alexander Dallas advertised his law reports by stressing their usefulness to students "for regulating the conduct of Referees, to whom, according to the present practice, a very great share of the administration of justice is entrusted."[103]

More welcoming than his companions in the law, Addison represented in a Westmoreland County case, *Dixon v. Morehead* (1794), that awards were "a kind of judgments, given by private courts" made up of the parties.[104] They were as binding as a contract or a court judgment so long as parties agreed to forgo instituting a suit unless the award was not honored by one of the parties.[105] *Dixon v. Morehead* involved settlement and improvement on abandoned land, a contest over title, and a subsequent ejectment. Brackenridge, for the defense, relied on the English rule restricting challenges to the award. Here, he argued against an appeal to the courts, contending that "[i]t is the general opinion, that awards are final, and the general interest, that they should be so." He added that under the rule of equity "what ought to be done is considered as done," concluding that the award "would operate as a title against the plaintiff."[106] In the event the case had been decided chiefly on the improved settlement (which since the Act of 1786 was protected against adverse title by warrant), the settlers represented by Brackenridge would have won the award. Unfortunately, the award constituted a transfer of title that was not allowed under common law in either England or in Pennsylvania.[107]

Despite overturning the award, Addison's opinion was notable as it expressed the high regard in which many westerners held arbitrations. First, the award was treated as a contract or equal to a judgment by the court. Second, Addison found contracts to be as binding as court judgments. Finally, he held arbitration up as a model form of dispute resolution: both parties had legitimate claims; they might enter into an agreement to settle the point between them; if the agreement was not in writing, the state would still consider it conclusive on the party out of possession; or the parties might submit their difference to arbitration, whereupon the courts of justice should hold the award conclusive. While arbitrations were not restrained by formal rules, yet they were "vested with ample powers for the most equitable redress to both parties." The authority of such a tribunal, Addison allowed, "ought not to be lightly impugned, nor its sentence easily evaded."[108]

The popularity of arbitration and private prosecution from the late 1780s through the 1790s suggests that regular courts and judicial proceedings in the backcountry were in a muddle. Jury nullification, officials afraid of popular blowback, conflicting state and federal legal systems, and outrage at removing suspects from the vicinage converged with the abandonment of trust in legal officials and courts. The way was clear for experiments in popular justice. Support for alternative courts was apparent, for example, in an April 1788 petition to the general assembly in which petitioners referred to themselves as "subscribers" and "citizens" and to the assembly as "Representatives of the Freemen of the Commonwealth." They blamed the people's distress on an economy of "abnormal status" and called for a law consonant with "principles of sound policy and national justice." The petition urged establishing a temporary court in which a sheriff could encumber real and personal property for debt valued by a jury of twelve men, the debtor's peers rather than a judge or a proper assessor. Creditors would be obliged to accept either the valuation or delayed execution on the debt for a term of specified years. The debt mediation court was intended to last until credit was more accessible.[109] Evidence in depositions from 1792 indicate that creditors complied with the court by dropping debt suits and paying penalties, with some five hundred settlements attributable to the extralegal system.[110]

Without bothering to seek the imprimatur of the general assembly, western democratic societies established courts under their own authority. The earliest of these courts, the Mingo Creek Society court, was formally constituted on February 28, 1794, but likely operated as early as 1792.[111] Building on public dissatisfaction in its proposed suspension of "the courts and the justices of the peace altogether," as Brackenridge claimed, it "actually drew causes to [its] own examination, and exercised judicial authority."[112] He reported that the society was founded by several office seekers frustrated in their desire to be on the bench and others harassed with expensive legal suits.[113] The society organized itself around Colonel John Hamilton's militia battalion, the nucleus of the district's militia. Its objective was to pressure litigants to bring their disputes to the society's court as a reaction to the imposition of judges appointed under the 1790 Constitution.[114]

A second society, The Mouth of the Yough, founded in Alleghany County on April 15, 1794, mimicked the structure of the Mingo Creek Society and was similarly intended to deter the public from using the established legal system. The secretary of the society, [John] McDonald, claimed that settlers were incensed by court costs and the salaries of judicial officers and that moderates among them thought the society could keep the people from acting out.[115] The society's constitution provided for "a republic, or society, in each colonel's district, throughout the four counties," signaling an intention to establish extralegal courts throughout the four rebellious counties.[116]

The Mingo Creek Society likely informed the rebel assemblies that many of its militia members attended,[117] though Findley (a respected political figure and author of a well-regarded history of the insurrection) made a clear distinction between the two entities. He claimed that Mingo Creek had the appearance of a permanent association conducted with "much system," whereas the assemblies were an occasional and temporary phenomenon.[118] Indeed, the society's founding document accounted for electing its officers (president and council), voting qualifications and vacancies, and the rules of the meetings.[119] It excluded those who held state or federal office from serving as officers and indemnified its officers and deputies, who were "*not to be questioned in any other place*" for speech or debate held in the society excepting those who were liable to impeachment if convicted "*of bribery, and high crimes, and misdemeanors.*"

The society's central function was to "*hear and determine all matters in variance, and disputes between party and party.*" As a precondition, no citizen within the district could sue another citizen in a court "before applying to the society for redress, *unless the business will not admit of delay.*" Collaterally, its constitution respected claims of the state and the United States, making clear that nothing in it could be construed to prejudice those claims. To accomplish that objective, the society retained the necessary books containing the laws of the United States, the Pennsylvania assembly, and Congress's minutes, implicit recognition that its processes were legally based and cognizant of the laws of other legally constituted entities to which its members were beholden.

There were those who objected to what they considered the coercion of the societies' extralegal courts, as "Democritus" made clear in the *Pittsburgh Gazette*.[120] Not everyone agreed to "one system either of a judicial or civil nature," nor, he hoped, would they accept that the common people were not "to argue but to obey." Likewise, he noted that the litigious, who wanted everything settled by the law, ought not to be compelled to have their disputes decided by the society. In concert with President Washington's linkage of the rebellion and the western democratic societies, others were convinced the Mingo Society was not as moderate as it pretended. Its members seemed to have provoked violence, according to Brackenridge, without having actually initiated it, as the "articles of their institution" intentionally produced a "licentiousness of idea, with regard to law and liberty," from which, he allowed, the rebellion "naturally sprung."[121] Findley shared the assessment, noting that while the rules of the society contained nothing unlawful, yet associating together led individuals to undertake acts they might otherwise have forsworn.[122] Harboring the suspicion that the society instigated the attack on tax inspector Neville's Bower Hill house, Findley was discomforted by the fact that the society was never "announced in the newspapers, and its existence was known but to a few"; this made the institution more dangerous in his view, for it "imitated the language, and assumed the forms of regularly constituted authority."[123]

While the societies did not affiliate with the rebel assemblies and they actively disassociated themselves from the violence associated with the rebellion, the courts established by the Mingo Creek and Mouth of the Yough Society constitutions owed something to militia members who were involved in the rebellion. Militia rendezvous provided early venues for meetings and assemblies that gathered at a "usual" place and a specified regular time, relying on a familiar gathering space when events became turbulent. Militia courts arose that one defendant referred to as "self-created, pretended court-martialls"; here, prisoners were subjected to "sundry harmless but insulting and humiliating degradations."[124] A militia court at Couch's Fort, for example, took seven men into custody, tried three of them, and saw two escape while two were released. Militia courts seem to have followed a common format. In a public place, a "self-appointed" court swore its prisoners, who were then sentenced to such punishments as tarring and feathering. The court proceeded to commute the sentence and "insulted [the prisoners] in a less severe manner."[125] Colonel Presley Neville, son of the infamous tax inspector and brigade inspector of the Alleghany County militia, apparently conducted such a proceeding, the notice for which read that a court would be held at a given time and place "where delinquents to the two last drafts for this brigade of militia, will have opportunity of offering their excuses, immediately after which the fines will most assuredly be levied according to law."[126]

Rebel Assemblies and the People's Rights

The people's participation in such a variety of popularly appealing legal forms demonstrated an authentic desire for a system that treated them as equals as well as brought order to the frontier on a sustainable basis. Extrajudicial arbitration courts, quasi-judicial society courts, and military-style militia courts highlighted the ordinary citizen's alienation from official courts and expressed a pressing need for relief from land title disputes, ejectments, foreclosures, and debt, the very stuff of which western life was made. By themselves, however, none of these accommodations fully satisfied the peoples' sense of disenfranchisement. Popular assemblies, on the other hand, spoke to the larger issue of justice for the body of the people. Through the assemblies, the people exercised customary liberties of speech, petition, and assembly, publicized their views, and debated questions of democratic representation. But they also played a consequential role in bringing the people into the law by providing a venue in rudimentary assembly courts that exercised a pragmatic form of rule enforcement and conflict resolution.

Because the assemblies play a central role in our discussion of the trials in chapter 5, the public debate over them—how they were defined, their political purpose, leadership, and factions—requires our attention at this point. We need, as well, to consider the people's rights of assembly and militia to establish a baseline for how the assemblies treated those issues before we can examine how they were treated in the trials. Then the workings of assembly courts need to be examined as a means of setting lawlike boundaries for the rebellion and giving substance to popular legal culture.

The term "assembly" expressed the convening of hired hands, homesteaders, the middling class, and a wealthy influential elite in a common setting. Politically, however, an assembly represented a traditional, crowd-based solution for common people to deal with conflicts over rights and redress of grievances. It was an efficacious means of moving from purely idiosyncratic acts of bands of men and the chaos of mobs to an outgrowth of community assuming responsibility for its own political well-being. Assemblies thereby provided the stability needed for a rebel narrative to develop.

With the imposition of the federal whiskey tax, antiexcise meetings emerged from 1791 to 1793 relying on voluntary attendance of elected or appointed participants appearing as delegates or meeting in committees. Ranging from township and joint-township meetings to district, county, and four-county meetings, large-scale formations developed organically in each year. Importantly, these western meetings constituted a pattern of self-governance reflected in the Washington County meeting in August 1791 (six districts), the Pittsburgh meetings in September 1791 and August 1792 (four counties), and the Fayette County meetings in August and November 1793 (eleven townships). As meeting minutes and other sources make clear, the western counties had an expansive view of the existential economic and political needs of their constituencies.

From 1791 to 1793, meetings and assemblies struggled to resolve internal conflicts, organize, and consolidate a message of justifiable dissent. In 1794, however, the rebellion took on a more hostile aspect as liberty pole raisings, tarring and feathering, and hangings in effigy gained in frequency to lend credence to government fears of treasonous conduct. It was thus unclear whether the rebellion would continue multi-issue gatherings such as the earlier meetings or commit itself to acts of outright rebellion such as the July attack on Bower Hill. The critical factor was the intervention of moderates who defanged the notion spread by the government of the people as a senseless mob at the margins of civilized life and developed the ideological and organizational structure of the assemblies that undermined mob-based violence. Three of those leaders (Albert Gallatin, James Edgar, and Hugh Henry Brackenridge, who are discussed later) were responsible for framing assembly resolutions, speeches, and petitions and for shaping the committees that constrained disruption of the assembly process during the most turbulent period of the rebellion.[127] Whereas Brackenridge was the only Federalist among them, he shared many of the Anti-Federalist sentiments that defined the rebel movement. A fourth figure, William Findley (referred to as "the political Nestor of the West"), was influential in developing the ideology of the movement, but his position as a legislator kept him away from the critical assemblies.[128] Born and trained in Ireland as a weaver, Findley was a captain in the Cumberland County militia and served both in the Pennsylvania legislature and, during the rebellion, in the U.S. Congress. He was known for encouraging debate in the public sphere, not mob action, and was a leading Anti-Federalist who came to support the Constitution.[129]

Two other figures, James Marshall and David Bradford, played a contrarian role in generating resolutions that sponsored radical actions and embraced secession.[130] Bradford (a well-liked and wealthy, if unstable, lawyer who became deputy attorney general for Washington County in 1783 and served as president of the Washington County Democratic Society) was known for inspiring the mob with incendiary speeches, which split the rebels into opposing factions. Bradford was an ardent proponent of secession from the Union, though he supported a strong national government to resolve western issues when he organized a Patriotic Convention to protest conditions in 1787. Gallatin, sitting with him in the state assembly (where Bradford served in 1793), considered him a "tenth rate" lawyer as insignificant as he was pompous. Bradford fled in a canoe to Spanish Louisiana when the federal militia rounded up rebels and appealed twice for a pardon, once in 1794 and again in 1798, pleading that he had been misunderstood or misrepresented and that he had fallen into a general frenzy that shaped the times. President Adams granted him a pardon.[131]

Marshall was Bradford's business partner, a militia colonel, sheriff, and justice in Washington County, and the first president of the Democratic Society. During the rebellion, he served as Governor Mifflin's register and recorder for the county and became a more moderate Anti-Federalist.[132] Born in Ireland, Marshall was a moderately wealthy lawyer and a captain in the Westmoreland militia who, notably, raised men to fight against the Indians. As a moderate Anti-Federalist, he was somewhat out of place among the radical rebels; he did not, for example, support founding a new state, declined to participate in the attack at Bower Hill, and found his home tarred and feathered when he tried to avoid the muster at Braddock's Field. His influence in the assemblies turned out to be a moderate one when those who had avoided meetings returned in greater numbers to declare their support for a popular form of democracy that was peaceful and within the terms of the Constitution.[133] Warring factions gradually coalesced in a western democratic republicanism supportive of a common position: constitutional resistance.[134] Like many political figures in the western country, Anti-Federalist moderates gradually moved away from the most radical version of local activism to align with adherents of state and national government responsible for the federal Constitution and the 1790 state constitution.[135]

As the assemblies generated a narrative of political subjecthood and popular governance that gave meaning to popular struggle, the critical question of leadership emerged. Several theories have been put forth, including that the common people were led, or misled, by the elite (the few), that unrest was class based (the many), and that the movement was essentially leaderless. Hugh Henry Brackenridge's son, Henry Marie Brackenridge, reports it was a mistake to hold "influential" men responsible for violent acts as the meetings actually repressed violence.[136] In fact, influential men, middling men, and the elites were deceptive about their positions in the face of rowdy crowds, and they shifted allegiance from one position to another with the aim of staying in the game or protecting their reputation.

In the debate over leadership, one view holds that the rebellion was riven by class conflict and that plebeian radicals took charge in the field and on the floor of the assemblies.[137] Whereas elites made gestures at interfacing with the rebel movement, opposition to the consolidation of wealth by a few was a central feature of many of the grievances the rebellion brought forward: a failed loan office, interest on debts, problems of a cash economy, official salaries, land speculation, and seizure of land from settlers and farmers. This view contends that a significantly larger lower-class element in the rebellion contested the agency of both the middling classes and the elite and that landless inhabitants of the frontier became principals rather than mere followers in the rebellion.[138] The assemblies served, in this regard, as a common man's political arena.[139] A less charitable reading of the assemblies faulted them for lacking ideological substance or discipline so that they were unable to deliver a clear message or to overcome class division.[140] Wealthy landowners, patronage networks, and upper-level office holders were unlikely leaders of such a popular movement as they could not identify with the small farmers, dependent tenants, and laborers from which the movement drew its strength.[141] As elite patronage disputes and state-building interests made them unattractive candidates to lead ordinary people, they were marginalized in the early assemblies.

It is undeniable, on the other hand, that many of the political and economic elite played prominent roles in the rebellion.[142] Certainly among those who presided over meetings or who served on elected or appointed committees, this group was disproportionately represented.[143] Still, a distinction needs to be made between those who were local elites and those who belonged to the "Neville connection" whose members held offices tied to state or federal government.[144] Those associated with John Neville collaborated with Hamilton's spies and the federal militia to inform on rebel activity, influence interrogations, and support charges against the rebels. By contrast, those disconnected from this lucrative patronage network did serve in the rebel assemblies. Many of them joined the radical faction of the rebellion, while others were responsible for organizing the scattered forces of the rebellion and developing a common political message.[145]

In sum, of the factions in the rebel movement a moderate middling class largely took on the mantle of chairs, secretaries, delegates, speakers, and committee members in assemblies.[146] Calls for expanded representation in the assemblies inevitably included them, based on their trustworthiness as respected members of the community. While many of them were identified with or were themselves people of property and wealth and some held local positions ranging from justices of the peace to elected representatives, their involvement in positions and issues of local importance ensured that they were well integrated into the community and had the trust of the crowd. Their work in the assemblies favored speeches and organization rather than violence to nudge radicals toward a lawful approach that expressed self-governance within the terms of the Constitution.

The leading spokesperson for constitutional resistance, Swiss-born Anti-Federalist Albert Gallatin is a case in point. A successful owner of a gun works and a glass works, Gallatin blamed the rebellion on "ignorant men" and distanced himself from radical populists and extralegal actions while he defended out-of-door politics and the involvement of middling men.[147] A petition Gallatin wrote for a Pittsburgh meeting in 1792 (August 21–22) provided an early instance of support for constitutional resistance. There he couched the meeting's demands within a framework of unresponsive government and liberty rights.[148] The law, the petition contended, was unequal (it fell more heavily on the poor) and immoral (it encouraged perjury and fraud). It pursued unconstitutional searches and seizures (trespass on properties, closing stills) and was thereby "incompatible with the free enjoyment of domestic peace and private property."[149] The rebels' exercise of their right "to criticize the government" and to disseminate their thoughts was no less legal, he argued, than the state legislature's own exercise of free speech, assembly, and publication.[150] The petition pleaded for a law whose principles were "more congenial to the nature of a free government, and its operation upon us less unequal and oppressive."

Reflecting an evolution from his earlier Anti-Federalism to a democratic republicanism that supported a national government responsive to state authority and popular sovereignty, Gallatin dealt in his speeches with constitutional issues, a theory of government, and the nature of the law. He reasoned at the Brownsville assembly, for example, that rebellion weakened liberty, which made "the people abject, and the government tyrannical." The speech distinguished the rebellion from the Revolution, holding that they were incommensurate: "In our case, no principle was violated; we had been represented, and were still to be represented in the body which enacted the law." Gallatin concluded that the republic was superior to "all that had been" and feared "the atrocity of undermining or shaking its fabric" both within the Union and the transatlantic republican cause.[151]

Gallatin's fellow Anti-Federalist in the ratification convention, James Edgar, spoke at Brownsville in 1794 (August 28) of the rebels' moral obligation to a government to which they had elected representatives and their "solemn allegiance" to a constitution whose laws protected them.[152] Edgar, an elder of the Presbyterian Church and a Washington County associate judge, called on those who refused submission to "answer at the bar of God for the blood that would be shed in a civil war." Referred to by Brackenridge as "a kind of rabbi," he elevated allegiance to a holy pursuit, making common cause with those who committed violence no more than an ungodly act relegating the rebels to savages.[153] Brackenridge, who shed his earlier Federalism to align with backcountry democracy, made a more immediate appeal at Brownsville to conditions specific to the geography of the assemblies. Questioning whether those assembled could overthrow the government, he warned, "We might as well think of tossing the Alleghany mountain from its base."[154] Could they secede? Without a seacoast they were at the mercy of the British forts. If the Union could not make peace with the Indians and free up navigation of the Mississippi, how might they? Even more pragmatically, were all those in the western country who clamor for war sincere? Some were cowards, others, unfamiliar with fighting, were moving on, had nothing to lose, and would flee: "If you depend upon these, you will by and by have to take the same course, *and defend the current with the frogs.*" Would they be able to beat back wave upon wave of armies over years? "I know your spirit," he answered with a rhetorical inversion, "but condemn your prudence."

Gallatin's declaration on behalf of Fayette County in September 1794 summed up the moderates' core argument: dissent required the ability to exercise the people's constitutional rights to free speech, publication, and assembly.[155] Following the legacy of the Sons of Liberty, he spoke of liberty with restraint to signify the necessary balance between individual rights and security of the state; infused with a consciousness of the demands of realpolitik, he spoke of submission as the best means of exercising legal remedies to achieve redress of grievances.[156] Gallatin drew a clear line between deliberative speech and violent conduct in arguing that principled resistance in a popular democracy was essential to good government, for liberty itself depended upon lawfulness and legality. He weighed in the scales the relative evils of the excise tax and acts of rebellion as he considered the legality of resistance by force and the prospects of an existential threat to the possibility of government itself. In this light, resistance within the Constitution, its laws, and its government was both justified and in the rebels' self-interest.

From the 1791 inception of the whiskey tax, it was clear that meetings and assemblies were preoccupied with citizens' rights in that they expressed the most important political concept of the Revolution—representation. By reopening the debate over representation that had characterized the ratification convention, resistance to the whiskey tax raised questions of what constituted the will of the people, how the people could legally express opposition, and the role of a minority. Further, representation spoke to questions of secession, disunion, and rebellion against the government.[157] From the popular sovereignty position, an underlying threat to the liberties enshrined in the Bill of Rights (ratified in 1791, the same year the whiskey tax was passed) made the insurrection a perfect test case for democratic constitutionalism.

Each of the rights claimed by the people to express their opposition to government—speech, petition, publication, and assembly—came under fire by the Washington administration in the early 1790s, though assembly was most at issue. Under the First Amendment guarantee of assembly, the question was whether the right to assemble was restricted to petitioning. Did it imply a politically organized, democratically constituted face-to-face meeting of a temporary nature? If the people were to exercise free speech, they self-evidently depended on such an understanding of assembly. Equally, assembly implied petition and speech, and even press, which were essential to popular participation in self-governance.

The discussion around these issues is illuminating. Assailing "advocates for ignorance" for presuming that one can communicate to a mass without forming into meetings, "The Watchman" asked in what other manner one might "at a very trifling expence, know and judge of the conduct of the agent he has entrusted."[158] The German Republican Society agreed, making the case that solitary opinions carry little weight until they have joined with the voices of many; maintaining "the equipoise, between the people and the government" required an association of some sort 'To obtain a connected voice."[159] As the linchpin of liberty rights, assembly enjoyed particular positive and negative protection; where it remained peaceful, it was shielded from government interference and imposed on the government a duty of protection.[160] The Whiskey Rebellion thereby served as a pivotal moment in the early republic in its assertion of associational expression in the public sphere[161] and its defense of popular constitutionalism's support for the multiple rights protected by the First Amendment.

On the one hand, Federalists such as John Adams saw dissenting meetings as a blur of transgressive groups. He referred to them as a virtual litany of "unlawful assemblies, Seditious societies, mischievous Conventions, pernicious Associations, dangerous and destructive Combinations," terms he would later use to justify the Sedition Act of 1798.[162] In congressional debate on Washington's censure of the democratic societies, Federalist Fisher Ames treated meetings indiscriminately, an affinity he shared with Washington. He conflated a Pittsburgh meeting of "Sundry Inhabitants of the Western Counties of Pennsylvania" with a meeting of delegates from the election districts of Alleghany County and subsequently with a variety of society meetings from Kentucky, South Carolina, and Virginia, tarring them all with the same brush.[163] As Washington expressed in a letter to Burges Ball, the people had the right to meet occasionally for the limited purpose of petitioning the government. The president refused, however, to accept that the societies, and by extension the assemblies, had such a right, as they constituted a "self created, *permanent*" entity that challenged the legitimacy of the elected legislature in a representative democracy. In toto, Federalists presumed that dissenting meetings were a subterfuge to invest authority in a popular entity presuming to represent the people and that their goal was to destroy confidence in the administration.[164]

Addison was a determined exemplar of the Federalist position. A Scottish-born emigrant licensed to preach, Addison apprenticed for the law in Washington County and began to practice in 1787. Within four years, having met with hostility from westerners for supporting the 1787 U.S. Constitution and the Pennsylvania Constitution of 1790, he was rewarded with the position of presiding judge of the Fifth Judicial Circuit. As a judge, he was preoccupied with grand statements covering republicanism and the nature of a free society that sounded much like jeremiads of a traditionalist who feared the marketplace of freely expressed ideas. Justice McKean referred to him as a "transmontaine Goliah of federalism."[165]

Addison held that citizens in a representative democracy do not waive their right to examine the way power is exerted. Without questioning the individual's privilege to discuss freely any political matter or citizens' right "to meet and associate together, for the consideration of any public question,"¹⁶⁶ he censured the abuse of those rights. He blamed those who conjured up grievances "which have no existence"; he opposed "all combinations not established by public authority" that presume to represent the public; and he disavowed "all associations" that considered their own interests separate from those of the nation.¹⁶⁷ The result of such a united Federalist front on the dangers of assembly was that the circuit court charged numerous misdemeanors related to conduct and expressions at assemblies; John Corbly, Robert Philson, and Herman Husband were, for example, among those charged on such grounds for conduct at Braddock's Field, Parkinson's Ferry, and Brownsville.¹⁶⁸

In contrast, Anti-Federalist western politicians Findley and Gallatin defended rebel meetings as political expressions intended to control the insurrection, not to cause disorder.¹⁶⁹ Findley reacted forcefully to accusations that popular meetings were criminal, "unlawful combinations" that led to insurrection, outraged that meetings conducted "indiscreetly" should be legally prohibited or denounced by the government. As he put it, egalitarian political debate might risk "mobocracy," but it enabled democratic input from moderates and prevented domination by elites. The potential risk of disorder at popular meetings was thus an insufficient excuse to prohibit the assemblies. "Doing so," Findley argued, "would be reducing the people to mere machines, and subverting the very existence of liberty."¹⁷⁰ The true risk was not impropriety on the part of the people but a loss of confidence in government that would itself lead to rebellion, "one indiscretion exciting another." Surely, Findley argued, the accepted right to petition against a law bespoke the right to assemble, which itself led to a right to "publish their sentiments and correspond" throughout the territory affected by that law, none of which justified "the imputation of combining against the government."¹⁷¹ He refused, like Randolph, to accept that any "meeting to petition government respectfully, was esteemed criminal in any country that had the least pretensions to freedom." And he insisted that Hamilton, who knew Randolph had found no criminal activity in the assemblies, had got it wrong in attacking rebel meetings.¹⁷²

Gallatin too found "nothing criminal" in citizens assembling nor in words as opposed to actions.¹⁷³ Not only were circulating opinions a privilege claimed by established bodies, but they were distinguishable "from declarations of an intent to act or persuade others to act."¹⁷⁴ To proceed otherwise was to destroy constitutional privileges of peaceful assembly, debate, remonstration, and the right to publish one's thoughts. By extension, citizens had the right to adopt resolutions that could then "be weighed and judged" on their justiciability as determinations to act. Should others who shared these views attach "reprehensible," "criminal," or "dangerous" measures to justifiable resolutions, the members assembled were not to blame. Findley and Gallatin agreed: meetings were legitimate expressions of popular dissent; they separated speech from acts of resistance and relied on public and legal rights of dissent.[175]

A final consideration in assessing assemblies is the role played by local militias that, by assembling with arms, complicated the right to peaceful assembly. First, the right to bear arms implied to some a natural and potentially a constitutional right of revolution against an unjust government.[176] Second, armed militias played a traditional security role in controlling Indian incursions, providing security for settlers, and mustering members of the community for self-defense.[177] Indeed, speaking in the context of the constitutional ratification debate, the Federalist Tench Coxe[178] conceded that "the powers of the sword" were in the hands of the militia, who were none other than "ourselves," rather than in the hands of the government.[179] In claiming that the right to arm was "the birth right of an American," Coxe denied the power of Congress to disarm the militia. Absent the involvement of the militia and its right to armed assembly, it seems clear, the rebellion was unlikely.

As an alternative to a standing army, militias not only retained customary privileges but were permitted under the state constitution to arm themselves with impunity. Their right to keep weapons was beyond dispute, a property right zealously guarded.[180] Moreover, serving in the militia was a community duty as much as a right and, unlike speech, petition, and assembly, could be compelled of a citizen by the state, which relied on the militia's police power.[181] The irony was that speech, by itself, did not qualify as treason under common law (it was charged as a misdemeanor in the rebel trials) whereas arming oneself did. In fact, prosecutors in the trials argued that a body of men appearing in a posture of war against the government constituted treason. By contrast, under a theory of popular sovereignty being armed to protect against an unjust government was "an insurrectionary right."[182] The sticking points were whether there was a natural right to revolution (as argued by William Pitt Smith and St. George Tucker); whether an armed mob constituted a well-regulated militia; and whether that conflation was not incompatible with the Constitution.[183] Radical, localist rebels were, however, willing to test the right in an insurrection;[184] the Whiskey Rebellion was that test.

In the hands of populists such as the radical faction of the rebellion, the right to bear arms had an atavistic appeal that reinforced extreme local democracy. It was posed by the western militia as a direct challenge to the government. In the backcountry of Pennsylvania, the formation of militia units was, in fact, beyond state control. Moreover, insofar as the western militia posed a direct challenge to the government, it hardly assured "the security of a free state" declared in the preamble to the Second Amendment.[185] The link between a right to bear arms and securing a distinctively democratic result was, consequently, a weak one. It only justified fears that the Washington administration would treat the local militia as a minority unwilling to submit to the will of the majority, supposing that the administration's true intent was to exploit the opportunity of the rebellion to support the need for a standing army.[186]

Once the federal government activated the Militia Act of 1792 to call together a federal force to march against the whiskey rebels, it became apparent that localist forces might support their own communities in a militia without feeling bound to serve a federal force.[187] Paradoxically, militia "nullification" asserted a right to foment an insurrection rather than to put one down as the Constitution provided.[188] The greater irony was that defendants in the rebel trials did not claim either a natural or a constitutional right to revolution; nor did they invoke a Second Amendment right to bear arms in their own defense once charged with treason.[189] Rather, supported by the general assent of the people their outlook was communitarian. They saw themselves acting as a presumptively legal body on behalf of the people, as the enforcement arm of local community.[190] In reality, the militia relied on existing officers and volunteers and had no clear plan or intent. Events associated with the militia were spontaneous and objectless, and the actions in which they engaged were of a self-organizing, temporary nature. Findley's observations about the militia are instructive in this regard.[191] He described rendezvousing "in a heterogeneous mass" with many listed who were never notified and plans executed as soon as they were conceived. Called out by their local community, the people were nonetheless obliged to muster and if they did not were considered delinquent. His description fed the government's view that the militia acted like a mob.

The right to peaceful assembly was clearly complicated by both the popular understanding of militia and the realities of how militias operated. The traditional role the militia played in providing frontier security had indeed made it the earliest popularly based form of organization westerners knew and the most natural recourse once the federal government intervened in western affairs. Combining its rights and duties with the right to assembly seemed to be a powerful, defensible resource for organizing and structuring resistance. Admittedly, without the force of arms it is unlikely that such a wide body of support for the antitax effort would have developed or been considered a threat. Yet, once the rebellion grew ideologically and organizationally, the right to bear arms became less of a weapon and more of a liability. The dispositive factor in avoiding bloodshed, expressing the rebel perspective on governance, and reaching a peaceful resolution would prove to be the right of assembly and the collateral rights of petition, speech, and press that it operationalized. The downside of assemblies was their appearance as a representative body posing as a legislative alternative. The upside was their ability to speak for the body of the people. The advantages of assembly became most apparent once moderates attended in progressively larger numbers, displacing mobocracy with controlled debate and the freedom to dissent. Moderate leaders fostered the ability to petition the government, to elect representatives, and to reach agreement by voting, forms of democratic process that ameliorated the criminal aspect of mob rule and military arms and represented the best fit for the rights-based narrative on which the assemblies depended for their viability.

Rebel Courts

The centrality of the assemblies to the larger picture of the rebellion is not limited to their defense of constitutional rights. Rather, the assemblies complete the story of the people's relation to the law, which constitutes the foundation for democratic participation in governance. In this regard, the rebel courts that arose out of the assemblies are important for what they tell us about that relationship. From the government's perspective, the assemblies were unwelcome extensions of extralegal courts that obstructed the operation of regular courts and their work of punishing rebellious parties. Extralegal courts influenced the assemblies to extend the populace's experience with adjudicating its own disputes, the likely result of the overlapping membership of western democratic societies, militias, and the assemblies as well as the example of debt courts and arbitrations. Assembly courts had the benefit of regulating the rebellion by establishing a rule-like boundary around the movement. They turned the tables on officials and those who resisted rebellion by subjecting them to the judgment of the common man in an inversion of regular order. They tried miscreants who undermined the reputation of the rebels or cooperated with tax officials. But most importantly, they preserved the authority of the assembly through recognizable, if imperfect, legal procedures and sources of law. In the government's view, holding officials culpable for doing their jobs and coercing citizens who supported the government was as intolerable as mobs who obstructed official courts and societies that indemnified their officers against harm for antigovernment speech and debates. For common westerners, however, assembly courts were of a piece with the popular justice meted out by local gangs, the summary justice of militia courts, and the arbitrated settlements of debt and dispute-resolution courts. They created the pretense that the people's customs were respected and their rights preserved.

The Braddock's Field Cases

Braddock's Field on August 1 was the first assembly to adopt a judicial role. The meeting was called by radical leaders David Bradford, James Marshall, and five other signers by means of a "circular letter" on July 28, 1794. The notice summoned armed citizens to come prepared to display their "military talents" and render "service to your country" resulting from the discovery of "certain secrets" intercepted in the U.S. Post.[192] Three deputies from each regiment made up a committee (of which Brackenridge and Bradford were members), which from the first was determined to retire to deliberate in private. Members of the camp followed them, and about a dozen armed men objected to their "counselling in mystery,"[193] which became a constant feature over the course of deliberations. Bradford opened by explaining that the cause for their assembling was "in order to chastise" those whose letters had been discovered expressing "sentiments friendly to the excise law." The charges included sending accounts of the "atrocity" of rebel "outrages"; revealing and giving insulting names to "authors of the disturbances'; exposing a motion to support those who committed violent acts; and providing a plan to apply the tax.[194] An extended debate ensued over the government's representation that Bradford had supported violence in obtaining the evidence. Brackenridge responded that it was unavailing to attack Bradford, "the Robespiere of the occasion"; he was, after all, a member of the committee.

In the first case emanating from the purloined letters, a committee making up the court accused Major Butler of corresponding with the government and, further, with "interfering with the civil authority of the people" by sending soldiers under the command of Major James Kirkpatrick (a brother-in-law of Neville's wife and part of Neville's patronage circle) to defend Inspector Neville's house. Brackenridge represented that, under the authority of the U.S. government, Butler was responsible "to the executive, for anything unconstitutionally done" and that the president would unquestionably remove him from his western command should he fail in his duty. Having determined that the president should recall Butler, the court referred his case to a meeting at Parkinson's Ferry on August 14.[195]

The court then took up the case of Major Isaac Craig, "an object of resentment with the people." Deputy quartermaster of military stores at the Pittsburgh garrison, Craig had served in the Revolution and, by virtue of his marriage to John Neville's daughter, was part of the army-supply operation and diversified business projects Neville populated with blood relatives and extended relations. Brackenridge acknowledged that Craig had been "overzealous" in offering to open an inspector's office in his own house, but that he had torn down the office sign and ripped it to pieces. A proposal to remove Craig from his post as army quartermaster, he added, could offend rebels in Kentucky since it might disrupt their efforts to control the Indians. Craig, like Butler, had been appointed by Secretary of War Henry Knox and had been providing him with information on the rebellion. After an extensive discussion, the court proposed that a solution like Butler's would suffice: "[Craig] should be superseded in his office."[196]

With two cases disposed of, the court turned to others whose "secrets" were discovered in the mail: General Gibson and Colonel Presley Neville. Brackenridge spoke favorably of Gibson as "a man of an inoffensive disposition." As for the colonel (the son of Inspector Neville), he was not only involved in the events at Bower Hill but acted as an adviser to his father and served as land agent for Washington's western land; opposing views were offered on his merits.[197] A soft-spoken man was eagerly for him; but a brash captain Murray was "strenuous for [his] banishment" and hanging, a reaction the younger Neville had anticipated on the way to Braddock's Field in expressing his hope "to escape assassination." Brackenridge equivocated when the possibility of exile was raised, arguing that exile would do the defendants' reputation more good than harm. Bradford stood firm for expulsion;[198] the sentiment of the assembly, he held, ought to prevail, as "[t]he people came out to do something, and something they must do." Some members preferred postponing the decision until the Parkinson's Ferry meeting, just two weeks away. A committee from Pittsburgh produced a mutually acceptable plan: announce at once the two men would be expelled; the committee would ensure it was done, and the men would be allowed several days to prepare their departure.[199]

Responding to the committee's decision, Colonel Neville requested passports and safe passage for himself and General Gibson, as well as publication of a statement explaining why they were not charged. The expulsion statement, published in Philadelphia newspapers, stated that three persons—Kirkpatrick, prothonotary Brison, and Edward Day—were expelled from Pittsburgh. Others, including Colonel Neville, were declared "obnoxious" for being friends of the excise tax, based on intercepted letters providing "sufficient evidence of [Neville's] enmity to the cause." The notice advertised that Neville and Gibson were also expelled; they should, accordingly, depart the country, a guard being provided "to conduct them to a proper distance." Neville apparently had second thoughts and asked that his case be reintroduced at Parkinson's Ferry. In his defense, he argued it was the town of Pittsburgh's fault he was sent away, and not any of his own doing. His sentence, he believed, should be repealed.[200]

In an unexpected turn of events, the younger Neville had arranged with Brackenridge to act as his counsel. Discounting his conflict of interest as a member of the committee, Brackenridge claimed he "never managed the case of a client, at the bar, with more flexibility" than on this occasion, having diverted "an enfuriated mob from coming in to seize [Neville]." Neville's cause was compromised by the fact that he had persuaded his father to refuse resignation when the people demanded it; he had further offended the people by accusing them of plundering "certificates and bonds" during the attack on his father's house. Brackenridge managed to reduce the mob to a committee, which then adopted the Pittsburgh delegation's offer "to execute the sentence." Neville so alienated the assembly that Brackenridge did not extend himself further on his cause.[201]

Brownsville and the Jackson Case

Endowing assemblies with a judicial function had by the time of the Brownsville assembly became an established practice. Adopted at Braddock's Field and used at Parkinson's, courts became normalized by Brownsville where the most elaborate case, that of Samuel Jackson, a Quaker, was tried. When the assembly's governing committee of sixty arrived at Brownsville, it encountered an armed band of riflemen intending to tar and feather Jackson and burn his property near Brownsville.[202] Jackson had referred in jest to the rebel assembly as a "Scrub Congress," but as the story spread abroad it was misrepresented to a drunken party of armed men that, but for the committee's interception, would have rendered its own justice.[203] Brackenridge explained to the riflemen, who were unaware an assembly had been convened, that "by the arrangements made at Parkinson's ferry, all complaints against offenders" were to be brought to the assembly which would decide "upon the criminality, and upon the punishment."[204] Prevailed upon to have Jackson "tried in form," the riflemen insisted upon escorting him with a file of men, whereupon the case was taken up as the first order of business. The riflemen were informed that the assembly's Committee of Safety had been "invested with plenary powers to administer justice and punish all offenses against themselves and the people of the four counties." Accordingly, the offender was brought forth that it might hear his case. The committee sat as a court under a cover made of boards to give the case a sufficient air of formality. Brackenridge undertook the accused's defense. His legal expertise lent him an air of authority, and his humor in resolving the matter appealed to the crowd.

The Quaker's "composed submission to the sufferings that might await him" made a tempting target for radicals anxious to make an example of any who opposed the rebellion. Two witnesses proved the charge, leaving only the question of a proper punishment for the crime "in the language of scripture, of 'speaking ill of dignitaries.'" Since the committee had leeway to invent law consistent with popular notions, Brackenridge composed a unique amalgam of legal traditions. First, he applied English common law (familiar to the "middling" men of the assembly) and an element of Scottish law (to appeal to the Scottish demographic that made up a large number of the attendees). Brackenridge explained that in Scottish law Jackson's crime was "called 'leese-making,' and subject to transportation," while common law might call it "sedition," a misdemeanor. But in the present "delicate situation" of the western country, Jackson's speech constituted dangerous language that undermined "respect due to the newly constituted authorities" and evinced "a bad disposition toward the cause of the people." Brackenridge then proposed punishment "according to the Jewish law—'an eye for an eye and a tooth for a tooth.'" Punishment in kind, proportionate to the crime, he recommended, was "the most just, reasonable and humane" of laws.[205]

To seal his case, Brackenridge amused the assembly with a touch of folk justice, building on the Code of Hammurabi, the Old Testament, and Roman law. He asked if one should send "a polite note requesting the honor of exchanging a shot" with a man who insulted you by pulling your nose, or, rather, should you "do to him precisely as he had done to you—that is, pull his nose." Going the extra mile, he cited historical precedent. Did not his fellow republican, the English Protector Oliver Cromwell, return the compliment "that his excellency 'may kiss his ——'" with his own compliment to the same effect? Brackenridge then recommended a verdict. Since Jackson had called them "the Honorable the Representatives of the four Western Counties of Pennsylvania, 'the Scrub Congress,'" Brackenridge moved "that we pay him in his own coin" and let him be known as 'Scrub Samuel as long as the world lasts."[206] Brackenridge's loose aggregation of legal principles and traditions proved as appealing to those who wished "to do execution on [Jackson's] person and property" as to those in the committee who resented the insult.[207] His performance had tempered common sense with populist mercy to the amusement of the assembly, leaving the committee satisfied, according to Findley, that the assembly had received "complete atonement for Jackson's offence."[208] For added value and as a ritual tribute to celebrate the event, Jackson supplied the entire body of prosecutors (reported to be "seventy") with whiskey while someone "cut his uniform" to mark that he had avoided a more severe sentence.[209]

As these cases demonstrated, assembly courts pleased the crowd, a decided improvement over the alienating technicalities and arbitrary treatment common people received in state and federal courts. The example of the Revolution was near enough to recall memories of the ex parte justice of bills of attainder where the accused had no right to a defense and no jury. Members of the assembly were more immediately aware of the unlawful search and seizure to which whiskey rebels were subjected, the denial of habeas corpus, and the infamous refusal of trial in their own vicinage. Assembly courts, by contrast, rebalanced the scales of justice in the common man's favor and were based on common sense; participants found themselves reflected in a vernacular justice they could understand and which felt familiar.

Like the extralegal courts envisioned by democratic societies and debt courts, and like the localism of justices of the peace and arbitration courts, assembly courts dealt in direct, concrete questions of right and wrong that did not require legal technicalities, paperwork, or formal venues. At the same time, they created the appearance of being fair, proportionate, disinterested, and conscious of analogies and precedents that did not have to be theorized or based on a chain of stultifying precedents. The accused could state his own case or seek an advocate, and members of the community who knew the accused rendered the verdict. Unlike the much-complained-of state and federal courts, the judicial apparatus was informal. There were no strangers on a jury nor distant courts to attend, no delays, bail, or detention before trial. Assembly courts avoided lawyers' tricks and legal language, offering justice of a type that a simple man might recognize. In theory, popularly responsive law constituted a social practice interpreted and enforced by those asked to obey the law; meaningful to those it accused, such law represented a way of building community. As an instrumental form of law, it enhanced respect for the law in terms of an instant case and a given act, creating the impression of a system that was immediate and demonstrable. Justice, of a sort, could be seen to be done. Positioned between the institutional order of government courts and the prelegal order of the wild world at the edge of settled land, assembly law exemplified a localism that fit the frontier's pragmatic sense of social justice and popular democracy.

This is not to say that popular courts on the whole delivered predictability in their verdicts or rationality in the process of delivering those verdicts. Not only was popular law impermanent, it was also idiosyncratic; its legitimacy depended on the acceptance granted it by an erratic populace. That its proceedings were public made them susceptible to community pressure. That its format lacked an impartial judge or jury made the verdict an imperfect solution. Moreover, conflicting customs made any law based on such courts variable.[210] Without a stream of precedents upon which to rely and without established procedural rules, legal standards, or written records, each case was unique and each resolution binding only on the case at hand.[211] But if popular courts were fraught with contradictions that rendered them as problematic as official courts, and if they left the people insecure in the law they delivered, common people had succeeded in producing a culturally present law that shaped social life.[212] The idea of an indigenous system that depended on common people deciding the law in gatherings[213] was apposite to commonsense justice. The mere fact that assemblies engaged in a judicial experiment that arose from the ranks of the people and spoke the "vulgar tongue" was as much a sign of their commitment to popular sovereignty as of the people's lost confidence in an unresponsive official legal system.[214]

Conclusion

This chapter has inserted the rebel perspective into the storyline of the western rebellion to underscore the importance of accessing its narrative. With a better understanding of the conditions on which rebellion would thrive and with an appreciation for the vision of egalitarian democracy and self-governing law sponsored by the assemblies, a legitimizing rebel narrative becomes apparent. The government's position is no longer the only game in town; its construal of the rebels as lawless and delusional is less appealing and ultimately less justifiable. What we have found is that conditions of instability, change, and conflict challenged popular participation in the law and that emergent forms responded to the demand for a process common people could understand and accept. Whether those forms inserted themselves into the legal system or appeared in spontaneously emerging popular courts and assemblies (as in the present chapter), or whether they survived in customary enforcement rituals, emerged as invented traditions, or were inscribed in propaganda and satire (the subjects of the next chapter), they constituted popular forms of law that fed the rebellion and became part of the rebel narrative. Legal forms responsive to the people did not arise one out of the other or express a continuum, though they had common ties to localism and backcountry democracy. Rather, the practices we shall examine next coexisted with private prosecution and arbitration. Legal primitivism, custom, and invented practices appeared alongside society, militia, and assembly courts; agitation-propaganda, satire, and popular literature ran parallel courses. Whether generated by official, extrajudicial, or extralegal systems or rooted in familiar customary practices, together they represented diffused mechanisms to restore a sense of justice and participation to the people. The most popularly generated of those forms, and those most directly implicated in the rebellion, are the focus of the following chapter. They demonstrate that resetting the picture of the rebellion requires an understanding of the legal culture of which it was a part. Fleshing out the nature and effect of that culture, we will arrive at a place where the rebel narrative represents a worthy opponent for government hegemony in telling the story of the rebellion. We can then in the last three chapters examine the clash of government and rebel narratives and the legal cultures they represented in the treason trials that were to follow.

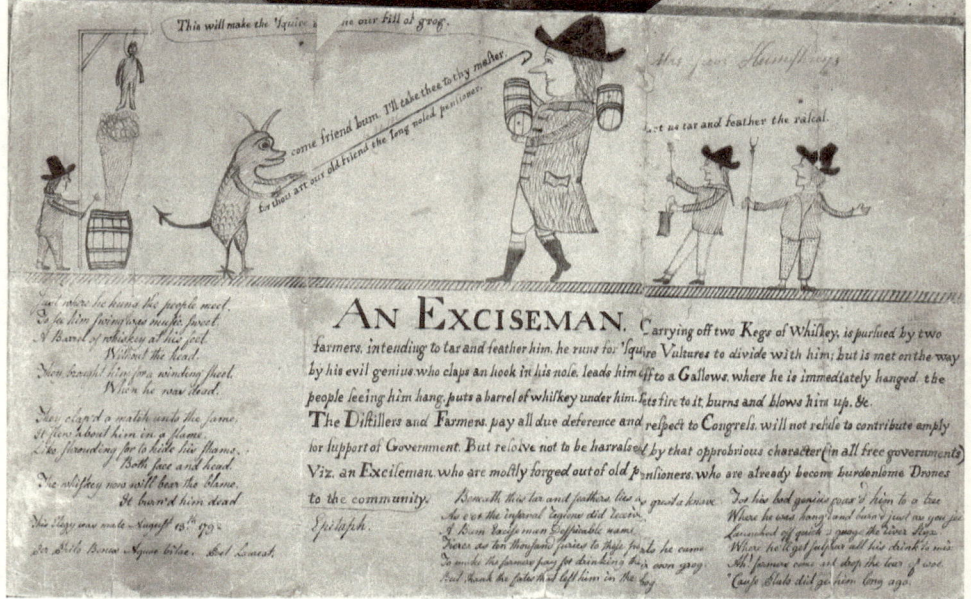

"An Exciseman," August 13, 1792. Bridgeman Images. Text on right side of image reads: "AN EXCISEMAN. Carrying off two Kegs of Whiskey, is pursued by two farmers, intending to tar and feather him, he runs for 'Squire Vultures, to divide with him; but is met on the way by his evil genius who claps an hook in his nose, leads him off to a Gallows, where he is immediately hanged. the people seeing him hang puts a barrel of whiskey under him, sets fire to it, burns and blows him up, etc. The Distillers and Farmers pay all due deference and respect to Congress will not refuse to contribute amply for support of Government. But resolve not to be harrassed by that opprobrious character (in all free governments). VIZ. an Exciseman who are mostly forged out of old Pensioners who are already become burdensome Drones to the community." The epitaph, just beneath that, reads: "Beneath this tar and feathers lies as great a knave / As e'er the infernal legions did receive. / A Bum Excise man despicable name / Fierce as ten thousand furies to these parts he came / To make the farmers pay for drinking their own grog. / But thank the fates that left him in the bog. / For his bad genius coax'd him to a tree / Where he was hang'd and burn'd just as you see / Launched off quick a guage the river Styx / Where he'll get sulphur all his drink to mix. / Ah! farmers come out and drop the tear of woe / Cause Pluto did get him long ago." And the text on the bottom left side of the image reads: "Just where he hung the people meet. / To see him swing was music sweet. / A Barrel of whiskey at his feet / Without the head. / They brought him for a winding sheet / When he was dead. / They clap'd a match unto the same. / It flew about him in a flame, / Like shrouding for to hide his shame / Both face and head. / The whiskey now will bear the blame. / It burn'd him dead. / This Elegy was made August 13th 1792 / Per Philo Bonio Aquae Vitae. Poet Laureat."

"The Bostonians Paying the Exciseman, or Tarring and Feathering," 1774. Library of Congress. Note the "Liberty Tree" on the tree and the upside-down sign on it that reads, "Stamp Act."

"New Hampshire: Stamp Master in Effigy," 1765. Engraved 1829. *Concord Monitor*, November 26, 2017, 35. Library of Congress. The presumed writing on the coffin in the background reads, "Liberty, Age 145, Stampt" (New Hampshire Historical Society).

"The Monstrous Hydra, or Virtue Invulnerable," 1789. William Dent. Library of Congress. The ideas listed in the art from top to bottom are "public good," "Ich dien ["I serve," the motto of the Prince of Wales]," "N-H Debts and Deficiencies," "Private Views," "Source of all Evil," "Regency Limitations & Restrictions," "American War," and "Pandemonium."

"Lawyers in Term," 1786. Library of Congress. Text along the top of the image reads (from left to right), "Get along In [...] you're quite done over aren't you," "Oh! The glorious uncertainty of the Law!" "Yes, you have brought this cause to an Issue indeed, and I am to pay all this merely to send the man to prison--this is recovery with a vengeance!" and "[Turnbelly against Menger] Attorney's bill." On the body being pulled: "action, Reverse of judgment, Execution TIME, Demurrer, Arrears, Habeas, Distress, Nonsuit, Certiorari." On the stones, "Exchequer, Chancery, Common Please, King's Bench." Just below the defendant, on the floor: "Part of Defendant," "AS if a Defendant were Dissected/To see how by Law he is affected," "Plaintiff's Case," and "Designed by Necessity Executed by Rapacity." At the very bottom of the illustration: "Others believe no voice t'an Organ / So sweet as Lawyer's in his Bar gown / Until with subtle Cobweb-cheats, / Th'are catch'd in knotted Law like Nets, / In which, when once they are embroiled / The more they stir, the more they're tangled. / And while their Purses can dispute / There's no end of th'immortal suit."

"Liberty Pole, New York," 1770. Pierre Eugene du Simitiere, Prints and Artwork, 1758–1790, box 10, folder 1. Library Company of Philadelphia. Text from left to right, top to bottom: "A fine prospect of liberty," "Scribbling post," "LIBERTY I am encompass'd with a ton and a half od Iron, Therefore can I relieve you," "All is well," "Ma-a-a," "Beef Stakes Hot & Hot," "Is there no other road to thee, Sweet Liberty," "[…]He seems to lay disconsolate at the foot of the pole," "We are [just] A 5 [all] go [up]," "39," "Road to Liberty," and "Road to Libel Hall."

"The Looking Glass for 1787, A House Divided Against Itself Cannot Stand. Mat. chap. 13th verse 26," 1787. Amos Doolittle. Library of Congress. The text reads, from top right to left, "Pay Commutation; Drive them to it; I abhor the antifederal Faction; Comply with Congress," "Gentlemen this Machine is deep in the more and you are divided as to its relief," and "Tax Luxury; the People are oprest; curses on to Foederal Govermt.; Success to Shays; Curse Independence." Text from middle left to right: "Parnassus; American Antiquities; CATO; I despise your Copper; Cur's commutation," "Takes all to pay taxes," and "Agricola; I fear & dread the Ides of May; S-H-P; A good shot." And from Bottom left to right: "Tweddles Studdy; as I sit plodding by my taper," "From Connecticut to New York Paying L40000 per annum Impost," and "New York." The bottom heading reads, "A House Divided Against Itself Cannot Stant. Mat. Chap. 13th verse 26."

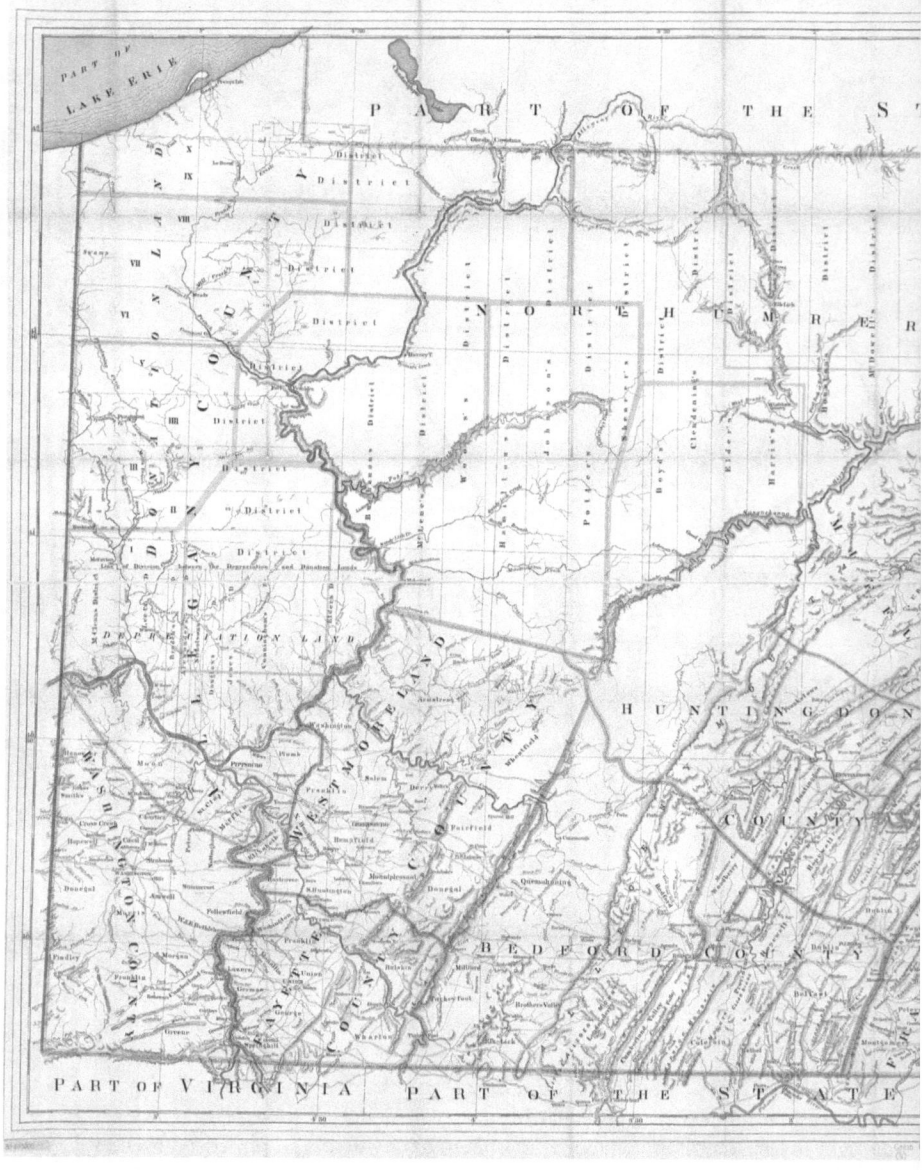

"A Map of the State of Pennsylvania," 1792. Reading Howell. *Pennsylvania Archives*, ser. 3, appendix 1–10, no. 4. 1792. See *Pennsylvania Archives*, ser. 4, vol. 4, 92–94; ser. 9, vol. 1, 455; ser. 3, vol. 30, 780; ser. 4, vol. 4, 246. Library of Congress. Inscription reads, "To Thomas Mifflin Governor The Senate and House of Representatives of the COMMONWEALTH of Pennsylvania The Map as respectfully forwarded by the AUTHOR." And from Samuel Caldwell, Clerk of the District of Pennsylvania (at the top of the map): "District of Pennsylvania to wit. Be it remembered that on the eleventh day of January in the fifteenth year of the Independence of the United States of America came Reading Howell of the said District [hath] deposited in this Office the Title of a Map, the right whereof he claims as Author in the words following to wit. 'A Map of the State of Pennsylvania (One of the United States of America) including the Triangle lately purchased of Congress and containing the Boundary Lines of the State [as] run by the respective Commissioners, with part of Lake Erie and Prequ'Isle. Also by actual survey the River

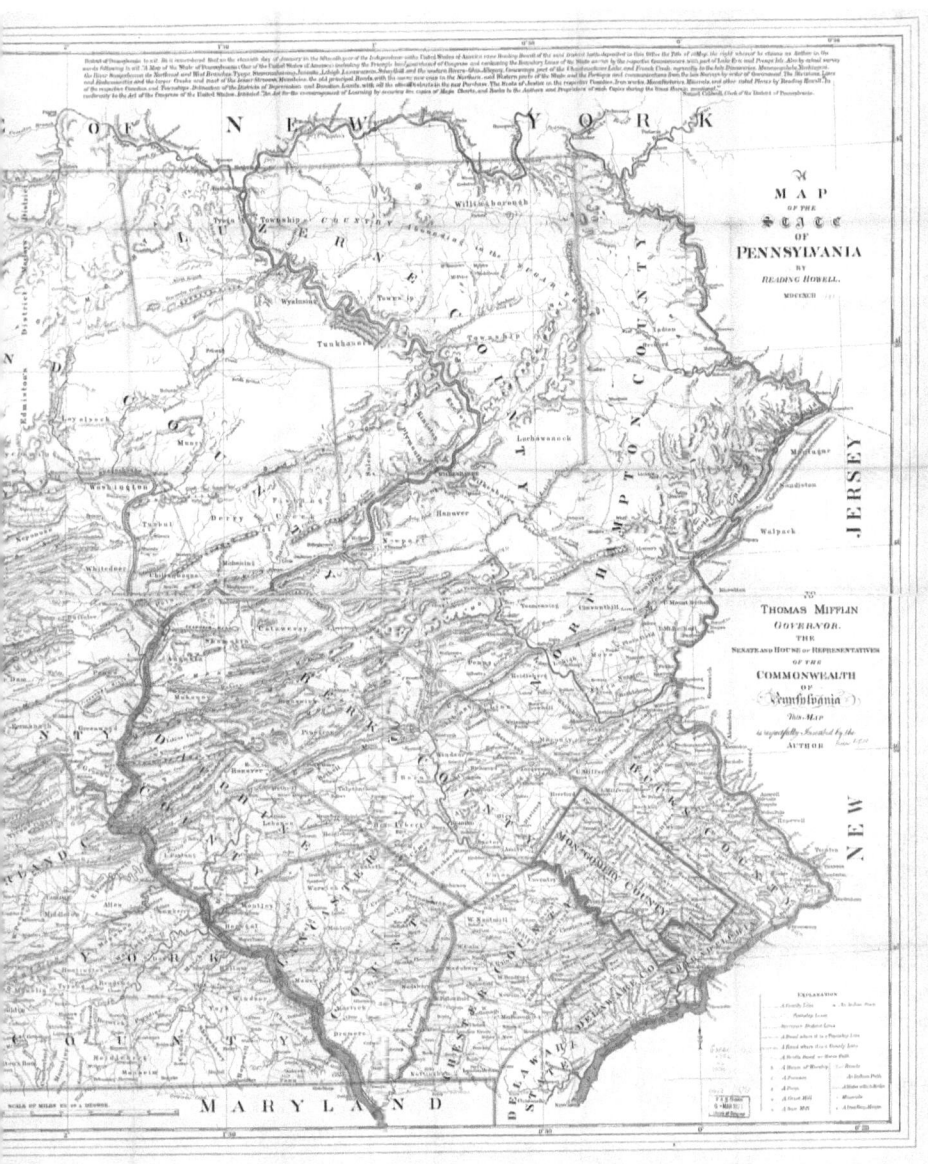

Susquehanna, its Northeast and West Branches, Tyoga, Sinnemahoning, Juniatta, Lehigh, Lexawacsein, Schuykill, and the western Rivers—Ohio, Allegeny, Conewango, part of the Chautaugme Lake, and French Creek: agreeably to the late Discoverie, Monaungahela, Yoxhiogeni, and Kiskemanelas and the larger Creeks and most of the lesser Streams, Mountains, the old Provincial Roads, with the many new ones in the Northern, and Western parts of the State and the Potages and communications from the late Surveys by order of Government. The Divisions, Lines of the respective Counties, and Townships. Delineation of the Districts of Deprec[i]ation and Donation Lands, with all the other Districts in the new Purchase. The Seats of Justice in the respective Counties, Iron works, Manufactories, Minerals, and other noted Places by Reading Howell.' In conformity to the Act of the Congress of the United States. Intitled. 'An Act for the encouragement of Learning by securing the copies of Maps, Charts, and Books to the Authors and Proprietors of such Copies during the times therein mentioned.'"

"A Peep Into the Antifederalist Club," 1793. Library Company of Philadelphia. In the box at the top left: "Creed of the Democratic Club[:] The People are All /and we are the People / All Power in one body / and that body Ourselves / Governments but another/ home for Arisstocracy [sic] / Liberty is the Power / of doing any thing we like / Laws are unwholesome/restraints on National rights / All means Justifiable / to a good end / This Society up / and all else Down." The figure in the bottom left is saying, "I never k[n]ew an Institution Equal to this since the Creation. What a Pleasure it is to see one's work thrive so well—." The box under their hand reads, "Sacred Records." Moving clockwise, the gentlemen say, "Oh! For the wreck of the matter and the crush of worlds," "Oh! For such a government as they have in Saturn," "To be or not to be, a Broker is the question whether tis nobler in the mind to knock down dry goods with this hammer; or with this head contrive some means of knocking down a government and on its ruins raise myself to Eminence and Fortune. Glorious thought this to Emerge from dirt to Gold," "Damn governments. I shall never be worth a dollar so long as theres any Government at all," and "Come here gobs. Dam———tion to the Federal Government." Papers in the right center of the image read: "Strictures on the Executive," and "Plan of an Entire Subversion." The figure seated says, "O my genny my genny and o my genny my diary such a sweet bassy as this is neither far nor nearby. If we can tickle the Lads and make em engage in the warey then it would see our frontieres Burst to a rag in a hurry There would be picking so nice That every dirty rascal might feather is nest in a trice (I don't mean you and ———. The little bassy might crow and flap flap flap his wings and then the hard dollars would flow and make in his pocket a gingy Get a gone Proclamation here's a Child that won't fear ye Pittle a little my Jewel and *** my deary." On the scroll: "Politics a better trade than Law." Folks in the top right (from left to right): "Will you Subscribe to this and faithfully observe all the articles of our Creed," "Well Citizen Mungo what think you of all this," "Yes. Damme he'll subscribe to any thing. He has nothing to loose," and "Tink I fine ting Broder Cockra our turn nese." And the date in the bottom right corner is "New York, Aug 16, 1793."

"Stop the Wheels of Government," 1796. William Cobbett, Frontispiece, *Political Censor*, vol. 3 (Philadelphia: Benjamin Davies, April 1796). See *Political Censor*, vol. 2, 9, in William Cobbett, *Porcupine's Works*, vol. 3, 253–256. The text refers to Albert Gallatin claiming in congressional debate in January 1796 that the House of Representatives has the right "*when they see proper*, to *stop the wheels of government*"; Gallatin considered the comment his only political sin. See William Cobbett, *Political Censor*, vol. 2 in *Porcupine's Works*, vol. 3, 253.

"The Times, A Political Portrait," [1795–1797]. *New York Historical Society Quarterly Bulletin*, 15, no. 4 (January 1932), 137. Middle left: "The cannibals are landing." On the banner: "Volunteers." Bottom right: "Stop de wheels of de government." Bottom heading: "Triumph Government: perish all its enemies / Traitors be warned: justice though slow is sure."

U.S. Circuit Court for Eastern District of Pennsylvania. U.S. Supreme Court building. 1790–1791. Builder, David Evans. Photo, Kostas Myrsiades. The U.S. Supreme Court, U.S. Circuit Court, and U.S. District Court sat here, 1791–1800. See Richard Webster, *Philadelphia Preserved*, 79.

"Washington Giving the Laws to America," [c. 1800]. Library of Congress. The tablet in Washington's hands reads, "The American Constitution"; the familiar eagle emblem in the flying angel's hands reads, "E Pluribus Unum."

CHAPTER 3

The Culture of Resistance and Its Agitation-Propaganda

As an adjunct to the legal culture informed by Anti-Federalism, the assemblies, and the official and unofficial courts of the western country, the present chapter considers the traditional rituals, agitation-propaganda, and satire that expressed less elevated efforts to participate in making the law. On the one hand, such activities complemented efforts of rebel assemblies to recruit members, resolve discord, and craft resolutions that would produce a legal culture subject to a congruent identity and system of belief.[1] Just as vernacular culture revealed popular imaginings of sovereignty justifying dissent, it publicized grievances that contributed to an arguable defense for the rebel trials. But it also functioned as a space where the rebellion itself was contested and its fault lines exposed, where factions emerged to splinter consensus. In this space, participants ranging from spontaneous mobs to propagandists and satirists converged to inform and carry on the process of political struggle and identity formation in the public sphere but without noticeable guardrails. This "sloppy surface" of culture did what law as a system could not—it revealed the deeper themes that underlay legal culture.[2]

In one sense, popular dissent subscribed to what has been called a hidden transcript and, in another, to an invented tradition.[3] That is, using ordinarily existing or invented weapons of speech and protest, a relatively powerless group acted to make its presence felt outside the bounds of accepted forms and genres. Resisters defined themselves through surreptitious practices or by turning the presentational tools of the powerful to their own use while defining the powerful by their resistance. For their part, the powerful used their own public rituals to maintain appearances and legitimize their mastery. Each party was thus adaptively strategic in relation to the other, allowing us to access and examine how the subordinated group staked its claim to a subject position and to assess how thick or thin hegemony was on the ground. In this reading, subordination is not inevitable, and dominance does not have a lock on defining those it subordinates. Resistance can stage-manage its self-presentation and instill legal meaning that creates value of its own. In concert, old symbols and rituals turned to new uses express compatibility with vague precedents while tacitly designing rules, values, and norms to sponsor newly emergent practices. This process expresses continuity with a largely factitious historical past to which older practices attached themselves. Thus, the void left by the rejection of old ways is filled both by adaptations of those practices and by cultural inventions generating new forms of cohesion and membership in a pseudo-community of understood rules, obligations, and rights.[4]

Explicating dissenting political actions requires delving into cultural activities that are the precondition of organized resistance but that fall outside conventional conduct. Since such activities constitute statements filled with many different contents,[5] the expressive potential of cultural materials can be exponential. Flags, liberty poles, and agitation-propaganda easily provided a flurry of meaning that contributed to broadly constructing the reality of resistance at the level of the common people. Displays, salutes, oratory, and processions all played a role in an architecture that seemed traditional even while it broke new ground, building on a chosen past and serving as a platform for future inventions. The rebellion thereby found its precedent and its continuity in customary practices but also substituted new practices for more formally established ones. Whereas previous traditions (like militia convocations) served as presumptive models, new or expanded practices (like rebel assemblies) adapted to contemporary needs and conditions. Elsewhere, a set of practices connected imaginatively with a preferred or relevant cultural history (such as the American Revolution) regarded as a touchstone to express social cohesion within a gestalt of ever-changing priorities. A cultural community of such practices could thereby affirm the rebellion in the present and imagine a new political regime for the future.[6]

Indians and the West

Within the set of cultural practices for which we have laid a foundation, studies of the rebellion have only marginally touched on the most central theme: the unique identification of the rebellion with Indian wars and of the rebels with Indians. Recognizing that the western frontier supplied the cultural materials and the ground on which the Whiskey Rebellion was played out, it is a short trip to realize a connection between the two most disruptive forces in the western country. Certainly, questions of security, identity, and racial exclusion were implicated in white relations with the Indians, who accounted for the most immediate problem facing frontier inhabitants and the largest part of the grievances addressed to eastern officials. The connection was more than the superficial one of economic grievances or victimization related to being forced off one's land, though there was a certain irony to both settlers and Indians suffering deprivation and discrimination at the hands of the wealthy and powerful who coveted territory in the West. Hugh Henry Brackenridge, for one, picked up on their being similarly situated in his comments on treaties, the excise tax, and the rebellion. In the same year the federal government initiated the whiskey tax, three Indian conferences took place in Philadelphia in which the Seneca Indian Cornplanter figured prominently.[7] The impact of the discussions was not lost on westerners such as Brackenridge, who compared treatying with Cornplanter to amnesty for the rash acts the rebels had committed at Bower Hill. "If Indians can have treaties," he asked, "why cannot we have one two [sic]."[8] His remarks led the U.S. district attorney to take depositions of his speech as evidence of his *mala mens*, or contempt, for national government. In a 1792 piece in the *National Gazette* on the Indian wars, and even later as a Pennsylvania Supreme Court justice, Brackenridge disavowed treaties with the Indians.[9] At the risk of further destabilizing the frontier, he emphasized that the Indians had no absolute right to the land; they did not work the soil and, having made no contribution to civilization, ought not to "hinder others to use it." Brackenridge could as easily have referred to squatters' rights to the land or to amnesty for the rebels.

Brackenridge recognized another connection between hostile acts of the Indians and reactions to imposition of the excise tax. Because the national economy from 1790–1796 had exhausted five-sixths of its budget on the western wars,[10] paying to defend the West complicated, on the one hand, the solvency of the federal government and, on the other, the survivability of its western inhabitants. Written just a year after the imposition of the federal tax on whiskey, his "Thoughts on the Excise Law" made clear that the excise law exacerbated the problems the frontier faced. Years of expeditions against the Indians requiring recruits and replacement labor at home were particularly burdensome. So too were the unsettled state of property rights and the burden of legal cases over titles on Indian land. Economically, the West was a critical counterbalance to the monied interests and urban influence of the South and the East; politically, Brackenridge offered, it offered a true republicanism emanating from "hewers of wood and drawers of water" who kept the Spanish at bay on the edge of the Union where they prevented inhabitants from navigating the Mississippi River. The strength of the common people of the western country, he wrote, was that of the nation: "cast this anchor to windward" and they will be safe; press the West further and "oppression will make the wise mad."[11] In this, Brackenridge was prescient; the rebels were in fact at the end of their rope, the excise tax being only the tipping point for manifold grievances.

The Import of the Indians

Going native was one way disaffected settlers expressed their angst. Mimicking Indian-style warfare was another. Both responses reflected the racism inherent in western solutions to the inequities of their situation, but they also expressed a shared sense of the inferiority Indians experienced. The North and South might have contended over racism entrenched in slavery, but in the West it was Indians who were considered inferiors.[12] On the one hand, white westerners elevated their own skin privilege to divide the civilized from the savage and "create the idea of an essentialized racial difference."[13] On the other, homesteaders identified themselves with Indian force and power in the form of "white savagery."[14] Indian imagery was thereby unpredictable, so that both identifying with and treating Indians as the "other" became useful tropes. A tradition of blackening and dressing in Indian garb had, for example, established itself in the West, having originated in England in raids on the king's hunting groups by blackened figures.[15] It was continued in the colonial period where black-faced gangs perpetuated a form of humiliation called "rough music."[16] Objecting to British support of trade with the Indians, the infamous Appalachian "Black Boys" of 1765 blackened their faces to attack a wagon carrying supplies to Indians at Fort Pitt. Captured, they were set free by a local mob, setting a precedent for the government to send future miscreants to distant courts for prosecution. Similar hostilities by Indian-clad settlers and militia interrupted trade and travel between Philadelphia, the Indians, and Fort Pitt, requiring merchants and British soldiers to obtain permission for safe passage.[17]

The ubiquitous Tom the Tinker's men, agitators in the Whiskey Rebellion, famously painted themselves like Indians, blackened their faces, or wore women's clothing to terrorize tax collectors and their collaborators.[18] A form of "ritualized community censure," the practice was repeated in other iterations where black-faced men wore hunting shirts and in one instance impersonated "Belzebub" who threatened to deliver an exciseman to devils who attended him.[19] In other forms of humiliation, bands of disguised men tarred and feathered those who assisted in executing the excise law, hung them in effigy, or stripped them of their clothes and marched them through the streets. Armed men waylaid tax collectors and chased them on horseback. They exposed officials to insults, threatened scalping, shaved off their hair, left them bound naked to a tree, and branded them with "marks of ignominy."[20] Such practices exploited perceptions that Indians might appear to be human but were really savages, "yellow devils" who lacked civilization and could not be converted.[21] Indian behavior was simultaneously internalized as many whites had "gone native" in the western country, while many Indians had assimilated.[22] White Indians of both types blurred racial lines and expressed symbolically the liminality of western identity and its political fungibility.[23]

Strikingly, the government perceived the rebels in much the same way it saw the Indians. Reflecting that the West was a "foreign" territory at the edge of the wilderness, its inhabitants were dependent on government forces much like a guardian-ward relationship. Indeed, the language of the U.S. Commission and communications from government informants in the West were expressed in terms that had become common usage in dealing with Indians.[24] Secretary Hamilton's agents, for example, reported that the rebels were whiskey-drinking, morally depraved inhabitants with poor comprehension of a citizen's duties.[25] The commission stubbornly refused to move beyond its narrow instructions, which obliged them to state, to say, to inform, to represent, to grant, and to require. They declined to open discussion, seek information, negotiate issues, admit to error, or reach agreement. The clarity, organization, emphasis, and bulk of the instructions expressed the government's reliance on the federal militia in principle and as a physical threat. Indeed, the instructions both began and ended with the power of the militia. In their discussion of the vicinage issue, for instance, the government's representatives made no admissions and suggested no awareness of the seriousness of the government's own contribution to instigating the rebellion. Instead, preemptive instructions had been provided should the rebels introduce a grievance or question the government's motives, indicating the government's denial of a space for the rebels to remonstrate or for the commission to fact-gather or negotiate. The commission's brief was detailed to the extent that, should it choose to speak, it was directed what to say; when the rebels spoke, no other reply was to be made than the script provided.

The first day of the commission meetings illustrated that the treatment of the Indians was the model for dealing with the rebellion, especially in its use of language typically applied to Indians. In the manner of an Indian treaty conference, the meeting went on at length as the government expressed its sense of the outrages committed by the rebels and its need to arm itself against its own citizens. Pennsylvania's commissioners communicated a sense of embarrassment that within its jurisdiction "violations of so flagrant a nature" took place against officers of the Union; in the spirit of reconciliation, they professed that they took "personally great pleasure" in returning "this country to the bosom of peace and happiness."[26] On the second day, the federal commissioners took a similar stance, speaking of the "extreme pain" of the Executive to hear of "deviations from the constitutional line" and of outrages that led "to having no laws at all." They referred to the "force of the Union" being exerted with great reluctance, having tried "all those lenient measures of accommodation" to obtain submission and restore peace. Thus, if pacification was found "impracticable," submission must be enforced.[27]

The Constitution was itself put forward as a type of treaty with which commissioners expected the rebels to comply. Force would follow if compliance was not forthcoming, a process of pacification comparable to that offered the Indians. The government's depiction of the rebels as outside the law and as "banditti" cast them, as it had the Indians, in the role of aliens on the margins of the civilized world. Rebel assemblies were not regarded as democratically elected representative bodies but more like tribal councils. Nor did the government consider the rebels criminals with rights or subalterns without rights, so much as a nation within a nation or wards protected by a guardian. The rebel representatives to the conference were "at all times [to] be obedient & submit to the laws of the State and also of the United States of America" and likewise to recommend "obedience and submission" to all "our fellow citizens,"[28] a position not unlike that of the Indians. The removal of rebels out of their vicinage and across the state for prosecution was itself on the model of Indian removal. Taken from their lands, they were placed at a distance from their communities and the presumed sites of their crimes to exclude those who could testify to their character and their grievances.

Captain Whiskey

It was no accident that an incisive satire of the Whiskey Rebellion used an Indian motif to go public with the story of westerners pitted against one another and the government over the impasse in the backcountry. The salience of the Indian theme gave the satire an unexpected resilience that drew attention to the malfeasance of all the parties involved, much to the annoyance of the commissioners, whose conference was the subject of the piece. The satire, titled auspiciously "The Indian Treaty," was described as "a very seditious libel."[29] It was instantly, and erroneously, attributed to Brackenridge, possibly because he had represented the Delaware Indian Mamachtaga in an infamous murder trial in 1785.[30] Published in the *Pittsburgh Gazette* on August 23, it bore a similarity to the "seditious and insulting dialogue" of the agitator Tom the Tinker, so that some supposed it might "be from the same quarter."[31] William Findley suspected the author was "a friend of the government" writing "in the character and manner of an insurgent" to incite the New Jersey militia, which made up the largest part of the federal army sent against the rebels. The *Gazette* ultimately disclosed that "a decided friend of the excise law" was the responsible party and that the printer could provide the name to any who wished to know.

Posted at the site of a market-house, the satire appeared on the eve of the first conference between the U.S. Commissioners and the rebel conferees. In preparation for the conference, the commissioners had put up at a house in Westmoreland; from behind a liberty pole, rioters shouted at the commissioners and threw stones, breaking several windows. As Brackenridge described the scene, "The commissioners were armed with pistols, and stood at their defence," leading to a confrontation (discussed in chapter 2) that became the subject of a court case.[32] "The Indian Treaty" parodied the meeting between the commission and the rebels in Pittsburgh (whose inhabitants supported the rebellion), which the character Captain Blanket sardonically described as "a lucky spot to hold a treaty meeting," no good presumably having come of meetings in Philadelphia.[33] The Six United Nations of White Indians at the treaty conference stood for the six protesting counties (the original four together with Bedford and Northumberland),[34] recalling the Six Indian Nations led by the Seneca chief Cornplanter at Philadelphia who conferred with "the Great Councillor of the Thirteen Fires" (the head of the original thirteen states) and "your great council," referring to Congress. The phrase "white Indian," a reference to the insurgents, was defined in a note to the satire as "[a] fashionable phrase, lately adopted by certain gentlemen in the service of the government."[35] In an alternative meaning, the phrase signified whites who had gone native, suggesting the rough music of blackface-disguised rioters.

The conference attendees included Captain Blanket, who took the position that the conference should address Indian demands and pay the Indians for attending, which was the British practice. These had been sticking points in the 1790–1791 Indian conferences where the Indian chiefs argued that the Cornplanter, Half-Town, and Great-Tree tribes received nothing for the sizable land they gave up in previous treaties with the "Thirteen Fires."[36] Captain Alliance (allied with Kentucky and the British), Captain Pacificus (who sought a cease fire and suspension of the tax until the next national council), and Captain Whiskey (the father of the six nations who rejected the tax and vowed to fight the federal militia) made up the other attendees.

Despite its likely origin, some believed the "Indian treaty" was a positive piece and that it accurately reported the rebel position.[37] It certainly reflected ideas about the government held by the rebels as well as the leverage they believed they exercised. For one thing, the piece expressed the sense of victimhood experienced in the West. A son of Saint Patrick (a nod to the western Scottish-Irish population who defended "their beloved bottle"), Captain Whiskey wished the same fate to befall eastern beer and cider that had been visited upon "homespun whiskey."[38] Nor had "the British about the lake" been visited with the same unequal tax or an army to collect it (a reference to the Lake Erie area where English forts still remained) for fear of "offending a nation with a king at their head." In a swipe at the president, the piece allowed that if the rebels had no king (Washington was regarded as a second King George), they had in Captain Whiskey "our monarch." In a reference to the government's two-pronged approach to managing the rebellion, Captain Pacificus argued that you come at the point of a bayonet and yet present as messengers of peace, whereas "I am more disposed to lay hold of the chain [to measure land] than the tomahawk," a likely reference to "tomahawk claims" as alternatives to land titles.

In fact, the Indian delegate Captain Pacificus maintained a posture much like that of the rebel moderates, holding that unlike others who were more desperate, he was open to "every reasonable proposition." But if the offer was merely that of a pardon, he argued, "we have not begged your pardon," referring to rebels who would not sign a submission and refused to admit wrongdoing. Knowing "our GOOD OLD FATHER" had the "duty to make proclamation, etc., etc.," Pacificus expected prudence and humanity (Brackenridge's view of how Washington would react), as he presented a belt inscribed "plenty of Whiskey without Excise" (a play on liberty pole slogans).[39]

In more pointed references to rebel intransigence, attendees spoke of secession, the politics of the Indian wars, and the imperial designs of foreign powers. Captain Alliance slyly implied they might, like the Kentuckians, take it upon themselves "to withhold supplies from your good old warrior Wayne [warring with the Indians in the Ohio valley] who is very often near starving in the wilderness"; with his army "immediately annihilated," the great white council could "bid adieu to [its] territory west of the mountains." Indeed, the rebels had withheld an attack on government supplies for General Wayne's troops on the very premise that it would interfere with the Indian wars. Or, he threatened, "some *evil spirit* might prompt us to a separation from the union" (reflecting David Bradford's secessionist stance). They could join the Kentuckians who, rather than lose access to "their darling Mississippi," might entertain a foreign alliance ("bow the knee to the Spanish monarch, or kiss the Pope's a——e and wear a crucifix"). Collaboration with Kentucky signified coordination with other organized resistance groups to spread the rebellion, mimicking the American Revolution's committees of safety. Posing another alternative, the great warrior Simco might employ "legions of white and yellow savages" to provide the rebels relief, indicating an alliance much like that pursued by the British and French with native tribes. Or they might make "a pleasing overture to the royal family of England" who might embrace the moment to "add again to their curtailed dominion America" and provide "their numerous brood with kingdoms and principalities."[40]

At the end of the piece, a figure called Jersey Blue, a surrogate for the federal militia, argued for a pardon. He represented that "our common Father" would have no problem brushing off the rebels' "cob-web argument," which could not be excused by the usual drunkenness of savages. He warned them to "send your swiftest runners" with a message of weakness and error, a common perception of the demeaning submission the government required of both the rebels and the Indians. And he advised that they pursue an amendment of the law "by constitutional [remonstration] and a change of representation," a gratuitous swipe at the fruitless efforts of the rebels to do just that and an indication of the failures of Indian tribes that chose to adopt the white man's form of governance.[41]

Whether the "Indian Treaty" really intended to be harmless satire (as Captain Whiskey openly suggested in speaking with "a smack of national tongue—Tongash Getchie [. . .] very strong man, me Captain Whiskey" and promising to "fight for our bottle till the last gasp") is open to question. Whereas the themes used in the satire ran the gamut of issues invoked in the rebellion, the piece nonetheless gave short shrift to the economic argument that whiskey, a luxury in the East, was both a necessity and an economic equalizer on the frontier. Nor did it press the complications or the desperation of the western position. On the other hand, the piece's familiarity with Indian culture aligned it with a similarly maligned people with comparable complaints and prospects. In using Indian spokesmen to treat with the "White Father," the satire signaled a residual notion of the rebels as a ragtag group of imbibing frontiersmen who had crossed over to barbarism. They might not have lost their link to popular sovereignty, but the satire undermined their claim to a constitutional form of resistance. It suggested instead that they were less worthy of being amnestied than they were of being dominated and made wards, an indication, as friends of the government suspected, that the satire was the likely product of an enemy of the western insurrection.

Among reactions to the piece, the satire attracted the outrage of the Jersey militia commanded by General Howell. Calling New Jerseyites the "water-mellon armies from the Jersey shores," the satire had allowed they would be better deployed battling the crabs and oysters of the Delaware Capes.[42] Brackenridge sent handbills to the rank and file by way of exonerating himself from responsibility for the piece, which the General tossed "instantly into the fire," support for the notion that the satire had "excited indignation and rage in almost every breast"[43] and made a poor impression on the commissioners. The printer of the piece, John Scull, defended publishing the piece and explained that his intention was to give the commission an idea of the "different ideas of the people in this country at that time" to mitigate the prejudice against them.[44] Caught in the maelstrom, the "Indian treaty" had toyed with heated issues to such effect that, like much else that occurred during the rebellion, it was used by all parties to the rebellion for their own purpose.

Liberty Poles

The impact of "The Indian Treaty" is a good indicator of the effect culture had on perceptions of the Whiskey Rebellion. Indeed, the satire and the riots that accompanied the arrival of the U.S. Commissioners did not occur in a vacuum. Rituals, displays, and ceremonies involving large, raucous crowds were a legacy of the Revolution's favorite themes: equality, no taxation, and the tree of liberty.[45] Liberty pole raisings had a history going back to Sons of Liberty in the 1760s and 1770s, which associated the poles with liberty trees, some as tall as a hundred feet, under which patriots met; poles reminiscent of ship masts to which banners and flags were attached were planted in the center of towns.[46] The origins of such poles are difficult to discern given alternative sources like May poles, battle standards, and Indian totems, though poles appeared to replace trees where the latter were unavailable, preserving the symbolic value of the association.[47] Liberty poles capitalized on the commanding imagery of beacons in the centers of towns, referencing yardarms from which miscreants might be hanged, crucifixes on which the worthy might be offered as sacrifice, or, indeed, a useful site for burning effigies. They resonated as life-renewing figurations of resurrection when they were torn down only to be remounted, reflecting transformational imagery like the tree of original sin or the tree of life. The poles were also signs, like crossroads, of places where opposed parties might confront each other.

Slogans on banners attached to the poles drew on prior usage, like the Sons of Liberty slogan "Liberty and Equality." They ranged widely, from "Equal taxation, and no Excise," and "Liberty and no excise, O, Whiskey" to "Liberty, no Excise and death to Traitors"; we find them as well in the inscription "Plenty of Whiskey without Excise" in the "Indian Treaty" satire.[48] On the top of poles, flags were flown as well, a practice likely informed by the flying of county flags or standards associated with local militias.[49] They were apparently small, the most widely known of which had six stripes, red and white (representing the rebellious western counties Washington, Westmoreland, Fayette, and Alleghany and two Virginia counties). Another, larger, flag featured an eagle, centrally placed, surrounded by thirteen stars, or in one case butterflies, representing the original states. This flag, often referred to as the Scenery Hill flag, might have been used in the rebellion, but in a minor capacity as it was probably a federal army regimental flag.[50]

Whether peaceful or riotous, the tradition of pole raising created opportunities to develop a culture of grievances. People ran from pole raisings to spread the word to other towns, as in Franklin County where five hundred men spread out to carry the news. Asked who led them, they replied, "[T]hey were all as one" and were bent on setting up the pole "if the Devil stood at the Door."[51] Discussions related to pole raisings expressed the popular sentiment that the people should not have their liberty until Congress was executed and that "[t]he Government had Carried themselves too high and must be taken down." They declared that the people of the West should separate from the U.S. government and "had better form a government for themselves who had no President, no King."⁵² "Productive of much riot and confusion," George Eddy informed Governor Mifflin, liberty poles were "erroneously" named and impossible to extinguish, for when citizens cut down one pole "Northumberland anarchists" produced a much larger "anarchy pole" to greater ferment than before.⁵³

Sources suggest that pole raisings involved intimidation but not real violence as the poles represented instances of collaboration and cross-class community supported by the agreement of sizable factions. In Northumberland, the people voted on all aspects of the pole raisings and circulated a petition to generate general support.⁵⁴ Communities designed, built, and defended them. Those assembled selected and cut the tree, gave speeches, and chose flags and slogans to adorn the pole. Neighbors participated in the particulars of design and saluted the poles with gunfire; those present passed around whiskey, torched effigies, and posted armed guards to protect the pole.⁵⁵

The ubiquity and resilience of poles was undeniable. Poles appeared at the homes of the wealthy, at commercial sites such as mills, at the offices of excise officials. They were gauntlets thrown down to contest court sittings as well as signposts of assemblies. Even the cryptically named agitator Tom the Tinker was associated with raising poles. As markers tracking the federal militia's progress, Findley allowed, they "were erected, through a great extent of the country, on the east side of the mountains,"⁵⁶ so that the militia was met by pole raisings in five counties (Cumberland, Franklin, Dauphin, Mifflin, and Northumberland) in support of the four counties in open rebellion. The *General Gazette* identified fourteen such sites on the way to Pittsburgh from Carlisle to Bedford and Greensburgh, declaring that their "alarming appearance" was "a token of the disposition of the people westward."⁵⁷ As an abstract message, they demonstrated the omnipresence of the rebellion; they rallied supporters, threatened enemies, warned those who refused to take a side, and called defenders to arms. But they also had the practical effect of impeding federal militia recruitment and spreading sedition; easily recognized, they marked the territory where communities supported the rebels. They were bound to impress Washington as he arrived to review the troops in Carlisle. Having traveled West, as he represented to Congress, to visit "the places of general rendezvous; to obtain more exact intelligence, and to direct a plan"⁵⁸ (not, as has been commonly supposed, to lead his army into battle), his decision to launch the army with dispatch into battle was clearly affected by the trail of poles. The erection of liberty poles evoked an even more visceral response from Hamilton who was so perturbed at the various poles guarded by armed groups that he concluded they were meant to terrorize the inhabitants; he denominated them "declarations in favour of a revolution."[59]

Pole raising was charged as a misdemeanor in the rebel trials, a catchall for minor crimes that nonetheless transformed symbolic speech into conduct. As a symbolic act encapsulating popular protest in a communal act of association and speech, pole raising fell into the awkward category of protected speech. Treated as conduct, however, it could be criminalized as riot. In practice, judges and prosecutors tended to discount the precedent of the Revolution and found that symbolic speech acts were, in fact, seditious conduct.[60] According to Attorney General William Bradford, when protests spread in Bedford until "near two-hundred men assembled, & in the very view of the court which was then sitting, erected a liberty pole," the county court responded by charging 125 men with riot.[61] According to Findley, state courts in counties on both sides of the Alleghenies laid heavy fines on those who erected liberty poles,[62] while those indicted federally from Cumberland and Northumberland counties escaped trial when their cases were delayed till the April 1796 session of the circuit court, at which time the district attorney withdrew prosecution.

The government's distaste for the disruptions occasioned by liberty poles was evident in twenty-six indictments in federal circuit court for "speech-related misdemeanors"; five cases resulted in failed indictments.[63] Seditious speech accounted for six of those indictments and a seditious letter for a seventh, though the government's main target was actually the newly created liberty pole–raising misdemeanor.[64] Findley observed that erecting a liberty pole, even accompanied by the heat and passion of "the most ignorant class," was no high crime.[65] Robert Porter, who was charged and acquitted of treason for other acts, complained as well that it was "too ridiculous to risk a trial upon." Prosecutors nonetheless treated pole raising as a means of aiding and comforting the enemy, and thereby as an indication of treason, even if it could only be charged as a misdemeanor.[66]

This was exactly what happened with two men, Robert Philson and Herman Husband, from Bedford County. After a failed effort to indict them for treason, they were charged in federal circuit court with a seditious speech misdemeanor for raising a liberty pole at the Parkinson's Ferry assembly. The case, discussed further in chapter 5, involved a flag inscribed with butterflies alluding to the rebellious counties and a banner whose inscription included the language "no asylum for traitors and cowards." That the federal court took the case to trial at all was less a question of the law than the government's ire at Husband's messianic speeches and writings and the president's conviction that Husband incited the rebels to revolt. Indicted for being "seditious persons," disturbing the peace, and insurrection,[67] the two men were charged in the indictment with levying war and being "armed in a warlike manner," "in a traitorous and hostile manner," and "confederate with certain other false and ill disposed persons," language similar to that which described a charge of common law treason or accomplice to treason rather than a misdemeanor. The defendants were acquitted.

Gallatin, the star witness in *Philson and Husband*, contended that pole raisings were intended as acts of "expression" and not conduct[68] and that the prosecution had overreached in its construction of the crime. From the prosecution's position, a misdemeanor charge obviated the need to reach the high constitutional bar of treason while it still allowed for a common law conviction. The lower charge left it to the court to decide whether the erection of a liberty pole was lawful expression or illegal conduct. Federal juries apparently determined it was lawful, as none of the nineteen defendants charged in the federal circuit court trials with raising a liberty pole was convicted. At the state level, meanwhile, those who erected liberty poles were successfully prosecuted under a charge of riot, including the six defendants in *Pennsylvania v. Norris Morrison et al.*, discussed in the previous chapter.[69] According to Judge Addison, pole raising constituted "an indignity and insult" to official representatives of the government (the U.S. Commissioners), serving "to the ill example of others." Without citing any law that might have been violated, the judge charged the jury that the rioters' conduct was sufficient to a guilty verdict. They had "made an impression very unfavourable to the whole country" and provoked the government to use force, thereby threatening violence and danger to the town. Addison's words constitute a sad commentary on the government's real motivation in prosecuting pole raising as a crime.

Tom the Tinker

Tom the Tinker was an invention positioned well within the tradition of liberty pole–raising festivities and humiliation rituals. Posters, handbills, and published appeals were promulgated in his name as a legendary figure who perpetrated acts of rough music against those who supported the whiskey tax. His identity was both unique—the rebel John Holcroft[70] was widely assumed to be Tom the Tinker—and shared by those who masqueraded as Tinker's boys. The true identity of Tom the Tinker was something of a mystery. Brackenridge identified Holcroft as "the very man [...] I am the most afraid of; he is Tom the Tinker" and indicated that Holcroft's sons had "threatened the town with Tom the Tinker."[71] But he did not persist in publicly naming Holcroft, noting that Holcroft had denied under oath any knowledge of Tom the Tinker and that he had "only copied some of the papers which had been put up on trees."[72] An advertisement[73] appeared to identify him when it indicated its author was a leader of troops "in the late expedition against the insolent exciseman John Nevill." It later appeared the pieces were not by Holcroft, though, as Findley claimed, "the inventor of them has never been discovered."[74]

Holcroft had, in fact, presented himself at Bower Hill as commander of a Mingo Creek militia made up of thirty-seven men.[75] Prosecuting U.S. district attorney for Pennsylvania, William Rawle, made notes on Holcroft for the trials but made no mention of Tom the Tinker in them; nor does it appear Holcroft testified, though he was noted to be a turncoat witness for the prosecution.[76] In Judge William Paterson's notes for the treason trial of John Barnet, an underlined marginal comment revealed that the government was interested in the Tinker's identity and that his work had been linked to the democratic societies: "*Generally understood, that Tom the Tinker's letters were the work of one man, and not of any association.*"[77] The government, in any event, took it that Holcroft was in fact the figure called Tom the Tinker. Hamilton wrote to Washington "of the apprehending of John Holcroft the reputed *Tom the Tinker*" and advised Rawle that Holcroft was one who must be brought to justice and not pardoned.[78] While Holcroft was among those specifically exempted from pardon by proclamation, he nonetheless avoided prosecution.[79]

The appellation "Tinker" derived from tinkers who cut up the stills of cooperative distillers[80] (the punishment for those who complied with the excise law by registering their stills), while the term "Tom the Tinker" became a popular call out for those who opposed the excise law. The cry "Are you a Tom the Tinker's man?" was generally met with favor.[81] The Tinker's boys engaged themselves in a "period of misrule"[82] that involved at the simplest level posting notices, disseminating handbills, and publishing incendiary letters. The ads they placed in trees "in the high ways, or on other conspicuous places" under the Tinker's signature admonished people to reject the law while the letters to the public were published by the editor of the *Gazette*, who thought it "imprudent to refuse to publish."[83] The Tinker's men soon moved on to erecting liberty poles, destroying stills, attacking excisemen, and burning their houses.

Intimidation was the Tinker's most distinctive trademark in compelling resistance to the tax and punishing those who supported it.[84] In one instance, an anonymous handbill distributed at Parkinson's Ferry threatened all those who might vote for submission and warned that the commissioners had brought bags of gold to bribe representatives sent to meet with them.[85] The campaign was especially effective at public shaming and harassment in trial by press. When the Tinker revealed in print, for example, that he had paid the distiller Cochrane a return visit, it raised the cost of supporting the excise law. Cochrane had already seen his still shot through with holes and several items (his still cap, a mill saw, and a loose iron) stolen; a note explained that the damage was punishment for complying with the revenue law. The Tinker's note directed Cochrane to go public in the Pittsburgh paper and reveal all that had been done to him; otherwise Tom's third visit would "make the hills give light to the vales." The entire exchange appeared in the following week's paper over the sign-off "Tom the Tinker, repairer of excised stills."[86]

John Reed—who had entered his still "on the excise docket"—was likewise instructed by the Tinker to publicize in the *Pittsburgh Gazette* an unadulterated advertisement of his iniquity, failing which he would suffer the "consumption of his distillery." Reed complied, appealing to Mr. Scull, the editor, that he was forced to request Scull "to put the following in your next paper. It was found posted on a tree near my distillery."[87] Reed had not only registered his still, but, more critically, he had failed to attend the militia muster which The Tinker identified as "under my direction in the late expedition," hinting at his own identity. He went on to demand that "if such delinquents do not come forth on the next alarm, with equipments, and give their assistance as much as in them lies," they would be declared enemies. The Tinker would not stand for any group eluding service in his district. The ad, which combined the attributes of a military tribunal and a summary proceeding, suggested the trappings of a court proceeding in that a survey was to be taken followed by findings and appropriate punishment. More immediately, the public nature of the notice exposed Reed to public shaming,[88] while its postscript directed more general future action: "To prevent a great deal of trouble, it will be necessary to repeal the excise law."

The friends of Tom the Tinker were generally successful in cowing the *Gazette's* readers. One subscriber, anticipating an advertisement against him, requested that the public withhold its opinion to give him an opportunity to justify himself. Preemptively, he "solemnly" declared, the charges were "entirely false."[89] Just a week later a complainant announced the circulation of a rumor by "some ill-disposed person" motivated by "a salacious design to hurt my character." He wished the public to suspend its opinion till he could defend himself against the accusation that he was somehow involved in the excise tax.[90] Similarly, John Lynne and Andrew Munro complained they had been falsely accused of collusion so that Munro might operate a collector's office in Lynn's house. In support of their public disavowal of the charges, excise inspector Robert Johnson attached a postscript testifying that he knew of "no such request." In yet another case, a friend of resistance addressed a "Gentleman" who shamed him for being against the tax. In his defense, he provided some "hasty thoughts" on what his accuser must prove: Were the demands "consistent with liberty and freedom" and "the principles of equity and justice"? Should the gentleman resolve those inequities, the author would then, he claimed, be properly ashamed and "even confounded."[91]

Activities associated with the Tinker phenomenon spiked in number and importance from the attack on Neville's house and the rebel march to Pittsburgh to the arrival of the U.S. Commissioners. What gave the name such a fearsome aspect was the easily imitated agitation-propaganda it sponsored, which spread like a virus. Like the reaction to the rash of liberty pole raisings, Findley noted, the Tinker's campaign had spread panic by means of a "description of people, whose voice is not heard in society in settled times." Even the rebel delegates at Parkinson's Ferry were "intimidated to a degree inconsistent with that calmness and reflection necessary for deliberation."[92] The Tinker had clearly prevented volunteers from coming forward to comply with the excise act or to cooperate with officers. Reports of officials victimized and enablers shamed over the years (from William Graham and Philip Jenkins to Robert Wilson, Philip Reagan, and John Neville) testified to the perception that spies and regulators were omnipresent to expose and punish those who broke with popular sentiment on the excise tax.[93] A statement on public perception that raised the stakes to a higher, indeed transcendent, level came from Judge John Lobringier of Westmoreland, an excise supporter, who postulated that "the Tinker was a new god added to the mythology at this time, and was supposed to preside over whiskey-stills and still-houses." A Judge Veech offered that Tom's "Olympus" was located on "the hills of Mingo or Peters Creek" and that he was a "multiform deity, or at least he was Briarean," a reference to the hundred-handed giant Briareus, a figure operating in the dark and impossible to detect.⁹⁴ This omnipresent Tom, the people believed, had many helpers.

Tom the Tinker was clearly not without his detractors. Prominently, the Federalist journalist William Cobbett satirized "Billets stuck upon trees!" He spoke of the gambit as "a romantic way of carrying on Treason and Rebellion," a poor match for 'the language of those gentle swains" of Parkinson's Ferry.⁹⁵ Zeroing in on "a sot like *Tom*," Cobbett could not imagine that ladies would love a man whose "scull had often been decorated with a liberty cap." He quoted the playwright Oliver Goldsmith to argue that like a man "eternally 'vociferating liberty! liberty!" Tom must "*in his own family*, [be] a most cruel and *inhuman tyrant*.'" Despite his grave misgivings, Cobbett conferred on Tom the honor of a certain "pre-eminence" among all his "partizans," though should he meet with the British "[t]hey would teach him how to set people together by the ears."⁹⁶

Tom the Tinker retired his position of community watchman for almost two months, with the hope that the country had been united behind his cause. Once the U.S. Commissioners arrived, however, he felt obliged to resurface. To announce his return, he commanded the printer John Gaston, printer of the *Pittsburgh Gazette*, to insert a note in the paper, a request Gaston felt he could not refuse given the situation in the country.⁹⁷ Addressing friends across the country, "Poor Tom" expressed his reluctance as well as his sense of obligation in taking up his "commission, once more." "[M]y friends see more need for me than ever," he declared, imploring them to reject the submission offered by the president's commission. Fair warning to traitors, he proclaimed, "[M]y hammer is up, and my ladle is hot. I cannot travel the country for nothing."⁹⁸ This time, his warning was to no avail; the commissioners' arrival had already turned the trajectory of the rebellion in a new direction.

Humor

Beyond shaming rituals and agitation-propaganda, a level of cultural manipulation attached to humorous speech had achieved a high profile in rebel circles, largely attributable to Brackenridge, a central, if eccentric, player in the rebellion. Brackenridge capitalized on humor as performance art in assemblies and conferences like those discussed in chapter 2. Borrowed from a popular tradition of moral tales, his astute use of anecdotes and exemplars calmed and guided obstreperous crowds, which found his stories easy to comprehend though sometimes disconcerting. Brackenridge used humor not only to conceal his insecure position in the assemblies but also to relate to the broad base of common people who attended the meetings; observing members of the crowd as he engaged them, if he could not change minds he would mold perceptions. Because humor cut across differences of class and political position, it had the potential to ease friction between factions and reconcile heterogeneous perspectives in the rebel narrative.

Brackenridge's task in the assemblies was complicated by the size of his audiences and the differing opinions he had to navigate, whereas in his dealings with individuals he could simply apply his skills at deflection. The collier Fergus Ferguson provided a case in point. Having failed to add his name to the amnesty, Ferguson feared he might be hung. But since his employment and residence were subterranean, Brackenridge advised, he could plead he did not belong to the earth. Should this fail to "bar the jurisdiction of the court," it might persuade the district attorney to dismiss the suit, "in as much as [Ferguson] had been under ground through the summer, and had not heard of the insurrection."[99] By contrast, at the Mingo Creek assembly the mob returning from the burning of Neville's house was at fever pitch. As they were at odds with one another and unable to agree on anything, Brackenridge tried flattery. Skilled as they were with their rifles, he offered, "[T]hey could pick an eye out of a squirrel on the tallest oak or hickory." He followed by role-playing the Seneca Indian Cornplanter's treaty-making with General Knox to demonstrate that rebels could make a treaty too.[100] Brackenridge's ploy paid dividends. The assembly came together to embrace such practical solutions as deferring a decision; the crowd withheld its support of those who had committed violent acts and left open the possibility of negotiating with the government.[101] According to Carnahan, Brackenridge "made a camelion speech" that adjusted itself "to the position of the hearer." It was unclear whether he was for or against the insurgents, so that neither moderates nor radicals could effectively oppose him. Brackenridge had set himself the modest goal of feeling out the temper of the crowd with a view toward protracted engagements over time. Discovering that talk of treason only angered people, he "told amusing anecdotes and threw down sallies of wit that men whose muscles had not been relaxed for days, were convulsed with laughter."[102] Brackenridge recognized that the crowd was divided in its opinion and, according to Findley, "drew their attention by amusing them and seeming to countenance their conduct."[103]

At Braddock's Field, as at Mingo Creek, the mob dominated the assembly only to be met with several anecdotes from Brackenridge intended to allay resentment. He countered Bradford's claim that Major Craig would open an inspection office by portraying Craig "to be a bloody man" who, hearing that the people were coming, ripped down the "obnoxious" office sign and ran off. Brackenridge explained that he knew "no better way than to turn it to a laugh," trading his partiality for Craig and lowering suspicion "by substituting something of less effect."[104] At the same assembly, he recalled a humorous, lawyerly anecdote to help resolve a dispute. It involved a man who, saved from drowning by a fellow traveler, sued for the damages he suffered in the rescue; he represented that he had not applied for assistance and his rescuer had not obtained his formal consent. The resolution offered the victim the choice of being returned to the pool where he almost drowned or being "satisfied with the act of his companion."[105] Brackenridge was even more diverting when dealing with the proposed march on the garrison at Pittsburgh, With the thought of storming the Bastille before him, Brackenridge "thought it the safest way to give good words, and good drink, rather than balls and powder." The cost of "four barrels of old whiskey," he mused, was worth "a single quart of blood."[106]

Brackenridge disclosed at the Parkinson's Ferry assembly that he consciously used humor to conceal his displeasure at Bradford's violent plans. To distract Bradford, he "amused him with pleasantry, and kept him laughing."[107] While Gallatin found Brackenridge's use of laughter disconcerting and contended that Brackenridge "laughs all by himself,"[108] Brackenridge himself said of a speech he gave at Mingo Creek, "I am aware of the delicacy of having any thing to say to people in the predicament in which these are." Although he had prepared to harangue the crowd on that occasion, he thought better of choosing "a moment between treason the one hand, and popular odium on the other,"[109] hoping to put his audience in a good humor that he might thereafter broach more serious subjects.

For Brackenridge, humor was a form of personnel management that sometimes required him to act the role of assembly jester. He found in this stratagem a means not of persuading but of making the crowd more amenable to the substantive discussions he and Gallatin introduced. Rather than a failure to understand the needs of his audiences, his delivery involved gauging their interest and exerting influence. Brackenridge, for example, played for time to reduce crowd tension, the biggest obstacle to coming to an agreement. The initial risks were significant and the prospects grim, but Brackenridge was hardly a novice at presenting arguments or leading groups to a decision. He was perhaps the most impressive litigator in the western courts and experienced in dealing with obstreperous juries. He recognized not only that words were a malleable medium,[110] but that the ability to convince depended on an accepting audience. His task was to lead his listeners to endow words with the meanings he had intended. The unintended consequences of speech that relied on humor made his task more difficult as did the need for ambiguous content to appeal to multiple audiences and to open alternative possible paths to a resolution. Brackenridge's ability to rescue an intended effect from an ironic statement might have yielded a more predictable response under more controlled conditions, but the assemblies presented speakers with the worst of all possible situations. Speakers had to reconcile conflicts among factions even as they developed the audience's trust if they were to reach a common understanding.

Exposing popular illusions to create a coherent position and creating persuasive appeals to reach common grounds led Brackenridge to adopt unusual and often extreme positions that confounded his audience. Humor had the benefit, in this regard, of removing obstacles to agreement. Brackenridge might have played an untrustworthy narrator or adopted ironic postures, but by doing so he introduced a turbulent crowd to alternatives through imagery and tales that broke open unyielding positions. In the end, his anecdotes offset the suspicion and outrage of his assembly audiences. He used ambiguity to provide a means for people to concede favored positions and entertain other ways of thinking. In dealing with difficult choices, he got them to defer decisions. Humor, as Brackenridge applied it, cut through the Gordian chaos of mob rule and offered the rebels a way back from the abyss.

Modern Chivalry

To fully account for the contribution Brackenridge made to the legal culture of the rebellion, it is useful to take a tangent to consider his satiric western novel *Modern Chivalry*. Here, Brackenridge moved beyond his disarming use of humor and affected ambivalence in the rebel assemblies and his effort to create a historical, if self-serving, chronicle of the period in *Incidents of the Insurrection*. He expressed in the novel his personal views on the rebellion with astonishing directness. This was hardly a new position for Brackenridge, who had been a propagandist since he wrote his bloody play "The Death of General Montgomery" during the Revolution, immortalizing Montgomery's torture and death at the hands of the British.[111] He went on to transform a captivity narrative in 1783 into a compellingly gruesome story of the Indian fighter Colonel William Crawford's capture and murder by the Delawares and to publish a screed against the Indians in 1792.[112]

The only writer of note to emerge from western Pennsylvania in the early republic, Brackenridge's participation in the rebellion became the stuff of events and experiences in the multivolume *Modern Chivalry*, a picaresque reflection on backcountry democracy, law, and politics. Brackenridge suspended writing the novel to work on his history, delaying the publication of part one, volume four of the novel (in which he features the rebellion) until three years after the events it treated and two years after his history of the rebellion and his participation in the rebel trials.[113] Despite its comic pretensions, the novel represented Brackenridge's most mature view of the Whiskey Rebellion.[114] His retrospective take on events expressed through the shifting personas of the novel's antihero, the irrepressible servant Teague O'Regan, was at once critical and forgiving as a kaleidoscopic view of a world in a state of transformation. The multiple points of view of its narrating voices (the author himself, the "narrator," a blind lawyer turned judge, and Teague's master Captain Farrago) sampled the multiple perspectives that informed the period, which, together with the animal imagery through which Brackenridge depicted the frontier mob and law courts, expressed the author's view of democracy as essentially an untenable congealing of mutually exclusive interests.[115] The most pervasive attribute, however, was the doublemindedness the novel exhibited in Brackenridge's innate sense of the irresolvable contradictions and split nature of the rebellion.

Brackenridge's satire centered on interactions between the protean figure Teague O'Regan, a servant promoted to an excise officer by President Washington, and a violent mob protesting the excise law. The mob bore the brunt of Brackenridge's attention, more for its use of force against an official than its "prejudices against the obnoxious law." Teague's master advised that "great allowance" be made for rash ruffians so that "[b]y soft measures, and mild words, prejudices may be overcome." Officials might then operate without "being under the necessity to attempt battery, or shed blood." Well-intentioned, Farrago at first compared the mob to a clumsy clown, only to discover in them pole-raising miscreants in a hanging mood.[116] Farrago compared the "sans culottes" of his mob to those of the French Revolution in a damning indictment that involved assembly committees, resolves to commit great violence, and flames of opposition demolishing inspection offices. Those obnoxious to the cause, or even lukewarm, were to be banished, their goods destroyed, or their persons injured. Indeed, the crowd had begun framing guillotines and talked of decapitating traitors.[117]

Feeling themselves deceived by election politics, the mob approached the excise officer with a tree "trailing after them," dug a hole to sink a liberty pole, and proceeded to tar and feather their victim, judging him, as the author observed, "by the opprobrium of opinion; and yet short of the coercion of the laws."[118] The scene depicted an outbreak of popular sovereignty, a form of "revolutionary punishment" that exceeded the justice of a steady state and its laws; little more than madness and prejudice, it was expected, in time, to pass, for it was an indefensible cause justified by neither principle nor reason nor natural law.[119] Mobs did not, said the captain, speak for the rights of the people; they represented the misguided patriotism of the uninformed and the destruction of republican government.[120] Contesting the mob, he held they were nothing more than "[a] few madcaps [who] get together, and call themselves the people; and talk of the majesty of the people."[121] Based on the mobs Brackenridge engaged in the rebellion, this mob was as tyrannical as bad government, leading him to question whether in a democracy terror issuing "from lamp-black, and patriotism" ought not to be put down.[122]

Brackenridge's view of mobs was linked to his exposition on the humanity of beasts. He had written *Incidents*, he confessed, to give "a picture of a people broke loose from the restraints of government, and going *farther than they intended to go.*"[123] Where fear was "the foundation of government, of man, as much as of a horse, or an ass," Brackenridge argued in the final volume of *Modern Chivalry*, the secret was not to govern as one would a beast prompted by its passions "but by *the fear of suffering a distant evil,*" signifying that man can anticipate his fate by reason.[124] As he explained to the blind judge, a visionary philosopher, if "[a] bull happening to roar, and a horse neigh at the same time, it was called out that it was the voice of the people." Should the herd's voice be honored, animals would have rights equal to those of humans, and thereby to manumission. They could not then be treated as beasts of burden or, for that matter, be ridden, skinned, or shot, "but on condition of taking turns, and letting them ride us."[125] The mob's call for equal rights was thus no more valid than that of beasts, Farrago (now a governor) pointed out.

As for Teague, the novel was no less forthright. Captain Farrago's Scottish steward, Duncan, regarded Teague as nothing "but a gauger," for no one able to live an honest life would accept the commission of excise officer. The captain, however, regarded the position as "a limb of the executive of the union" whether he was "styled, your worship, your honor, or your reverence,"[126] a dig at the elevated aspirations of local officials tempted to side with national government. The nature of Teague's appointment was itself a matter of controversy, as the president, having anticipated resistance to the office, chose the Irish "bog-trotter" for no better reason than that he could repel insults. The president, the captain offered, was "said to have the virtue, or rather the excess of [some]one" who stood by his appointees, likely "an unwillingness to have it thought his judgment could be fallible."[127] The novel's narrator did not, however, berate the president (a beloved figure) or the government's implementation of the excise law (which met with considerable hostility). Nor did the narrator describe the people's conduct in treasonous terms since it lacked the intent that would rise to the level of a serious threat. But he did deride the excesses that arose from the conduct of the excise officer Teague and the corresponding abuse to which the mob subjected him. Brackenridge was, beyond all else, a proponent of the need for good citizens to honor the law and its execution and to support good government and honest officials. Virtuous citizenship and respect for the law were for Brackenridge crucial elements of a sound republic. Indeed Duncan, the good citizen, conceded to the authority of the excise officer, "for I ken the law better than to stand out against the civil authority."[128] And the captain would honor his former servant because a republican government demanded obedience to the law and its officers. If Teague's conduct was beneath the dignity of his commission, the captain would not have his own "attributed to any secret grudge, or dislike of public measures, or persons at the head of our affairs,"[129] a reflection of Brackenridge's public position during the rebellion. That is, because republican government required majority rule, individuals must submit.[130] In sum, a citizen's duty to respect authority was a necessary complement to the laws if reason was to prevail over violence.[131]

In the volumes of *Modern Chivalry* published in 1804 and 1815, Brackenridge continued to be preoccupied by a state of affairs in which the authority of the law lost popular support.[132] About to be elected governor of a new state that desired more permanent legal principles and institutions, the captain considered "they are going to burn the lawyers, as they did the witches in New England, and as to judges, it is as much as a man's life is worth to resemble one."[133] But if each man was his own lawyer, the law would not survive.[134] Satirizing Erasmus Darwin by making the point that man descended from "a cray-fish, or a flying squirrel," Brackenridge set the stage for a near-perfect test of man's great achievement, the law, in part two, volume four of the novel: the law would be conducted by a court of animals. "[H]ave you not heard it said," the novel posited, "that judge this, or judge that, is an ass, that another is a horse, and of even a juris consult, or barrister, for instance is a panther; a bear"?[135] Informed by his experience litigating in the early years of western courts, Brackenridge's experiment replaced the barking, braying, and false eloquence of lawyers with leaping monkeys, a browbeating wolf, and a clever fox admitted to a bar where growling was well tolerated and, indeed, taken for ability.[136] The general feeling, as a sober observer said, was that "it was as easy to make a judge of law as to make a bird-cage, or a rat-trap." Observing western contempt for American practices based on the common law of England, the blind lawyer added his voice; he raised the prospect of having no laws at all, "a burlesque" that would tend "naturally to the overthrow of justice." Intrigue would in that case "come to be employed in the management of causes" to render persons and property precarious. The bottom line was that security in the law depended on settled rules that were known and properly applied.[137]

Throughout *Modern Chivalry*, Brackenridge used the faults of the judicial system as a teaching tool and the courtroom as a metaphor.[138] The blindness of justice had left the western country bereft of fair courts and judges, which Brackenridge demonstrated through a blind lawyer who becomes a judge and then chief justice. While his blindness walled him off from the influences of fear and favor,[139] he was capable of being deceived or misled, deprived of the knowledge possessed by those who could see. The judge, in other words, was an image of the western lawyer, an imperfect character whose view of the law was a mix of naivete, insight, and innovation. Reflecting the broken system of which he was a part, the judge gave Teague lessons in being a judge and oversaw the legal experiment that substituted beasts for humans. He advised his student that far from having to learn the law, it would suffice to have a steady gait, wear spectacles, and maintain a grave attitude to cover his stupidity. Nor need Teague take notes, though it was the fashion to do so; rather, notes must only seem to be taken, for "*justice itself is said to be blind* and can take no notes."[140] Whatever else, Teague, like Brackenridge himself, must pretend to be listening to satisfy those who expected to be heard, though they should lose their case.

With Teague's lessons over, it was clear the ignorant servant would make a sad figure on the bench in a court where, as the judge said, each man could "state his own cases, and speak for himself. No Hooks and Crooks reports; no Hawkins; no Bacons; or Blackstones; [...] no law of evidence." With the jury free to believe what it liked and judges to state the law as they wished, judgment might "be according to the light of nature; but not according to the law of nature."[141] Like Brackenridge, the blind judge was no fool. He was a philosopher of the law who recognized the importance of its legacy. He argued that deserting established courts and reverting to a simple set of legal practices might free people of the shackles of the law, as it did in the rebellion, only to leave them in a primitive state of liberty, draining law of its content and displacing justice.[142]

Conclusion

The examination of legal culture in this chapter and the preceding chapter emphasizes how legal culture interfaces (law in culture and culture in law) to create a framework that contests, displaces, or stresses the rule of law when social conflicts and legal issues confront each other. Legal culture provides the space for that interactivity. We discover this in the popular enforcement rituals and the agitation-propaganda practiced in the Whiskey Rebellion, which constituted a means of enacting and redressing grievances, whether in speech acts or conduct and whether borrowed or invented. Functioning as extensions of a ground-level legal culture, traditions and inventions turned impotence into power and made real the expressive content of the rebel narrative. Common people mastered the means of defying authority and stage-managing their own order of meaning and experience by constructing practices that violated old norms and established new ones. They generated cohesion to create a rebel community that could write itself into history, linking to a preferred past and the prospect of an ideal future of rights-bearing political subjects.

Identified as white Indians, the rebels adopted a persona that, on the one hand, was of a piece with their frontier environment but, on the other, defined them as victims of a more civilized power. "The Indian Treaty" satire which greeted the U.S. Commissioners built on the belief that settlers had in fact gone native. The treatment they received responded to a long history of land grabs and exploitation that benefited wealthy easterners as westerners entered a Union of which they did not feel a part. Erecting liberty poles transformed symbols into speech acts of a substantive character; it collectivized individual resistance in communal rituals to organize whole towns in solidarity. Like pop-up trees, the poles rose, fell, and resurrected to dog the route of an invading army and spread news of the rebellion. For his part, Tom the Tinker gave personhood to a pseudonymous rebel anyone could impersonate and who could recede into the population and disappear like a lord of misrule or some modern-day deity.

The propaganda and enforcement arm of the rebellion embodied a culture of resistance that amplified the rebel message in living terms to extend its impact and reach. It represented both the furtive conduct of resistance in the context of hegemonic power relations and the use of ordinary weapons by relatively powerless groups that could ill afford the luxury of open rebellion.[143] Legal culture thereby provided forms of everyday resistance for common people to make their political presence felt. Indeed, these forms were both a precondition to organized resistance and a collateral form of action, arising out of contests that were not always aimed against the government. While the use of blackface and Indian motifs as well as mock hangings in effigy (like that of Justice McKean in chapter 2) ruptured the playing field for government authorities, the audiences for such displays often splintered into factions that faced off against one another; some raised liberty poles and others razed them.

Retaliatory image-making—as in welcoming celebrations that attended the president's progress across the state—underscored that legal culture was not monolithic or predictable. Federalists celebrated the president's arrival as a grand cavalcade; in such an instance in Carlisle, the courthouse featured a transparency inscribed "in large, illuminated characters," which read "'WASHINGTON IS EVER TRIUMPHANT' On one side, 'THE REIGN OF THE LAWS,' on the other side, 'WOE TO ANARCHISTS.'"[144] Still, the quantity of western public rituals on its home ground favored rebel displays as strategic behavior demonstrating self-mastery in the face of the government's organized political and military resources. Bradford's entry into a militia muster presented a visual image on point: "Mounted on a superb horse in splendid trappings, arrayed in full martial uniform, with plumes floating and sword drawn[. . . .] Never was mortal man more flattered than was David Bradford on Braddock's Field."[145] The cultural presence of resistance revealed that subordination was not inevitable and that objectively the subordinated could appropriate tools of domination to legitimize popular struggle in the eyes of a wider public. Cultural resistance thus staked a claim to a subject position in the political dialogue ensuring that hegemony was never as "thick on the ground" (in the Gramscian sense) as the government hoped.[146]

Operating within the guise of such agitation-propaganda as handbills, satires, and rituals, the rebellion engaged in political mobilization, but it also served as entertainment. Tom the Tinker's notices were not merely informational directives or threatening missives. They were also an amusing, innovative way to reach rural folk who failed to follow the dictates of the rebels. The tie-in that required recipients to publish a notice in the gazette, typically expressing a demeaning capitulation, also invented an energizing form of outreach that turned recalcitrant distillers into live advertisements for compliance. This unique form of agitation and message sending began as an individual handbill only to turn into mass distribution. Their dark humor tinted with threat, the notices' shared authorship allowed for communal participation that generated a groundswell of approval and solidarity. The Tinker's mysterious persona proved puzzle-like, allowing for various interpretations and guesses; at the same time, the appearance of a notice at any time or place, by anyone or everyone, lent the practice a game-like aspect based on its omnipresent and ephemeral quality. Endemic and characterized by high connectivity, the Tinker's posts kept the rural population off-footed in a seriously playful game of catch-as-catch-can. It was nothing if not an invented practice of high ingenuity.

With their roots in traditional lore, cultural forms of resistance capitalized on a common cultural language. They might not have overcome differences in social status, but they had the potential to extend across the spectrum from political gossip to social criticism; using performative means that were as celebratory as they were transgressive, they were hard to resist. Spectacles like Bradford's theatrical horseback entrance at Braddock's Field or the counterrevolutionary pomp attending the president rendezvousing with the troops at Carlisle carried messages as sensational in their effect as symbolic idioms such as liberty poles. Rituals imagined the rebellion as armed violence could not, and they carried a palpable sense of meaning that petitions could not deliver. They were part of the unofficial, nonprofessional discourse in public spaces, expressions of politics-out-of-doors that told a complementary, if politically contentless, story. On the rebel side, they enacted popular grievances in a physically present form, of the moment and as a mirror that captured popular sentiments unavoidably and without mediation.

Agitation of the sort that characterized the Whiskey Rebellion was, in sum, legal culture in its most politically transparent, popularly accessible manifestation. That it did not reason with its audience was its strength because it touched their emotions. That the people participated in rituals and spectacle and were the intended audience of broadsides, handbills, and print satire made them part of the picture. Whether they were sympathizers or not, they were part of something larger and more exciting than themselves. Ordinary people experienced the message of rebellion and the response to that message in ways that spoke through them, that were infused with their emotions. The immediacy of such expressions reflected the force of cultural history as a worthy competitor for political professionals.

As we pursue the storyline that runs through this study, it becomes more and more apparent that the authentically untidy realm of popular expression within legal culture provided a proper counterpoint to the discourse of the official world of courtrooms that we shall visit in the next three chapters. Typically protean, it might at one time have appeared frivolous and at another coercive; but its most common feature was its expressive potential as an aspect of rebel self-presentation. The pluralistic, localized nature of rebel democracy, however, complicated its position relative to the government's broader, homogeneous message when it became a question of treason charges, indictments, and trials. The legal process that will dominate the remainder of this study appeared to be the perfect venue for the government's argument. Certainly, the circuit court featured a Federalist predisposition in its grand jury proceedings. But that unopposed presentation of the prosecution's case did not account for the passion of defense counsel or the independence of a trial jury. It could not anticipate the complications introduced by a poorly prepared prosecution team's reliance on English common law and constructivist reading of constitutional law.

Importantly, as the next part of this study will indicate, there is more to the story of the trials than the broad brush of existing studies has suggested. Part two draws a picture of grand jury charges, circuit court trial arguments, jury statements and pardon petitions, and a rebel defense that indicates the government narrative was not as dominant as has been supposed. It will become clear that the rebels demonstrated narratively they were more than a disorganized, hapless, unprincipled, treasonous mob. We have already seen that the rebel position constituted a complex political statement about rights-based democracy that has gone unrecognized; and we have seen that the government had exposure as counterrevolutionary, elitist Federalism focused on the security of the state and unresponsive to individual rights. The storyline of the next three chapters will demonstrate how this clash of perspectives played out in the rebel trials.

Part II

CHAPTER 4

Judges and Grand Jury Charges

In the second part of this study, chapters 4, 5, and 6, we turn from official and unofficial legal culture in the struggle between the people and the government to the legal scene of grand jury indictments and treason trials. These chapters take the clash between government and rebel narratives from political and cultural venues to a federal law court whose Federalist judges wrote their own script on nationhood, citizenship, and treason to condition what the jury would hear in the trials. In an immediate sense, the trials represented the contest of a government and its citizens over the stability necessary to state power as against the liberty rights of the people. In a larger sense, the trials completed a longer story: a government intent on establishing its legitimacy and the country's viability as a democratic experiment; a people determined to resist hegemony and assert the right of self-governance; and a court system struggling to turn English law into American jurisprudence.

While the Whiskey Rebellion has been treated as the first act of treason against the new United States, few sources, either primary or secondary, have shed much substantive light on the first treason trials under the U.S. Constitution.[1] Comments such as Hugh Henry Brackenridge's comparison of the Philadelphia trials to the French Reign of Terror have left historians feeling that the trials were bogus or that they were no more than hanging parties.[2] There was another side to the story. Thrust into the limelight, federal judges who indicted and tried the cases or who charged grand juries before and after the trials framed the rebellion for a national audience through their addresses to citizen-jurors, law reports, and bench notes. It became difficult, as a result, to consider the Whiskey Rebellion from outside the Federalist perspective. The government had turned a relatively simple protest against a discriminatory tax and other consequential western grievances into an assault on the Constitution, the laws, and the nation.

This chapter departs from a common view of Whiskey Rebellion judges that holds they were merely partisan Federalists, challenging it by examining their judicial principles, theory of government, and views on the welfare of the Union. Federal judges, this study argues, were engaged in resolving questions of governance and law as the legal world was undergoing a transition that reflected the contest of political thought over the new Constitution. From the American Revolution till the end of the century, a Federalist judiciary engaged to balance law, politics, and government while it expressed judicial concerns about the insurrection and tried to deal not only with threats to public order but also questions of popular sovereignty, federal-state relations, and preservation of the Union. U.S. Supreme Court justice William Paterson, like the two other judges most intimately involved in trying the rebels (state President Judge Alexander Addison of the Western Courts of Pennsylvania and federal district judge for eastern Pennsylvania, Richard Peters), would pay a heavy price in the judgment of his peers for the role he played in defending national government, a role which resulted in his being much maligned and distrusted. Faced with public fears of disorder that had the potential to turn the law into a joke or make it deeply hated, these jurists found themselves shackled with a thankless task. They shared certain ideological predispositions as Federalist judges but not a mere propensity to just do the government's bidding or toe a purely partisan line. Rather, they operated as a political conscience within a judicial narrative. That narrative, it is true, expressed a perspective on the law that was heavily invested in validating a conservative discursive community predisposed to believe its arguments bore an authority beyond which no reasoning was thought to be necessary. And it interpreted an understood text beneath the language of the law that expounded a preferred theory of the political relationship of the people and their government. Their role, as they saw it, was to uncover such understandings in the Constitution so to ensure the survival of that community.

The treason trials would be the first true test of the government's concern for stability and security and for preserving a tenuous Union underpinned by a constitution under challenge. The federal courts had to prove themselves as a new institution in a new form of government, but they had to do so in the presence of a residual set of laws—that of the English customary constitution. Where English laws and decisions operated under a vague set of variously understood precedents and principles, Americans saw themselves as a sovereign people who had given their consent to a written document. In this complex, changing world, simple partisanship on the part of Federalist judges might help explain the politics of the judges, but it does not address the ambiguity under which grand juries and the trials operated. Changes in the American legal system ran from the establishment of federal courts and shifting roles for counsel, judges, and juries to more rigorous rules of evidence and standards of proof. They invoked the questionable viability of English common law and statutes and adapted precedents to a new constitutional framework.[3] The broad nature of those changes makes study of the Whiskey Rebellion trials an exercise in exploring a powerful episode in transitioning legal processes, structure, and thought. The problematic precedent of the American Revolution, the challenge of a new form of government, and the threat that democratic populism posed in the struggle to balance liberty and power, all argue for a more nuanced understanding of a developing judicial narrative of law and government, including, importantly, the role of judges in forming that narrative.

The story of the Whiskey Rebellion has yet to take account of the judge's work in guiding grand jurors to indictments and trial juries to verdicts. Grand jury charges have been little studied for the insights they offer on governance and legal authority, issues which go unaddressed in the selective, truncated law reports of the trials. This chapter studies sixteen charges by seven judges over an eight-year period from 1792 to 1800, from the initial events of the insurrection through six years after it.[4] They address the Whiskey Rebellion leading up to, including, and in the aftermath of the trials and reflect how the rebellion affected judicial thought and the political culture of the early republic. We shall find that, like other federal judges, Paterson took the opportunity of his grand jury charges to serve the new government and its courts by educating grand jurors on citizenship and their role in this new structure. It is grand jury charges that reveal the judicial framing of the rebellion and that explain how treason law was applied in the trials. More broadly, the light shed by grand jury charges exposes the dilemma judges faced in clarifying clashing political narratives of the insurrection.

The Grand Jury

Before we get to the grand jury charges, however, the questions of shared legal knowledge and the function of the grand jury need to be addressed. How early American legal opinions were shared within the profession tells us a lot about the development of and access to the legal precedents that judges relied on to frame their opinions. Leading up to the Whiskey Rebellion, judges were dependent on oral opinions from the bench, which meant they knew little of American court precedents.[5] During the Revolution, various media—pamphlets, broadsides, and newspapers—printed legal debates and trials in the vernacular, informing a public that in important cases tried to influence trials. In the 1790s, the advent of irregularly published law reports returned the law to a professional elite and cut back on public access. Brackenridge reported on the state of the process from the time of his appointment to the Pennsylvania Supreme Court in 1799, noting that he often neglected to deliver his opinion to the reporter. In one case, his reasons for concurring were thus omitted from the report. In other cases, he delivered his opinions verbally and "it was left to the Chief Justice to deliver the opinion of the court."[6] While some written opinions were destroyed, others were "given to some of the bar, or [had been] lost." As a result, he concluded, even opinions drawn up with some care were never shared even among his colleagues on the bench.

Despite the unreliability of and lack of access to judicial texts, judges in the early republic had to balance the pressures of legislatures, public opinion, and political factions. They did so by defending republican virtue and asserting the judicial authority upon which the court depended.[7] It did not hurt that they controlled interpretation of common law in their courts and aggregated to themselves the power of judicial review. James Kent, an early law reporter and author of an influential treatise on American law, wrote that lawyers, many among them the founding Federalist elite of the Revolution, took over the role of "sentinels over the constitutions and liberties."[8] In that capacity, they served as gatekeepers of the common law to determine what parts of it applied.[9] Republicans, by contrast, preferred fixed statutory law and objected that common law changed "simple justice into a professional mystery."[10] In line with the deference Federalists assumed, judges charging grand juries took on the aspect of teachers disciplining unruly students, especially in political trials like those of the whiskey rebels. Whereas grand jurors were often at variance with the presiding judge's preference, judges provided the prevailing vision of the law. By the time of the 1795 trials, it was clear that Federalist judges represented a professional class placing limits on citizens' influence over government. Their jury charges were routinely published in newspapers, rather than in law reports, with or without jury statements attached, allowing them to communicate their views of legal issues directly to the people.[11] In this discursive community, the judge had no need to convince on particular facts and acted as a bastion of Federalism to reflect on the public good.[12]

Instructed by judges, grand juries were not, however, as easily impressed as judges wished. They represented a force for citizen participation in government through "a jury of neighbors"[13] asserting a community's values, beliefs, and traditions. William Blackstone's view of the English grand jury, upon which the American version was based, described the grand jury as a "barrier [...] between the liberties of the people, and the prerogatives of the crown."[14] Relatively independent in the colonial period, the likely result of limited local government, grand juries had a history of opposing authority to the extent that judges during the Revolution appealed to juries to gain their support for the war effort.[15] Grand juries had the power to impede the government's ability to enforce the law by refusing to indict, even discouraging authorities from seeking indictments in matters such as taxation that met with local disfavor. While its power of indictment could check legislatures by disregarding existing law, the grand jury could also shield against political prosecutions and officials who neglected their duty or who pursued "promiscuous prosecution" in periods of disorder.[16] Its role in this regard was to maintain the stability of local government by investigating corruption to ensure public order and to address complaints of official abuse brought by private citizens.[17] In practice, its powers extended from fact-finding and law-finding to mitigating sentences, effectively determining the crime for which a defendant could be tried.[18]

During the first decade of U.S. courts (1790–1801), circuit court judges used their grand jury charges to promote support for federal government locally. Even those who were overtly political established more federal legal principles and created more legal consistency than the Supreme Court, which delivered thirty-eight opinions to their ten thousand. Circuit courts thus had the effect of enhancing judicial nationalism, which included interpreting the meaning of the Constitution and creating uniformity by subjecting state laws and state court decisions to judicial review. Since supreme court justices sat with district judges on circuit courts and developed familiarity with state law and local courts, circuit court opinions reflected a better fit for the locales in which they operated. Circuit opinions depended, however, more on English law (partially explained by the absence of U.S. statutes and federal court case law) and followed other circuit court opinions more often than decisions by state high courts.[19]

In light of the growing pains experienced in establishing a national court system, jurists expected grand juries to act as a tool of government.[20] Even more to the point, because their career ambitions would profit from government support, judges were tempted to pack the jury with members of the elite upper class and to threaten those who refused to serve.[21] They had the power, moreover, to refuse to call a grand jury, to reprimand those that refused a directed charge, and to ask juries to reconsider their verdicts.[22] For their part, jurors profited from the presumption that, being "inscrutable," they could not be interrogated on their refusal to indict and could not be relied on to enforce unpopular laws or indict political defendants.[23] In times of unrest, when rioters might serve as jurors and make it impossible to deliver indictments, both judges and juries found it easier to fall in line with locals than with the needs of a government authority hundreds of miles away.[24] It was also more likely that a panel of neighbors asked to indict neighbors would deliver a bill ignoramus (refuse to indict) rather than a true bill (to indict), recognizing that the presumption of guilt that attached to an indictment would prejudice the petite, or trial, jury that followed.

The importance of the makeup of grand juries leads us to consider the extent to which they were stacked by class or wealth and whether their composition might not have differed from that of petite juries. During the Revolution, grand juries were, in fact, made up of men wealthier than most Philadelphians (within the upper twentieth through the tenth percentile of wealth); by 1789, the Judicial Act of Congress (section 29) democratized jury selection by relying on state law for jury composition.[25] The jury was to be chosen by lot from a pool made up of qualified jurors called up by a sheriff or marshal. No distinction was made between jurors for a grand jury and those for a petite jury, and there were no landholding or voter requirements for either kind of jury. As a result, a mixed grand jury was possible unless the marshal summoned only those of a certain class.[26] Fines for not appearing encouraged poor jurors to attend,[27] though the geographical composition of a jury was a matter of concern for cases where the crime did not occur in the same vicinage as the trial. The presence of jurors from nearby Philadelphia, Delaware, and Chester counties alongside western jurors for the Whiskey Rebellion trials in Philadelphia suggests that grand juries might have been similarly constituted.[28] The difference between the rate of grand jury indictments (73 percent) and trial convictions (20 percent) for the Whiskey Rebellion trials, and the fact that for death penalty cases the 1789 Act of Congress only required representation from the counties in which the crime occurred, suggests that jurors from the western counties might not have served on the Whiskey Rebellion grand jury.[29] Still, as the rebel Albert Gallatin (who observed and reported privately on the trials) offered, the grand jury displayed its impartiality in refusing to act as an arm of the prosecution and indict in all its cases. All the jurors, he claimed, were taken from Philadelphia and its neighborhoods and with one or two exceptions they all came from one party, "so that they cannot be accused of partiality."[30]

Beyond the composition of the grand jury and the procedural machinations of which judges were capable, the most potent instrument in influencing a jury was the judge's charge. Grand jury charges were intended to educate the jury on self-government and the Constitution as well as to advise jurors on the law, so that similar charges were commonly delivered in different court terms.[31] Typical charges, like those of William Paterson, might inform jurors about the branches of government and the types of offenses they would deal with, or they might cover the humanity of U.S. laws and their proportionality. Federalist judges took the opportunity to exploit the theme of national government, including admonitions that popular sovereignty applied to the responsibilities of a government of laws, not men, and that when crimes were committed they were directed against the people themselves as the source and the guarantors of the written law.[32] Charges were also used to inform and provoke discussion, reflecting the usefulness of patriotic sentiments to generate public support. Charges thereby commented on issues as widely ranging as partisan factions, fellow justices and courts, citizenry and education, even the influence of the French Revolution on American politics.[33] Covering both moral and political messages, charges tended to be rhetorical and forswore impartiality.[34] Especially in cases of sedition and treason, Federalist judges were prone to haranguing juries from the bench with their party views, political biases, and the government's position, recognizing that their words carried weight with jurors and that the combination of political charges and packed juries made insufficient evidence less of a problem and indictments easier to manipulate. Even an ignoramus bill had its effect as the mere fact of calling a grand jury had the power to silence public opposition.[35]

Alexander Addison and Richard Peters: Grand Jury Charges

Our examination of grand juries focuses on their most significant aspect for the purposes of this study, that is, the judge's charge to the jury. The grand jury charges that had the greatest effect on creating a judicial narrative for the Whiskey Rebellion trials were those of William Paterson, the U.S. Supreme Court judge who sat alongside a U.S. district judge, Richard Peters, on the circuit court trying the whiskey rebels.[36] Before we consider Paterson's grand jury charges, however, we need to look at those of state judge Alexander Addison and those of Richard Peters, which provide a crucial context. Addison had charged a grand jury in September 1792, the early days of whiskey tax resistance, so that the development of his views from "democrat" to Federalist can be traced over time.[37] In September and December 1794, the year of full-blown insurrection, Addison delivered two charges in state courts,[38] one just before and the other just after the federal militia's October incursion into western Pennsylvania, just as important trials were being moved to the federal circuit court in Philadelphia. Peters's charges occurred in federal courts in August and September before he and U.S. district attorney for Pennsylvania William Rawle accompanied the federal militia to round up the rebels in the West. For the trials in Philadelphia, Peters sat with Paterson while Rawle prosecuted the rebels along with U.S. attorney general William Bradford.

Addison's 1792 grand jury charge called upon the duty of the grand jury to preserve the peace, a continuing theme across all three charges. In the wake of an August 24 attack on excise inspector William Faulkner[39] in Washington County, he evoked the passion, state of nature, and private interest (natural liberty) expressed by the rebels to create a portrait that contrasted riot and sedition, on the one hand, to an exercise of social, legal, and public good (civil liberty), on the other. Minimizing the threat to public order, Addison spoke of the excise tax as an inconvenience that no legal means could remedy and which had led to a false sense of liberty that inspired the use of force. He characterized the protests as riots that dangerously combined private citizens "under specious pretences of justice."[40] The principles Addison laid out were simple and direct. The grand jury need not consider rebel intentions (since blackening their faces and carrying arms had "proved their design unlawful") or whether the force used was necessary (since "every use of force implies, that the cause is bad"). Nor need it consider whether an act had a good purpose ("the thing itself is criminal, whatever be the object") or whether an individual in a group was guilty (in the law, "its authors, their advisers, and abettors [...] are all guilty").[41] His approach not only obfuscated several critical legal issues, but it also simplified the process of interpreting the facts for the jury, smoothing his judicial narrative. That the defendants were indicted for riot is worth noting, as the offenses were the same as those the federal court would later indict as treason.[42]

By September 1, 1794, in a grand jury charge in Pittsburgh, Addison had reached a watershed moment. In the face of several fitful years of unrest, he was faced with accusations that state courts under his authority were incompetent. The arrival of the U.S. Commission forced him to concede that the western counties now confronted a national crisis so awful that they risked any forgiveness by the national power.[43] Resistance to the excise law had become conflated with resistance to all laws, a crucial construction that had already led the Washington administration to procure authorization to activate the militia act from Supreme Court justice James Wilson (who would later serve as a judge for procedural motions in the Philadelphia trials).[44] "[I]f one law is repealed at the call of armed men," Addison now held, "government is destroyed: no law will have any force."[45] The nation must either exert the "whole force" of its authority or it "must cease to exist"; either the rebellion would defeat the United States (a possibility he explored at length) "or the United States will subdue us," he ominously declared. Addressing the jurors as "guardians of the public peace,"[46] Addison called on fellow westerners to consider whether they could survive as an independent people if the government "cast us off," an argument that resonated with western Pennsylvania jurors as it reflected rebel demands. How, he asked, would the Indians on the western frontier be repelled? How would the frontier withstand the British and the Spanish? How would the Mississippi River be opened to commerce?[47] His queries, interestingly, synced with the assembly speeches of Gallatin and Brackenridge, with which he would have been familiar.

By the time of Addison's next grand jury charge, in December, the federal militia had arrived in the West. Here he delivered his most powerful indictment of the insurrection. With the federal government taking over prosecution of the most important cases and stung by federal accusations against the western courts, his charge concluded that the people's alarming use of force demonstrated the "inefficiency of a free representative democracy" in America.[48] Addison was most exercised over an "atrocious class of offenders," those who prevented others from submitting to the president's conditions for pardon and peace. He held equally culpable those who abused property and persons and those who exercised symbolic speech with their liberty pole "standards of rebellion" as they terrorized "all the well-disposed and peaceable part of the community."[49] Individual neighborhoods, he complained, mistakenly used the word "people" and spoke in their name, each assuming a right to do as it pleased; allowing any individual to prevail in a group, any combination in a state, or any state in the Union permitted a part to dictate to the whole. By implication, Addison concluded, the rebels exhibited the very dangers of republican government that Federalists most feared, disunion and minority rule.

In retrospect, the central constitutional problem for Addison was the rebels' recourse to force,[50] which entailed their failure to respect the Constitution and the law. Presenting itself more like a legal brief than a charge to a grand jury, the December charge asked and answered whether "forcible resistance to law [was] never justifiable?" "Never," according to Addison, so long as "the law be consistent with the constitution."[51] Not only was the Constitution "entitled to obedience," but if the law was "repugnant" to it, the Constitution itself would silence the law and make it void. With the present storm over, Addison's valediction announced that the recent troubles exhibited "an awful lesson" of anarchy, lawless bodies, and riotous assembly "under the semblance of zeal for the public good."[52] He went so far as to hold even words criminal, for "[i]mpunity begets offences, as corruption begets maggots."[53] As for the jurors, he reminded them that they were bound by their oath and would answer to God, indicating they had no discretion in their verdict. By the time he delivered the December charge, Addison had adopted the position that the rebellion was to blame for exposing the weakness inherent in representative democracy; obedience to law was his watchword and anarchy his nemesis. Addison had identified the central themes that defined the federal judiciary's concerns about the Whiskey Rebellion and had shifted his own position from one that enabled local institutions and popular resistance to one that stood with national government. He had completed the process of converting to a Federalist.[54] A letter published in 1795 in the *Aurora* by "[a] Militia Man"[55] addressed Addison's change of heart. Whereas the first seeds of sedition saw him "hidden in obscurity whilst it was in his powers to bring the offenders to justice," the author avowed, once the government had taken them to trial the judge turned on them to protect himself. The author attacked Addison's publication of a September 1794 grand jury charge as well, holding that it inflamed the public and demeaned "the characters of individuals in the eyes of their fellow citizens."

By this point, Addison's position vis-à-vis democratic populism had become inextricably complicated. The federal government distrusted him, and he was much maligned by Alexander Hamilton, as we see in chapter 1, who considered the president judge guilty of misrepresentation. Having seeded the doubt that Addison lacked independence and catered to the people, Hamilton claimed that Addison had by his own admission deviously undermined adherence to the law in a way that was nothing short of violence against the government.[56] As a state judge supporting federal authority, Addison was caught at cross-purposes. His grand jury charges in Alleghany and Westmoreland Counties went unendorsed for publication by jurors "who were under such apprehensions from the country" that they thought it unsafe to approve of his sentiments in the charges. On the other hand, just two weeks later both Washington and Fayette Counties embraced a charge with "explicit approbation," while the Fayette County charge was said to have "brought forth a favourable account of the impressions of the people."[57] In the August 1794 assembly at Parkinson's Ferry, as well as a meeting in Berlin, Somerset County, one of his grand jury charges was, notably, read in conjunction with a fiery pamphlet of a charismatic utopian preacher, Herman Husband.[58] Of some interest, according to Justice Paterson's notes from Husband's trial, "The people thought more of Husband's piece than of Addison's charge," likely the result of Addison's change in attitude about the rebellion.[59]

Federal district judge Peters anticipated Addison's increasing concern for constitutional democracy in his August grand jury charge. Peters had been speaker of both the Pennsylvania House and Senate, so he thoroughly understood the political nature of government. As a U.S. district court judge with jurisdiction over admiralty matters but without guidance on what law should be applied, Peters had considerable leeway as a judge. He took the position that an independent America could make its own law as a sovereign power and did so from a broad sweep of sources, commercial considerations in the law, and some creativity in expressing new principles. While he expanded the law, he was unwilling to confront popular sentiments, a political instinct that would affect his judicial conduct following the rebellion.[60]

In his August charge, Peters effused on the unequivocal responsibilities citizens have to the government, the laws, and the Constitution. While "[t]reason [was] a crime of too high a nature and of too deep a dye" to fall within the district court's jurisdiction, Peters held that the district jury was mandated to address breaches of the law that had led to the "unjustifiable, disgraceful and much to be lamented disturbances."[61] Framing a shift away from the American Revolution, Peters recruited the grand jury to embrace an interest that rose above the right to resist oppressive laws (the revolutionary republican legacy) and to restore the jury's duty to defend the people's government. Local interests were to be laid at the feet of the nation, which would fully compensate that sacrifice by its defense of the whole of the Union. Peters's theme reflected that of an earlier charge by Pennsylvania Supreme Court chief justice Thomas McKean, who wondered at a people "just rescued" from the bondage of a foreign power which had raised up a government "framed by themselves" only to "trample on laws of their own making." Having escaped "a despotic government," McKean added, yet they would "not submit to one free and equal."[62]

In his September charge, Peters weighed power more heavily than liberty as he affirmed the role of his court as an agent of public police, prosecutorial rather than merely judicial: "this branch of Jurisprudence," he offered, stood "between the heavy hand of government, and the liberty and rights of the people"; it ought to bring "the offending citizen to make atonement for his transgression."[63] Encouraging the grand jury to join him in defending American exceptionalism and the public will, he called on God, nature, "our common country, and [...] the majesty of the law" to ensure the blessings heaven had bestowed on this free government. He condemned treason against the government and, adverting to the angel who fell out of God's grace, rebellion against the heavens.

Following this charge, Peters was assigned to head the judicial unit accompanying the federal militia. In that role, he rounded up prisoners, investigated crimes, and laid charges against the rebels under the unrestricted powers he had been granted by the president in his orders to General Lee.[64] Accused by such moderates as William Findley and Hugh Henry Brackenridge of prejudice and favoritism in allowing biased testimony and corrupted evidence, Judge Peters's management of his task in the West would undermine subsequent prosecutions. Peters had already demonstrated an ambition to insinuate the district court into issues that touched on the rebellion, whether the court had jurisdiction or not. As a trial court for minor civil and criminal matters,[65] the district court had no authority over appeals from state courts or jurisdiction over larger federal questions. Once he took his place on the bench beside Justice Paterson in the circuit court trials, however, Peters found himself perfectly placed to apply his views on the insurrection. Albert Gallatin reported to his wife in a letter from Philadelphia that Peters, whose temperament Gallatin found prosecutorial, was not impartial on the circuit court bench and was unimproved by his colleague Justice Paterson's excellent example as a sound lawyer and judge.[66] Peters's preoccupation with threats to public order had left him open to criticism for apparent unfairness and for a jurisprudence that has since been described as "arbitrary and tyrannical,"[67] accusations supported by the fact that he never considered recusing himself from his circuit court position despite his activities in the West.

Peters's attitude on the bench was apparent in two of his trial jury charges. In *United States v. Insurgents*, where his charge went unsupported by fellow jurist Paterson, Peters famously weighed "all the inconveniences to the defendant" as nothing compared to "the delays and obstructions" faced by the government.[68] His penchant for exercising personal discretion on the bench, which he would later express in *United States v. Mitchell*, became an issue again in the 1799 Fries's Rebellion trial, where he also presided.[69] In *Fries*, Peters brazenly declared that while he had rejected constructions of treason that ran afoul of "justice, reason and law," he was of the opinion that "[i]t is not fair and sound reasoning to argue against the necessary and indispensable *use* of constructions, from the *abuses* it has produced."[70] His reading of what was both necessary and indispensable expressed a means-to-an-end rationalization that authorized juries not to be "so much alarmed about *abuses*" and not to refrain from using interpretations that were "proper and necessary," placing him squarely in the ideological and political mode of partisan Federalist judges.[71]

Treason Law

Addison and Peters give us a good idea of how grand jury charges functioned as political theory. But the charges needed to act as primers on treason law, as in Paterson's charges, if they were to result in indictments. "Treason" was a familiar term in both common law and American colonial statutes, which relied on aspects of English law important to Americans.[72] In fact, agreed-upon areas regarding English common law represented the general lines along which colonial law understood treason. Common law largely derived from judges' decisions but also incorporated statutes to constitute an unwritten constitution. It generally allowed prosecution wide scope to expand types of treason and considered treasonous intent sufficient to prove levying war against the government.[73] Under common law before the Constitution, constructive treason (whereby judges created new kinds of treason) became established. The doctrine on levying war was thereby expanded, government power broadened, and individual rights narrowed.[74]

In colonial America, preserving government superseded protecting individual rights, but with proofs and procedures designed to protect the accused against official oppression and to retain rights of political activity that were balanced against the security of the state.[75] The common law of treason, however, was general and "very uncertain," according to common law commentators, and it could not be easily proved or defended against;[76] the difficulty in clarifying such imprecise concepts as conspiracy, subverting government, and accroaching power led to abuses of judicial discretion. Matthew Hale, among others, considered the assembly of a large force without arms a doubtful "constructive levying of war"; treason required a posture of war, intent, and overt acts to rise to the level of levying war.[77] Riot with intent was not treason until the rioters who had assembled "had actually begun the execution of that intent"; without an overt act, a riot only touched levying war in relation to its manner.[78] As generally understood, words alone might constitute a treasonous act but they could not signify intent as they might be misconstrued.[79] They ought not, therefore, to be prosecuted under common law without an overt act to demonstrate that intent had passed from thought to action.[80] Critically, under common law, treason distinguished between general acts of a public nature, as in preventing the general execution or repeal of a particular law (which were treason),[81] and private, particular acts, as in preventing the collection of particular levies or acting against a particular person (which were not). William Blackstone warned that treason required a "general defiance of public government" and a "universality of design" to determine "a rebellion against the state, an usurpation of the powers of government."[82]

During the America Revolution, the colonial common law of treason was replaced by a bill of attainder, which allowed for capital punishment by legislative act rather than by trial. Such bills responded to the immediate danger to the nascent state and the unavailability of courts to execute swift justice.[83] Whereas the 1696 Treason Act had required numerous protections against abuse of government power (two witnesses to an overt act, defense counsel, compulsory process for defense witnesses, pretrial disclosure, and defense witness oaths), revolutionary authorities discarded them.[84] Executive, military, and county committees, associations, and assemblies adopted the British practice of bills of attainder,[85] which precluded rules of evidence and due process and denied the right of the accused to answer charges. Resolutions to suspend due process legitimized the right to demand loyalty from colonials, so that those who benefited from the laws of the colonies owed an allegiance that made counterrevolution a treasonous act. Bills of attainder were, consequently, considered a necessary, emergency means of asserting authority.[86]

When proper court trials were reintroduced in 1778, legal process continued to be restricted thereby broadening the range of conduct that constituted an overt act. This led to the only convictions for treason (Abraham Carlisle and John Roberts) in the American Revolution, on a charge of aiding the enemy under a 1777 Pennsylvania state law that dealt with the allegiance of loyalists who resisted joining the American cause.[87] Treasonable offenses identified under that law (among them levying war, aiding the enemy, communicating and conspiring with the enemy, and sending arms or intelligence to the enemy) reflect the political nature of many of the cases tried in 1778.[88] The results of the law cut two ways: the law was restricted in its application and the trials broadened the kind of conduct that constituted an overt act of treason.[89] In the law report for the Carlisle trial, for example, the court found it sufficient to indict the defendant for sending "intelligence to the enemy, without setting forth the particular letter, or its contents."[90] As to the charge of levying war, the court found "assembling, joining and arraying himself with the forces of the enemy" sufficient for an overt act of levying war, though that conduct did not bear on the case.[91]

When the U.S. Constitution became the prevailing law on treason in 1788,[92] it still relied on common law to specify the definition of treason. Whereas the Constitution limited treason, its definition was vague, which left it open to abuse by judicial construction. Judges still had to determine which of the prolific options available in common law cases were compatible with the Constitution. Much of the expansiveness of English common law, as it happened, hung on acts against the king that produced doctrines intended by the framers to be barred from American law.[93] It was not clear, as a result, what aspect of government had to be breached, and to what extent, to constitute treason. Defying execution of the law could describe any of a number of acts, from usurping the legislature's general authority to make law to merely opposing a single law, violating established procedures, or resisting officials.

Complicating the search for certainty, the Constitution failed to specify those who owed allegiance and the entity to which allegiance was due, critical functions of any definition of treason. Without a king, sovereignty had to reside within some version of the state or the people. The Constitution's preamble—the people forming "a more perfect Union"—made the people members of a nation. The natural predicate of "a nation" was not divine right, royal power, a president, or a particular government, but the union of the people in a republic. Treason in this sense would be against a people, a nation. In his law lectures, James Wilson, the architect of the Constitution's language on treason, made the reciprocal case that those protected by the nation owed it obedience as a duty and that "[o]f obedience the antipode is treason."[94] The ambiguity that arose from the effort to clarify allegiance would plague government through the Revolution to the Whiskey Rebellion both in terms of secessionist movements and preserving the Union.[95]

The same lack of clarity applied to what constituted treason. Treason was restricted in the Constitution to "levying war against [the United States] or in adhering to their enemies" (Article 3, Section 3), phrases adopted from 25 Edward III, the English statute from which the Constitution borrowed its definition of treason.[96] In Wilson's law lectures, that statute replaced creative common law judgments on treason as "the governing rule."[97] Wilson held that acts were not treason unless they were constitutionally qualified, so that "there can be no treason" except that which the Constitution defined.[98] Thus, where the legislature was only given power over the punishment of treason, Article 3's intent, according to Wilson, was to safeguard from "legislative tyranny" and "the arbitrary constructions of courts."[99] The Constitution thereby prevented expansion of the definition to "other cases of like treason [that] may happen in time to come."[100] As Madison framed the question, the constitutional convention had opposed "a constitutional definition of the crime" as a barrier" to that "peculiar danger."[101] Nonetheless, St. George Tucker's commentary on Blackstone echoed Wilson's fears in finding that constructive treason permeated American treason cases; referencing the Federalist Papers, he added that "new fangled and artificial treason drove the violence of factions against each other."[102]

Despite its lack of clarity, the Constitution had broken from English influence to narrow government authority, enhance individual rights, and diverge from English common law.[103] Riot became more distinguishable from treason, words alone could not constitute a levying of war, and compassing the king's death was eliminated to curtail the wide scope of prosecution it allowed. Importantly, the Constitution improved on English law by requiring two witnesses to the same overt act or a confession in open court, making it more restrictive than in 25 Edw. III.[104] Constraining the legislature to "the power to declare the punishment of treason"[105] ensured treason "shall consist only" in levying war and aiding the enemy and could not be redefined. Distinguished from English tradition, the Constitution did not intend to apply to political opponents or domestic disturbance;[106] rather, it was intended to protect against government interference. The Constitution might not have specified the definition of treason, but it clearly circumscribed it.[107]

William Paterson:
Grand Jury Charges

Having considered the grand jury charges of other judges who tried Whiskey Rebellion cases, and with a general understanding of contemporaneous treason law, we can consider Paterson's grand jury charges and anticipate his judicial approach to the trials treated in the next chapter. Paterson had served as attorney general of New Jersey during the years of the American Revolution and became governor in 1791, at which time he gave up his postwar legal practice.[108] He was well received for the role he played in the constitutional convention of 1787 in which he defended equal representation of small states and affirmed state interests in western lands over private ones, thereby easing the ratification process.[109] George Washington appointed Paterson to the U.S. Supreme Court in 1793, which reflected the president's regard for the court as a central support for the legal system that would cement national government. Washington was intent that this body seat only the fittest of men to illuminate the national character: nominees ought to have actively supported both the Revolution and the Constitution; men with judicial knowledge and legal experience were preferred, as were those who had served politically or in the military.[110] In nominating the New Jersey governor, Washington disregarded his own practice of geographically balancing the court, as he bypassed three possible southern nominees. The Senate approved Paterson unanimously,[111] a common procedure for the president's nominees at the time. Paterson was not firmly Federalist in his views, but he supported a strong national government and adherence to its laws. His failed proposal in the constitutional convention of a plan authorizing drastic measures against a popular rebellion made his position against destabilizing democratic movements clear. His appointment was, as a result, a function of both his political leanings and his legal views.[112]

Paterson was well respected on the U.S. Supreme and U.S. Circuit Courts and was known for his "basic moderation and open-mindedness."[113] Indeed, a Georgia grand jury statement in 1793 appreciated Paterson's "elegant, concise, and republican charge," even though jurors had complaints about some of the issues in the charge.[114] But as the Whiskey Rebellion trials approached, Paterson's political opinions began to encroach on his judicial impartiality, leading to Paterson's statement that the trials were "a disagreeable necessity"[115] and to controversy over his contribution to them. The trials were commonly held to be politically expedient and Paterson's heavy-handed instructions to the jury were credited with making "the verdicts inescapable."[116] Accused of having weighted the interests of the state over those of individuals in the trials, he was thought to have behaved in a volatile and excessive way.[117] A review of his jury charges and a relevant court opinion will provide an opportunity to address this mixed picture of Paterson's conduct on the bench.

Three grand jury charges by Paterson in the year of the Whiskey Rebellion trials (in April, May, and June 1795) offer a picture of his state of mind in the months immediately surrounding the critical April trials. These charges can be juxtaposed to his trial jury charges in *United States v. Mitchell* and *United States v. Vigol* (delivered in May) and supplemented by both his Supreme Court opinion in *Vanhorne's Lessees v. Dorrance* (delivered in April) and a report he sent to the president (in June). Grand jury and trial jury charges cannot, of course, be regarded in the same light. The two juries had different purposes (grand juries indicted and trial juries tried a case) and operated according to different legal standards (grand juries used a lower standard of probability and allowed only prosecution evidence; criminal trials used a higher standard of proof and allowed prosecution and defense arguments and evidence).[118] The two were, however, connected by an explanatory framework Paterson developed for the grand jury that justified politically the legal position he would later take in the petite trials.

Justice Paterson's views on the insurrection first appeared in the lead-up to the trials with a grand jury charge to the circuit court of New Jersey in April 1795. Taking on the paternal role of an educator in good citizenship, Paterson complimented New Jerseyites, who had supplied the largest number of militiamen to the federal army, for distinguishing themselves by "their love of social order, and submission to the laws" and for suppressing "that dangerous insurrection." He stressed a "preventative justice" that educated the uninformed to identify "hostile but colourable schemes and views" and that enabled republican virtue by means of the Constitution and laws as "articles of our political faith."[119] Poles apart in its appeal from Peters's American exceptionalism and public police, Paterson's April charge was still a manifesto. It wove together a tapestry of belief, nation, citizenship, the Constitution, republican character, and education to which one could subscribe as a member of a community in which a citizen thought, acted, and judged for himself, unswayed by rabble factions or political parties.

Just a month later, Paterson's May 4, 1795, charge was another matter entirely. He now addressed the grand jury called upon to indict the whiskey rebels. Gone were the high-minded appeals and the deeply felt beliefs; they were displaced by outrage and fear that entreated the jury to use the law as a weapon to castigate the rebellious and compel them to submit. In a nation of republican character, law was sovereign, not men. Paterson spoke of a "trying emergency" that endangered political existence, the peace, and "the majesty of the people themselves." And he contrasted those more dreaded "than hosts of external foes" to citizen–grand jurors, recalling destabilizing pressures from France and Britain. Waxing eloquent, he called upon "[y]e disorganizing spirits from henceforth [to] obey" and to reverence the supreme law while he condemned "discontented and turbulent public men" who spread rumors to alarm the public and stir up sedition. He reaffirmed this charge in other undated charges that reflected similarly harsh judgments and published it in the *Genius of Liberty & New-Jersey Advertiser* in October.[120] In one undated charge, he argued that obedience to the law was "mistaken for slavery by the thoughtless and ill-formed."[121] In another, Paterson invoked a higher authority, indicting the insurrection's rebellious miscreants for refusing to acknowledge that "[o]rder is Heaven's first law." That such defiance could only end in "political slavery and death" left the rebels, in Paterson's construction, outside the protection of heavenly as well as secular law.[122]

With his May charge, Paterson's vitriol resonated with that of Peters, exposing a heavy-handedness that would reappear in the trials. The charge was also the first inkling of the jurisprudential approach he would use in the trials. In this critical address, Paterson laid out the options for how he would apply Article 3, creating a framework that would inform his crucial analysis in *United States v. Mitchell* (addressed in chapter 5) and yield a rare conviction in the treason trials. Paterson's charge was compatible with the English common law commentaries of Michael Foster, Hale, and Blackstone that served as the basis of the prosecution's case in *Mitchell*. He identified two approaches to defining treason, both of which constructively expanded the constitutional definition to include acts that might have been misdemeanors or felonies, such as riot or misprision of treason (knowledge of treason and concealment), but did not qualify outright as levying war against the U.S. government. The first approach relied on a litany of English common law instances of acts that described assembling with leaders in a military manner and in numbers; it reflected as well Wilson's discussion of assembly in levying war in his law lectures, the only analysis of substance that survived from a member of the constitutional convention.[123] The second approach focused on resisting the administration of justice or the execution of laws, including rioting under the pretense of redressing public grievances, forcing the repeal of a law, and altering government measures. This definition leached into an arbitrary denomination of uncertain and ambiguous offenses that were not actual insurrection.[124] Embedded in the judge's charge, Paterson's alternative versions gave the grand jurors two options: choose one over the other or toggle between the two to capitalize on aspects of each and enhance the prospect of an indictment.

Confirmation of Paterson's idiographic approach appeared in a June 1795 report solicited by Secretary of State Edmund Randolph to inform President Washington's consideration of pardons for Mitchell and Vigol. Here, Paterson represented that he had "given a short narrative of the cases made out in the trials of Mitchell and Vigol."[125] He excused himself for dashing off the report without "more detail" in his haste to attend the Circuit Court of Delaware. Here again, Paterson merely recited without interpretation a litany of acts, leaving them to speak for themselves and omitting legal citations and analysis: the rebels "assembled in the appointed place"; they "found themselves in a line"; they "commenced their attack"; Mitchell "appeared with a gun, throwing out threats and spreading fear and alarm"; Vigol was "among the most zealous and enterprizing," the most "intemperate in language, and violent in behavior and action."

In the April term of the U.S. Supreme Court, Paterson provided an opinion in *Vanhorne's Lessee v. Dorrance*[126] that cast a new light on his thinking. Here Paterson drew a bright line between what was constitutional and what was not constitutional. As a representative of New Jersey in the constitutional convention of 1787, he was a supporter of a strong Constitution. In his judicial opinions, he held to a constitutional standard that he referred to as "ultimate adjudication," indicating he was a proponent of judicial review.[127] In *Vanhorne*, of course, Paterson delivered an appellate court opinion, rather than—as in the Whiskey Rebellion indictments and trials—a grand jury or trial jury charge. Nonetheless, the opinion addressed two areas of consequence to the trials. First, Paterson was clearly mindful that "no opinion of a single judge can be final and decisive."[128] He argued that a justice's charge in a trial had limitations and that there were often times when it became necessary for a jury to take a broader role, impinging on a judge's responsibility to decide the law. Here he expressed the view that when decisions were properly rendered, "it gives stability to judicial decisions, and security to civil rights,"[129] indicating sensitivity to the future weight an opinion carried in preserving the grounds of principle and the path of precedents.

The opinion in *Vanhorne* indicates that Paterson maintained in the Supreme Court's April term a respect for jury independence that could easily have informed the May circuit court trials. As a gauge of his reaction to the refusal of grand juries to indict and trial juries to convict in many of the Whiskey Rebellion cases, the opinion suggested a greater respect for self-direction by the jury and less insistence on directed verdicts than Dallas's law reports of the trials suggest. Even if Dallas, a Pennsylvania Republican and secretary of the commonwealth, had access to Paterson's unpublished bench notes (taken up in full in chapter 5), which is very likely, or combined them with his own observations, which is even more likely, Paterson's notes suggest that Dallas's emendations would have been substantial.[130] In fact, Dallas's *Mitchell* and *Vigol* reports created the impression that Paterson was determined to direct the jury to a guilty verdict and that he left the jury virtually no choice in the outcome, an account that was out of sync with accounts by trial watchers, who did not cite Paterson for intemperance, unfairness, or manipulation of the jury,[131] and with Paterson's less quotable language in the law reports, which generally indicated a jurist struggling to deal with common law on treason, Article 3 of the Constitution, and an unsettled body of residual state law on treason deriving from the Revolution.

The second area of consequence in *Vanhorne* touched on Paterson's understanding of how the Constitution should function. A written constitution, he was quite clear, must always precede in importance a legislated law: "The one [the Constitution] is the work of the Creator [the people], and the other [laws] of the Creature [the legislature]."[132] Law that was inconsistent with "principles of reason, justice, and moral rectitude," laws out of line with the letter and the spirit of the Constitution, were void: "[T]hus far ye shall go and no further. Not a particle of it should be shaken, not a pebble of it should be removed. Innovation is dangerous."[133] Paterson was, of course, testing legislative law against the Constitution in *Vanhorne*, while in the Whiskey Rebellion trials he was distinguishing Article 3, Section 3 of the Constitution from common law. Should he allow encroachments and precedents, as common law did, the Constitution would eventually be destroyed, he warned in *Vanhorne*. Paterson's dilemma implicated his use of judicial discretion in the trials and his construction of two critical aspects of the constitutional definition of treason: the two-witness rule and the phrase "levying war." Given his earlier representations on the loyalty due the Constitution, Paterson had exceeded its limits. One of several explanations seems likely: he believed his analysis in the trials was consistent with the Constitution; he did not think the Constitution spoke to the issue; or he so desired a given verdict that he allowed himself more discretion than his jurisprudence justified. His conduct of the trials themselves would provide a better read on which alternative was more likely.

In June, with the bulk of the Whiskey rebellion trials just completed,[134] and two days after his report to the president, Paterson addressed the grand jury of the Circuit Court of Delaware where he looked forward to the citizenry having learned certain lessons. He ended his series of grand jury charges as he had begun them by echoing the language of his April and May charges. In his appeal to the jury, he proclaimed, "May no factions nor disorganizing spirits arise within thy peaceful vales [. . .] may insurrection never more rear her crest; may neither foes at home nor foes abroad disturb this our rare and high felicity."[135] The June charge presented a judge who had survived the spring and early summer trials clear in his own conscience; he was not about to be moved. The safety and welfare of fifteen states diversely constituted and loosely linked, he represented, depended on "co-operation and confederacy" to ensure "the prosperity and happiness of the Union at large."[136] Paterson moderated the tone of threat that had infused his grand jury charge at the opening of the trials to celebrate the happy situation in which the United States now found itself as a land of peace and plenty. He hoped a policy of neutrality in foreign affairs would maintain the peace, but he was clear that the happiness of the nation depended on its having learned the lesson of rebellion. Returning matters to the grand jurors, he advised them it was their task to ensure that "such transgressions" against the nation "be proceeded against and punished." So far as the judge was concerned, he was content that "the justice of the nation [...] is committed to their care."[137]

Collateral and Aftermath Narratives

Among the grand jury charges related to the Whiskey Rebellion, a number were delivered by judges who had not tried the rebels at either the state or federal levels, suggesting Paterson was not alone among the judiciary in his concern for the state of the Union, his presumed devotion to the Constitution, and his conviction that the country needed an example. Fellow justices in other venues drew similar conclusions about the significance of the rebellion in their grand jury charges, suggesting not only solidarity among brothers of the robe but also a common judicial perspective—considerably Federalist in that they were administration appointees—that many criticized. As much as Paterson might have been criticized for his approach to the Whiskey Rebellion trials, however, he did not amplify the importance of punishing the rebels or resetting the order of the community with as much heat or as outsized a manner as some judges. Richard Peters was among these judges, but it was U.S. Supreme Court justice John Blair who proved the most acerbic. Compared with Peters and Blair, Paterson showed a restraint that not only signaled his sense of responsibility for conducting the trials, but which argued that he actually tamped down much of the heated rhetoric of the times. Blair, by contrast, engaged in an extended screed in his grand jury charge about the events that emanated from the western country, digressing from the admiralty issues before the Georgia Circuit Court where he presided at the cusp of the trials.[138]

In a charge embodying what would come to be the Federalist line in the Whiskey Rebellion trials, Blair warned of an "an overstrained conception of liberty" appropriated by combinations who assumed 'all the sacred rights of the people" in their name and under the "authority [of] their own pernicious systems."[139] His unique prose accused whoever opposed "with pertinacious petulance private to public opinion" or threatened "the eversion of our happy government."[140] Blair constructed a narrative of salutary lessons. However infinite the evil of the law, the evil of rebellion decidedly outweighed it. However untenable the principle of law, forcible resistance was a function of a state of nature, not of civil society, and repugnant "to the principle of every consociation."[141] Should force be directed against tyranny, it was justified, indeed entitled to legal protection, Blair contended, surely his answer to the continued need to address the problematic precedent of the American Revolution. But the present use of power, with a "cruelty and distraction inseparable from civil war," derogated the authority of a constitution that the people had themselves deliberately enacted. Adopting a popular sentiment, Blair argued that whatever the pretense, such presumption usurped the sovereignty of the people.[142]

The broad sweep of Blair's brush anticipated the sentiments of grand jury charges in the aftermath of the trials. U.S. Supreme Court justice James Iredell was a central figure in this regard. Slated to sit on the circuit court that tried the whiskey rebels only to be reassigned at the last moment, his charges served as a guide to the political lessons of the rebellion. Iredell aptly reflected the Federalist aftermath in three charges that addressed the rebellion, with the perspective of half a year, a year, and four years after the trials.[143] He cast treason as one of the three objects of criminal law. The other two forms of law (universal law and international law) were implicated by way of a strong dose of political precautions against both Francophiles and Anglophiles. An offense against the national character and the Union, Iredell held, treason was "the greatest accumulation of public and private misery any crime can possibly occasion."[144] Yet it was defined so loosely by the "great engine of Judicial tyranny" that subterfuges allowed for charges that the Constitution never intended.[145] Iredell was referring to the abuses of English courts and the French Revolution "that allowed suspicion to replace evidence" and led American sansculottes to punish publicly men of great virtue. The last of his three charges, in fact, took place under the politically inspired Alien and Sedition Acts targeted by the Federalists at Republican journalists.

The slim results of the recent Whiskey Rebellion prosecutions proved an ironic counterpoint to what Iredell depicted as American improvements over English and French practices. Still, a beneficent government had, according to Iredell, provided "every indulgence which humanity as well as justice could declare" and extended to those convicted "the scepter of Mercy," a rejoinder to the French Revolution's bloody treatment of victims of its justice.[146] Placing Americans at the center of an improved and more equitable process, Iredell broadcast to all governments and all people a lesson "displayed on the theatre of the world" that ought to have its effect on other countries and never "be obliterated from the memory of our own."[147]

Justice Iredell's final comments on the Whiskey Rebellion came on April 11, 1799, in a charge seeking indictments for Fries's Rebellion. He delivered it in the same venue, the Pennsylvania Circuit Court, that had tried the whiskey rebels four years earlier and alongside District Judge Peters, a relic of the Whiskey Rebellion trials. Peters dreaded the pernicious precedent set by the Whiskey Rebellion in a state "twice disgraced by infamous Insurrection," fearful that a wrong turn could end in a conflagration by spreading "to all the combustible Matter too generally dispersed in other Quarters."[148] The crux of Iredell's charge, by contrast, was the preservation of government, a theme that could not fail to resonate with members of a Pennsylvania jury still smarting from lingering recollections of the events of 1794. Restating threats expressed in grand jury charges from Addison to Blair, Iredell warned of chaos should the jury fail in its duty: "If you suffer this government to be destroyed, what chance have you for any other? [. . .] Anarchy will ride triumphant [. . .] and justice be trampled under foot." In an argument that resonated with Peters's August 1794 and Paterson's May 1795 grand jury charges, Iredell's sentiments threatening catastrophe warned the jury of no less than a jeremiad called down upon a nation that had risked its blessed state by rebelling against authority. His final plea was to a "God whose peculiar providence seems often to have interposed to save these United States from destruction"; his hope was to preserve their "care and protection by a conduct best calculated to obtain them."[149]

Renewed as it was by Fries's Rebellion, the specter of the Whiskey Rebellion had clearly not subsided in the imagination of the republic. The activities of the democratic-republican societies, protests against the Jay Treaty, and the press turmoil leading to the 1798 Alien and Sedition Acts had exacerbated the sense of threat against the Union. In this atmosphere, U.S. Supreme Court justice William Cushing's charge to the grand jury of the Circuit Court of Virginia on November 23, 1798, tied the Sedition Act directly to the Whiskey Rebellion and linked both to publications of the democratic societies that supported France and incited the overthrow of the Union.

Three and a half years out from the trials, he likened contemporary events to a latter-day construction of what he called the Pittsburgh insurrection. The earlier threat, he charged the jurors, arose "under the groundless pretext of opposing an arbitrary law about a small matter *of excise.*" Echoing what had become a common refrain, he declared the attack was really on the fundamental power of the Constitution to provide "for the support of government, for the common defence and for the general welfare."[150]

A Federalist's Federalist,[151] U.S. Supreme Court justice Samuel Chase, offered a final iteration of the message of the Whiskey Rebellion trials (now refreshed by the Fries's Rebellion) in a grand jury charge on April 12, 1800, once more in the Pennsylvania Circuit Court. In reflections he attributed to "the *former* and *late* insurrection in *this* Common Wealth of Pennsylvania," Chase took a position recalling that of Noah Webster: a burdensome, even oppressive law cannot be opposed by force if there is to be a government. Chase's "political truth" was embedded in a basic Federalist principle: the only security for the Union, for the impartial administration of justice, and for the protection of lives, liberty, and property was the law. The repeal of an act whose execution one section of the country finds objectionable can only, in a federal Union, dissolve the government; every other section, Chase declaimed, will exert similar resistance: "it will be the height of folly to expect afterwards to see any law executed."[152]

Jury Statements

With the full weight of the Federalist judiciary having weighed in, juries had their say. Jury statements were commonly attached to judges' charges if they recommended them for publication. In truth, Federalist judges directed their judicial narrative at an audience of jurors potentially responsive to a story of good governance and unity under conditions of instability both domestic and foreign. The narrative reflected the framework established for the public sphere by Alexander Hamilton and elaborated by President Washington for national and international consumption. But the judges themselves ran the gamut from ex-Republicans and states' rights jurists (Addison) to moderate (Paterson) and rabidly partisan Federalists (Blair), while their charges ranged from more extreme versions (warning of pernicious and chaotic spirits and threatening retribution) to more conservative renderings (celebrating the jury's care for justice and the nation's rescue from internal discord and external threat). Overall, nonetheless, a certain consistency of political theory emerged as well as a relationship between judges and juries that bespoke a sometimes-begrudging commonality among them and with the government narrative.

The judicial narrative that arose out of grand jury charges reflected an understood agreement that judges and juries had a duty to educate on citizenship and the law, to make decisions that preserved peace for the common good, and to balance individual rights against those of the state. Working out the demands of the people and guaranteeing the stability of the people's government in terms of the Constitution was treated as a patriotic labor whose principles were few and easily grasped. Thus, to preserve the Union, the whole and not the part must govern; civil war, secession, and the forceful overthrow of the government must be prevented and punished; and representative democracy must speak for the people through elected officials and institutions, not through self-organizing groups and assemblies. In sum, the enemies of republican government were disunion and minority rule; its guarantor was the Constitution.

A general theory of reciprocity infused the narrative. The Constitution, the laws, and the government had a duty of care for the people, as individuals and as a nation, and the people had a duty of loyalty and obedience, but also of vigilance in being aware of both abuse of power and rebellion. Representing a chosen nation and a chosen people, the narrative read, the government and citizens were mutually beholden to the majesties of the law and God as the price of the twin blessings of liberty and order. The supporting pillar for this overarching message was republican virtue grounded in citizenship and education, an expression of political faith that jurors were presumed to represent in serving as agents of their communities.

Jury statements recorded the reception accorded judges' charges. Largely intended as a means of recommending or withholding publication of the charges in the newspapers, the statements responded in several ways.[153] Those that survived express remarkably consistent support for the judicial system and routinely recommend the publication of grand jury charges to edify fellow citizens about the Constitution and laws, as well as to disseminate "moral and patriotic lessons."[154] Grand jurors charged by Pennsylvania Supreme Court chief justice Thomas McKean[155] in a 1792 rebellion case, for example, expressed an enthusiasm about and a characteristically deep pride in jury service. Jurors generally took the opportunity of their statements to express the depth of their concern in language that often seemed to have been lifted wholesale from a judge's charge. They found it useful as well to express embarrassment that assaults on the "public happiness" occurred in their jurisdiction and to communicate their district's innocence of rebellious motives. Jurors trusted that the rebellion would remain a solitary event and ensured "we have not failed to exercise our vigilance and zeal in making diligent enquiry of all such offenses."[156] They defended the reputation of their state and their loyalty to the republic; they voiced their disapproval of riot, anarchy, and subversion; and they took on an active role in calling on friends to oppose enemies of order and to encourage minorities to respond to the general will.[157] Jury statements thus reflected the extent to which a judge's charge convinced a jury, but they also represented an opportunity for jurors to express their own republican virtue by countering the spread of sedition and "ruinous attempts" against the government.[158]

Answering Judge Peters's circuit court charge at the height of the rebellion in August 1794, a Pennsylvania jury statement passed the charge on to the printer "deeply impressed with the truth and excellent doctrine contained in the charge," without commenting further on the passion the judge had exhibited in his charge or the sense of immediacy it communicated.[159] Grand jurors of the more distant Circuit Court of Georgia were more congratulatory.[160] Responding as the rebel trials were ongoing, they appreciated the excellence of Judge Blair's severe charge as well as "the restoration of peace and tranquility" that they attributed to fellow citizens generally. They construed the rebellion as a daring "attack on the liberties of a free people," accompanied with the jury's hope that a like attempt would not occur again; the jurors endorsed publication of the charge as a "moral and patriotic lesson." Similarly, a jury statement in the Circuit Court of New Jersey, made near the trial venue a year after the trials, derided western Pennsylvanians for failing to subordinate themselves to the Union.[161] With the resulting discord, anarchy, and consequent evils suppressed, the jury hoped this "outrage upon law, order and true republicanism" would prove instructive to history and that the rebellion would "remain a solitary instance in the annals of our country."

In 1796, a Pennsylvania Circuit Court jury registered a full-throated expression of grand jury sentiment,[162] suggesting that, over time, the narrative had crystalized into a declaration that the rebellion was a disgraceful warning "of the folly and danger of such unavailing and ruinous attempts," put down by "friends to order and good government." Here the jury congratulated itself and "the patriotic exertions of our fellow citizens" for supporting the laws, which had earned them mutually the gratitude of the nation. The goodness of the result gave proof, if proof was needed, of the president's benevolence and wisdom and alerted "a once deluded people" to its "true interests." Those interests, the statement intimated, included support for efforts to make treaties with foreign powers, "namely that with Great Britain." Clearly the story of the rebellion in the final chapter of the judicial narrative included a place for the nation on the international stage, a position denied it so long as internal dissension left the country vulnerable as a democratic experiment in government.

Four years after the trials, with the nation facing its third rebellion since the Revolution (Shays's Rebellion in Massachusetts in 1786, the Whiskey Rebellion in 1794, and now Fries's Rebellion in Pennsylvania in 1799) and its second since constitutional ratification, a final jury statement from the Circuit Court of Pennsylvania put its imprimatur on the judicial narrative, recommending the publication of a grand jury charge by Judge Iredell to counter the spread of "false philosophy and the most dangerous and wicked principles [. . .] under the imposing garb of liberty."[163] The influence of the French Revolution, according to the jurors, had been countered by the "highly beneficial" example set by the United States through its Constitution and laws as represented in Judge Iredell's charge. The meaning was clear to those "too easily led" by the French to threaten "the peace and dignity" of the United States. The message from these jurors—in the final iteration of a jury statement in the same venue where the western Pennsylvania rebels had been tried—was that the experiment in democracy and the state of the Union were sound, despite the existential threat to their survival. In some ways, the Federalist judicial narrative was a success; jurors were remarkably attuned to its message, if not indoctrinated, with the added benefit of enhancing the role of the federal court system.

Conclusion

The grand jury charges of the Federalist judges expressed a common judicial perspective, despite differences of intensity and rhetoric. The judicial narrative they generated diverged from the revolutionary republicanism of enabling local institutions to act in defense of a people's government. Rather, it positioned the citizen within a community in which republican virtue meant veneration of the law and obedience to an elected government, endorsing at the same time the need for education to ensure citizens acted independently of the rabble or political factions. Here the law stood above the people to ensure that a strong, centralized Union was sovereign. Above the law, a superordinate deity blessed the nation and the majesty of its laws as a statement of American exceptionalism. To ensure that blessing, citizens had to accept a form of restrained liberty and remain vigilant; to deserve the intervention of providence, their role was to protect government from being destroyed and justice from being struck down. In the grand jury, citizen-jurors adopted the familiar role of a posse comitatus,[164] answering the community's call to punish outrages against true republicanism and to warrant that rebellion was an aberration in the democratic experiment. Within that frame, the narrative demanded that rebellion be judged and punished, that it be made an example. The lesson was a judicial version of evil brought low and public happiness restored, of wickedness masquerading as liberty exposed, lest the small matter of a whiskey tax undermine the fundamental power of a great nation. This patriotic labor would preserve the whole and defy minority tyranny. It would guard against disunion from within and threats from without to resolve the dissension that made democracy vulnerable; it would reclaim the nation's standing on the world stage as a beacon of liberty. The judicial narrative was in this sense a perfect wedding of politics, culture, and law operating in tandem and complementing the government narrative as a foundation for the legal theory and preferred jury message that would follow in the trials.

The example of the grand jury charges and the jury statements that responded to them infused new life into the effort to develop a constitutional identity separate from that of English common law. As part of a gradual judicial evolution, this movement toward the authority of the courts and the written federal Constitution was incremental across the 1790s. As the leading jurist in the grand jury proceedings that produced the indictments for the Whiskey Rebellion trials, Justice Paterson sent a message of social order, citizenship, and obedience to the law that still acknowledged popular democracy and volunteered its respect for "the majesty of the people themselves."[165] Paterson also sent a message of his sensitivity to changes in the law that would affect the Whiskey Rebellion trials in his contemporaneous *Vanhorne* decision. There he signaled his acceptance of the shifting roles of judges and juries and the importance of appellate review. He was clearly mindful in *Vanhorne* of the transition represented by changing legal rules and the criticality of the Constitution. The principles and precedents applied in this decision would inform Paterson's performance across the spring of 1795 in procedural and substantive matters that arose in the rebellion trials.

At the same time, Paterson never fully deserted the conservatism of his fellow Federalist judges, for all that he was willing to entertain a certain openness in his jurisprudence. Part of a community of meaning whose audience was jurists such as himself, Paterson spoke with conviction in reducing complexity to simplicity and ambiguity to certainty, basing his moral authority on an inherited common law that justified their preeminence. Paterson understood, for example, that the popular sovereignty embraced in the Continental Congress's consensus constitution was not dead and that popular forces had not yet committed to a written Constitution entrusted with the law the people had created. His solution was to protect the legacy of the Revolution by curbing democratic populism when he sensed it had turned against the contract the people had made. Supporting the Union and reverencing the Constitution and the law it founded would, he was convinced, honor the sacrifices made by that Revolution. His choice of solution conformed to a judicial narrative that pitted a good (government) against an evil (populism) in a discourse of authority speaking from a position of enlightened power. Here, judicial authority presumed to know best what the country needed and who was best positioned to deliver it, consistent with Paterson's moral rectitude in coloring his judicial thought with a political theory of government focused on the relationship of governance, law, and the common good.

In one last look at the Whiskey Rebellion grand jury charges, we find they were delivered at a special time in American history when rebellion was a dominating motif. Rebellion and the Constitution were interactive from Shays's Rebellion to the so-called whiskey insurrection. Where Shays's was a catalyst for the constitutional convention,[166] the Washington administration plainly conceived of the 1794 rebellion as both a test of the Constitution's viability and an experiment in governing under it. Just as the Constitution was a tool for democracy in working out democracy's possibilities and needs, grand jury charges by Federalist judges were a crucible for contested concepts and partisan factions that arose in the process of applying the Constitution in the early years. Grand jury charges were in some ways like the rebel assemblies in that they gauged the rights of citizens and their justifiable limits in relation to the responsibilities of government and its potential overreach. The charges weighed individual liberties at risk in the rebellion against the risk to government stability and the security of the nation. They denounced the passion of a part of the people, which, weighed against the good of the whole, risked minority tyranny. Where rebellion took the form of counterrevolution, charges attacked them for wasting the victory won against England and reducing the nation to anarchy. Most portentously, grand jury charges warned of a continuum in which local grievances and popular sovereignty devolved into mobocracy and threatened secession.

In many ways, Shays's was a kind of archetype setting the precondition for rebellion that informed the Whiskey Rebellion.[167] Anarchy led to more rebellion, which fed recurrent bouts of tyranny. Despotic democracy was not the only ominous prospect fostered by continual rebellion; monarchy, too, raised its head with conservatives looking to Washington as a model. One could argue that in both rebellions the federal government was fighting the same war. The government needed something like the Whiskey Rebellion for convincing proof of the need for a strong central government, much like its earlier counterpart. The implication was that the government provoked the rebellion or, in the alternative, that a rebellion required a belligerent government that refused to accommodate the people.[168] Undeniably, the government made much of the dangers emanating from organized resistance.[169] Washington, drawn out of a three-year retirement by Shays's Rebellion, wrote to Henry Lee anguished that it exhibited "a melancholy proof of what our transatlantic foes have predicted": left to themselves, men were unfit to have their own government.[170] "Precedents are dangerous things," he warned. Thus, the government must brace itself and reprehend "every violation of the constitution." Yet in a letter to James Madison he feared embracing too severe punishments that might "give birth to new, instead of destroying the old leven," anticipating the very playbook he would later actualize in the Whiskey Rebellion.[171] Beginning his presidency in 1789 with the country just emerging from Shays's Rebellion, Washington would have been loath to end it with one. But that was what was about to happen. His retirement came just one year after the trials of the whiskey rebels ended the insurrection in western Pennsylvania.

Persistent talk of anarchy and secession counterpointed to the Constitution and strong central government was the very stuff of which the grand jury charges were made. Isolating the rebellions that ran through the early republic without appreciating how connected they were to the government's need to centralize power diverts us from gauging how preoccupied the federal courts must have been in putting rebellion to bed. The Whiskey Rebellion trials seemed like the government's best bet to exorcise that special demon, and the grand jury charges—with their goal of educating Americans in citizenry and their bully pulpit in the public sphere—must have seemed the ideal first act for a meaningful Federalist judicial narrative that would do just that.

The present chapter has drawn certain conclusions about the judicial narrative. First, it overlapped with the government narrative, both in Washington's words to Congress in establishing the need for an "inseparable union" and in John Jay's words in the Federalist papers that "[n]othing is more certain than the indispensable necessity of government [. . .] the people must cede to it some of their natural rights in order to vest it with requisite powers."[172] The judicial narrative was not, however, identical with the government narrative across the range of judges who addressed the Whiskey Rebellion in their grand jury charges. Not only was there a split between justices such as Paterson and Wilson as opposed to Addison, Peters, and Blair, reflecting the difference between moderate and conservative Federalists, but between state and federal grand jury charges, indicating the persistence of the state-federal conflict we observed in chapter 2. In a more general sense, the government and judicial narratives differed in terms of their politics and their use. Grand jury charges yielded a more principled narrative and were grounded in a theory of democratic governance often lacking in the government narrative; the government narrative, by contrast, manipulated public perceptions to serve the interests of the Washington administration and its pursuit of national power.

The second part of the study has thus far established the position of the federal judiciary relative to the rebellion and explored the grand jury role as a precursor to the trials. Together they created the parameters for a judicial narrative. While it was rejected by the trial juries of all but two treason trials, the circuit court judges and the government prosecutors would be guided by that narrative. In terms of the progression of the storyline of this study, several other things were about to happen. As chapter 5 demonstrates, for the first time the rebels would face the government on an even playing field. The dominant government story would have to prove itself in court, where coercive military force could not dictate the trial verdict. National power was no longer a necessary advantage for the government; nor was the heterogeneity of the locally dispersed settlers who made up the rebellion any longer a disadvantage for the defense. The rebel defense would demonstrate it had a legitimate, defensible argument that resonated with common man juries whether they were made up of westerners or easterners. The rebel perspective would be equally represented, and it would get a fully argued hearing under the protection of evidentiary and procedural rules. With the rebel perspective reinstated, the history of the rebellion was reset as a balance of popular rights and state security. That becomes fully evident in the final chapter where defense notes make clear that backcountry democracy did not reject the Constitution and the laws so much as engage to check a counterrevolutionary interpretation that would erode them.

CHAPTER 5

The Trials, 1795

The clash of government and rebel narratives in the trials occurred within the parameters drawn by the Federalist judicial script produced by the grand jury charges explored in the preceding chapter. The influence of this judicial narrative demonstrates the continued prominence of judges in the late eighteenth-century courtroom, a phenomenon that would prove as critical to the trial jury charges as it did to the grand jury charges. As applied to the subjects of the present chapter—constitutional and common law, but just as importantly procedural and evidentiary challenges—that mix of narratives would determine whether prosecution cases would succeed. Study of the trials in this chapter considers how with the emergence of federal law legal questions were addressed constitutionally and under residual English common law; these interactive bodies of law shaped the legal constructions to which trial judges were prone and to which trial arguments would address themselves. The competing objectives, as we shall see, were to enhance the authority of federal over state law and to generate an American law that weaned the courts from dependence on English common law.

It is useful to provide a sense of how the trials proceeded before we discuss them. The judicial arm of the militia charged the rebels it had rounded up, and the prisoners were delivered to the Walnut Street jail (on the corner of Walnut and Sixth streets) in Philadelphia on Christmas Day, many without having a hearing. They were joined by other captured or surrendered rebels and were held awaiting indictment and trial for months. Defense counsel William Lewis petitioned the U.S. Supreme Court on behalf of several prisoners to hold a special circuit court in western Pennsylvania. The change of venue would allow the accused easier access to their witnesses but would also permit them a "jury of their neighbors" familiar with the issues, the witnesses, and the accused. Justice James Wilson rejected their request. While the court was addressing this issue, Lewis made a motion to the Supreme Court for a writ of habeas corpus (the first such grants in U.S. history), with the hope of getting several rebels discharged or put on bail. Although two received bail, none of the three who petitioned was indicted for either treason or misprision of treason. Brought before a grand jury of the eastern Pennsylvania circuit court, the first group of those who were indicted were tried in May and June 1795.

Indictments for treason had been sought by U.S. attorney general William Bradford against thirty-six men. In a third of the cases, indictments were rejected; only ten of those indicted were tried, the others having fled. Still others had signed a submission statement that entitled them to presidential amnesty, while some traded their testimony against fellow rebels for dismissal of their cases. The resolution of procedural questions moved forward with a focus on empaneling western jurors and resolving whether state or federal law would dictate procedural aspects of the trials. Justice Paterson ruled favorably on a number of defense motions and suspended the trials for three days so the prosecution could comply with his rulings. Jury selection followed, whereupon the defense team used its thirty-five peremptory challenges to select juries more to its liking, an exercise that met with mixed success. Trials were held from May to June and resumed in October of 1795 but yielded only two convictions for treason. Frustrated at the ineffectiveness of the trials, the prosecution withdrew those cases that had been held over until the April session of 1796.[1]

Problems of Evidence

One of the most significant factors affecting the Whiskey Rebellion trials was the conduct of the judicial arm attached to the federal army that marched into the western counties at the end of October.[2] Washington visited the army under the command of General Henry Lee in Carlisle and then pushed on to Bedford, where he delivered a farewell to the troops in a letter to Lee that he intended "to be published in orders."[3] As he expressed in his diary, he had "prepared his Instructions and made every arrangement" in order that he might return to Philadelphia "to meet Congress, and to attend to the Civil duties" of his office. The president had not come to lead the army into battle. Several things are of note here. Visiting the troops personally, Washington displayed a fatherly solicitude in ensuring their proper conduct and limiting their role to support the judiciary, not to usurp its functions. The first of two "objects" he set for the military force was to subdue those in arms, to which he added "a special recommendation: that "every Officer and soldier will constantly bear in mind that he come[s] to support the laws." In so doing, they owed a duty to "preserve th[e] blessings of the Revolution" that had made the nation "free & Independent" and to provide to the world an example for humankind, the double obligation that he felt for himself in serving both a national and an international role as president. The second object, and for the purposes of the present study the more important, was "to aid & support the Civil magistrate in bringing offenders to justice." Washington made clear to General Lee that "[t]he dispensation of this justice belongs to the Civil magistrate—and let it ever be our pride, and our glory, to leave the sacred deposit there, unviolated."[4] William Findley, who was present in Carlisle, reported that the army had been recruited with passionate speeches suggesting "that the whole country would be given up to miliary execution and plunder." Washington's appeal to good order among the troops, consequently, met with serious resistance. Indeed, any who favored subjecting the military to civil law or having them answer to the courts for the murder of civilians "were in as much danger, and equally the object of threats, as the whiskey men, and in fact were called so."[5]

Washington left behind a draft of his "Instructions" which Hamilton then communicated to General Lee.[6] What happened between Washington's letter to Lee and Hamilton's communication (the draft is not available other than as it is reflected in Hamilton's letter) is informative in suggesting the influence Hamilton exerted over the relative balance of military and judicial functions as well as his ability to assert his self-interest in carrying out the president's directives. Where Washington's letter to Lee had established that the army was to support the "[c]ivil magistrate in bringing offenders to justice," a judicial function, the language used in Hamilton's instructions was to "support the civil officers in the means of executing the laws," an executive function, which displaced the emphasis from a single chief judicial figure to a shared responsibility of multiple figures. The sacred inviolability of the civil mission was omitted.

Departures from Washington's letter to Lee further diminished the authority of the judicial function. "You are aware that the Judge [Peters] cannot be controuled in his function," Hamilton allowed, speaking on Washington's behalf, "But I count on his disposition to cooperate in such a general plan as shall appear to you [Lee] consistent with the policy of the case." Peters's inviolate "dispensation of justice" was not only subordinated to Lee's "general plan," but the instructions now inserted an intermediary, the district attorney, so that Lee's "method of giving a direction to legal proceedings" was to be through "instruction" to Rawle. The instructions, moreover, had already circumscribed the district attorney's function by directing that "He ought particularly to be instructed" in the categories of those who should be arrested, issuing process for penalties, where prisoners should be jailed, and where different offenses should be prosecuted.

Whereas Hamilton had accompanied the army without a designated role, the instructions had inserted roles for Hamilton's agents (the supervisor of the revenue and officers of inspection); in addition, it prohibited pardons of those against whom the revenue laws had a claim. Both directives made the secretary of the treasury's presumed right to interfere in the judiciary process a matter to be reckoned with. Another instruction (that Peters's work be guided by "a list of the persons" who accepted amnesty) smacked of "favoritism and prejudice," according to Brackenridge,[7] while the pardoning power of the president added yet another burden under which Peters and Rawle had to operate.

Both Brackenridge and Findley took issue with the activities of the judicial arm and the pressure from the troops to exact punishment. As a soldier writing home to his wife expressed, the troops had "daly taken our enemies and confining them" and expected that trials would follow and some would soon be hanged; short of that, the author anticipated that should any violence be offered, "I expect we shall put many to the sword."[8] Findley particularly pointed to the influence of the army's meddling. Having seen many prisoners "dismissed without atonements being made,"[9] he offered, the troops threatened mutiny and revenge and silenced witnesses, which, with the prospect of escapes by the rebels, led Peters to take large numbers of prisoners and file large numbers of treason charges. The judge, Findley claimed, was easily imposed upon "[o]wing to the hurry and confusion of the camp" and to his own desire to protect himself,[10] so that many cases would be unwinnable once brought to trial. None of these factors led Peters to recuse himself from serving on the circuit court in Philadelphia that conducted the rebel trials.

It was Hamilton, however, who posed the biggest obstacle to Peters's control of the process. Hamilton behaved as if he was representing the president, indeed even more like the commander in chief himself. As we see in chapter 1 with Secretary of State Randolph and his French connection,

Emissary Fauchet, this criticism was a shared concern. Findley put it that Hamilton was "generally taken" as director of the army's judiciary based on his insistence that many of the prisoners be brought to trial without examination or a cause of action.[11] Hamilton himself interrogated Brackenridge and Findley at length as suspected rebel leaders, leading Brackenridge to complain of "indiscrete zeal on the part of the prosecution."[12] No friend of Hamilton (having published a critique of the secretary's financial plan just a year before), Congressman Findley feared Hamilton's willingness "to prove me a bad man, as well as a criminal" in relying on non-existent proofs and discounting testimony offered by Judge Peters and Judge Baird on Findley's behalf.[13] Both Albert Gallatin and John Smilie, members of the state ratification convention who refused the government amnesty, were faced with investigations "accompanied with the most illegal inducements to promote discovery" and with Hamilton's repeated assertions to witnesses that there was proof of their guilt. Nonetheless, "no testimony," Findley reported, "was found even to lay a foundation for suspicion."[14] Hamilton saw to it that Findley, Gallatin, and Brackenridge were not among those to be amnestied.[15]

Brackenridge represented that Hamilton and Rawle were not the only problematic figures in the investigations. Excise inspector General Neville, together with his lawyer John Woods, was, he complained, given "so facile an ear" that his influence was unlimited. A combined witness, investigator, and prosecutor, Neville assisted the judiciary arm by identifying and interrogating witnesses.[16] Having provoked the most violent event of the rebellion, he proceeded to mislead the investigations and corrupt the cases in which he provided evidence. Woods, according to Brackenridge, had spared no pains in collecting information "with denunciations that he would have me hanged."[17] Like Findley, Brackenridge had made himself a target; in his case, it was by pursuing prosecutions of Neville's father-in-law General Morgan (who described Brackenridge in general orders as "busy in fomenting difference, and urging prosecutions of a vexatious kind") and of Neville's brother-in-law by marriage Major Kirkpatrick (who sold a free Black into slavery). Brackenridge complained he was being persecuted for "having instituted suits, and directed prosecutions against unprincipled, wanton, maurauding pandours of [Neville's] corps."[18]

Brackenridge felt the judicial arm was well aware that charges it was being induced to bring were fraudulent, including those from parties with influence, reputation, or status who sought opportunities to settle scores. Their unsupported testimony was nevertheless treated as sacrosanct. In other instances, enticements were offered for more "pardonable frauds"; these involved dangling amnesty as a reward for testifying against other, more desirable targets.[19] Overall, the evidence-gathering process failed to generate proof worthy of depriving a person of his life, according to Brackenridge, who determined "to trace the source of information" and charge those responsible for making unfounded accusations.[20]

Although Brackenridge and Findley's complaints were, to be fair, self-interested, they were reinforced by Hamilton's cavalier attitude toward the gathering of evidence. In an especially revealing letter to the president,[21] Hamilton dismissed out of hand information from those familiar with the local legal scene, including the state's governor and judges. He excused himself at some length for neglecting to gather formal evidence further afield given the unsafe conditions in the western country, and he admitted to lacking "a formal exhibition of the evidence" on the excuse that he could not foresee what cases the governor would consider "proper for that animadversion which he seems to contemplate." Decrying, further, the delay that collecting formal evidence would entail, Hamilton complained he had to deal with unreliable and fearful persons "liable to specious controversy" who were unlikely to volunteer as witnesses."[22] He represented that testimony and witnesses were "[s]usceptible of different interpretations" and begged off providing proof on the specious grounds that it was so often disguised and duplicitous that it could not be "rendered palpable by precise specification and proof."[23] Other problems with evidence surfaced in the reports Hamilton's network of spies and informants sent to him and upon which the Washington administration relied from 1791 on.[24] According to Findley, Hamilton's officers reported the smallest slights to the law or themselves which they arranged "in the most criminal dress suited to [their] design," a practice common to spies in any country.[25] That revenue officers could not produce evidence that led to convictions, he concluded, indicated how "evidently fabricated or doubtful" the information was.[26]

Spies, collaborators, and opportunists were not the only parties to have falsified or accepted dubious evidence. Justice James Wilson had no depositions or witnesses to examine in his official certification of the Militia Act of 1792 to vouch for Hamilton's account, only "some private letters containing information of the facts and the general notoriety of the outrages."[27] Even so, Hamilton complained that Wilson wasted time on getting "the hand writing proved" on "Sundry papers," apparently the sole effort Wilson made to test the evidence provided by Hamilton's cohorts.[28] Judge Wilson's truncated statement avoided the term "treason" and offered Washington a mere eleven lines restricted to the narrow terms of the militia act; he simply applied Hamilton's information to the requirements of the militia act. "From the evidence which has been laid before me," Wilson declared, the execution of the laws were "obstructed by combinations too powerful to be suppressed by the ordinary course of judicial proceedings or by the powers vested in the Marshal."[29]

Members of the president's administration (Secretary of State Edmund Randolph and U.S. attorney general William Bradford) distanced themselves from Wilson's certification. Bradford hedged his bets and would not say that Wilson's certification was more than "sufficient in point of law."[30] He allowed that it "does not preclude the President's Judgement upon the facts," suggesting the president might revert to "the ordinary means of enforcing the law."[31] Randolph went so far as to question the insufficient legal form of the testimony and expressed concern that the certification "specifies no particular law that has been opposed."[32] Reporting that Wilson "did not yield to my reasoning," Randolph withheld his confidence in the certificate's validity. The president might, he advised, "[u]pon the supposition of its being valid" still conduct "a calm survey" and choose not to call immediately on the militia as the certificate might prove by itself sufficiently terrifying to the insurgents.[33]

Pennsylvania governor Thomas Mifflin was the most forceful of those advising the president. Representing the state's perspective based on his own prodigious sources of information, he counseled care "on the evidence as it appeared at the time of our conference,"[34] referring to the critical August 2 meeting of state and federal officials convened by the president. Mifflin complained that the affidavits he had seen before the certification were hearsay and "vague narrative" and that testamentary letters were "not written under the sanction of an oath or affirmation." Moreover, they "could not acquire the legal force and validity of evidence" from a mere signature. Mifflin advised Washington to "use his judgement" in choosing to approve evidence on which "an act of Government was to be founded."[35] An instance where civil law would be suspended and martial law imposed, he counseled, required "a much higher degree of caution" as military might would replace "the Judicial instruments of coercion" and involve numerous citizens "in the implication of Treason or Felony."

President Washington nonetheless endorsed Hamilton's construction and left Randolph to make the administration's case. Declaring that Wilson was in possession of "all the information which had been received," Randolph stipulated that federal law would control in this case, leaving it to

Wilson's conscience and on his responsibility to determine "what kind and degree [of evidence] should suffice." Indeed, the acts committed might fall short of insurrection, but they still supported "riots, assassinations and murders" within the community and defied "ordinary judicial means."[36] Cutting off further discussion (with the implication that Mifflin had crossed a red line with his criticisms), Randolph proclaimed the decision would "be made by the proper organ of the law for that purpose."[37]

By the time of the Philadelphia trials, it was clear that the evidence relied on to justify the militia and the trials was problematic and that the parties involved in certifying the evidence were aware of its inadequacies. Witness, court watcher, and "elected" but unseated U.S. senator Albert Gallatin[38] held that the long stream of errors in evidence would make cases difficult to prove. Thus, from among the contingent of rebels marched to Philadelphia from Gallatin's home county, Fayette County, Attorney General Rawle sent only two bills to the grand jury; "not a shadow of proof appeared," Gallatin wrote to his wife, "although the county was [ransacked] for witnesses."[39] In the very first treason case tried before the circuit court, that of Robert Porter, defense counsel Lewis found the trial so confused that he "would not even take the trouble to call any witnesses on [Porter's] behalf"; prosecutor Bradford "acknowledged that the evidence did not [amount] to what he expected"; Paterson "declared that the prosecution was not supported by the evidence" and directed the jury to find for the defendant. Porter was found not guilty.[40] Evangelist and the first principal of Dickinson College, Charles Nisbet predicted "that the prisoners in Philadelphia will have a sham Trial," after which "it is expected that they will soon return home in Triumph."[41] Brackenridge shared Nisbet's premonition, intimating that the trials in Philadelphia would "differ little from a revolutionary tribunal of Paris."[42]

The Vicinage Question

Before the rebels could be tried, several questions had to be resolved: whether the trial would be held where the crime was committed; from which area jurors would be selected; which court had jurisdiction; and which crimes, charges, or procedural questions would be implicated. The writs served in June and July to recalcitrant distillers (the immediate and inciting cause of violence in the rebellion) was itself questionable as Rawle had no intention of prosecuting the sixty rebels initially identified in writs he had procured in Philadelphia. In fact, the writs were "technically invalid" as the eastern district court was not scheduled for a summer session. Still, Rawle sought indictments.[43] Fellow prosecutor U.S. attorney general Bradford supported Rawle's stratagem in a private letter that read, "The suits that were brought were merely for the purpose of compelling an Entry of the Stills"; the suits were eventually discharged either as a general rule or because of any of a number of legal or procedural obstacles.[44]

Rawle calculated that whereas Congress's change in the excise law in 1794[45] allowed for local trials, there was "no reasonable expectation" that would happen. Still, in a line crossed out in a letter to Randolph, he speculated that he could afford a delay as it "might operate favorably upon the minds of the people."[46] Rawle knew he had the upper hand and that not only was "vindictive delay" to his benefit but also he was at liberty to set his own rule having "found none of any kind established in the court." Thus, though he had previously required witnesses to appear in Philadelphia for their depositions, he felt he had the discretion to pursue a more lenient course of action and afford "a reasonable time to the opposite party."[47] The U.S. Commission, of which Bradford was a member, expressed the benefit as well of giving way to local control, claiming Congress's modification of the excise law acknowledged "[s]tate courts had been vested with a jurisdiction over offenses against those acts, which would enable the President to remove one of their principal complaints."[48] In any case, and as both Rawle and Bradford had privately revealed, the government's jurisdictional interests were less about a principled legal position than about political leverage.

Reacting to a possible change in vicinage, the rebel assembly at Parkinson's Ferry wrote a resolution protesting the removal of the trials to Philadelphia, declaring it "a forced and dangerous construction" and "a violation of the rights of the citizens."[49] Brackenridge, who participated in writing the resolution, argued that the move would have a prejudicial effect on the defendant. Moreover, using the entire state as the venue for trying a crime was "a hard construction" since before the Constitution the vicinage was the county.[50] Transported for trial to the other end of the state and having witnesses travel that distance, he maintained, meant that the accused's character and that of the witnesses was "not impressed on the minds of the jury."[51] The government in fact made minor concessions to the state judiciary. Hamilton's instructions to General Lee, for example, had laid out the parameters under which the judicial arm of the militia was to handle prisoners. The first directive was "[t]o cause *offenders*, who may be arrested, to be conveyed to goals where there will be no danger of rescue; those for misdemeanors to the goals of York and Lancaster; those for capital offences to the goal of Philadelphia." Thereafter, the plan was "[t]o prosecute indictable offences in the Courts of the United States—those for penalties on delinquents [...] in the courts of Pennsylvania."[52] As Brackenridge reported, Judge Addison of the western courts would have the responsibility of handling minor offenders tried for misdemeanors in their respective counties at courts of quarter session which would judge their penalties.[53] That state courts took seriously their responsibility for misdemeanors is demonstrated by entries for the November 1794 Bedford County Court of General Quarter Sessions where twenty-nine rebels were held for indictment on charges of raising liberty poles "in sign of treason [...] or other bad language against the United States"; only five forfeited the sum (thirty pounds) pledged for their appearance.

Historically, the contest over which court—state or federal—had priority was integral to the nation's system of laws from as early as the constitutional convention of 1787. There James Madison led a faction which suggested federal courts would remedy the problem of "improper Verdicts in State tribunals obtained under the biassed directions of a dependent Judge, or the local prejudices of an undirected jury."[54] Randolph put it that the central question was whether state courts could be trusted to administer national laws or would national and local policy be in conflict.[55] Federal courts, Madison and Wilson concluded, were essential.[56] Following a Madison proposal, the convention added "the national Peace and Harmony" to the jurisdiction of federal courts, and the final version of Article 3 of the Constitution gave supremacy to national law, though it would face significant state challenges.[57] Wilson had denied at the convention that states retained any sovereignty and held that the formation of the United States had extinguished it.[58] Wilson, it should be noted, would preside over and deny the request by the rebel defense that a special circuit court be held in the western part of the state.

The law regarding the venue for federal whiskey tax violations is illustrative here. The federal courts were empowered by the 1791 Excise Act to prosecute violations in federal district court, with allowance thereafter for state court jurisdiction. Precedence thus went to federal courts, but in the absence of a U.S. action or suit the trial was to be "laid in the county in which the cause of action shall have arisen."[59] A June 1794 amendment to the excise act raised the hope that rebels would be tried locally (an experiment the U.S. Commission appeared to support); it gave "the judicial courts of the several states, and of the territory of the United States" equal authority to try violations, indicating overlapping jurisdiction.[60] Capital cases were covered by the 1789 Judiciary Act (section 29), which designated state courts for those cases unless "that cannot be done without great inconvenience."[61] A follow-up Judiciary Act in 1793 would, in criminal cases, have permitted special circuit courts closer to where a crime occurred should the regular circuit courts prove inconvenient.⁶² Despite these options, and faced with rebel resistance to sign submission statements and Washington's decision to send a federal army, the government precipitately charged the rebels under the 1791 Excise Act, disregarding the 1794 amendment and foreclosing the possibility that state courts would try any but the lowest level cases.⁶³

As for which federal courts were candidates for the kinds of crimes charged in the rebellion, instructive insights appeared in District Judge Peters's grand jury charges. Peters complained that criminal law was not as precise as he hoped it would be in the future; the district court, which lacked powers on the criminal side, was thus "confined in its jurisdiction."⁶⁴ Treason, for example, was too high a crime for the district court to consider. On the other hand, the district court was mandated to address breaches of the law like those that had led to the "unjustifiable, disgraceful and much to be lamented disturbances." In Peters's view, federal courts had a public police role to play in holding citizens accountable.⁶⁵ The mandate for the federal courts was thereby to preserve stability against political crimes such as sedition and treason, which indeed constituted Madison's proposal at the constitutional convention and the judicial philosophy of the 1795 Circuit Court of the Eastern District of Pennsylvania (which had jurisdiction over major criminal cases) in trying the whiskey rebels.⁶⁶

A major obstacle for the choice of a court was the language on "inconvenience" that appeared in the excise and judiciary acts. In *United States v. Stewart and United States v. Wright* (1795),⁶⁷ defense counsel Lewis reminded the circuit court of the inconveniences to the defense, basing his argument on the 1789 Judiciary Act.⁶⁸ He added that twelve jurors should be summoned from the county where the crime occurred should the government proceed in federal court, citing the great distance and the absence of material witnesses in a capital case. Absalom Baird—a member of the state legislature and a witness at the trials—added in a letter home that the government refused to specify the charges to prevent the defense from sending for witnesses. A marshal had "been out some time to the western country to summon witnesses" for the government, while the prisoners had to summon their own, which he calculated would "not be less than 100 or 150 witnesses from the four western counties" as well as a number from three other counties (Bedford, Cumberland, and Northumberland).⁶⁹

The debate over inconvenience took on a different meaning in *United States v. The Insurgents of Pennsylvania* (1795), where Judge Peters argued that on balance the burden on the defense paled in comparison to that on the prosecution; in *United States v. Stewart*, prosecuting attorney Rawle found the defense's complaint a problem of its own creation.[70] Rawle cited poor preparation and a lack of "due diligence" by the defense as the source of its inconvenience. He claimed to have disclosed sufficient information on the motion for a special court to show that "the indictments would be presented at *Philadelphia*," adding, with more than a hint of sarcasm, that it would have been "mere speculation" to think the trials would occur elsewhere than in Philadelphia.[71] In *United States v. Hamilton* (1795),[72] Justice Wilson's procedural argument resolved the question of venue based on timing. Despite section 3 of the Judiciary Act of 1793,[73] which would have permitted the Supreme Court to call a special circuit court, Wilson found timing an "insurmountable" problem. He argued, first, that a special court could not begin and complete its work before the next regular court. Second, even if a special court were called, there was no provision for remitting to that court an indictment arrived at by the regular court. Finally, he questioned whether the two courts "could both be in session at the same time." Not only was the prisoner's request denied in this case, but Lewis and Moses Levy lost their petition for a change of venue in the cases of John Corbly and John Lockery,[74] which would have established special circuit courts in each of the five counties where the acts were committed. Had the Judiciary Act of 1793 prevailed on the issue, it could have allowed the petition on the grounds that regular circuit courts were "inconvenient."

As a test of the "goodness" of the venue decisions in the Whiskey Rebellion trials, it is worth noting how the same issue was treated in the *Fries* rebellion trials in 1799 (reprising Lewis for the defense, Rawle for the prosecution, and Judge Peters on the bench and tried in the same circuit court as the Whiskey Rebellion trials).[75] There, Lewis argued passionately that Wilson's decision (which the judges held was "in full force and founded on true principles of law") was not a good precedent, for it had been rendered it on the grounds of timing that did not now apply. More broadly, a local trial was an "inestimable right," the deprivation of which had contributed to separating "from the mother country." In terms of "inconvenience," whatever "judges might feel in traveling, or the time spent" weighed no more heavily on them than on the prisoners. Did the inconvenience make it "improper or impossible" to try the case where the offense occurred; could a fair trial not take place there? Were there corrupt judges in that place? If the safety of the United States or of the court was at issue, he reminded the judges, U.S. troops were still present to enforce the law.[76] Without providing a rationale,

Peters offered that "while a doubt remained, it would never do" to move the case[77] and he would refuse to do so even if "applied to, in his official capacity." Equally obdurate, his fellow justice on the bench, James Iredell, decreed it "exceedingly improper" to return the case to the seat of insurrection where justice "of the sword" would likely be guided by intimidation, if it was to operate at all.[78]

Vicinage in the Whiskey Rebellion trials was not in the end to be settled on procedural or statutory grounds, on trying a crime where it occurred, or as a question of inconvenience, the court's safety, or the defense's lack of "due diligence"; rather, it would be decided on the nature of the crime. As the threat was against the Union and the federal Constitution, not against an individual state, the federal court charged treason against the U.S. government. While the law might allow crimes to be tried in either state or federal court, the underlying presumption for a venue on a charge of treason under the Constitution would be federal where treason against the nation had a different meaning. Federal courts had an interest in the overthrow of the general government. Too high a crime for the federal courts to ignore, or for the states to preempt, treason was the true test for the constitutional convention's resolution that a republican constitution should be guaranteed by the United States to each state. As Wilson argued, "The object is merely to secure the States agst. dangerous combinations, insurrections and rebellions," a position Madison reinforced: "the Constitutional authority of the States shall be guaranteed to them respectively agst. domestic as well as foreign violence."[79] The Whiskey Rebellion was just such an instance.

Procedural Issues

With vicinage decided, the trials could proceed. The bulk of the trials were not, however, reported, which means that for the most part examination of the trials has focused on Alexander Dallas's law report of the John Mitchell trial and to a lesser extent the trial of Philip Vigol, in both of which the defendants were convicted of treason and subsequently pardoned.[80] Four transcripts of trials taken down by Justice Paterson and preserved in manuscript bench notes have, however, never been studied and a series of procedural cases have been only summarily discussed, which indicates the need for a fuller examination of the trials as a whole. The procedural cases, which we shall take up first, are of interest for two reasons. They provide a picture of early applications of the law when the Constitution was still an untested document, the federal government's authority was still unsettled, and the law still required alteration to establish principles and practices.[81] They have additional value in their use of technical procedures to win or shape cases, much like the approach abolitionists took in fugitive-slave cases and in emancipation cases under Pennsylvania's gradual emancipation act of 1780.[82] Indeed, in these Whiskey Rebellion cases, common law pleading on technical errors was a productive area for the defense, including bail applications, access to defense witnesses, venire and jury selection, witness lists, and copies of indictments. The defense's choice to plead on procedural grounds was not surprising considering the short cuts to which the prosecution admitted,[83] among them due process violations (failure to hold hearings and unsupported detentions), constitutional violations (searches and seizures), and abuses of the rules of evidence (prejudicial testimony and the reward system used to entice witnesses).

Importantly, the court heard several habeas corpus petitions. In that of John Hamilton, defense counsel Lewis argued that prosecutors did not hold a hearing before jailing the defendant and that the accused was not informed of the names of witnesses against him or the scope of their examination. Rawle admitted that District Judge Peters failed to hold a hearing before issuing a warrant committing Hamilton, offering in extenuation that it was not a question of oppressive treatment or indifference, given the number of suspects and "the urgency of the season," and citing the "established character of the Judge."[84] Because section 33 of the Judiciary Act of 1789 covering arrests did not require a hearing, the prosecution argued that the court could not override a detention order without new evidence or judicial misconduct. Hamilton and several other prisoners were granted bail.[85]

In the absence of a change of venue or a special court, James Stewart and Edward Wright sought to have their cases postponed citing the need to procure witnesses from a great distance and decrying "the poverty of the witnesses"; otherwise "an immediate trial would be a mere *ex parte* proceeding." Nor could they prepare for trial until, like Hamilton, they knew the charge and the names of the witnesses against them, in which case they needed time to bring forth proof against their accusations. Rawle countered that the accused ought to have known the nature of the charge and what proof was "necessary to their defense," and that they must show they were not guilty of neglect in procuring their witnesses or of delaying the proceedings. Although the court sided with the defendants, Lewis decided to continue with the testimony already available in Stewart's case. The court accepted as a principle that no negligence, unreasonable delay, or prejudice should attach to defendants who took time to gather their witnesses, but it found that was not the case with Stewart. Stewart, as a result, had no further claim on its "legal discretion" and the court denied bail.[86]

United States v. The Insurgents of Pennsylvania concerned disclosures to which the defense was entitled: the indictment, panel of jurors, and list of witnesses. The defense went further, however, relying on Pennsylvania law to demand the caption (which stated the judges, the time, and the place of trial) for the indictment and specifics of the occupations and residences for jurors and witnesses. Judge Peters denied the request on the grounds that the federal judiciary ought not to be controlled by "strict adherence" to state regulations, especially where the defendant argued "inconvenience." If such inconveniences existed, which he much doubted, they "weigh lightly when set against the delays and obstructions [... to] the execution of the laws of the nation." Justice Paterson, on the other hand, was willing to acknowledge that section 29 of the Judiciary Act of 1789 referred federal courts to state laws. The material in question, he held, was naturally part of the same instrument and should be provided to the defense, except for occupations (as they were not among "the niceties" incorporated into federal law) and the venire (the list of names from which jurors were to be selected), central aspects of the defendants' case.[87]

The final, and potentially most critical issue in question, was jury selection. In early May 1795, Gallatin noted that the remaining delays to the trials chiefly regarded the jury.[88] The number of local jurors to be called from the affected counties to form jury panels was a critical issue for the defendants. Lewis relied in *Insurgents* on the provision in the 1789 Judiciary Act that twelve jurors be summoned from the locale where the events had occurred. Justice Paterson conceded and established separate jury panels for each trial; twelve jurors were returned in compliance with federal law and sixty with state law to reconcile the concurrent jurisdictions of state and federal law.[89] Nonetheless, four-fifths of each jury panel was made up of jurors from outside the affected counties.[90] While Paterson found there had been no abuse of authority or discrimination by the marshal, only twelve (16 percent) of the seventy-two jurors ultimately empaneled for each of the Whiskey Rebellion trials were from the western counties; the rest were from eastern Pennsylvania.[91]

The trials told a somewhat surprising story about the effect of the makeup of juries. Rawle, for one, discovered that the prosecutions preparations were largely unpersuasive to circuit court juries. He confided to Addison that there was "a great unwillingness to say too much against their fellow citizens, a reluctance in the jury to convict the smaller engine on the testimony of their ringleaders, and a natural repugnance to capital convictions." Contrary to what he had expected, there were more ignoramus bills and acquittals, which he attributed to "the difficult distinction necessary to be made between the different jurisdictions."[92] Rawle reflected not only an aversion to independent-minded jurors and a lack of appreciation for conditions in the West, but also an inability to navigate the difficult question of jury composition.

Whereas Gallatin, who not only observed but was also a witness in the trials, called the grand jury "respectable" and not "suspected of partiality,"[93] his comments on trial juries were more discriminating. Regarding western jurors, he reported that those from Fayette were good, from Washington middling, and from Alleghany such that defense counsel in *Porter* "challenged all of them but one and chose rather to trust his life to the decision of jurors from the counties in the neighborhood of Philadelphia."[94] The defense's strategy proved prescient as the jury delivered its verdict within minutes of the judge directing a verdict of not guilty.[95] Gallatin later cited Lewis's choice of "a jury of a different complexion" in *Barnet*. In that case, the evidence, pleadings, and charge lasted from one morning until three o'clock the next when the jury retired for fifteen minutes and brought back a verdict of not guilty.[96] In truth, efforts to exclude jurors from Philadelphia and neighboring counties in favor of western jurors were largely unavailing, as Lewis and Thomas saw in *United States v. Porter*. Those from the West, Gallatin claimed, "had been picked up with such care" that they were of no use to the defense.[97] At the same time, many eastern jurors were not in line with the government or convinced by the prosecution. Gallatin expressed his sorrow that Vigol was convicted, on the grounds that "[h]e had a very good and favorable jury, six of them from Fayette, for although he is from Westmoreland County, the fact was committed in Fayette." That is, even with a jury made up of 50 percent westerners, Vigol was one of only two defendants convicted of treason.[98]

A review of trial documents, however, suggests that when western jurors were selected they were in fact favorable to the accused.[99] Although twenty-four jurors from Northumberland and Washington counties never served on a jury,[100] none of the Alleghany County residents who served ever voted guilty. Unfortunately, defense counsel Thomas excluded all those from Alleghany from the *Mitchell* jury. Indeed, that jury included no one from the West, potentially a deciding factor in Mitchell's conviction. Lewis did not make the same mistake. He selected the same juror from Alleghany who had voted innocent in the trial of Marmaduke Curtis for the *Barnet* jury. Unlike Mitchell, Barnet was acquitted, as was Thomas Miller on whose jury a countryman from Alleghany County served.[101] Jurors from York were equally amenable to acquittals; when no western jurors were available for four trials in the October term of the circuit court, York jurors acquitted in all their trials.[102]

Despite the disparate picture on juries across the trials, Gallatin concluded that jury selection was more likely to account for an acquittal than choice of counsel. Because the defense in *Mitchell* had rejected all the jurors from Alleghany, Thomas had "left the case to twelve Quakers (many of them probably old tories)," under the presumption that Quakers would not condemn the prisoner. In this, Gallatin allowed, "[Thomas] was utterly mistaken,"[103] though he admitted that Brackenridge, a seasoned litigator who also observed and served as a witness in the trials, had a different view of the matter. Brackenridge, he noted, "always chose a jury of Quakers or at least Episcopalians" in such "common cases" as murder and rape, "but in every possible case of insurrection, rebellion and treason, give him Presbyterians as the jury."[104]

Predicting a verdict based on the makeup of the jury was, in sum, complicated by the discretion of marshals to choose selectively those admitted to the western venire of jurors. Voir dire played a role as well, considering the thirty-five strikes for no cause that defense counsel used wisely in selecting jurors. Finally, the pool of jurors from the eastern counties were unpredictable in their preferences; many of them were sympathetic to the rebels (a sentiment also demonstrated in eastern Pennsylvania's Fries's Rebellion trials) while others were simply unsympathetic to the Federalists. The effect of jury composition and defense strategies on verdicts was in any case part of a larger climate that included the poor showing of the prosecution, ongoing changes in the influence of judges on juries, and a general political climate in which the development of political parties and the declining political pull of the old-guard revolutionary elite were in play.

The Trials

Whereas issues related to procedural matters demonstrated dependence on state and federal statutes (an issue introduced in chapter 4), statutory treason law that might have been applied has been neglected in studies of the trials in preference to constitutional and common law. There was, in fact, a history of treason law dating in the United States from the time of the Declaration of Independence. We are speaking here in particular of Pennsylvania's 1776

Treason Act, superseded by the 1777 Act. Although it was largely unused after the Revolutionary War, and was not referred to in the trials, it remained part of the legal knowledge base informing the trials.[105]

A review of Mitchell's treason trial reveals only one reference to a U.S. statute (the penal code), leaving the rest of the legal citations to common law. On the issue of the two-witness rule, the prosecution's argument referred to a variety of English authorities, while the defense spoke directly to the established constitutional rule, having earlier argued the intent of Congress (the constitutional definition of proof) and warned of the "dread and scourge" of constructive treason. The procedural cases (*Hamilton, Stewart and Wright,* and *Insurgents*), by contrast, referred to acts of Congress and Pennsylvania statutes with frequency, though they did not refer to Pennsylvania's treason laws. In *Insurgents*, for example, acts of Congress were cited on such issues as providing copies of indictments, captions of indictments, and places where jurors resided; drawing up panels of jurors; including jurors from the western counties; and trying crimes where they occurred.[106] The application of state rather than federal statutes was treated at length in *Insurgents* for consistency between them as well as the relative weight that should be given to their provisions, especially as regarded requirements that state rules guide federal practice in matters of procedure. The prosecution objected to incorporating all the state provisions into the practice of the federal court rather than substantially complying with them, presuming that federal law had been passed with full knowledge of existing state law.

Several things are noteworthy here. First, the court took the opportunity of the trials to assert that the national government "should not be fettered and controuled in its operations by a strict adherence to State regulations and practice."[107] Second, that the treason trials would not regard state laws "as rules of decision" in common law federal court trials. That is, where an act of Congress did not fix a procedural rule or expressly adopt a state rule or practice, the court would revert to common law, and where state practice and an act of Congress differed the latter would prevail. It is no surprise that federal statutory law played only a small part in the trials as there was little federal law as yet. What was unusual was the reluctance to rely on state statutes, as a body of developed state law was available from the colonial period, the period of the Revolution, and after ratification of the Constitution.

Equally interesting, Pennsylvania treason law had played a defining role in the treason trials of 1778, which made it the only true precedent the new nation had for American treason law other than the Constitution's Article 3, which was untried. On the one hand, two parts of the Pennsylvania

1777 Treason Act should have clarified the work of the Whiskey Rebellion judges. First, the exclusion of statutory English treason law ought to have limited the freedom with which the trials applied English common law, of which the statutes constituted a part. Second, the Treason Act had resolved the sticky point of allegiance (a matter of significant contention in the 1778 trials), as it specified allegiance to the country as a union of states as well as the state.

On the other hand, proof of a treasonous act was clouded by the treason act's failure to require an overt act of treason or two witnesses to the same act, which the precedent of the English statute of 1696 had left open by allowing for a witness to one act and another to a second act. Although constitutionally two witnesses to the same overt act was required, because of the earlier statutes the critical issue of proof was vulnerable to mischief by the judges. In addition, the treason act's definition of treason through the enumeration of seven types of treason and specifications for misprision of treason complicated its adherence to the liberal tradition limiting treason inscribed in 25 Edw. III, which the Constitution had adopted. With the 1778 trials applying common law together with the treason act, the judges were provided as well with a precedent to use common law to interpret the Constitution. This gave the Whiskey Rebellion judges an opening to expand treason constructively to include acts never intended to be considered treason, as the defense would complain. Finally, a 1782 act extended treason further, incorporating language that prohibited attempts to secede and reaching deeply into conduct that made 1791 Bill of Rights' freedoms such as assembly and speech treasonous acts.[108] American statutory treason law as applied in the Revolution thus acted in the background of the rebellion trials, even if it was not specifically cited by judges; the judges, it is important to note, had immediate or referred knowledge of the law applied in the 1778 trials and their aftermath.

The Treason Convictions

UNITED STATES V. VIGOL

With questions of vicinage and procedural issues largely behind them, the circuit court shifted to address the charge of treason head on. *United States v. Vigol* (May 23, 1795), one of only two treason trials to be reported at any length in a law report, was tried just a week after the government lost its first treason trial, *United States v. Porter*. Philip Vigol (Wigle) had no property and was considered a simple man. After the assembly at Braddock's Field,

Vigol hid in the bushes with a party of men and then surprised tax collector Benjamin Wells, taking him prisoner and frightening him into taking an oath not to operate an office of excise or to prosecute those who assaulted him. Vigol admitted to being of the party that burned the house, but not that he joined those who set it on fire. A "rough, ignorant German," according to Gallatin, he "had certainly no idea that [engaging in a riot] amounted to levying war and high treason." Gallatin had no doubt Vigol was "guilty in a legal sense of levying war against the United States" but found him to be "certainly an object of pity more than of punishment."[109]

The judge charged the jury that the crime with which Vigol was charged was intended "to render null and void, in effect, an act of *Congress*." As Paterson related, "[T]here is not, unhappily, the slightest possibility of doubt" of the party's intent. Paterson relied on witness testimony that Vigol was part of the group, but there was no evidence he committed an overt act himself. In fact, the law report asserted, Vigol's guilt was entirely dependent on witnesses who testified to overt acts by other members of his party. Although prosecution and defense counsel arguments do not appear in the report, Paterson makes clear in his jury charge that the defense's efforts to justify Vigol's presence at the attack did not constitute reasonable doubt or any other standard of certainty as he felt "the whole scene exhibits a disgraceful unanimity." Paterson discounted as well a defense of acting under duress, as such a defense would enable any "crafty leader [. . .] to indemnify his followers, by uttering previous menaces"; it could not, consequently, be considered an excuse. As "no question of law arose," the prosecution and defense mutually agreed "to submit to the decision of the Jury, under the charge of the court."[110] The jury requested a copy of Foster's *Crown Law* and the *Acts of Congress* and deliberated from 9:30 p.m. until sometime after three or four o'clock in the morning before delivering a verdict of guilty. The jury was satisfied that violence had been committed and that there were two witnesses to an overt act, despite lacking evidence of an act of war by the party or an overt act by Vigol. The verdict in *Vigol* thus left the impression that the judges had directed the trial process toward a guilty verdict to make up for the court's loss in *Porter*. Certainly Paterson's language in the charge appeared to leave the jury little choice in the outcome.[111] To its credit, the jury took its time in consulting the law and deliberating on a verdict, to the extent that the court twice refused to accept its presentation, first in a sealed written version and then "viva voce," an indication of the court's impatience with having to deal with a jury reluctant to accept the judge's charge at face value.

UNITED STATES V. MITCHELL

United States v. Mitchell, tried just after *Vigol*, provided the fullest elaboration of the prosecution case and gave the government its second treason conviction. As members of the radical faction of the rebellion, rather than leaders of the rebellion, Mitchell and Vigol were indicative of the type of frontiersmen taken prisoners by the federal militia. Brackenridge reported the two were "not worth hanging, on a charge of treason. I do not think that two more insignificant creatures could be found in the western country." Among those in custody, Mitchell and Vigol were "of better character," Brackenridge held; Gallatin added that there were "others who were more important than Vigol being either absconded, protected by the authority, or not taken notice of."[112] John Mitchell, a farmer, was from Westmoreland and had a small plot reduced from a hundred to thirty-five acres. Findley considered him "a very ignorant man, said to be of an outrageous temper, and subject to occasional fits of insanity." Mitchell not only gave himself up to the authorities and confessed his role when others fled, but, given a pass to proceed on his own to Philadelphia, he delivered himself to stand trial. A turncoat witness, "the principal leader in the riot," was said to have been the main witness against him.[113] Mitchell was convicted and sentenced to hanging for attacking and burning Neville's house.

In this case, Dallas's law report was extensive; it provided prosecution and defense counsel arguments in addition to Justice Paterson's charge. Rawle argued for the prosecution that it was enough for a treason charge that four witnesses proved Mitchell was at Couch's Fort where he "originally combined with the conspirators, in a treasonable purpose, to levy war." Mitchell confessed to having offered to reconnoiter Neville's house. It was unnecessary, according to Rawle, that a treasonable purpose be thereafter executed by Mitchell to convict him of treason. Mitchell need not be present where treason occurred (one witness saw him "within a few rods" of the burning house), "which was the consummation of their plot"; nor must he have acted on the purpose himself. Rawle considered it sufficient that the conspiracy of which Mitchell was a part had led to a treasonous act by another conspirator at Neville's house, under the prosecution theory that the act consummated a treasonous intent and that an act by one made all guilty of treason.[114] Rawle extended his argument to a subsequent assembly at Braddock's Field, where Mitchell's conduct (which fellow prosecutor Bradford referred to as Mitchell's "hasty declarations of the *quo animo*") corroborated his *mala mens*, "that dark and dreary turbulence of soul, which is regardless of every social, moral, and religious obligation."[115] Mitchell's state of mind at a subsequent assembly could thereby, Rawle claimed, serve as evidence of his intention at a previous assembly.

The approach taken by the prosecution was founded on English common law, which, Rawle represented, bound American courts. Common law "uniformly and clearly" defined treason, the evidence for which left "no room for excuse or extenuation,"[116] he claimed, ignoring that common law on treason was contradictory, indeterminate, and expansive and that the Constitution itself incorporated a restricted definition of treason that could not be expanded. Attorney general Bradford, the architect of the prosecution's constructivist approach, had first proposed it to the president for the trials.[117] Bradford laid out that the insurgents' acts were in fact "settled by uniform judicial construction" as a treasonous levying of war, a position that endorsed judicial discretion in interpreting common law. He defined treason as armed uprisings that "by their own authority and *with force*" rose up to "alter the lawful missions of government" and change established law. His definition included redressing grievances, real or pretended, and achieving "innovations of a general concern," using the excuse that such acts dissolved social bonds and destroyed property and government; this, he claimed, made them "cognizable in the Courts of the United States" as high treason. Bradford's description (dissolving bonds, innovations, withstanding authority, and altering the mission of government) avoided clear criteria of treason (intent, questions of allegiance, and overthrow of the government) and thereby presumed to jump the hurdle of the Constitution's restricted view of treason. His choice of terms ("lawful missions," "the established law") sidestepped particular resistance to one law by implying the dissolution of social order and the authority of government generally in order to meet the common law standard of resistance to all law. By the same argument, he morphed lesser forms of resistance (specific threats against officers and interference with serving writs) into general obstruction of the legitimate operations of the government in the execution of its laws and the administration of public affairs.[118] Had Congress been forced to repeal the excise law, he argued, excise offices would have been suppressed throughout the Union. In Bradford's estimation, irrespective of when or where it began or ended or how "any man became an agent in carrying it on," it was all "one great insurrection."[119] He used phrases such as "universality of object" and one "single, traitorous, motive" to signify that Mitchell need not have been present nor have committed an overt act to have been implicated in treason. While a man must be present and take part in a crime to render him a criminal, he contended, yet "if his intention was taiterous, his offense was treason." Along the same lines, he reminded the jury of Michael Foster's common law commentary, which held that "war may be levied, though not actually made."[120]

Defense counsel Tilghman and Thomas rejected Bradford's argument as an attempt to eliminate distinctions between types of crime and their punishment.[121] Magically, a mob became a conspiracy, and a riot became treason.[122] This was not what Congress had expressed. Suppressing one officer—a mere misdemeanor—was not to suppress all officers. A bare conspiracy to levy war did not amount to a treasonous act. Nor should a crime against a government agent be counted as "a crime of the same denomination" as compelling Congress by violence to repeal a law. Indeed, if a risk to all law was claimed where the excise law alone was resisted (abrogating the common law generality principle regarding "all laws"), "one must equally [do] so, in relation to every other law."[123] By extension, the government's proclivity to compound descriptions of treason "incautiously, into a system"[124] would lead to the "too easy admission of future cases" that was guarded against by Article 3.

On the issue of the assembly at Couch's Fort, counsel argued that it did not convene to achieve "a compulsory repeal" of the excise law nor to suppress the excise offices. Rather, those assembled at the meeting composed a committee to consider what was their best course of action, and they decided to send Neville a flag. The defense's posture was thereby that the prisoner's conduct at Couch's Fort was immaterial to a charge of treason.[125] Likewise, at Braddock's Field no plan for levying war was devised or executed and no act of treason committed;[126] the prisoner might have declared "a traitorous intention," but that intention was not proof of "having levied war against the government at another time, and in another place." The defense's most pointed legal challenge, however, was to the prosecution's construction of the two-witness requirement for proof of a single overt act of treason: the requisite two witnesses to a presumably treasonous act were not present at the place where the treasonous act was alleged to have occurred, and where there were two witnesses no treason had occurred. Furthermore, the defense added, an act such as reconnoitering that did "not amount to an overt act of treason by levying war" was not treason, no matter "if it were proved by fifty witnesses."[127]

Justice Paterson's charge to the jury mirrored the prosecution's argument. It promoted the idea that a single law signified all law and a usurpation of government authority "of a general nature,"[128] in effect dismissing the Constitution's restricted definition of treason. In this reading, mere political willfulness could be construed as treason and the people's refusal to obey a single law rendered the nation just as ineffectual as if they had overthrown its established laws by violent, direct attack, that is, the effect would be the same with or without an intent to subvert the government. This was the very model of doubtful construction of a treasonable act English authorities had warned against.[129] Here, a "connected course" of individual acts preventing the execution of a law constituted a general usurpation of government authority; being seen at a meeting (where the conspiracy took place) and then marching to Neville's house (to carry it out) constituted a composite transaction, a single act, that would satisfy the two-witness standard for "a competent number of witnesses."[130] Paterson reminded the jury that Foster regarded the very act of marching "as carrying the traiterous intention into effect";[131] he recommended a process whereby the jury might weigh "circumstances, which carry irresistible conviction to the mind" against the most positive testimony and "consider how far this aids the doubtful language of the second witness."

Paterson's efforts to finesse the two-witness rule and confound the generality principle were supported by his idiographic approach to Mitchell's presumed treason.[132] The defense had warned that weaving "various descriptions of treason" into a system contorted resistance to executing a law into a violent act compelling Congress to repeal a law.[133] Paterson saw no harm in the construction. Rather, he placed Mitchell in scenes related to the conspiracy and attack on General Neville's house and made Mitchell's appearance in arms at Braddock's Field, after the fact, by itself an overt act of treason "if his design was treasonable."[134] Whether the conspiracy at Couche's Fort was deemed treason or whether that conspiracy and the acts at Neville's house were considered one act, he argued, the accused would thereby still have been guilty.

The prisoner's presence at the assemblies before and after the events at Neville's house—rather than being present or having acted at the site where the violence occurred—was nevertheless the critical element of the prosecutor's case and the judge's charge. Being present at assemblies had implicated Mitchell in a conspiracy and rendered him an accomplice to an act of treason committed by another party, even if, as Paterson admitted, a base conspiracy by itself was not treason; still, where others "execute the plot" all are guilty.[135] Not only did assemblies play a large role in Mitchell's trial, but many of the failed indictments and numerous misdemeanor charges referred to seditious speech and symbolic speech associated with attending a meeting. For example, John Corbly was charged for his "expressions" at meetings and Herman Husband for reading an incendiary pamphlet.[136] The presence of several figures (John Barnet, Thomas Miller, Robert Philson, and Husband) at specific meetings (Couch's Fort, Braddock's Field, Parkinson's Ferry) was prominently remarked upon by Paterson in his bench notes.[137]

Reflecting the government's preoccupation with assemblies, not only as a form of organization but as a vehicle for crafting and expressing oppositional speech to undermine confidence in the government, the effect of Paterson's effort was twofold: to create a crime out of the right to assemble and petition for redress of grievances; and to allege a conspiracy between rebels who did not commit violent "outrages" but supported a common cause. An even more explicit signal occurred in an aside to the defense in *Mitchell* where Paterson asked counsel to address two considerations related to the assembly at Couch's Fort: "Whether the conspiracy to levy war at *Couche's Fort*, was not, in legal contemplation, an actual levying of war"; and "Whether the *proceedings* at General Neville's house were not a continuation of the act, which originated at *Couche's Fort*."[138] This unusual and direct assignment exposed a preoccupation of the trials as a whole. That is, if charges of treasonous assembly and speech proved unsuccessful in indicting and trying the rebels, they might contribute to a charge of levying war, which was a proper constitutional standard for treason.

Just as the rights of assembly and speech were implicated in *Mitchell*, so was the right of a local militia, which constituted the operational arm of the rebellion, to bear arms. Here Paterson and Rawle shared a convenient strategy. It worked in two ways: attacking the militia undermined the right to assemble; attacking the assemblies neutered the right to an armed militia. What could not be successfully attacked was the right to bear arms, though Paterson's bench notes for *Porter* indicate that if Federalist judges could have done so, they would have. There were several complicating factors. One was that the militia musters were a customary practice tied to local democracy. Another was that several of the assemblies were actual extensions of militia musters—Mingo Creek, Couch's Fort, and Braddock's Field—and the militia remained tied to assemblies throughout the rebellion; John Hamilton's Mingo Creek militia was, for example, responsible for the destruction at Bower Hill.[139] Yet a third complication was the connection between the Mingo Creek militia and the Mingo Creek Democratic Society, which was formed by militia members many of whom participated in the assemblies.

Thus, when the prosecution made a case for treason based on a posture of war or the people being armed, as Paterson's bench notes clearly indicate, it not only went against common usage but it transgressed a right that was beyond dispute, a property right zealously guarded.[140] Depending on common law precedents such as those that prosecutor Rawle indicated in *Mitchell* ("raising a body of men," "an assembly armed and arrayed," "they affected the military forms") and Justice Paterson emphasized in his *Porter* notes ("stand to their arms," "generally armed," "appeared to have command") represented an indictment of the militia and the commonly accepted right to bear arms.[141] The very language, rituals, and gestures, the very forms of militia organization—majors commanding battalions and captains their companies—were necessary to create the appearance of war demanded by a charge of treason. But they were also an integral part of a self-defense tradition on the frontier. This was the horns of a dilemma on which the prosecution was stuck. As defense witness testimony in *Porter* demonstrated, the rebels themselves were torn over attending assemblies: Should they obey a call to join their unit or risk being delinquent; should they wear their "military accoutrements" or not? Officers were conflicted over whether to issue "regular militia orders" or to refuse, like Porter, to take command of their troops. As a result, charging treason for levying war was bound to be a hard sell to a common man jury. It raised too many conflicting feelings, making an attack on arms and militia less a weapon than a liability, as the directed verdict to dismiss in *Porter* would demonstrate.

Paterson's Bench Notes

Mitchell and *Vigol* gave the government the only wins it would get in the treason trials, which largely explains the dearth of law reports for rebellion cases. But there were four other substantive accounts of the rebel trials. Three of them dealt with treason charges (*Porter*, *Barnet*, and *Miller*) and one with a misdemeanor (*Philson and Husband*).[142] None of these trials resulted in convictions, and Paterson's bench notes (which exist only in manuscript) were not used in law reports or otherwise published; the bench notes have, consequently, gone unnoticed. That they are being analyzed here for the first time both deepens our understanding of how the Whiskey Rebellion trials were conducted and substantially expands the number of cases open to examination. In providing the actual testimony offered by witnesses, they elucidate the importance of establishing the facts to complement legal arguments made in the law reports, where such testimony is non-existent.

Of even greater consequence, they provide insights into Paterson's process in drawing conclusions about the cases, a matter of some interest given the importance of his role in the trials. Because the notes have yet to be studied and because they expand the number of cases now available to us, Paterson's bench notes are examined in some detail. It will then become possible to answer with greater confidence the question posed about Paterson in the previous chapter. That is, we can determine whether the common view that he was a partisan judge stands up to scrutiny in the face of what we learned in the preceding chapter of his judicial principles, theory of government, and views on the welfare of the Union together with a fuller assessment of his conduct in the trials.

Paterson's bench notes were taken in the midst of the trials, so that, of necessity, they were selective and incomplete. Nonetheless, Paterson's habit of making marginal notes and marks as well as sidelining and underlining testimony reveal much about his predispositions in handling the cases and his application of common law. Only *Barnet* includes counsels' opening and closing arguments and the judge's charge to the jury, so that the bench notes largely express an unmediated view of the judge's in-the-moment reaction to the trials through the testimony he transcribed and his emphases. The fact patterns that emerge create a unique picture compared with jury charges and legal arguments, particularly in the cases that cover the attack on Neville's house (*Barnet*, *Porter*, and *Miller*),[143] which supplement the law report version of that critical event in *Mitchell*.

The notes are from twelve to thirty-two manuscript pages in length: *Porter* (sixteen), *Miller* (seventeen), *Barnet* (thirty), and *Philson and Husband* (thirty-two). The trials include testimony that ranges from twelve to thirty witnesses: *Porter* (twelve prosecution witnesses, no defense was offered); *Miller* (thirteen prosecution witnesses, two defense); *Barnet* (nine prosecution witnesses, four defense); and *Philson and Husband* (ten prosecution witnesses, twenty defense).[144] In the misdemeanor trial, the number of defense witnesses outnumber prosecution witnesses two to one, and yet the number of manuscript pages devoted to the prosecution was two and a half times that of the defense. In *Miller*, prosecution witnesses exhausted seven times as many pages of testimony as defense witnesses and in *Barnet* eight times as many, suggesting that Paterson was significantly more attentive to the prosecution case in the treason trials (justified by the seriousness of proving a death penalty case) than to the defendant's case. Jurors appear to have disagreed with Paterson on the value of the prosecution witnesses and the judge's charge in *Barnet* (where he argued that the accused was guilty) as they acquitted in both that case and in *Miller*. One could argue that Paterson's inattentiveness to defense witnesses in *Miller* was a function of his having concluded that the prosecution failed to make its case, as in *Porter*, where there was no charge to answer, and in the *Philson and Husband* misdemeanor case, which was dismissed. Another consideration was the difficulty of procuring witnesses from the western end of the state, considering the distance and that many were afraid to testify for fear of being associated with the rebellion. More immediately, the appropriation of turncoat rebels who bought themselves relief by testifying for the prosecution (two in *Porter*, four in *Miller*, and one in *Barnet*) compromised much of the testimony.

Paterson's notetaking indicates that the judge made a concerted effort to exercise judicial restraint in his handling of the trials. He did his own summaries of individual testimony, witness by witness, and marked his text in a variety of ways, a sign that he reread his summaries more than once and re-emphasized testimony that struck him as significant. He placed a sideline alongside testimony to pick out material that interested him, that clarified events, or that he wanted to focus on. In many instances, he appeared to be creating a file of evidence that painted a picture of events. He isolated items with potential legal significance such as intent, planning, conspiracy, buying and selling arms, and the conduct of assemblies; he noted the presence in assemblies of slogan-bearing flags, proposals, and petitions, as well as public readings of papers, pamphlets, or jury charges; and he detected the logistics of calling and organizing meetings, marches, and assaults. Finally, he preserved evidence of character, provocation, or coercion, as well as the assertion of individual rights and religious or political beliefs. His summaries of testimony were much like a historical chronicle as they produced substantive material but lacked shape or coherence. The sidelining minimized the amount of material he needed to account for, but it was still largely informative and contextual, indicating but not clearly delineating the judge's thinking.

Peterson's highlighted material honed and focused his understanding of events, sometimes within the sidelined text and at other times as stand-alone underlining, as if to note items he might have originally missed or wanted to isolate. The underlining put the sidelining in context and kept track of items that Paterson wished to follow, including details of importance (wounds, ammunition needs, presence of spectators) and incriminating notifications and letters (to mobilize forces or to direct conduct). He identified characterizing psychology (character traits that mitigated or incriminated the accused's conduct) and commitments made or reinforced (which indicated the level of involvement). He demonstrated not merely attention to details of fact but also of human psychology and legal requirements, showing a significantly stronger sense of the complexity of rebel activity than the limited picture provided by law reports of the trials.

In his margin notes, Paterson narrowed the material he had identified. He made notes to himself on rebel drunkenness, exasperation, purposeful actions, and demands for the resignation of officials together with notes memorializing their support for peace and constitutional remedies, protection of captives and property, and actions that provoked them. Finally, a limited number of items were marked with an X or double-marked (for example, an underlined note in the margin) to garner special attention. These constituted an emphatic form of reference potentially identifying criteria to be addressed in a charge to the jury. Thus, the judge referenced the prisoner being present at the edge of a site where violence occurred; he identified members of the mob as terrified rather than terrifying (indicating they were coerced); he referred to the agitator Tom the Tinker as not many men but one man (limiting general culpability). Paterson allowed that buying and selling arms was much spoken of, but that such talk was common practice (mitigating the threat of being armed) and noted that persons and property were not meant to be hurt (speaking to intent). As to accomplices, Paterson noted that whatever capacity one served still made one part of a whole (for the purpose of conspiracy or treason) and that defendants had committed themselves to be present as part of the whole (speaking to intent and making common cause).

The detailed consideration Paterson gave to his bench notes suggests, in total, that he was a conscientious jurist intent on attending to the facts without prejudging or prejudicing a case. That his bench notes for the four trials never appeared in law reports and yet survived indicates that while they were personal notes not open to general scrutiny by the legal community, they might have been among those materials that judges commonly shared with colleagues to compensate for the irregular appearance of law reports. Whatever else, his notes reveal a judge who was scrupulous in his approach to trial testimony and who appeared to value his judicial independence over rote adherence to legal technicalities or precedents, relying heavily on a judge's discretion. They reveal as well, an approach to trial law that kept close to the facts and what one could infer from them, something we saw in his grand jury charges in chapter 4 and his trial work in *Mitchell*. As we shall see further in his bench notes, Paterson's idiographic approach in the bench notes lacked an explanatory framework or a clear legal rule, proceeding by inferring intention from the facts and generating his legal standard by assembling actions to create a fact pattern (a form of enumerative induction comparing fact situations). His process was inherently a descriptive effort to aggregate acts until they reached a perceived critical mass rather than an application of a legal rule. The bench notes thus provide a portrait of Paterson antithetical to Dallas's picture in the law reports. As an addendum to the law reports, they offer a unique perspective into his working process and insight into his sense of basic fairness.

UNITED STATES V. PORTER

United States v. Porter (May 18, 1795), was the first treason case to be tried. Porter, who had been an officer in the Revolution, later commanded a militia company on the frontier against the Indians, which led to his being accused of involvement in the rebellion. His greatest sin was that he neglected to sign the amnesty, because, as he said, he had not done anything for which he would have been liable. He nevertheless gave himself up to the federal militia, having heard he was accused by someone named Pollock of being an insurgent. Pollock, a drunkard, was dismissed as a witness as he had no support for his accusation, though Porter was still required to answer to the charge. Two other men who presumed to have evidence never appeared at the trial as witnesses.[145]

The trial ended in an acquittal that embarrassed the prosecution and persuaded it to change its trial strategy;[146] that change resulted in convictions in the next two treason cases, *Vigol* and *Mitchell*. There were several reports of Porter's trial, in different formats. Two short versions appeared: extracts from the defendant's journal and Dallas's law report of the trial.[147] The most extensive sources for *Porter* are two sets of bench notes (one is eight manuscript pages and the second sixteen), in different hands. The longer of the two is consistent with Paterson's characteristic format (a longer, narrow strip of testimony with a deeply indented left margin in which witnesses' names appeared and any handwritten comments) and in his handwriting (the writing is similar to the bench notes for other cases); but it does not use the markings that typically appear in the other bench notes. Witness testimony is lengthier and more detailed in the longer version, which references physical evidence (flags, messages, a proclamation, processes, papers, and an affidavit) but does not mention assembly minutes, resolutions, or petitions. As in Paterson's other transcripts, the testimony yields fact patterns but no analysis and few legal citations, while the legal approach relies on common law, rather than constitutional or statutory law. In both the longer and the shorter, truncated version, a prosecution statement by William Rawle is provided, though of different lengths, and the judge does not sum up the case but directs the jury to acquit.

The differences between the two transcripts serve as an exemplary lesson in framing events in trial accounts. The relative weight the bench notes give to the testimony of different witnesses and the omissions tell different stories of the trial. In what we can take to be Paterson's version, for example, David Lewis (the first and longest testimony for the prosecution) was treated as the most critical witness at one hundred seventy-one lines; in the reduced version, his testimony was cut to a mere sixty-five lines, while John Baldwin was cut from thirty-two lines to a modest thirteen lines, diminishing the relative importance of the two witnesses.[148] Moreover, cuts in Lewis's testimony shielded the testimony of turncoat witnesses David Phillips and David Hamilton. Apparent discomfort with the use of turncoat testimony was supported by the insignificant length of testimony for two other turncoats, Arthur Gardner and George Parker, and the fact that turncoat John Holcroft did not testify as a witness, even though he was present at the events at Neville's house and was suspected of being the infamous Tom the Tinker.[149]

Neither did the shorter *Porter* version align with the longer transcript in the accuracy or detail of its reporting. More clearly focused, it suggests the hand of a reporter creating a purposeful narrative. It has all the earmarks of a clerk's scaled-down version as it is more legible and omits considerable strategic material that would be of interest to a jurist. Witnesses are framed in the third person and their testimony is treated more like a straightforward narrative. The text reads as if it was written at leisure and as a synopsis of original notes rather than notes taken down in the moment. The reduced version does not, as a result, appear to be useful as a basis for a charge to a jury or as a draft for a trial report, but possibly for shopping around to a newspaper. Prosecutor Rawle's statement in the shorter version, for example, reads in toto "the law itself decides how it is to be enforced, or changed—if necessary." By comparison, the longer version opens with, "To decide not by their feelings as men but by their duty as citizens. The law decides." It then goes on to cite the endeavor "by numbers and with force to prevent the execution of a law, or to procure its repeal" and the "necessity of submission to the United will of the community." The statement continues with details of the establishment of offices, rebel meetings, and the attacks on officials, noting, as well, the circular letter convening a rebel meeting at Braddock's Field and the proclamation issued by the president that set the government's terms with which the "prisoner at the bar" did not comply.

In general, the reduced version's framing of events reflected the government narrative in diminishing mitigating factors and steering the text in the direction of the rebels' contempt for authority. It underplayed the flags, proposals, and messages that went back and forth at Neville's house and the "friendly interference" of the rebels in protecting their captives. Reductions diminished Porter's indecision, his refusal to order his men to join the attack, his efforts to distance himself from events, and the coercive effect of the crowd on individuals who were reluctant to join rebel activities. The inadequacy of the evidence used to convict Porter was, however, reported, as was the lack of proof by two witnesses to a single act.

Porter's journal extracts were entirely different in tone from the transcripts. More expansive in defense of the accused, the journal claimed that a rebel named Pollock, a drunkard, busied himself in branding Porter an insurgent. While Pollock's motives were spiteful and he had no proof of his charges, Porter was compelled to face trial, "as something might turn up yet to implicate him in the insurrection," according to a colonel Campbell. Campbell was not called to testify for the prosecution. Two other men, from Pittsburgh, were said to have evidence, which Porter considered a subterfuge as they never appeared to testify.[150] Witnesses did, however, testify that Porter was at Neville's house; it appeared that Porter's command of a militia company supplied a "circumstance against him." John McDonald testified that he "[s]aw Porter at Couch's fort, was on a stump, had an instrument of writing [addressed 'From the citizens west of the Alleghany mountains to General Neville'] and was reading it to the people." It demanded that Neville withdraw from acting as a tax collector. Porter refused, however, to join in armed resistance, nor would he sign the amnesty, on the claim that he was not conscious of having acted against the government.[151]

At the close of the trial, Porter's journal recounted, defense counsel William Lewis and Joseph Thomas declined "to examine a single witness for the defense, so groundless was the prosecution"; Rawle declared himself satisfied upon examining twelve substantial witnesses. It went on to relate that both sides agreed the judge might charge the jury without any further comment. Judge Paterson proceeded to direct the jury that the charge against Porter "has not been supported by one single evidence. The court is of the opinion that he is not guilty. You will, therefore, show mercy on the favorable side"; without leaving the box, "the jury made a bow, and in one or two minutes" agreed Porter was not guilty.[152] On this point, Dallas's abbreviated law report added that the jury found Porter had not taken part in the insurrection and was not, in fact, "the person liable to the charge, but another person of the same name."[153] Paterson's transcript simply noted there was "[n]o summing up. The court charged the jury to acquit the prisoner."

The loss of a case on a lack of evidence, despite a substantial number of witnesses, was not to be repeated in the next two cases (*Mitchell* and *Vigol*), though in *Vigol*, as in *Porter*, the case was submitted to the jury without argument by mutual agreement of defense counsel and the prosecution. In *Vigol* and *Mitchell*, however, the judge and the prosecution had agreed on an interpretation of the Constitution's two-witness standard that would ensure the conviction of both defendants.

UNITED STATES V. BARNET

United States v. Barnet (May 29, 1795), the most complicated of the treason trials for which Paterson provided bench notes, was tried after the convictions in *Vigol* and *Mitchell*. Gallatin considered Barnet "as guilty as Mitchell who has been condemned," allowing that "there were not sufficient legal proofs against either."[154] Paterson's notes included his jury charge as well as a brief indication of the arguments by Lewis and Rawle. Here, Paterson began marking his text to highlight critical events or his perspective on them, creating a narrative of events. The narrative emphasized that the rebel committee had not issued orders about arms but that it raised a combination of armed and unarmed men at Couch's Fort to go to Neville's house. Notice of an unsuccessful attack circulated calling for a second meeting at Couch's Fort to raise more men and decide what to do next. The first attack, intended to compel the surrender of the excise office, was deliberate, to which Inspector Neville's son, Colonel Presley Neville, testified. The younger Neville had been informed of it beforehand and had warned his father, who armed himself. The narrative, supported by the highlighted testimony, thus rebutted the argument that the rebels had merely responded to fire from the excise office and supported that the inspector was defending himself from a preplanned attack.

The *Barnet* bench-notes testimony drew a picture that spoke both for and against Barnet's having played a treasonable role. In Barnet's defense, a witness saw him at a distance from Neville's house unarmed and guarding the horses. Testimony revealed that he disapproved of burning Neville's house and refused to raise a liberty pole when approached to do so. Moreover, he had planned "to turn out for congress" to work on repealing the excise law; Paterson sidelined testimony that Barnet "was willing to turn out any day to support government." Paterson's margin mark identified prosecution testimony that the defendant's "conduct was for moderation and civility" and that he had spoken out against any harm being done to the marshal serving writs or to Neville. Witnesses also testified that Barnet had been seen at Braddock's Field with other rebels who were armed and marched as a military unit and that, importantly, he came "forward as a general spokesman ag.st signing" the submission. Once he surmised who might sign, he threatened "he would use it, as they were now in cond.n to know the Whig from the Tory," friend from foe. On the totality of evidence, Paterson could have used his discretion to treat Barnet's incendiary speech as words spoken in heat (like military array without a treasonable act); on the other hand, he could treat it as a levying of war by means of a questionable construction of treason.

With Vigol and Mitchell already convicted, Paterson indicated in his *Barnet* notes a greater attentiveness to the defense than the prosecution on what constituted the elements of treason and how they were to be connected; one and a half manuscript pages were reserved for Lewis compared with a mere thirty-three words for Rawle, though none of Lewis's argument was marked in any way. The notes on Lewis outlined a two-part argument. The first part asserted that the charges against Barnet were "[a] question of constructive treason." The notes then presented Lewis's conception of treason: it had to be "an offence ag. the sovereignty of a state—Apt to be pursued with keen ardor," presumably responding to Rawle's depiction of Barnet's conduct as menacing. What Lewis meant by state sovereignty followed: "If men combine to affect the alteration of governmental measures or to repeal a law, by force, it is treason." By this argument, going to Couch's Fort did not "amount to treason," though "a battle [was] not necessary."

Lewis's argument required that a full set of events—intention or predetermination, conspiracy, an array of war, an attack on state sovereignty, and an act to implement intention—was necessary to prove treason. The intention would have to include "a view to make war" pursuant to a previously determined common agreement. Marching to Neville's would have to flow from that intention and the acts intended ought to include the element of force; in the case of Couch's Fort, they had to implicate an attack on the government. Lewis argued that whereas treason required "1. A predetermination 2. A marching for war in consequence thereof,"[155] he was unwilling to concede that consultation and conspiracy were the same kind of act. Consultation did not indicate agreement, as conspiracy did, with the implication that Lewis did not concede to there being a conspiracy, or even a common cause, at Couch's Fort. If, however, "the party determined at Couch's to proceed to Neville's to compel him by force, or to intimidate him by numbers to resign his office, then all [were] guilty of treason." Convicting Barnet, based on Lewis's propositions, would require a chain of events with each link proved to be true, common agreement among the parties to a purpose (a particular "intention of design"), and general participation in that purpose. The jury appears to have found Lewis persuasive, as it acquitted Barnet.

Paterson's charge offered a contrary set of insights into the case and the analysis he felt the jury ought to be guided by. As background to his charge, the bench notes emphasized a sense of chaos. Brackenridge, a witness for the defense (in testimony sidelined by Paterson), offered that it was generally held "there was a revolution and no law in force." Paterson underlined that it was "not the terrifying people [who] made the mob" but those who were terrified. Second, the judge discounted any possibility that an overt act was necessary on the part of the accused. As Rawle had construed and Paterson wrote in a margin note, Barnet was not absolved by his role as a horse guard at Neville's: "different duties required of different persons," he wrote, indicating that it was all part of a common cause. Paterson also made a margin note ("on the general purpose, he is guilty") on Rawle's construction of intent, by means of which the defendant was guilty if he was "concerned in carrying [on] the general purpose."

While seventeen pages were devoted to prosecution witnesses and two pages to defense witnesses, Paterson's charge to the jury took up eight pages or almost 30 percent of the *Barnet* manuscript. He divided the charge into facts and intention and thereafter subdivided intention "into a general and a particular intention of design—The general intention goes hand in hand with the facts." Without citing a single authority on the law (his notes on Lewis had citations from Foster, Hale, and Blackstone, whereas his notes on Rawle had no citations), the charge relied on what Paterson referred to as harmonizing the facts and inferences regarding intention, from which "the law arises."[156] This approach was consistent with Paterson's trial jury charge in *Vigol* and his approach to indictments in his May grand jury charge.

In his discussion of facts, Paterson detailed a process at Couch's Fort that included gathering there and appointing a committee for the purpose of drawing up a paper for Neville to sign ("that he should resign his com.n, no longer executed his office of inspection, and give up his papers relating to the same"). This was followed by the attendees approving the resolution, proceeding to Neville's, and tarrying at Painter's Run to case bullets. Subsequently, the party obtained "a little more regularity in their line of march, but still not under very good command." On these grounds, Paterson charged the jury that the rebels knew the object of the visit to Neville's and had marched there with intent to use force as many were "offended" by the marshal (Lenox) serving process and were "exasperated" at Neville acting as his guide.

Paterson's recounting of the events at Neville's depicted a body of men "drawn up in military form and array, each company under the command of its respective officers." Negotiations commenced and a message was sent to the house, followed by "a 2.d and 3.d message or flag." The response "not being satisfactory, an attack was concluded upon." Paterson cited one witness's remarks: "To battle—and for what—why to compel a compliance with the paper" demanding Neville's resignation. Led by James McFarland, the party "commenced upon the house." The charge made no mention of the party acting in self-defense or of shots being fired from inside the house to precipitate the rebel action. Thus, Paterson simplified the fact pattern to claim that the intention behind the march was "clear and uncontestable"; it was to compel, to intimidate by numbers, to force Neville "to resign his office, and to surrender his papers respecting the same." Indeed, a margin note specified that all were guilty, "whether as watchmen, as guards, or in any other capacity." Concluding his notes on the general design, a margin note read, "on the general purpose, he [Barnet] is guilty."

Having dispatched facts and intention regarding the party as a whole and Barnet as a part of the whole, Paterson moved to "the particular case of the p.r at the bar; and to examine how far he was traitorously concerned." Here, he directed the jury to the "mind" of the prisoner which "must be manifested by some overt act"; it was the jury's responsibility "to collect or infer the intention from the testimony laid before you" and to discover through some overt act the state of Barnet's mind and his individual intention. Paterson was clear that without conduct that indicates "a traitorous spirit or intention, he is not to be criminated." But if the jury believed Barnet knew the object of the rebels' actions and willingly aided them, "his guilt rises into treason." Barnet, he said, had to know that the rebels' object was either to intimidate or force Neville to resign, "to suppress the office of excise, to resist and prevent the execution of the law, or to procure its repeal by intimidation, by violence, by numbers, by an armed force." Paterson had provided the general grounds for Barnet's individual guilt as part of the party (presuming their acts were treasonous); Barnet's knowing concurrence (his mental state, an essential element of treason, whereby Barnet knowingly and willingly aiding the rebels) would make him guilty of treason as a part of the whole.

Paterson's pattern of facts painted a picture in which two acts constituted Barnet's guilt: levying war against the operation of the government (the excise office standing for the sovereignty of the state) and the intimidation of government officers conducting the government's business (the officers standing for the government and the intimidation for a general purpose against the government). In this regard, Paterson's margin notes pointed to the verdict he wished the jury to find: "The pr. was at Braddock's field and armed"; "He was active in warning others to go to the same place"; "All persons that went to Braddock's field and there appeared with arms, and marched in military array, in execution of a traitorous object or design, are guilty of treason."

Whereas his margin notes also considered that "[p]ersons or prisoner may have gone with good intent," Paterson's general pattern did not favor the possibility of a "good intent" so much as it sponsored the idea of Barnet's knowingly or willingly aiding the rebels' insurrectionary purpose. Importantly, if "the intention and the act" truly had to "concur" and the facts and the law had to harmonize (Paterson's analysis in *Mitchell* as well), weighing Barnet's "good intent" would have provided the jury an opportunity to acquit. That Paterson did not in fact mean to offer the jury such an option might be inferred from his argument in *Mitchell* that marching to Neville's was an overt act capable of standing for intention.[157]

On the other hand, under common law an act without purposeful intent was not treason just as purpose alone did not constitute a treasonous act.[158] These were lines of law with which Paterson was clearly familiar. Moreover, Paterson's jury charge had held that an "act" must make manifest the intent. Without reverting to constructive treason, marching in a common law "posture of war"[159] was not necessarily dispositive. The events could thereby qualify as riot as much as a levying of war. The collateral items of enlisting others, furnishing weapons, and casting bullets were not, furthermore, so much a levying of war as actions that qualified as "adhering to the enemy," a treasonable act with which Barnet was not charged. Equally, Paterson's charge presented acts (Barnet's conduct as a horse guard at Neville's and his "conduct at the day and place proposed for signing the submission paper") that suggested not all assembly, resistance, or disturbance was treason absent expansive constructions, which left a path for the jury to acquit. In fact, Barnet was acquitted.

UNITED STATES V. MILLER

Paterson's bench notes in *United States v. Miller* (June 1, 1795) were in many ways comparable to those of *Barnet*, in that they consistently set off testimony about the appurtenances of war and featured the facts without mediation by legal analysis. As in his charges for the grand jury and the *Vigol* and *Barnet* juries, Paterson's template was one in which fact concurred with intention. His process was to focus on fact patterns that fit common law examples of treasonous acts without noting or arguing the law; as in *Mitchell*, the law would follow the facts. In underlined testimony, Paterson emphasized the elements that were to prove crucial to his thinking: the attack against Neville's excise office, a general design to burn houses, threatened use of force, and opposition to the excise act. He was particularly focused on testimony concerning the violent events at Neville's house that exposed the determination of the rebels to meet, raise more men, and decide the next step after the failure of the first attack.

Following Rawle's statement that overt acts presented themselves in various guises, Paterson's bench notes reinforced a particular narrative about Miller: he was a man, armed, who held horses in a nearby field and was not present at the attack on Neville's house; nevertheless, he appeared the next day with a small wound on his neck (which Paterson underlined in two places in the testimony). He regarded Miller as part of a party that committed violence, even if he was not present and could not thereby have participated in an overt act himself. As in Rawle's argument in *Barnet*, since different parties performed different tasks in the overall effort Miller was an accomplice, though he was not charged as one. Testimony also showed that the rebels returned fire in self-defense once Neville's men began shooting and that most said they did not intend to fire and their arms were merely to frighten Neville. Still, their preparation in "running bullets" and their participation in a scheme to pay money for lead and to buy arms at Painter's Run were set off by a sideline in the bench notes, offsetting the exculpatory language that indicated lack of intent in overt acts of preparation. The notes ended without a charge by the judge and Miller was acquitted.

UNITED STATES V. PHILSON AND HUSBAND

In the last of the trials for which Paterson provided bench notes, *United States v. Philson and Husband* (June 3, 1795), the defendants were initially charged with a treasonable felony (an act with intent to commit treason),[160] which was returned *ignoramus* by the grand jury. They were subsequently charged with disturbing the peace, a misdemeanor under common law. The downgraded misdemeanor charge concerned "disorderly tumultuous assembly" conducted without "any of the ordinary shew and apparatus of war," as distinguished from an insurrection that had an appearance of an army (the latter described the content of the *Miller* and *Barnet* trials).[161] Whereas

Philson and Husband were not tried for treason, the government's use of lesser charges to curtail individual liberty rights (particularly speech acts and by implication the right of assembly) by charging them as treason deserves attention. *Philson and Husband* provides the most prominent instance of such cases.

The more influential of the two defendants, Husband, was a leader and political thinker in the 1760s North Carolina Regulators—a popular democratic movement that agitated against government abuses. A radical democrat, he wrote fiery political and religious pamphlets about a New Jerusalem and was such an inciting figure for his incendiary petitions to the legislature and pamphlets read at assemblies that Washington demanded his name be withheld from the list of those who were to be amnestied in the Whiskey Rebellion.[162] Husband was reported in the trial to have encouraged "the people [. . .] to petition in a vigorous manner"; Philson, too, "insisted upon petitioning" and proposed that those attending assemblies "should sign a petition for a new convention." Paterson underlined as well liberty pole inscriptions that recalled the revolution against Great Britain ("liberty and no excise," "united we stand, divided we fall") and that were meant to incite the rebels. He sidelined Husband's spoken words openly attacking President Washington and his administration (recorded three times in witness testimonies), which called them "a gang of horse thieves" and warned that if the militia was called out "God damn you, I will fight you."[163] He sidelined as well testimony reporting that Husband had written about the president "ruling with an iron rod" and that Congress imposed more laws than England ever did. Philson was said to have read a paper at Parkinson's Ferry that called for a "convention to form a new const.n" or to make amendments, which Paterson also sidelined. Other sidelined testimony revealed that Philson felt submitting to the government meant withdrawing all support and friendship from the people, who ought to be assisted. What appeared to be the greatest threat of such speech was its ability to generate agreement on a common cause and to incite armed activity. Noting the connection, Paterson sidelined as well as marked in the margin testimony that identified Philson as a storekeeper who sold rifles. This testimony specified his actions as buying, selling, and providing arms and ammunition, conduct that was nevertheless prevalent among storekeepers in the backwoods where ownership of arms was considered a common right.

Paterson's markings in this case tended to be highly selective. While he sidelined mitigating testimony where Philson said that standing against the government would ruin the country and that the destruction of property was "a very ill done thing and [those who did so] ought to suffer for it," he did so only once even though such testimony permeated the notes. Among other testimony Paterson did not mark, witnesses generally supported Philson and Husband for focusing on the conduct of meetings: representation by committees, running for elected office, speaking against the use of force, and of course writing petitions and reading papers and pamphlets. Husband, for example, was reported to say of the burning of Neville's house that "if they could resist and overpower govrn. Then there would be no security at home, and they w.d be left without protection. Whatever was the will of the people right to be the law of the land." Philson, according to testimony, consistently avowed "none but const.l measures should be pursued," while Husband was acknowledged to have said "opposition to govern.t—but meant const.l measures." Testimony routinely reported that the defendants stated they would only join those who were for peace and that the rebels, while denying they were a mob, would tar and feather any who said they were. Once more, the jury was convinced that the evidence did not call for a conviction; both men were acquitted.

In sum, Paterson's pragmatics in his bench notes were not the result of abstract principles and precedents; they represented the working process of a judge faced with the immediate needs of a high-profile series of trials. Paterson's transcription and markings were meant for him alone, so that they show the jurist working hands-on and in the moment, presenting us with unique insights that law reports are unable to provide into how a judge might actually work. Because the pragmatics of presiding over a trial are less performative than charging a grand jury, the judge's bench notes did not express the same educative relationship with its audience of jurors, nor did they anticipate a jurors' statement to encourage publication of a charge. Overall, Peterson's transcription of trial testimony appears, in the first instance, to have been faithful to what witnesses actually said. He followed by editorializing about the text through his markings. The mechanics Paterson utilized to apply the law were not evident in legal principles but in the facts of the case and the patterns they formed. Nor were they untethered from a theory of governance (as in the grand jury charges) or political ideology (like the government narrative).

The predominance of prosecution over defense testimony, the relative weight given to certain witnesses, and the selective marking of testimony in Paterson's bench notes appear to be related to determining whether the prosecution made its case on the facts. A certain rigidity, however, arose from his process. His preoccupation with common law instances of treason fit testimony into categories and patterns based on themes like common agreement among the rebels, forceful interference with official acts, and the formation of bodies of armed men. He was alert to the practical details of holding meetings, large numbers of people, and communications as well as contempt for authority, state of mind, conspiracy, and predetermination in deciding intent and overt acts. Paterson's working process created a narrative of events out of such evidence, noting mitigating factors within a patchwork system of common law, constructive treason, and judicial discretion. It was sufficient in the end that acts of varying kinds aggregate to a plausible act of violence whether they connected to levying war or whether individuals truly intended to become a viable part of some larger culpable whole. What is not evident is a judge who thoughtlessly or narrowly prejudged the facts or imposed a procrustean mold on trial testimony. Indeed, what the notes most clearly evidence is a judge whose engagement with the facts belies the pretense that juries were tasked with deciding the facts and judges with charging them on the law. Rather, Paterson reflected the mixed, if residual, modality in the late eighteenth-century of a courtroom in which those functions were still not clearly divided and the judge continued to play both jury and judge.

Postscript

As a postscript to this discussion of Paterson's bench notes and taking into account his grand jury and trial jury charges, his Supreme Court opinion in *Vanhorne*, and his report to the president on the *Mitchell* and *Vigol* cases, we can return with greater finality to the question of his potentially partisan conduct in the trials. We need to do so, however, with some sense of the context in which he had to operate. Paterson and his contemporaries were deeply concerned that a combination of internal and external enemies was poised to destroy the Union. Not only the democratic-republican societies, the Indian wars, and the Shays's and Whiskey Rebellions, but the irresolvable international conflict between Britain and France converged to threaten the new nation-state. Paterson's cognizance of this combination of forces was reflected in his Horatius essays in October 1795.[164] The essays were the culmination of events initiated in early 1795 by U.S. Supreme Court chief justice John Jay's negotiation of a treaty with Britain. The furor over the treaty erupted in March when details were publicly leaked, just as the trials were about to begin.[165] Public assemblies, protests, and libelous attacks such as those that incited the Whiskey Rebellion were aimed at preventing the government from signing the Jay Treaty, leading Paterson in one of the essays to acknowledge the right to public assembly while attributing assemblies themselves to the effects of summer sunstroke, disordered brains, and hallucinations.[166] The partisan politics that threatened the stability of the nation were, however, his larger worry. He recognized in the treaty protests a rejection of government authority and in the French Revolution a move to overthrow the elite in power that correlated with the Whiskey Rebellion. Envy of one's superiors and unthinking partisanship were the same forces Paterson struggled with in the May and June trials.[167] It was a short step to conclude that legal action to prevent rebellion was justified against opponents who disrupted society and sought popularity by vilifying others and undermining the republic.

With the advantage of his Horatius essays, it is difficult to relegate Paterson to the status of an ill-tempered partisan who arbitrarily held the line on Federalism or of a jurist gone bad who betrayed his characteristically thoughtful and temperate self. Rather, Paterson navigated the judicial community of which he was a part by applying what he believed was a reasonable jurisprudence in the face of formidable national forces, significant and unresolved state and federal conflicts, and international interests pulling America in diametrically opposed directions. Although his grand jury and trial charges were intermittently emotional and reactive, Paterson typically expressed principled positions as a judge. Those principles underpinned Paterson's rejection of Peters's irascible charge in *United States v. Insurgents* and his choice of a procedural resolution that walked back the promotion of state power at the expense of individual liberty; and they explained his treatment of rebel procedural rights in *United States v. Hamilton* where he exhibited judicial restraint and reasonableness. Still, his general inclination as a Federalist judge was to interpret constitutional law through established common law and constructivist reasoning based in English rules, doctrines, and precedents as it was understood at the time. In his jurisprudence, this meant respecting history and tradition as it was rooted in custom and precedents commonly applied in American courts. Paterson's analysis in his jury charges was, by this argument, closely aligned with a mainstream Federalist theory of government and the Constitution and tied to the common law rather than common logic or party politics.

As for Paterson personally, his performance in the trials neither exonerated him from serious criticism nor condemned him. This does not mean he was ambivalent about the criticism leveled at him. In fact, in the aftermath to the trials he became defensive about Republican objections to his performance, which partly explains the dismissive, almost ungracious tone of his report to President Washington.[168] It is apparent in his report to the president, if merely suggested elsewhere, that Paterson was confident about taking a common law, constructivist approach to the trials and that he was certain of his own rectitude in the part he played. The two men he sentenced might thereafter have been pardoned, but Paterson had the example of the Revolution before him; there, treason trials set examples while juries petitioned for clemency and reprieves followed.[169] Paterson did not question whether he had acted properly or whether justice could be said to have been done.[170] In the end, he did not look back to re-examine his jurisprudence or his politics. This does not mean that history was on his side, as we shall discover in the next chapter in considering Justice Marshall's veiled criticism in the 1807 *Burr* trial of Paterson's jurisprudence.

Conclusion

Studies of the rebellion suggest there was a wholesale association of the judicial narrative with the government's obsession with punishing the rebels. In truth, the assumption they were coterminous simplifies the statement generated by grand jury charges and the expanded view of the trials offered in the present study. Overall, the Whiskey Rebellion trials represented a test of how and for whom the early republic's courts should work. Several aspects of the system conduced to a privilege for the prosecution, for the eastern establishment, and for the government and the elite. This included obfuscation of constitutional law in the charges, priority given to the inconvenience of the prosecution, and inadequate concern for the terrible finality of a capital sentence. The lack of access to jurors and witnesses from the vicinity of the crime and the distance of the court from where the acts took place produced a decontextualized narrative isolated in a system in which the technical niceties of professionalized discourse displaced the real consequences for dislocated figures. Problematically, the judiciary's Federalist perspective reinforced that of the prosecution to enable further legal distortions. Acts elevated to a plane of generality essentialized the law applied in the trials, while judicial constructions created the impression of a system-wide threat victimizing government officials; at the same time, they obviated the responsibility of government to balance the rights of its citizens with the security of the state. The judicial narrative, in this sense, can best be described as underdetermined and open to a preference for authoritative voices.

Considering the trials more directly, they might be regarded as closed books (given the comparative uniformity of judicial analysis) or as closet dramas (given judicial adherence to the precedential value of the verdicts). They did not tell a story that had collective buy-in from the public or that reached much beyond its narrowly intended audience of professional jurists, friends of the elite, and the federal government. But in the end, the number of ignoramus bills of indictment and failed convictions disrupted the ability of the judiciary to dominate the final chapter of the insurrection. Just as English common law was being displaced to create an American legal culture, so too was the Federalist judicial narrative revealing its fault lines. The coherence that tied together themes of order and stability at the macro level of grand jury charges was not recursively repeated at the micro level of trial bench notes. In the trenches of the jury trial, Hayden White's discussion of chronicles comes back to haunt us, for facts alone cannot tell a story.[171] Induction may have utility value in common law reasoning, but it does not identify a significant underlying principle that can also account for differences; to derive a rule from a case by inductive inference and use it as authority revealed itself to be a flawed process.[172] From the juror's perspective, the effort to reduce a number of testamentary voices to a single thread exposed itself as a fool's errand. Equally, the lack of explanatory legal reasoning in preference to fact patterns left jurors adrift in the search for meaning. What we are experiencing is the collapse of a master narrative in the story of the trials. If the government narrative carried off a hegemonic telling, and the Federalist grand jury narrative remained persuasive as a tale of strong central government, the trials themselves proved fragmented and unconvincing. The judicial construction lacked sufficient coherence to command acceptance as a common reading that was both satisfying and apparently necessary. It remained for a rebel defense to fill out the story by supplying an alternative construction of the insurrection that authorized insurgency.

Another way of gauging the relative persuasiveness of the judicial narrative is to consider the public reaction and that of the trial juries that convicted Mitchell and Vigol. The struggle to twist constitutional law into a common law pretzel, as in *Mitchell*, worked only so far as it achieved token convictions. But public discomfort with the two death penalty verdicts led to a campaign to pardon Mitchell and Vigol that destabilized even this tentative coherence. The pardon campaign undermined the ability of the courts to secure the support of the public for the verdicts. Clergy of the Lutheran and German Reformed churches led petition drives, and citizens of the Grand Inquest for the City of Philadelphia as well as the jury of the *Vigol* trial appealed for mercy. One anonymous suppliant, "Incog.," called on the president as the only man on earth who could restore these men to their families. May "*He* who has made his angels encamp around you and I," the writer beseeched, lead the president to that joyful approbation, "Well done good and faithful servant."[173] Influenced by William Bradford's pamphlet against the death penalty and subsequent legislative reform, ministers Henry Helmuth and William Hendel forwarded as many as 264 names, including those of the grand jury that indicted and the petite juries that convicted Mitchell and Vigol, on four petitions asking the president not to carry the death sentences into effect.[174] Two *Vigol* petitions argued that Pennsylvania had led the way in improving the penal laws but that the United States had "not yet arrived to an equal degree of perfection."[175]

While the jurors claimed that their oaths and the letter of the law bound them to convict Vigol, they found the case "a hard one" for which he should not "forfeit his life." The Constitution, they entreated, gave the president the power to correct such hardships. Citizens of the Grand Inquest, while pleased by restoration of the law, asked that the chapter "be fully closed" without the loss of two more lives; two more deaths would not make the community any more remorseful or strengthen its security against such crimes in the future.[176] The general sentiment of the campaign, in the words of citizens of Philadelphia, was that suppression of the recent rebellion rendered "public examples of justice unnecessary." As God's goodness had foregone Washington's use of "the military sword," so ought the president show his gratitude by withholding "the Sword of the Law."[177]

The two men were reprieved in June and pardoned in November. In his address to Congress, Washington celebrated the auspicious "Providence" which the nation enjoyed and he engaged to preserve. Here he inserted a draft paragraph that John Jay had crafted to extend clemency and pardon. The scene of insurrection was now tranquil and the "misled have abandoned their Errors," it read; exercising the president's constitutional powers was a sacred duty, permitting "every degree of moderation and tenderness which the national justice, dignity, and safety may permit."[178]

While the president's words in his address to Congress were intended to close the book on the rebel trials, to fully complete that story one voice remains to be heard: the rebel defense. Recognizing that the treason trials have not received the kind of in-depth research they deserve and that the defense of the accused has never been properly foregrounded, the rebel voice is recovered here in the final chapter. The statement made by defense notes constitutes a remarkably thoughtful conclusion to the story of the first clash in the new democracy between those with the power to govern and those who must agree to be governed under a democratic constitution. In terms of pulling together the storyline of the present study, the rebel defense offers us the proper complement to the rebel assemblies' assertion of a rights-based vision for rebellion. It does so through its attention to volitional allegiance and to the subjectivity and agency guaranteed by the rights granted in the grand democratic experiment produced by the Revolution. The defense notes preserve, for good or ill, an argument for the protection of participatory democracy as it was interpreted in the backcountry.

CHAPTER 6

A Rebel Defense

Choosing to end the story of the trials with Washington's closing remarks would have left us with the impression of an orderly judicial narrative and a coherent legal culture in which a nationalizing Federalist representation overcame localism and popular democracy. Its exceptionalism reaffirmed, the country would have justified the blessings of providence to pursue its imperial destiny. But this construction failed to account for the inchoate nature of legal culture. More immediately, it glossed over the countervailing rebel defense. Giving history its due, this chapter fills the vacuum unaccountably left by these omissions by arguing that the rebel position represented a principled, if unruly, return to the country's revolutionary origins. The Revolution had justified the threat of secession by raising questions about the legitimacy of allegiance and the arbitrariness of government power that minimized individual rights. In their declared independence, the people asserted a right to choose a government from whose laws they benefited in return for their consent to be governed. The Whiskey Rebellion continued that legacy, undermining an inherited law dependent on a judge's discretion and common law constructions and refusing to sacrifice state sovereignty to the encroachments of federal law. The rebel position looked forward to a more representative American law that valued democratic participation and treasured individual rights over state power.

To argue its case, the defense, and indeed the prosecution, needed trained lawyers, which meant having access to legal literature, an organized law office, and admission to the bar.[1] But within that superficial picture, a legal profession had yet to be established. Bar associations existed largely as gatekeepers to keep the number of lawyers from expanding beyond a limited number, while lawyers constituted an elite guild or practice made up of groups of practitioners and political allies. Informal relations and shared legal understandings framed the social, political, and professional mutuality that developed within that small elite, a mutuality that thrived where a common body of law and legal sources was still fluid. Indeed, the organization of informal knowledge operated as part of a consensual community of law talk responsive to unofficial norms and practices and to formal ones at the same time. This world would change with the officialization of law reports and the publication of legal treatises, together with a later development of law schools and a legal profession in the nineteenth century; in the eighteenth century, however, the legal system operated as a self-organizing, self-reinforcing entity.[2]

The small circle of lawyers working in Philadelphia that supplied prosecutors, defense counsel, and judges for the county court, Pennsylvania Supreme Court, circuit court of eastern Pennsylvania, and U.S. Supreme Court constituted a group that had intimate knowledge of one another's work. They consulted with one another and shared information, sources, strategies, and notes of court cases, supporting one another reputationally as a confederation of practitioners both within their law offices and within rudimentary associations.[3] We find, for example, that lawyers prepared collected local cases in manuscript volumes that circulated among members of the bar, eleven having survived from 1792 to 1830 for the state of Delaware alone.[4] Many attended the law professorship lectures of James Wilson at the Philadelphia College, whose inaugural lecture in December 1790 was attended by President Washington and members of his administration, as well as members of the Pennsylvania state legislature, "together with a great number of ladies and gentlemen [. . .] the whole composing a most brilliant and respectable audience."[5] In the law courts, as well, lawyers and their apprentices joined gentlemen and the interested public in an occasion that was as much a social or political event as it was legal, resulting in an entertainment that joined spectacle to adversarial argument.

The state of the law was such that lawyers had little access to law reports, which only began to be officially published in 1789.[6] Those that were available were the work of entrepreneurs and appeared as poorly subscribed, selective, unreliable editions irregularly published.[7] In self-defense, lawyers kept notes on court findings and judicial preferences[8] to use when appearing before a given judge in a court case. Judges' notes were frequently mislaid or written on odd pieces of paper. They were often withheld from being reported, filed, or published, so that judges lacked accountability. In truth, some judges were embarrassed at their lack of knowledge of the law while others wished to retain possession of their intellectual property.[9] Commonly forgoing legal reasoning, judges maintained considerable discretion in their oral opinions, which loosely applied common law and were responsive to local practices and political contingencies.

In addition to trying to salvage notes from judges, prosecutors, and counsel for their law reports, law reporters transcribed directly from court proceedings. They "caught arguments on the fly," according to Hugh Henry Brackenridge, so that "the pen of the most ready writer, will not be able to keep pace [...] with the oral expression." The resulting text captured the rudiments of an opinion or charge but unavoidably omitted or misconceived essential content.[10] Connecticut court reporter Ephraim Kirby contended that early law reports served as poor precedents for future decisions since "every attempt by judges, to run the line of distinction between what was applicable and what not, proved abortive" while the principles behind decisions were often lost, misheard, or misrepresented: "Hence arose a confusion in the determination of our courts."[11] Alexander Dallas "found such miserable encouragement" for his law reports that he wished in the end "to call them all in, and devote them to the rats in the State-House." He considered it would have been better to commit them "to the *flames* instead of the *press*."[12] Law reports were, consequently, infrequently studied or cited by counsel who wanted guidance in American common law.[13] As a result (as we found in discussing grand jury charges in chapter 4 and as became evident in considering statutory law in chapter 5), the development and acceptance of doctrine that might have emanated from them was impeded and cases were largely received individually, underpinned by uncertain legal principles rather than a string of precedents.[14]

Regarding legal commentary, little was written about treason, not surprising in a country established by a revolution. Even James Wilson, author of the constitutional language on treason and a respected lecturer on the law, provided limited public interpretation. Moreover, there was no American case law from the revolutionary treason trials until 1795 or body of legal commentary to test or explain how legislative, judicial, and constitutional law interfaced in devising and applying treason law. More immediately, the "not particularly detailed" Whiskey Rebellion law reports left the impression among recent scholars that the trials had "limited importance."[15]

In sum, the late eighteenth-century legal world was characterized by insufficient and inefficient legal resources and relied on intuitive responses and informal relations; lawyers practiced according to the norms and values of a small, relatively closely knit group that shared information and where reputation was a form of capital. From such a resource-scarce world, little has survived to indicate a defense theory of the trials, leaving us with piecemeal insights. Counsel aggressively raised technical and procedural issues and zealously argued for local vicinage in *United States v. Stewart and Wright*, *United States v. Insurgents*, and *United States v. Hamilton*. They made pragmatic choices to accede to a judge's charge or to withhold argument where there was insufficient proof of a crime, as in *Porter* and *Vigol*. And they resorted to constitutional arguments to controvert common law analysis and constructive treason, as with Edward Tilghman and Joseph Thomas in *Mitchell* and William Lewis in *Barnet*. But nowhere is it made clear that counsel had a wholistic view of treason or that they had as developed a view as the prosecution, for neither Tilghman nor Thomas nor Lewis left evidence of their work in their papers.[16] It seems hardly possible, however, that the defense was not at least as well schooled in treason law as the prosecution, particularly since William Lewis was reported to have defended "in nearly every treason case" in Pennsylvania till the end of the century.[17]

Hugh Henry Brackenridge's Notes

To resolve this question, we turn to Brackenridge's unstudied treason defense notes for their insights into the defense team's case. Brackenridge not only theorized an approach to treason law that both encompassed the legal language of the courts and the popular law talk of the assemblies, but there was no one better situated to bridge formal and informal venues of the law, embody western interests, and address questions of treason.[18] Not only had he been intimately involved in the rebel assemblies, been a spokesperson for the rebels, and been investigated by the federal militia for his role in the rebellion, but Brackenridge had litigated cases for the rebels in the western courts. Given the state of the legal profession at the time, one can make the case that his notes were not marginal to the contemporary legal process but part of an essential core of practice that was common to lawyers of his period. Moreover, they constituted a necessary corrective to what law reports had to offer, considering the shaky, unofficial nature of their collection and publication.

Published no less than a month after the most critical rebel trials and three to four years before Alexander Dallas published his six law reports on the trials,[19] Brackenridge's notes on treason responded to a request by the insurgents to represent them. "Let it be understood," he wrote, "that the above are the notes of the arguments, I had projected in my mind, had I appeared in defence of the prisoners."[20] Two decades after the rebellion, Brackenridge explained further that he was republishing "a note of the argument I had intended to have made on the law points which might arise in their case."[21] Comments he added to his original notes when they were republished reinforced the validity of the notes, which had not been widely read and which he hoped, by republishing them, to give a "chance for preservation."[22] In neither version were Brackenridge's notes summarized or redacted—a practice to which law reports were routinely subjected—so that, having never left Brackenridge's control, they retained his original language and thoughts. As an added measure of their responsiveness to the trials, Brackenridge had collected testimonials for his own use and he had access to prosecuting U.S. attorney William Rawle's notes "taken in the Course of the Trials," some of which he published in the appendix of *Incidents*.[23]

Whether Brackenridge's notes were composed as he deliberated on the possibility that he might serve as counsel or while he observed the trials is of some interest. While he seems to have shared the general reluctance of counsel to making their arguments available in print Brackenridge had expected that a law report would be published "with advantage from the argument of that very able lawyer, and distinguished philanthropist [William Lewis],"[24] which would have obviated the need for him to publish anything. Brackenridge relied on Lewis's assertion that "had an argument with the jury taken place, he had been prepared to shew this,"[25] but two obstacles impeded that prospect. Edward Tilghman and Joseph Thomas defended in *Mitchell*, not Lewis, and Brackenridge had little confidence in or affinity for their arguments. Where Lewis did defend, in *Vigol*, "no question of law arose" and the case proceeded without argument; Lewis, "a careless man, negligent of his papers," kept no records of his trial notes.[26] Despite his disappointment, Brackenridge indicated that he had a full record of the trials (which he attended and where he served as a witness) and that "without having that testimony with the most perfect exactness, *which has been obtained* in court" he could not have made his own argument.

To summarize, Brackenridge's treason notes were contemporaneous with the trials. He provided a motive for his notes, explained the process of writing them, and offered evidence of the timing. He waited until all the testimony and evidence had been given in court before he, like the estimable Lewis, concluded definitively that there was no treason. He thereafter put his notes into manuscript form based on all that was presented in court. Brackenridge was clear: he was publishing his notes in lieu of being able to defend the rebels in court; as well, he wished to offset any responsibility he might have felt for their welfare and to express his humanity in supporting "the Expediency of a Pardon."[27] His notes appear, as a result, to have been published after the May 1795 convictions of Mitchell and Vigol and before their pardon in June of that year. Given their fullness, it is likely that he began preparing the notes when he was asked to represent the rebels, presumably in November (when they were arrested and marched to Philadelphia) through April (when it became clear that he would be testifying in the April session of the circuit court in Philadelphia). Since he knew he would not be representing the rebels before the April term began, Brackenridge would have had no need, or indeed reason, to write up the notes until he could capitalize on the testimony the trials would offer him. This would have enabled him to craft his argument in direct relation to prosecution and defense testimony and arguments and the jury charges. Not only were prosecutor Rawle's notes for the trials available to Brackenridge, but, as a trial observer and participating witness, he had access to defense counsel arguments and took his own notes on the trials. His publication of his notes followed common practice at a time when law reports were not generally available and members of the legal profession shared their notes.

It is important to clarify what exactly Brackenridge's notes offer us. They are not the actual working notes of trial counsel for, as events transpired, he was not a formal member of the defense team. One could argue that his work had no impact on the trials, nor did they inform the work of those who defended the rebels in court. His defense in these terms could be considered a hypothetical one and of limited importance to the conduct of the trials. One might argue as well that Brackenridge's work could not have served as a precedent nor have had an impact on the development of American law that fed into subsequent trials—the *Fries* trial in 1799, the sedition trials of 1800, or the later treason trials of Aaron Burr in 1807.[28] But such objections fail to account for the larger legal culture in which Brackenridge operated.[29] His history of involvement in the western courts, the events of the insurrection, and later as a witness in the Philadelphia trials, took place within an informal network of relationships maintained over time with defendants, their supporters, and other lawyers in the trials. At the same time, the courts in which Brackenridge litigated were creating an American law to rival English common law on a case-by-case basis without the benefit of a systematic or official written record. Critically, his treason notes were part of a larger debate on treason that lasted into the early nineteenth century. They were situated in context as part of the debate on treason law as it circulated orally within the informal world of law of which he was a part and as it was understood and practiced in the late eighteenth century. It was a world where a small circle of lawyers and judges litigated and presided over court cases, men whom Brackenridge had heard of and admired (James Wilson), studied with (Samuel Chase), served with in the courts in the West (Alexander Addison), or knew at Princeton College where he earned two degrees (James Madison and William Bradford). He had in addition observed lawyers in court in his earlier practice of law in Philadelphia and in the cases he litigated in the western courts. He served as a witness in *Barnet*, *Miller*, and *Philson and Husband*, where William Rawle and William Lewis as well as William Bradford, Moses Levy, Joseph Thomas, and Edward Tilghman argued the cases. Tellingly, Brackenridge had attended the sentencing of Abraham Carlisle and John Roberts, convicted of treason in 1778,[30] and had accessed there a network of acquaintances in support of a failed pardon effort. Such connections not only served to develop a rebel defense that was meaningful in the chain of eighteenth-century treason law but also later proved helpful in facilitating his appointment to the Pennsylvania Supreme Court just four years after the Whiskey Rebellion trials.

As Defense Counsel

Born in Scotland in 1748, Hugh Henry Brackenridge settled in York County, Pennsylvania, when it was a frontier community. He studied law with the notable Samuel Chase and was admitted to the bar in Philadelphia in 1780. He migrated to the "second" frontier in Pittsburgh, where he hoped to make his fortune, and was admitted to practice from 1781 to 1788 in the newly established courts of the four western counties (Alleghany, Fayette, Westmoreland, and Washington) in which the Whiskey Rebellion arose. Brackenridge represented western Pennsylvania in the state legislature from 1786–1787 but was more important as a lawyer than a politician, having become the most accomplished practitioner on western court dockets. In Pittsburgh, the county seat of the Alleghany Court, the number of lawyers litigating cases in the Court of Common Pleas from 1793 to 1795 rose from 7 to 14 and the number of cases from 129 to 251. Brackenridge's cases represented 82 out of 129 in 1793, 142 out of 190 in 1794, and 99 out of 251 in 1795, or 64 percent, 82 percent, and 40 percent of the cases tried. In Alexander Addison's law reports for 268 western cases across the four counties (which included Brackenridge's cases from 1791 to 1798), Brackenridge was named in 54, or 20 percent, of the cases (of which he won a third), suggesting the volume of his practice and his desirability as a litigator.[31] His reputation as a western Republican together with his legal contacts and an effort to offset eastern Federalist influence on the court would prove critical to his appointment to the Pennsylvania Supreme Court.[32]

With the trials approaching, Brackenridge recognized that having played a prominent role in the rebellion and having forfeited amnesty left him targeted for a hanging by the government and open to persecution by his opponents in the West.[33] At this point, and with little confidence in the fairness of the upcoming trials, he began to prepare notes to "bring the calumniators to justice."[34] He insisted he "was willing to have rendered service as an advocate in the court if I had conceived that it would have served them," but it was clear he was conflicted and even felt he might contribute to the convictions of *Mitchell* and *Vigol* and the prospect of their hanging.[35] To redeem himself, he supported their pardon, on the claim that they were "not worth hanging, on a charge of treason," and hoped that his "observations may be of use to induce the public to interest themselves for their pardon."[36] It did not help matters that Brackenridge was called as a witness for the prosecution in the *Miller* trial and for the defense in *Barnet* and *Philson and Husband*, which created the appearance that he had made a separate peace for himself. His adversaries spread rumors that he had turned state's evidence and presented him as a spy for the government who had been granted immunity. As Brackenridge put it, "now I was come down to fulfill that dark engagement of giving testimony."[37] In fact, Justice Paterson's bench notes made little of Brackenridge's largely anodyne testimony.

Brackenridge had yet another hurdle to overcome. He had publicly portrayed the rebels' acts in the inciting event of the rebellion (the attacks on Neville's house) as "outrages [...] in construction of law, amounting to high treason."[38] He later qualified his comment by contending that the acts were treason in terms that "always struck me *in bulk*, as, by the decisions of the judges of the English courts."[39] Mirroring the broad common law position taken by the government, Brackenridge accepted "this is treason that has been committed; and in treason there are no accessories, before or after the fact, all are principals."[40] He offered that if rebel acts opposing one law, rather than all law, were not considered treason, "they would finally oppose all [law], and demand a new modeling of the Constitution; and there would be a revolution."[41] The rioters, he clarified, were legally, if not morally, wrong; the temper of the mob at a rebel assembly (presumably Braddock's

Field) had rendered the law useless, so that "[i]t was a case within the power of the President to call out the militia."[42]

Brackenridge was not, however, supported by Lewis in this finding. Lewis confided to Brackenridge that he had concluded "*no treason had been committed in the country*" (regarding *Vigol*), but only after "*a view of the facts*, now fully come out in evidence."[43] Lewis's "confidence" in the matter extended to whether Neville's killing of a rebel (Oliver Miller) before the attack on his house was justifiable or criminal. That Lewis found no justification for treason either in his defense of the rebels in *Vigol* or his prosecution of excise inspector Neville (for killing Miller)[44] concerned Brackenridge who was familiar with Lewis's treason defenses in cases from *Carlisle* (1778) and *Roberts* (1778) and thought highly of him. That opinion would be confirmed by Lewis's lawyering in the 1795 Whiskey Rebellion cases (*Hamilton, Stewart, Insurgents, Porter, Corbly and Lockery*).[45]

Considering these areas of contention, Brackenridge was convinced that his ability to represent the rebels was on shaky grounds. As a fellow rebel, his representation as counsel would "stand ill with the jury [...] as the pleading of one criminal for another."[46] Brackenridge readily admitted that, being "involved in the insurrection, a crime aggravated a thousand fold in the case of a man who knew the law," he would be considered unworthy of serving on the defense team.[47] Yet he was seated as counsel, "not without hesitation" for a short time, "only just to shew myself and retire again."[48] His withdrawal might well have represented a missed opportunity. The addition of Brackenridge as counsel would have allowed the defense to capitalize on his experiences within the rebel assemblies and his unmatched familiarity with riot and excise cases in the western courts. Brackenridge had, moreover, legal dealings with those informants who provided advice and direction to the government team (among them Inspector Neville and his lawyer John Woods) as well as intimate knowledge of circuit court prosecutor Rawle and presiding judge Peters from their interrogations of subjects and evidence collection in the West. Moreover, Pennsylvania Supreme Court justices riding the western circuit had some regard for Brackenridge for cases he tried from the 1780s through 1794, and he had become well known in Philadelphia.[49] Brackenridge was well positioned to anticipate the prosecution's predispositions and the case it would mount in the trials.

Brackenridge's conflicted role in the insurrection, however, had created barriers of trust with the rebels.[50] This contributed to the appointment of Philadelphia-based lawyers Lewis, Thomas, Tilghman, and Levy for the defense.[51] Thomas was not regarded as a particularly astute choice, according to Albert Gallatin, who considered him "young, inexperienced, impudent and self conceited" and blamed him for the death sentence in John Mitchell's trial, a case he considered "poorly defended." Gallatin did not remark on Tilghman but thought highly of Lewis for having provided a "very good defence."[52] A prominent Philadelphia litigator with experience defending in treason trials during the Revolution, Lewis's expertise and reputation were likely the best match for prosecutor Rawle's deep roots in the metropolitan legal community.[53] As for Brackenridge, in the end he felt redeemed: "The people began to talk less of having me hanged instead of the accused, and the gentlemen of the bar became sociable; and the court complaisant."[54] By any argument, it seems clear that by the time he wrote his defense notes he had regained the trust of the rebels and moderated the views he reported in *Incidents*.[55]

On Treason Law

In making the case for a rebel defense, Brackenridge's commentary defended constitutional law on treason, put common law precedents in their place, and attacked constructivist treason. It located the precondition for treason in a social contract between man and state by means of which one owed a duty of allegiance (which was voluntary and capable of being withdrawn) and not one of obedience (which was imposed and fixed). Critically, Brackenridge's commentary clarified the limitations and requirements presented in the Constitution. In short, he took on judicial construction, precedent, the Constitution's definition of treason, and allegiance.

Judicial Construction

The largest issue Brackenridge took on was the question of judicial constructions. He opened his treason notes paying homage to Blackstone, for whom forced constructions were nothing more than the "creatures of tyrannical princes" who rendered offenses treason "which never were expected to be such."[56] Following Blackstone, Brackenridge found constructive treason too inclusive, too expandable, and "rendered sanguinary" by judges; "even a single trespass," he submitted, "tends to the subversion of the government."[57] If one was to argue that legislation "sanctioned the interpretation" of the English courts, Brackenridge answered that American judges could construe the law "on principle of reason" and thereby disable precedents as if they did not exist.[58] He held that discretionary law created in cases by English judges was neither the "law itself" nor evidence of the law; guided by the Constitution's "meliorating spirit," American judges should thus depart from it "in all cases, warranted by reason."[59] Indeed, he declared, jurists should resist such liberal interpretation as it would multiply treasons and relay more rigorous interpretations into an uncertain future.[60]

Judges handling Whiskey Rebellion cases were no exception to constructivist tendencies.[61] Judge Addison's September 1794 grand jury charge,[62] for example, construed one law synecdochically for all law, declaring that discrete acts of disobedience would enumerate until the government, the nation, and the citizenry itself "must cease to exist."[63] His was a posture adopted effortlessly by federal judges such as Richard Peters, whose August 1794 grand jury charge denied any dissent against a legitimate government, even one acting illegitimately. Peters weighed the duty to defend the government more heavily than the right to resist oppressive laws; power, by Peters's description, superseded liberty and circumscribed participation by the people in democratic processes.[64] Justice Paterson, too, adopted an expansive English version of treason in several undated circuit court grand jury charges where he construed obedience to government, which he acknowledged might be "mistaken for slavery," as a function of "Order [. . .] Heaven's first law."[65] Thus, he found that resisting the execution of the law or the administration of justice was a tolerable construction of a treasonous act, which excused a jurist's aggregation of nontreasonous acts to reach treason.[66] Not much had changed from "ancient common law"[67] to the Whiskey Rebellion trials if the trial judges were to be believed. Constructions by English judges would have made the attack on Inspector Neville's house and the rebel march to Braddock's Field two weeks later clearly treason.[68] Brackenridge disagreed. Treason was to be confined to a meditated intent and a direct attack, which he defined as "a fixed, formed, deliberate intention of subverting the government." Only such an offense "will construe high treason, and punish with the loss of life itself." Since the bulk of those at Neville's house "had no looking forward of mind to more than a redress of what they called grievances, under the government,"[69] no jury could find they had a treasonous design.

In the context of a tradition going back centuries, common law ran in two directions. It proliferated options for interpreting what was treason at the same time it embraced stare decisis (the power of precedent); these trends reinforced Blackstone's warning that constructive treason was indefinite and it gave judges great latitude.[70] By comparison, the preamble of 25 Edw. III limited the "divers pains of treason" that statutes had previously ordained, as no man could know how he ought to behave "for doubt of such pains."[71] Brackenridge was concerned by the dichotomy, as was Wilson. Disquieted by the uncertainty of common law, Wilson argued that indeterminate treason "is sufficient to make any government degenerate into arbitrary power." It provided the unprincipled with an opportunity to harass citizens with prosecutions that are "constructive, capricious, and oppressive."[72] Indeterminateness was the very doubt against which 25 Edw. III stood—the doubt that constructive treasons left in the minds of men as to their conduct and fate.

The numerous inclusions and indefiniteness of the common law that Americans inherited ran counter to the certainty demanded when punishing a capital crime that threatened the existence of the state. Like 25 Edw. III and the Constitution (which based its definition of treason on 25 Edw. III), Brackenridge was intent on curing indeterminacy. Toward this effort, he reviewed how common law treated the treason of levying war. Assembling in the manner of war could, he considered, determine a treason charge "where the trespass is with numbers, and with arms" and threatens social order.[73] But riot and treason must be distinguished. Where risings involved maintaining a private right—even to breaking persons out of prison—these were not treason by levying war.[74] Resistance to an officer serving a process of a U.S. court was no more than "an aggravated trespass" and thereby no more than a maximum twelve-month sentence and $300 fine.[75] So too, resistance of a particular and not a general design was not a levying of war. Brackenridge's review of the law dismissed altogether any form of constructive treason that did not confine "the law to a direct attack upon the government [...], an attack *animo subvertendi*," an intent, or conspiracy, to overthrow without which no outrage may be punished.[76] Thus, unlike common law reasoning that aggregated instances or circumstantial inferences resulting in a fact pattern, constitutional reasoning required defining levying war and deducing what constituted an overt act to subvert or overthrow government by obstructing some necessary part of its operation and stopping the whole machine; this definition was productive of an underlying explanatory principle.[77]

Brackenridge held that correcting the arbitrary nature of judicial constructions that contributed to the uncertainty of treason law was insufficient without a uniform explanatory framework based on reason.[78] On the one hand, courts lacked a competent legal system and judges learned in the law; "[m]uddy waters," Brackenridge represented, "produce ignoble fish."[79] On the other hand, legal culture had yet to adhere to the Constitution in correcting the prejudice expressed by illiberal judges against the accused; legal culture had yet to set limits in defining treason "on the basis of reason," saying in effect "hitherto the law will go, and no further."[80] As Brackenridge expounded, a purposeful intent (in the mind of a person to subvert the government), an overt act (of treason not riot), a levying of war (not mere conspiracy) were the pieces of which the treason framework was to be constructed.[81]

Precedent

Brackenridge took up the second part of the dichotomy regarding common law—stare decisis—asking whether Americans were bound by common law constructions of levying war. For Brackenridge, levying war was a double-edged sword: the hard English edge (which he considered "to the last degree sanguinary") and the soft American one in determining the nature of the proof to fix the crime. His concern was whether American law was "at liberty to depart" from the English view and "what ought to be the construction."[82] He considered common law binding in Pennsylvania along with those statutes convenient and adapted to the commonwealth, following Blackstone's view that colonists carried with them as much of English law "as is applicable to their own situation."[83] Brackenridge himself considered common law settled and known but particular to a given application; flexible, yet capable of preventing arbitrariness in judges. Yet he also spoke of decisions following the revolution that were "as if men who had set out from the same place and having travelled together a certain distance, had parted."[84] They should compare their notes of the path traveled and, where they parted company, correct them and cooperate in making improvements. These were the parameters within which Brackenridge wished to retain English common law.

Brackenridge took up common law not only in his treason notes and *Law Miscellanies*, but in his novel *Modern Chivalry*, where he treated the matter in a vernacular manner that reflected law talk on the ground in the western counties.[85] The blind lawyer in *Modern Chivalry* (an imperfect surrogate for the author) noted in his newly appointed role of chief justice, for example, that replacing English common law was a question of rewriting the wisdom of the ages, "the means of governing, from time immemorial."[86] Abolishing common law merely because it was the law of England, as if, somehow, it was the worse for having originated there, meant giving up the birth right for which Americans had fought a war.[87] Its very name spoke to its essential political value. It was called "common law" as a system of universal justice "common to the whole people."[88] It was embedded in the very foundation of society—state constitutions—whose outlines were filled in by those portions of common law from which the United States drew.[89] But if creating a common law of one's own was a fool's errand,[90] such reasoning also precluded holding blindly to common law precedents. Even conceived as the wisdom of the ages, precedent cannot be binding, the negative side of Brackenridge's legal dichotomy in which the "modern chivalry" of American law eclipsed the "iron crown" of English law.[91] Underlying principles of common sense and equity became, instead, Brackenridge's good-faith brokers. It was one thing to prefer judgment that withstood "the examination of law and reason" and quite another to substitute legal cases for sense. Just as "[g]eneral reason, is a safer ground, than doubtful decisions," the problem for Brackenridge was "an enchainment of texts" repeating the same thing rather than arguing by reason and upon principle supported by the authority of precedent.[92] Once a case became common law, another of Brackenridge's alter egos in the novel (his peregrinating hero, Captain Farrago) complained, no judge can undo it or question its reason: "If [Sir John] Holt has once said it, the game is up[. . . .] It is a knock'im down argument, that [William] Paterson has ruled it; or [Bushrod] Washington, or [John] Marshal. It is the construction of the judge that makes the law[. . . . T]here is no more to be said about it. Positive institutions are arbitrary things."[93]

As Brackenridge wrote in *Law Miscellanies*, once again reflecting the imprint of Blackstone's liberalizing perspective on common law, stare decisis ought not to mean permitting the nonsense of one man to guide another.[94] The exercise of judgment was "as necessary as the recollection of precedent." Reason should deduce the principle applied and the principle should be the guide: "Unless the case is precisely the same, the analogy is imperfect and the application erroneous."[95] Considering servility the enemy of reason, judges ought to depart from senseless decisions "unuseful to their end," to the extent of deserting their own decisions.[96] The guiding principle already resided within English common law in its "classical" sense, that is, congruent with principled jurisprudence, common sense, and reason,[97] which Brackenridge privileged in his focused discussion of intent, his critique of the preservation of government, and his analysis of allegiance.

The Constitutional Definition

Brackenridge's animus toward constructive treason and common law precedents conditioned his response to the two most contested provisions of the constitutional definition of treason: proof of an overt treasonous act and "levying war," both of which proved problematic in the Whiskey Rebellion trials. Brackenridge argued that "*the leaning of the [English] judges to convict on a charge of treason*" employed a false witness standard since the Constitution required two witnesses to a single overt act necessary to rectify "illiberal constructions."[98] He cited 7 William III as support, which stated that "both witnesses must be to the same overt act of treason, or one to one overt act, and the other to another overt act, of the same species of treason."[99] But this still left room for constructive treason among judges, as Brackenridge had feared.[100] In *United States v. Mitchell*, Justice Paterson proved Brackenridge correct by compounding different events so they might be considered a single overt act to get to the requisite number of witnesses.

As to the second constitutional provision—treason as a levying of war—prosecutor Rawle breached two of Brackenridge's norms: that American law was not bound by English authority and that the common law definition of treason was contradictory, indeterminate, and expansive. Bradford went on to include what Brackenridge had excluded as forms of treason: executing the law and administrative operations of the government. Brackenridge rejected such slippage. As we have seen, he held that every act that did not directly attack the government with the purpose of subverting or overthrowing it was a riot and could only be "repressed and punished" as such.[101] As applied to the attack on Inspector Neville's house, Brackenridge denied that treason without intent applied to the facts; the facts might imply trespass, a breach of the peace, a riot, but not treason.[102] Brackenridge rejected as well Paterson's construction whereby the effect of an act might stand for its intent; treason, Brackenridge argued, required intent not effect. Instead, he asked "whether it be necessary for the preservation of the government, that the treason law be carried so far?"[103] His answer was clear: treason could not be declared by inference, and mere political willfulness did not constitute treason; nor was a citizenry treasonous if it declined a duty of care to government institutions.

As a political matter, American law from its founding excluded domestic disturbance and political opposition as treason when it discounted compassing the king's death; they were displaced by an intention to overthrow the government or conspiring to do so. Brackenridge's baseline was simple: to be charged as treason any such attack must first "attempt to shake the foundation of the government" to which one had sworn allegiance. One must intend to overturn "the existing order of society" and to install, first, anarchy, and in the end tyranny.[104] Intent required that one knew an attack was meant to overthrow the government and that one knowingly engaged to commit such an act. Only then would the act be "the act of the mind, which is the man."[105] No rebel present at Neville's house, Brackenridge concluded, would have accepted such a presumption of intent. Further, given that treason was an act punishable with one's life, it must contain a direct line in the mind to a subversion of the government: "The accused had meditated death to the government, and the law in this case, and in this case only, will meditate death to him."[106] Without the paramount factor, "the *quo animo*, the mind with which a thing was done," he argued, the government could consider acts of force "in the light of an aggravated riot only," which was not an overt act of treason but merely treason by inference.[107] In short, Brackenridge held firmly to his North Star: no act was treason without intent, and intent had to be attached to an overt act.[108]

Allegiance

Brackenridge took up English common law and judicial constructions well before he addressed allegiance, expatriation, and secession, for several reasons. First, pragmatics. In his defense of the rebels, he was faced with the immediacy of the trials, including his desire to join the defense team and his involvement as a witness for both the prosecution and the defense. Second, politics. Confounding allegiance and secession with the immediate question of whether violence and riot rose to the level of treason would have been prejudicial to the defense in the trials. Finally, jurisprudence. Judicial philosophy demanded an examination of allegiance to complete his treason analysis, but the task required hindsight and reflection. Brackenridge arrived at a place where he could provide those missing pieces when he became a Pennsylvania Supreme Court justice in 1799. With the advantage of the experience he would gain in 1807 in examining English and Pennsylvania law, and in 1814 when considering the War of 1812, he could give his full attention to the issues of common law and expatriation.[109] His legal thought here took him from the immediate needs of trial practice to longer-term considerations of legal culture.

Nonetheless, two years after the Whiskey Rebellion trials Brackenridge had already advanced a theory of allegiance that offered philosophical underpinning for his view of treason. Appearing after the immediate pressures of the trials and the practical necessities of defending his tattered reputation had abated, his picaresque treatment of travels through Pennsylvania's western frontier, as we saw in chapter 3, devoted itself in volume four of *Modern Chivalry* to the Whiskey Rebellion. There, he satirized the social conditions leading to acts of treason and featured a debate on man's right to revolt. That debate would seed the commentary on allegiance attached to his reprinted notes in *Law Miscellanies* in 1814, by which time the War of 1812 had raised serious questions about expatriation and British impressment of American seamen.[110]

Brackenridge's political views, as Robert A. Ferguson notes, were in flux. He had begun *Modern Chivalry* with a Jeffersonian perspective that saw democracy as a test for enlightenment reasoning and republican virtue. But he ended disappointed by democratic weaknesses that produced not a Jeffersonian farmer, like the novel's hero, but a mix of irrationality and opportunism, like that of the servant Teague. Democracy, Brackenridge concluded, was only as good as its subjects were honorable and educated, a recipe for chaos under frontier conditions in western Pennsylvania where local democracy had collapsed in an admirable but failed experiment. The rebellion in this sense was a failed test of the common man's nobility and the pretense that in a pure democracy the people could rule themselves.[111]

In a final comment on the rebellion in the novel, Brackenridge reflected on the *sansculottes* of the French Revolution (an obvious parallel to the whiskey rebels) in a debate on social theory between Farrago and an émigré nobleman, the Marquis de Marnessie. The marquis was a Rousseauist and French émigré whose real name was the Marquis Claude Francois Adrien de Lezay-Marnezia.[112] Like Farrago, the marquis of the novel never considered the West his true home. Detached and philosophical, he saw himself as a "disembodied spirit," like the ghosts in Hades visited by Ulysses.[113] His visitor, Farrago, was a captain in the local militia (like some of the principal figures in the rebellion) and a Pennsylvania farmer with an academic education (like Brackenridge).[114] Farrago had read Thomas Paine's pamphlet *Rights of Man* and was disposed to subscribe to its doctrine that no pact undertaken by an ancestor can take away the right of a descendant to a government of his choice.[115] Comparing Paine's premise to the right of the French to overthrow the monarchy in favor of a republic,[116] the marquis demurred. As a member of the French elite, he had much to lose in a revolution. Here he compared himself to Achilles in the underworld, who would rather live a slave than rule among the undying. Such was his "predilection for [his] country"[117] that he would rather dig the soil in France than be president of the United States. Whatever else might happen, he argued, no Frenchman by natural right or the "artificial establishment of society" could remove himself from his ancestry, a position Blackstone would have admired as we shall see below. The people ought "not pull the house down about our heads,"[118] said the Frenchman, for they were joint tenants and owners; to demolish the edifice was thereby a question of mere power, not of right. Making use of a typically western image, the marquis referred to himself as a hunter in the woods: "I take the raccoons and rabbits, not that I conceive myself to have any right [...] to make these depredations, but that having come, I have the skill to do it."[119]

Amused at the émigré's misanthropy in equating men to brute animals, the captain attributed his companion's views to having lost his ancestors' fortune to the "dreadful outrages" of revolution. Asserting that a man's fortune was not his to lose unless he had earned it once he came of age and by his own labor, Farrago questioned whether a man could possess by birth a right to the soil or whether he committed an injustice by emigrating to lands belonging to others. In this, the captain mirrored Brackenridge's own affinity for homesteaders who chose to improve and settle on the frontier in the face of Indian attacks and absentee land speculators. Change "from despotism to liberty," Farrago reasoned, was as impossible "without violence, as to dislodge a promontory from its base, by any other means, than mining and gunpowder."[120] In this respect, he recalled Rousseau's formulation that freedom required living "under a law which one has oneself enacted" and Robespierre's use of Rousseau's theory of the "general will" to justify the French Revolution's Reign of Terror.[121] A people that ruled itself was free, Farrago appeared to argue, even if forced to be free by virtue of popular tyranny. Whether Rousseau's "principles of justice" thereby justified violence (as the rebels would have claimed) or whether a democratic constitution superseded popular action (as the Federalists alleged) set the implicit terms of the debate,[122] leaving open the prospect that popular sovereignty, and all the inanities for which it was responsible, could legitimately prevail over government.

Expatriation

In the commentary attached to his reprinted treason notes in *Law Miscellanies*, Brackenridge embellished his social theory in a more serious venue to interrogate natural law and the foundational question of allegiance: Who owed allegiance? And to whom? As background to his developing theory, and concurrent with the tax rebellion and the appearance of the Francophile democratic societies, expatriation had become an issue in the 1793 trial of Gideon Henfield.[123] A special circuit court in Pennsylvania charged Henfield with expatriating to the French (having joined as a privateer in France's war against Britain); the animus against him, like that against the societies, was rooted in Francophobia.[124] Chief Justice John Jay made the connection in the grand jury charge he delivered in indicting Henfield in the Middle Circuit Court, District of Virginia on May 22, 1793. He argued that, despite the people's right to use force in their own defense, the "establishment of political societies" made the exercise of that right too dangerous. Furthermore, those who aided or abetted foreign interests prohibited by their country forfeited its protection on the grounds of the country's absolute "sovereignty within its own dominions."[125] Jay's argument accused Republicans of being disloyal not only to the Revolution and the Constitution but to President Washington as well.[126]

Justice James Wilson in his trial jury charge for *Henfield*[127] reiterated the chief justice's reasoning, allowing that emigration in support of a foreign power was "inconsistent with the duty of a citizen" and treasonous. Even a Francophile Republican such as Thomas Jefferson agreed. He held that the commission of a crime (treason) did not amount "to a divestment of the character of a citizen" or free one from the authority of American law. Nor could treason be rendered "innocent by giving it the force of a dissolution of the obligations of the criminal to his Country."[128] Jefferson argued further that if one citizen can claim a right to go to war, then all may do so. And if all may do so, then the nation ("by the authority of its individual citizens") is free to do so. The U.S. Constitution, however, gave that power to Congress, not to the people. Jay agreed; since the will of the people chose the form of government under which the people lived and which formed the "general compact" to which they were all bound, no man or body of men could involve the whole in a war.[129]

Brackenridge took a diametrically opposed tack. He began by rejecting Blackstone's dictum, *ne exære patriam* (one cannot escape from subjugation by the parent society), just as he had rejected the marquis's doctrine of the priority of ancestry. Allegiance, according to Blackstone, was fundamental to the relation between the ruler and the ruled, "The first and most obvious division of the people."[130] In common law, that division represented, as Matthew Hale said, mutual trust between master and servant and mutual duties, to protect and to serve respectively.[131] Blackstone went further. He bound the subject by an "implied, original, and virtual allegiance, owing [. . .] antecedently to any express promise."[132] He called the relationship "a principle of universal law" that could not be altered or forfeited by any act of one's own: "it is written by the finger of the law in their hearts."[133]

Brackenridge considered Blackstone's view "a slavish principle," making the subject the property of the king or the country and his allegiance perpetual.¹³⁴ Citing Plato and Cicero, Brackenridge contrasted Blackstone's doctrine to "the principle of republican government" and found it "repugnant."¹³⁵ Such allegiance neither allowed free will nor did it constitute a proper social compact, rendering society's entitlement to a man's service anathema.¹³⁶ Having rejected rank feudalism, emigrants to America had left behind unalienable allegiance, "this badge of servitude," serving as a reminder that Blackstone had at least supported the colonies' right to appropriate the law that was fitting to their condition.¹³⁷ Here Brackenridge threw down the gauntlet: "*Ubi libertas, ibi patria*, where liberty is, there is my country."¹³⁸ Man was more than vegetation that "must belong to a bed of loam," just as he happened to find himself. Must he who is "willing to shake off the clod" (a claim to land in exchange for service), he queried rhetorically, be held to "the whole clod of the dominion, so that he cannot put it off?"¹³⁹ "[T]he *prohibition to expatriate*" and allegiance that "cannot be forfeited," he concluded, were "contrary to the laws of nature."¹⁴⁰ By extension, Brackenridge considered it lawful to remove from a chaotic situation by expatriating and added that it was even more lawful to resist a parent society that has wronged one. Moreover, since one's allegiance was a natural right, the choice to secede was not treasonable once one reached his majority.¹⁴¹ In Brackenridge's view, the critical qualification in American law was that the Constitution could only premise treason on a duty of allegiance¹⁴² and that one's allegiance was based on the right to resist being wronged. Thus, an individual's choice to secede was no more than protecting one's person or property from trespass by the parent society. The key to this framework was that allegiance was a question of choice and character (not obedience and duty, as Wilson had put it) and that under those conditions it did not constitute the predicate for treason.

Notwithstanding his strong views on allegiance, Brackenridge had a complicated view of collective secession. By implication, federal authority in the Whiskey Rebellion was comparable to that of a foreign power and secession represented the prospect of a free state, an argument that resonated with Brackenridge's experience in rebel assemblies where dissolution of the Union and secession were linked to separation from Great Britain in the American Revolution.¹⁴³ Thus, he supported individual separation and the right to fully emigrate,¹⁴⁴ for otherwise a nation was turned into a prison. As he mused, "The example of the iron, or any other crown, will not paralize the American spirit, in contending for the freedom of mankind, in opposition to this *imprisonment of any one in an enchanted island*."¹⁴⁵ But he did not accept, citing Peter Du Ponceau, that separation could serve as "mere cover to evade or violate the laws of our country,"¹⁴⁶ a position, as Jefferson indicated, that would have covered those Pennsylvanians who fled at the end of the rebellion. Collaterally, he questioned the collective right to self-govern or secede when refusing allegiance, for the social contract, as in St. George Tucker's understanding, did not support the secession of land. Land remained with the sovereign (the commonwealth), which cannot lose its interest without its consent. It was the sovereign, not the subject, who had to consent to secession, just as it was the subject's right to consent, or not, to allegiance; the land could not secede with the individual, nor could "the multitude [secede] together." The only way, Tucker said, citing John Locke, that one could enjoy what his predecessors had was to give consent to be part of their society.¹⁴⁷ Brackenridge declared himself in agreement "in totis" with Tucker's analysis, expressing that he had portrayed in *Modern Chivalry* "a picture of a people broke loose from the restraints of government[...] to show the *danger of even talking of a severance of the union*."¹⁴⁸ In this sense, Brackenridge's literary account of the rebellion was nothing less than a recollection of "the earlier disintegrating tendencies in the West"¹⁴⁹ despite his flirtation with backcountry psychology and mob actions.

John Marshall and *United States v. Burr*

Having dispensed with questions related to allegiance, Brackenridge had essentially completed his supplementary comments. He did, however, add a codicil to his treason notes on a case that he might have hoped would clarify his application of treason law—Chief Justice John Marshall's opinion in the 1807 trial of Aaron Burr. In 1806, Burr conspired to conduct a military expedition against Spanish territory in Louisiana in violation of the 1794 Neutrality Act, for which he was charged with treason by President Jefferson and tried before the U.S. Circuit Court for Virginia with Marshall presiding. The case has been positioned as the first truly high-profile case the new nation faced while its ideological importance as a question of public justice has been considered more important than its legal issues.¹⁵⁰ Certainly, John Adams was concerned about the trials' effect, for while he regarded Burr as "a Nondescript in natural History," yet he felt that "something must come out on the Tryal, which will strengthen or weaken our Confidence in the General Union."¹⁵¹

In line with treason trials going back to the Whiskey Rebellion, Jefferson and his lawyers felt that Justice Paterson's opinions had opened the way to a broad indictment against Burr.¹⁵² This left Justice Marshall with the task of clarifying the differences between the circumstances of 1795 and Burr's involvement in the events of 1806. Marshall has been represented as resolving the dilemma by discounting English constructive treason and relying on the U.S. Constitution, thereby undermining Jefferson's theory of the case.[153] Jefferson was embarrassed with the result. First, there was the peculiar public attraction of pitting a founder and president of the republic against a recent vice president. Separately, Jefferson had privately represented that the Shays's Rebellion in 1787 was an evil "productive of good" under a government in which "the will of everyone has a just influence"; "a little rebellion now and then," he impoliticly offered, "is a good thing."[154] The Burr case, unfortunately for Jefferson, was just such a "thing."[155]

Marshall has been accused of vacillating between his view of treason in *Burr* and his view in *Ex Parte Bollman* and *Ex Parte Swartwout*,[156] cases connected to the Burr conspiracy. One reading contends his vacillation is wrongly cited as evidence of a political motive rather than legal principle, while another attributes it to his effort "to *build* a national consensus on disputed constitutional questions."[157] The controversy was rooted in *Bollman* and *Swartwout*'s broad statement that those who provide for an assembly without committing a treasonous act by overtly levying war are guilty of treason. But Marshall's restrictive language in *Burr* suggests another reading: that those accused must have some proximity to the crime. As treason law expert James Willard Hurst renders the qualification, they must have "some minimum capacity-in-fact, sufficient to at least make them dangerous, to do harm."[158]

Brackenridge was convinced that Marshall had confirmed the defense team's view in the Whiskey Rebellion trials that treason required an overt act. Certainly, Marshall had expressed equivocal language relative to Paterson's opinion in *Mitchell* that suggested as much. First, Marshall considered that Paterson was "inclined" to think that marching to Neville's house was in itself an act of war though he did not "precisely state" it. Moreover, though Paterson, according to Marshall, held in one instance that the crime depended on the intention, in another he contended it required "combining actual force with a treasonable design."[159] Marshall then stated that the Whiskey Rebellion and Fries's Rebellion judges "seem to have required the actual exercise of force, the actual employment of some degree of violence." To justify this supposition, he intuited, "This, however, may be, and probably is, because [...] the design not having been to overturn the government, but to resist the execution of a law" would have required an assemblage capable of rendering "the object unequivocal."[160] Marshall could not be certain because, as he said, the judges implied "'an actual assembling of men, though they rather designed to remark on the purpose to which the force was to be applied than on the nature of the force itself.'"[161] It is noteworthy in this regard that Marshall consistently used conditional phrases or otherwise qualified his interpretation, citing throughout that the judges "are said 'to imply,'" they "indicate," "it must have been," and "it must have given"; he "estimated Paterson's opinion" and indicated what they "seem to have required" or what "would be" sufficient to the need at hand.

The larger obstacle for Marshall, however, was Paterson's construction of the overt treasonous act. As Marshall framed it, Paterson was disposed to think that "the assemblage at Couch's and the marching from thence' was the act of levying war, where Mitchell was seen by two witnesses.[162] But Paterson proceeded "without deciding this to be the law" and considered the assembly, the march, and the attack on the house as all one transaction.[163] Finding more than two witnesses to "that transaction," according to Marshall, Paterson "declared it to be unnecessary that all should have seen him at the same time and place." Marshall certainly had questions about Paterson's approach: What if no one had seen Mitchell at the fort or house or on the march? What if Mitchell had been "notoriously absent in a different state"? Could anyone who knew how cautious Paterson was, Marshall asked, have believed he would say Mitchell was "constructively present, and might, on that straining of a legal fiction" find him guilty of treason?[164] Marshall was less forgiving on this point than on the issue of force. Had Paterson, he noted, "given this opinion, it would have required all the correctness of his life to strike his name from that bloody list in which the name of Jeffreys is enrolled."[165] Marshall's indirection on this point might well have been informed by Paterson's thirteen years as a colleague on the court and his recent death.[166] In any case, Marshall was hesitant to accuse Paterson of having constructed a treason that was unprovable by way of witnesses, even if he appeared ready to admit that Paterson's model was untenable as a general principle for application to other cases.

In sum, Marshall had mined a reformed definition that made the employment of force, rather than the mere purpose to use force, a central consideration for a charge of treason and a necessary element of the crime. He made treason dependent upon intent; if an act of force was charged against an assemblage, the actor must have assembled with the intent to use force. Moreover, any act of treason must be proved by means of the constitutional standard of two witnesses to a single overt act; the proof could not be "constructively present" or "a legal fiction"; nor could an act of assembling in levying war be "an equivocal act." While Marshall did not extend his opinion to require that treason must intend to overthrow the government, he came close to it. And though he did not eliminate constructive treason, he put it on notice.[167] In addition, the *Burr* opinion clarified the law on conspiracy. It was not the case, Marshall held, that in levying war where many conspire and one of them acts on that conspiracy that all were guilty of treason, for that provision in the law did not cover all treason, merely the treason of counterfeiting. Had Hale, who offered the dictum, intended to apply the rule "universally he would have stated it as a general proposition."[168] Marshall thereby justified those whiskey rebels who were considered part of a treason because they had conspired but not acted. More importantly, he confirmed Brackenridge's earlier assertion that no act was treason without intent, and intent had to be attached to an overt act.

Justice Paterson's loose constructions on constitutional concerns such as the proof for treason, the question of intent, and the necessity of an overt act thus prevailed in the Whiskey Rebellion trials only to be disavowed within a decade and a half when Marshall brought the law on treason back in line with thinking in the constitutional convention. "I consider the principles laid down in that trial [*Burr*]," Brackenridge wrote, "as gaining much to the citizen of the United States." Referring to the debate over the legacy of English common law and English statutes in American legal practice, Brackenridge considered *Burr* "a barrier against the application of British rules in the construction of treason." Speaking as a good Republican, he added that Marshall's opinion "contains some excellent landmarks, that may serve to guide in aftertimes, when [political] parties may prevail, and [Federalist] *judges may have the same leaning with the prosecutors for the state.*"[169] Marshall was indeed quoted as a precedent in subsequent opinions on the questions of overt act and levying war in an acknowledgment that treason law had moved past the Whiskey Rebellion trials.[170]

Conclusion

Law in the early republic was admittedly in a state of flux. American legal institutions were unformed, and in terms of "frontier theory"[171] the law in early America was considered rude and unsophisticated. The "transatlantic connection" was imperfect,[172] and English law was a question of America's picking and choosing. Against this background, the social position, judicial authority, and political leanings of Federalist judges were expressed through judicial constructions to control the law. That these judges presided over newly established federal courts exacerbated the conflict between the general government and state jurisdiction and contributed to the contest over the law between the people and the government, each claiming sovereignty. Law was thereby at the center of what the nation would become; it did not exist in isolation but was interconnected with and positioned within culture and society.[173] Consequently, there was perhaps no other time in its history that the country's legal system was more dependent on its legal culture as a "matrix of values, attitudes, and assumptions" to shape its understanding of the law.[174]

Hugh Henry Brackenridge was perfectly positioned to capitalize on the conjunction of law, politics, and culture at a time when the nation was at loggerheads over the foundational values of democracy; a man of letters, social critic, politician, and legal mind, he read the law through the prism of American democracy, culture, and legal practice.[175] Brackenridge confronted William Blackstone's feudal understanding of allegiance, on the one hand, and, on the other, Jean-Jacques Rousseau's formulation of a tyranny of the general will. He rejected the "iron crown" of an inherited law unresponsive to the needs of those it would rule,[176] but, equally, he refused the view that an unregulated mob could dictate separation from an orderly society. Averse to the technicalities and strings of citations to which the law was prone, Brackenridge spoke with simplicity and directness to underlying principles and "common sense," deradicalizing Thomas Paine's vision of the American Revolution in preparing for an orderly legal system.[177] As a man of law, he supported the antiexcise resistance in a way that mediated between the world within the rebellion and the world without, stepping forward to assume a leadership role to express as well as contain dissent in the rebel assemblies while he advised elites and negotiated with the government to peacefully resolve the rebellion.

A contentious figure who nevertheless had a considerable legal reputation in western Pennsylvania, Brackenridge was a moderate in a time of immoderation and a defender of the rights of those whose rights were not regarded as consequential by the national government. If the rebels in western Pennsylvania presented themselves as citizens of the Union, the government narrative depicted them in the language of "banditti," disguised and secretive insurgents participating in unwarranted and extralegal proceedings. By contrast, Brackenridge crafted a defense for them rooted not in the context of mob rule but in common sense and reason to endow them with the right to choose their own allegiance and reject mere obedience to the state. He located in the jury the equity and democracy that he found lacking in elite constructions and historical precedents routinized in the law by judges' constructions. And he embraced an Americanized law that resonated with the legacy of the first principles of the Revolution and the natural rights of man.

Brackenridge's treason analysis can best be understood in the context of a response to rebellion in which an ad hoc bill-of-attainder approach still resonated. That approach ranged from illegal searches and seizures and interrogating defendants without due process to detaining them in custody for months before, or even without, bringing indictments or charges. The government oversaw an emergency judicial process characterized by warrantless mass roundups of suspects, denial of habeas corpus, lack of judicial process, and arbitrary and inconvenient removal of cases to federal courts across the state. The process limited access to defense witnesses and jurors familiar with the character and credibility of the defendant and his witnesses, permitting the prejudice that such treatment attached to the presumption of innocence. Such procedures smacked of nothing so much as the arbitrary privileging of government power against the rights of the individual.

Compared with the often pragmatic and reactive technical and procedural arguments that defense counsel offered in the rebel trials, Brackenridge's defense was more akin to a principled declaration of independence. He reminded his readers of the people's right to actively pursue a government of their choosing, softening received law. In the process, he made some critical distinctions in the law of treason that left open the route to secession that terrified the Federalists. As a function of popular sovereignty, he contended, a citizen's allegiance was neither natural nor perpetual; nor was it part of an obligatory exchange of obedience for protection by the government. In his rethinking of the philosophical underpinnings of allegiance, Brackenridge undertook to neutralize the argument that a subject owed automatic submission to the authority of the state, or even that benefiting from its laws obliged a subject to be loyal. He offered instead the possibility that a rebellious subject of the United States might renege on his allegiance and still not be guilty of treason. For Brackenridge, consent of the governed was key to meaningful allegiance, a position stubbornly aligned with an American view of the right to revolt against oppression. As a result, what appeared to be a straightforward social-compact issue provided analogues for Brackenridge that enabled him to link the disparate elements of his legal thinking.[178] The central analogy was between citizens held in perpetual allegiance and American law being condemned to English precedents. Analogy linked the "iron crown" of English law to the "badge of servitude"[179] expressed by tyrannical allegiance. Dissent from English common law mirrored emigration from England and secession from the Union, just as resisting the encroachment of inherited English law on American law was symmetrical with defying the encroachment of federal law on the states. Adopting only that common law that applied to a state's situation was confining in the same way as holding English constructions "to the constitutional orbit."[180] Similarly, state sovereignty in relation to the federal government was reciprocated by secessionist aspirations in the western part of the Union. By the same reasoning, independence in one's political allegiance corresponded to independence in legal judgment; what might not, in the words of Brackenridge's biographer, "govern in precedent" might "guide in reason."[181]

Brackenridge was in other ways a conservative jurist with a penchant for tradition but without being entirely beholden to the past. Thus, he appreciated the wisdom of generations embedded in English common law and depended on principle in departing from precedent. He rejected the idea of disavowing inherited English common law and statutes that were applicable to American conditions and useful to the purposes of American courts. Conversely, he emphasized revising the legal process to discourage robotic reliance on strings of precedents and legal technicalities and to enable recourse to underlying principles of equity, reason, and common sense. He spoke powerfully against abusive constructions of the law and the tendency of judges to support pro-government prosecution positions, a tendency that reflected the embedded nature of a conservative English law that had much more interplay with American law than many would admit.[182] In doing so, he re-enforced the liberal part of the English legacy that resisted a wide scope of prosecution and constructions that weakened limits on treason.

The improvement of American over English law was a point of pride for Brackenridge who embraced those aspects of common law that privileged intent or supported the Constitution's narrowed definition of treason, its constraints on government authority, and its protection of individual rights. Brackenridge's theory of constitutional democracy disallowed political redefinition of treason by the executive and expansion of treason by legislation. In his defense of a restrictive constitutional definition of treason, stretched beyond recognition by Federalists, it was the overthrow of the republic and not the common law fact pattern of posture of war, array of arms, and conspiracy that controlled treason law. The American Constitution and U.S. laws based on it, and not English common law precedents or judicial constructions, were Brackenridge's guiding light.

Discounted by the Whiskey Rebellion and Fries's Rebellion trials (which found its precedent in the errors of the whiskey trials), Brackenridge's views had broken with practice in American courts that would take another half a century to restrict judicial constructivism, limit government power, and protect individual rights.[183] Still, the core of his views on treason were justified by Justice Marshall's opinion in the Burr trial, an opinion that would count as the last word on treason in the early republic. Where the late eighteenth century might not have had a defined perspective on treason, Brackenridge had examined it as a social critic and legal analyst on both a practical and a theoretical level. His work on treason might not have been cited in law reports, just as Brackenridge himself did not have an opportunity to comment on treason law in his role as a Pennsylvania Supreme Court justice. Yet, as an element of a larger legal culture, his work had resonance. It recalled the rebel assemblies' return to first principles in challenging allegiance to authority and resisting limitation of the legal right to reject oppressive laws; and it resonated with the legacy of the American Revolution and its principled defense of a natural right to popular sovereignty. Brackenridge's treason notes, his satire of the rebellion, and his social theory of allegiance expressed the humanism of the law, literature, and politics of late eighteenth-century legal thought along the western frontier. Importantly, it captured the democratic vision of America spread through its history from the 1760s to the 1790s.[184] Brackenridge's independence, even his idiosyncratic politics, contributed to an astute legal analysis and insight into how the new nation thought about its approach to treason law under uniquely American conditions.

The rebel defense gets the last word in this final chapter because it has not hitherto been examined in any detail in studies of the rebellion, whereas, in fact, it is essential to preserving a holistic view of why the rebellion happened and what it meant as a legal matter. We focus on it as well because it caps our understanding of resistance to hegemonic power as it was revealed in the people's relation to the courts, their agitation-propaganda, their traditional and invented rituals, and the assemblies that organized and expressed dissent during the rebellion. These insertions into the history of the Whiskey Rebellion are not, however, the most compelling reason for revisiting and repositioning the contribution popular values add to the conflict between liberty and order. Nor are they merely useful because they challenge a prevailing view of that conflict (the Hamiltonian view) or question the interpretation of the event that returned it to its place as a salient moment in early American history (Thomas P. Slaughter's work). Rather, they allow us to go places where previous studies have not gone, using the rebellion as a frame that opens out onto a view of the law and legal culture of the early republic. In this effort, the study restores to history the perspective of westerners as a competing approach to the law at a time when a new national judicial system was just emerging and the Constitution was just asserting itself as the law of the land.

What follows in the conclusion provides an afterword of sorts, with attention to tying together the themes of the book, but also to page-marking ideas in relation to the rebellion that take us beyond the time and space of the rebellion itself to other considerations. There, we attend to questions of language and culture that connect to our own times while they look backward to warnings from a rebellion that captured the imagination of the 1790s in much the same way that problems with democracy have captured ours.

CONCLUSION

An Afterword

On Monday last we had a party of *liberty boys* in this town. About three hundred of them raised a liberty pole in the middle of the streets, and their motto on their flag is 'Liberty or Death.' They likewise have a paper on the pole with this inscription—"Liberty, plenty of Whiskey, and No Excise." Although it was court week, the judges took no notice of them. Every four or five miles along the road, there are liberty poles raised, with the same inscription as above.
—"A Letter from Bedford County," *New-Jersey Journal*, September 10, 1794

[U]pwards of 120 of the *pole gentry* were confined in that town, and more hourly collected—information had been received at Hagerstown of the erecting of a pole about seven miles from the town, a party of the horses went in pursuit and took them prisoners—their principal they compelled to cut a sapling of a tolerable size and carry it on his shoulder to Hagerstown.
—"Extract of a letter from a gentleman in Hagerstown," *Carlisle Gazette*, September 24, 1794

That there is such a person as *George Washington*, and that he is President of the United States, are historical relations, within the bounds of probability—He preaches most excellent politics, and the equality of man, but he preaches against insurrections and rebellions, and this drew upon him the resentment of the "*Whiskey boys*." They accuse him of endeavoring to support good government, and to remain at peace with all nations; which is very probably the case.
—"No. 6," *The Medley or Newbedford Marine Journal*, June 5, 1795

The legal culture that enveloped the Whiskey Rebellion, this study has argued, was made up of state and federal courts, as well as extrajudicial arbitration courts accommodating such parties as Quakers, merchants, and settlers in personal, debt, commercial, and land disputes. It included extralegal popular justice that ranged from democratic society courts to those of rebel assemblies, the primitive law of effigies, liberty poles, and tarring and feathering. Where it surfaced as a tool of government, legal culture found itself in its most naked form in the bench notes of judges and opinions unofficially shared between practitioners of the law and more formally with the published law reports that serviced the profession. In its official guise it appeared in grand jury and petite jury charges, in trials, and in jury statements. The legal culture that informed resistance to government appeared in rebel assembly petitions, resolutions, and speeches expressed with an affinity for the western Anti-Federalism of the ratification convention. In the out-of-door politics of popular activism, that culture manifested itself in the agitation-propaganda of posted and printed notices and vigilantism. It emerged pseudonymously in newspapers to conduct political debates and to proselytize and recruit, even to humiliate and threaten. In sum, the legal culture that emanated from and informed the Whiskey Rebellion pervaded the western Pennsylvania counties at all levels and across a spectrum of official and unofficial activities and sites. In a backcountry rife with Indian wars, land grabs, and economic disrepair, legal culture acted much like a spine linking the skeletal parts of life on the frontier.

Whereas leading up to and during the Whiskey Rebellion the people had lost confidence in unresponsive official courts and experimented with popular forms of justice, the federal government was at work creating a national system of courts, and state courts were intent on reforming themselves and defending their own viability. Federalist judges in federal grand jury charges delivered an educative public message of constitutional governance that was supported by citizen-juries. The message spoke of fealty to national government and weighted the balance of liberty rights and order on the side of institutional stability and representative government, not direct democracy. Social order, citizenship, and obedience to the law were their judicial watchwords in a nation under siege internally and threatened externally. The very meat of grand jury charges was directed at countering anarchy and secession with a message of union and national government.

At the level of popular law talk, dissent expressed through public assemblies, protests, and libelous attacks undermined respect for the Constitution and its laws to make the Whiskey Rebellion both a test of the Constitution's viability and an experiment in governing under it. Some considered that the real challenge to the government was that the Whiskey Rebellion was a necessary and convincing proof of the need for a strong central government, as if a strong government needed the excuse of a rebellion just as rebellion depended on a belligerent government. Thus, while the grand jury charges directed themselves at creating a citizenry amenable to constitutional governance, the Whiskey Rebellion trials tested how and for whom the early republic's courts should work, whether for the government, the elite, proponents of Federalism, and the eastern political establishment or for debtors, the propertyless, populists, and those accused of resistance.

On such questions of political interest, the expectations of the eastern and western parts of the country clearly diverged. The East expected peace and order on the frontier, free access to speculate on land, and gratitude for the gains of the Revolution. Westerners who wanted to take possession and improve the land as settlers had no wealth, landholdings, or political status. In that sense, they had no distinctive identity and were invisible. Their removal to the East for trial following the rebellion was an iconic statement meant to deny them their regional autonomy and disassociate them from the land that endowed them with their historical consciousness and spatial reality. It was both an involuntary removal and a physical displacement intended to dislodge them psychologically and socially from the people and places from which they drew their meaning, much like the treatment given to the Indians. Denigrated as "whiskey boys," "liberty boys," and "pole gentry" in the press,[1] and as rabble, bandits, and disguised dangerous combinations by the government, westerners were reduced to an identity that marginalized them regionally, ideologically, and in terms of class as inferiors. Westerners were vulnerable to the government's "race-ing" of their regional character, which considered them lower on the human scale and closer to half-caste savages than their skin-privileged betters on the east coast. Their perceived condition rendered their claim to rights part of the larger problem of the stability of white identity.[2] Framed in terms of the mutability of white Indians, they presented a problem for the new nation in terms of "fit." They were tied to an atavistic fear of aborigines on the dark frontier that recalled for free whites on the eastern coast the case of Black African slaves whose various stages of freedom under Pennsylvania's Gradual Abolition Act of 1780 would take sixty-five years to resolve. These were the deeper identity stakes of the rebellion that put the question of vicinage at the heart of western resistance to federal government.

Before the trials, the people convened in assemblies to petition, debate, and make speeches, while in the public sphere the propaganda arm of the rebellion discoursed through popular demonstrations and speech acts as well as creative uses of the print medium from handbills and posted notices to coercive newspaper publicity. But narratively speaking, resisters were positioned on the margins of a discourse that considered their claims illegitimate, that appropriated their rights, and that controlled their narrative tropes. Their cultural power was silenced by rhetorical strategies that allowed for powerful misconceptions and shrunk access to public approval.[3] The rebellion fought back. It countered with a narrative that cast off the disempowering fictional role to which it had been assigned and created a reading based on rights-based constitutional dissent together with shared revolutionary stereotypes, myths, and lineage. The rebellion revealed itself in a plot of self-discovery in which the people restored the former greatness of the American Revolution by throwing off demagoguery to participate in governance as rights-bearing subjects. Between idiosyncratic opposition to the excise tax and the opportunism of defenders of the tax stood a rebellion that became potent once it recognized its ability to speak to a body of the people and not to a radical subset of westerners. This was the value of the rebel assembly, which narrated idiosyncratic acts into a groundswell through a discourse of dissent reminiscent of revolutionary popular movements. It discovered its strength in the genius of asking members of meetings to vote on representation and resolutions and in its ability to connect groups through committees of correspondence. And it inserted itself into popular traditions of petition, speech, and assembly that capitalized on a theory of popular sovereignty requiring the people's consent to govern, a theory solidified in a founding document to which the people as a whole had given their consent. If the rebellion ultimately resulted in failed trials, a change of government in new elections, and repeal of the offending excise act, it was because of the connection to constitutional resistance made possible by the assemblies.

With the advent of the trials, the judicial narrative directed itself to reducing discursive chaos to a tentative order by settling the struggle between the government and rebel positions over the meaning of democracy. The social position, judicial authority, and political leanings of Federalist judges nonetheless controlled what law was heard in the courtroom, a venue where the Federalist grand jury narrative remained persuasive as a tale of strong central government. Still, the trial narrative proved fragmentary and unconvincing as appearing in the courtroom humanized the rebels, endowed them with legal rights, and provided an opportunity for the first time to present an authorizing structure for insurgency before an attentive public. The challenges to judicial constructions and the legitimacy of common law interpretations thus took place on a more expansive public stage where the voice of the people could be heard in juries' refusal to indict or convict large numbers of the rebels and in the popular cry for pardons.

The government's narrative, by contrast, exposed a less noble picture. In selling a funding scheme to the government, Hamilton's counsel on the rebellion was essentially a reflexive reaction to protecting his brainchild. His government spies followed suit in indulging their appetite for a federal appointment and connection to an elite network. Cabinet secretaries' political fortunes were tied to the survival of the Federalists, who considered the threat to centralized government greater than the threat to the nation posed by international wars. The president, looking at the uprising through a military lens, engaged the rebellion in person through the spectacle of a military cavalcade intent on suppressing internal dissent. In each instance, government actors had little motivation to see the rebellion in terms of its complexity as a story of a political body asserting its identity through popular struggle and aspirations for self-governance. In the end, the greatest danger did not happen; there was neither secession nor a civil war. The denouement was not like the compromise over the Stamp Act nor the win enjoyed by the American Revolution. The rebellion ended in a confused invasion, a chaotic process of submission and amnesty, and the ignominy of show trials, all without bloodshed.

This study maintains that studies of the Whiskey Rebellion miss something of importance when they concentrate on the violence and the outrages of rebellion. It is more revealing, sociopolitically, legally, and historically to look at the rebellion as a contest of narratives embodying contending interests. Where the government narrative capitalized on oppositional themes and characterizations informed by national concerns, western-differentiated rebels held fast to their claim of a local identity. They intensified their insistence on a regional common cause and refused to disavow a cultural distinctiveness that was a tenet of their political faith and a pillar of their narrative. They were not about to be marooned, as former slaves were,[4] nor degraded and tainted by their association with the Indians in a land whose bespoke values did not include or describe them. They felt they deserved, if not wealth or political status, rights and a land in which they belonged.

Rebel legal culture defined itself against an eastern elite, Federalist-dominated narrative that discounted popular dissent. Whereas the eastern elite fixated on opposition to French influence in the East, the authorial western voice told a story whose setting was purely frontier based, a locale populated not by French diplomats and Francophile political figures but by Indians, land grabs, forts, and rivers. Its intended audience of settlers and local officials placed allegiance at the center of its preferred plot and replayed the Revolution's values with a cast of unregenerate characters who rejected inherited legal bonds to retell their story on more familiar grounds and with identity themes of their own making. Common law was common sense, precedent was local, and constructions were social. They cast themselves in the garb and disguises that characterized the ambiguity of the terrain in which their narrative played out, attuned to traditions of tricksters, folk figures, and rituals that registered their opposition to alienated state and federal practices.

Pure democracy, equality, and regional independence resonated across their narrative with a reconstituted perspective on natural rights that returned western Pennsylvania to first principles. Pragmatic reaction to received law argued for the original right to contract for allegiance by choice and not duty or obligation. Pragmatism spoke to its intended audience of the reciprocal responsibilities of subjects and officials and a route to secession when that connection was abrogated. To build their brave new world, the people participated directly in activating their collective right to craft their own story, first through cultural resistance and acts of force but ultimately in legally defensible acts of speech, assembly, petition, and dissent to prevent alien judicial constructions from rewriting the story of their legal rights. Narratively, the rebel story operated within the present as its functional frame, discounting the far feudal past as a point of reference and rewriting the more recent revolutionary past to provide the hindsight that justified its storying. Nascent democracy tested both the frontier's propensity for chaos and the common man's nobility while it contested the undying authority of their forefathers. The people were willing to pull down their own house about their heads to assert their right to rebuild it and to destroy false freedom to make change happen. They would prove permanent allegiance an ephemera, a self-defeating prophecy, not a constant feature of man's condition. This was a narrative of nation building within a nation that had just proved its right to exist, but it was also a narrative in which the people ran the government and not the government the people. It argued that freedom was its own parent in an act of self-creation and that secession was implicit in every act of self-assertion. Like the Revolution, if the people had no right to abolish all law they were willing to obey appropriate laws and maintained the right to reject laws that served the needs of a coercive state.

In narrating the early republic, this study has positioned legal culture as a frame that plays a decisive role. Robert A. Ferguson begins his classic study *Law and Letters in American Culture* with the statement "The centrality of law in the birth of the republic is a matter of national lore" and goes on to say that Blackstone's *Commentaries* were second only to the Bible as an influence on American institutions.[5] Legal historian G. Edward White presents "law as culturally 'special' in America," not as a cultural artifact or "a product of its historical setting" but as a binding force rooted in a rule of law central to democracy where social conflicts were presented as legal issues that tested the "nation's collective identity."[6] In early America, not only did those with talent almost uniformly go into the law, but revolutionary rhetoric "was patently legalistic." Legal thought gave American history its context; legal terminology informed political debate; and the law rationalized the new nation, rendering religion a secondary force. In every sense, law—natural and divine—connected the affairs of the country and gave it its order. If there was an American king, Thomas Paine famously declared, it was the law.[7] By this argument, law was an innovating force in a changing world that had no tradition of its own.[8] It is a small step to say that the center that holds does so because of what and how the law speaks. This is nowhere better exemplified visually than in a late eighteenth-, early nineteenth-century print titled "Washington Giving the Laws to America,"[9] where the president appears in neoclassical garb, the Constitution in hand, the god Ares at his feet with his hand on the lion of war. Washington's place in history assured (the figure of History appears holding a mirror pointing to the future, a city on a hill), an annunciating angel floats overhead with an eagle on its shield. The military and religion are combined under one authority, the law, which controls the whole. The import of law narrating the early republic is here made manifest.

But law, as we have said, does not stand alone in this study; it is paired with culture. Culture shapes our understanding, but more than that it creates and sustains how we engage with the world. It is embedded in the very phrase used to identify the subject of the present study where the Whiskey Rebellion of 1794 becomes the descendant of Alexander Hamilton's contemptuous denomination the "whiskey insurrection."[10] While newspapers called them the "whiskey boys," Hamilton's agent George Clymer attributed their poor citizenship to a depravity of morals occasioned "by the intemperate use of the favourite drink."[11] The phrase distinguished the western tax revolt on the one hand from, on the other hand, widely revered mob actions like those protesting the Stamp Act and the Boston tea tax and from Regulations, popular efforts to regulate ineffective government.[12]

Culture informs not only Hamilton's appellation but also the power of the myths that framed President Washington and against which the rebels had to contend. Washington was the defining figure of the early republic—embodied in the myths of the titan Atlas and the Roman general Cincinnatus. Atlas's punishment in the failed Titan revolt against the Olympians—supporting the weight of the cosmos on his shoulder—characterized Washington as a figure of superhuman stature. Washington's substantial height and strength and the burden he carried in taking on command of the Continental army and assuming the presidency confirmed him as the American Atlas.[13] Washington reprised, just as fortuitously, Cincinnatus's example as the citizen-general who answered the call of his country to lead its troops to victory and then retire from public life to farm his land; he did so three times over: as a British officer in the Seven Years' War, as commander of the Continental army, and again as president. Stepping away from power, Washington exemplified the public man without ambition. An iconic nonpartisan figure, he carefully crafted his association with the Roman general, including as president-general of the Society of Cincinnatus.[14]

Washington enjoyed the stature of not only a mythic or classical figure but also the father of his country, liberator, and patriot-king, which carried an authority ranking him with monarchs. Indeed, the press reportedly wrote that when Washington traveled to rendezvous with the militia set to engage the rebels, it was an "artful attempt" to present himself like an English monarch assuming the right to direct "the force of the state."[15] In an inauguration that some considered a coronation, the Senate debated what title he ought to assume, with some feeling his new role should require the "obeisances" of messengers moving in and out. John Adams wanted a title that would elevate the president to "His most benign Highness." An appointed Senate committee recommended the title "His Highness the president of the United States of America and Protector of their Liberties," while Washington was reported to have considered favorably adding "His High Mightiness" to the president and Protector titles. A joint House and Senate conference committee ultimately resolved the matter on the grounds that it would be improper to add any title beyond that plainly stated in the Constitution. Washington and all future presidents would simply be called the "President of the United States," avoiding any taint of British monarchy or aspirations to kingship under another name.[16]

Alas, the rebels had no such standing. They were for the most part mere plebeians, a status encapsulated in language that condescended to backcountry democrats who dared to assert their sovereignty. Hamilton's network of spies portrayed a rebel movement of "sordid shopkeepers, crafty lawyers, or candidates for office"[17] and pictured a three-part division of a disobedient elite, an enraged mob, and a cowed general populace to define the moving parts of the rebellion. The government reconceptualized its amorphous enemy in the language of "banditti," "violent and unwarrantable proceedings," and a "seditious confederacy," equating politicized economic resistance with the criminal acts of highway robbers such as the Appalachian "Black Boys" and violent gangs such as the infamous Paxton Boys, reinscribed by Ben Franklin as "Christian White Savages."[18] Critically, the addition of the term "combinations" upscaled "banditti" to include multicounty meetings whose structured activity organized large groups in concerted antigovernment actions. Moreover, the language of the Militia Act of 1792 ("combinations too powerful to be [judicially] suppressed") became a recurring mantra that resonated with the legal requirement to authorize a federal militia.[19] Identifying assemblies as illegal "combinations" elevated the threat of secession from the Union, a powerful argument against the assemblies. Applying the term to a range of activities (from plebeian mobs and local meetings to bourgeois democratic societies and pseudo-legislative assemblies) amplified the danger to constitutional democracy and legitimized a forceful government response. Naming preemptively transformed a vague, unfamiliar threat into an imminent certainty.

The image of the Hydra was emblematic of that threat. The many-headed Hydra had a formidable mythological meaning involving the second of Heracles's labors where, having had a head cut off, two more sprang up in its place; to slay the beast, Heracles cauterized its stumps and dipped his arrows into its blood, endowing them with a fatal power. If Washington was Atlas supporting the burdens of the new republic, the rebellion was a monstrous Hydra endlessly reproducing itself. Described by an expert in backcountry sociology, the image was a "favored elite metaphor [. . .] a monstrously fused mass that is simultaneously hideously dispersed."[20] The public iteration of the Hydra was no homage to the serpent in flags of the American Revolution ("Liberty or Death," "Join or Die," "Don't tread on me"). Rather, recontextualizing the earlier image required an act of collective amnesia about the value and meaning of revolution after the war of liberation against the British. In the public sphere, the Hydra came to figure Anti-Federalist dissent. Eighteenth-century readings of the myth typically pictured the "motley rabble" of a polymorphic mob resisting authority.[21] The Federalists' friend William Cobbett referred to the image as "the many-headed Hydra of republicanism," a "system of anarchy" rooted in the French Revolution.[22] Transplanted in the Whiskey Rebellion, it was "[a]n Hydra in a free and republican country justly to be feared."[23]

In an inversion worthy of the contested meanings that battled one another in the rebellion, the Hydra was itself contested. Thus, while Washington recalled a Heraclean task that called for cutting off the heads of secession and anarchy to preserve constitutional government and Federalists associated the image with the spreading poison of rebellion, dissenters gave the image a diametrically opposed meaning. There, the Hydra signified the many voices of the people and the fight for their liberties; it represented undying resistance to the established order and the hegemony of monarchy. Thus, the Hydra of monarchy was to be "decapitated by the battle ax of liberty" and insurgents were called on to "be a Hercules to crush despotism and monarchy."[24]

Culture, it was evident, counted in the Whiskey Rebellion even if its meaning could not be contained. Hamilton took pains, according to William Findley, to "impress the public mind"[25] with ideas based not on facts but on language or constructions dependent on pregnant circumstances. An illustration of the government's "pretense" in magnifying dangers, disfiguring views, and attributing falsehoods,[26] the government's determination to put down rebellion as an "experiment" was itself a function of provocative "naming." Overall, transforming the meaning of revolution and rebellion was intended to exclude backcountry democracy from association with the sanctified American war for freedom and allowed the government to place rebel grievances under erasure. Importantly, it neutralized the potency of the language of "constitutional resistance" by tautology: law is not law, Hamilton had contended, when it is lawfully exercised to resist the law. Understanding culture, in the end, is undeniably crucial to how we conceive of events historically, but it is not an easy thing.

On a personal note, the present study has examined the people's loss of faith in law and government in the 1790s as a sign of a time when democracy was in danger. This exploration of a clash within legal culture between competing narratives of order and disorder resonates with where we are today—a test for the conditions under which democracy itself is under threat of erasure. Where leadership is no longer trusted to protect the people and where an elite takes its opportunity to enrich itself in power and wealth, national unity is sacrificed. The erosion of democratic norms and abuse of power, rather than reason and law, become the weapons of choice. Demonizing one's opponent becomes the rule because honoring one's enemy is not possible where partisanship reigns. Some common focus, some higher good is necessary. In the Whiskey Rebellion, that force became the Constitution. If the people, left to their own devices, subscribed to disintegrating tendencies and if judicial interpretations of common law become tyrannical, the text of the agreed-upon founding document superseded both tendencies. It endowed the people with the right of resistance so long as that resistance was constitutional. And it endowed the government with the authority of a law to which the people had given their consent. The Constitution allowed for uncomfortable political opposition while preserving civil order and the stability of the state, allowing that popular dissent was not treason so long as it did not intend to overthrow this agreement.

The warning of the 1790s is that such a touchstone might no longer be available to us. With a loss of faith in institutions, a political crisis like that of the present-day partisan divide might well be incapable of taking the lesson of the 1790s to heart. A bifurcated community is the new constant of contemporary politics, making unity, an essential attribute of democracy, inaccessible. Where the incentive to cooperate is minimal, the body politic's hydra of partisan conflict looms larger than Atlas's feat of bearing the weight of the world on his broad shoulders. The takeaway might well be to keep one's eye on the horizon where a more sweeping trajectory prevails and where consensus might be brewing. This could easily be the legacy of a failed rebellion that gave back to the nation its hope for unity. Failures, we are reminded, are often as important as successes, a necessary form of changing-by-learning in the historical present.

One can profitably apply lessons of the 1790s to the present day. Examining how democracies emerge and die, recent studies have contended that American democracy today is at risk of "regime fragility" like that which has occurred only five times in the country's history, the 1790s being one such period.[27] In the space created by a critical juncture, governments make choices and close off alternatives, establishing or reinforcing institutions.[28] National unity or agreement within the political community, a critical feature of democracy, depends on how such transitions are negotiated by the opposing powers of political elites and social forces. The clash over leadership and the criminalizing of political opposition, this study has suggested, are powerful signs of a threat to the very survival of democracy. It is, indeed, democracy's Achilles's heel.[29] Ideological conflict combined with autocratic tendencies is precisely the issue that resonates with the Whiskey Rebellion's contest between elites and backcountry democrats and the erosion of democratic norms in the 1790s.

Suzanne Mettler and Robert C. Lieberman make the point that of four threats to democracy the largest in the 1790s was polarization (the other three were conflict over who belongs, rising economic inequality, and executive aggrandizement). Certainly, polarization had the greatest capacity to undermine early democracy if one considers the assault on liberties and the attack on dissent. But with frail constitutional protections and weak commitment to the rule of law, with inequality in the status of women, slaves, and Indians, and with overweening executive power, elements of all four threats were implicated in the earlier period. Mettler and Lieberman, in fact, conclude that "the nation came precariously close to its first decade being its last."[30] That seems to be about right for our times as well.

The interfacing of partisan activity and electoral politics that began in the 1790s is a remarkable prototype for present-day conspiracy theories and riotous activity in the United States. In fact, in the period of the 2010s we see all four threats in play. We are reminded, moreover, that these abuses of democratic practices are neither new nor particularly surprising, for America has had a partisan tradition of dissent that goes back over two and a half centuries in the country's experiences with crowd politics and mobocracy.[31] Plebeian activists proudly identified themselves with party causes at a time when the populace at large construed political parties and their conflicts as destructive forces, and even as organized street crowds, political clubs, and militias were common, attracting ordinary people into the public sphere and giving rise to riots that purported to give the disenfranchised a voice in governance. The contest, as John L. Brooke depicts it, was between "the state, civil society, and the outlaw 'uncivil,'"[32] so that alongside gentlemen's politics there coexisted a politics of disruptive political mobilization. In "Trumpian" terms, Isaac Ariail Reed reminds us, "It is simultaneously about economic disenfranchisement and a kind of reassertion of whiteness and then also a cultural alienation from the world of a cosmopolitan globalization [multicultural, global, multiracial]."[33]

Historians since Richard Hofstadter have labeled conspiracies that ran rife among revolutionaries the "paranoid style," finding, like Gordon S. Wood, that they run through American politics among minorities and the marginalized. Wood even considers whether the Revolution had predisposed resisters to think in terms of conspiratorial dark forces as a feature of national identity and to believe in plots as "a rational attempt to explain human phenomena."[34] There is a long history of paranoid thinking in the United States from the American Revolution and the Whiskey Rebellion to the Ku Klux Klan, Senator McCarthy, and present-day extremist conspiracy theories. Internationally, it extends across history from fears of witchcraft and Freemasonry to the Illuminati.[35] In a meta-analysis of eighty-eight studies, in twelve countries, over forty-four years, involving twenty-two thousand subjects, social scientists Saunder van der Linden and others demonstrate that extremist ideologies on both the right and the left (though more significantly on the right) are vulnerable to conspiratorial thinking. Their study concludes that such thinking is tied to paranoia and feelings of powerlessness, as well as a lack of education and even "magical thinking."[36] These dangers threaten the stability of liberal democracies that require a level of trust to allow people to share power and consent "to being governed by others with whom they disagree."

Democracy in all its permutations, we can conclude, is a work in progress, forever unfinished, always contested. In one meaning, all those who enter are reduced to abandoning hope; in another, we are encouraged by the possibility of change to continue to engage. Grudgingly, some align themselves with party, others with the powerful; some with conspiracies, others with truths that bear the appearance of facts. In whatever guise, the trajectory for democracy is uneven, even Sisyphean. While democracy represents a terrible choice, except for all the others, it promises to make us stronger, if we do not kill it first.

APPENDIX A

Trial Research Sources

Court Reports

United States v. Hamilton, 3 U.S. (3 Dall.) 17–18 (C.C. Pa 1795).
United States v. The Insurgents of Pennsylvania, 2 U.S. (2 Dall.) 335–342 (C.C. Pa 1795).
United States v. Porter, 2 U.S. (2 Dall.) 345 (C.C. Pa. 1795).
United States v. Stewart, 2 U.S. (2 Dall.) 343–345 (C.C. Pa. 1795).
United States v. Wright, 2 U.S. (2 Dall.) 343–345 (C.C. Pa. 1795).
United States v. Mitchell, 2 U.S. (2 Dall.) 348–357 (C.C. Pa. 1795).
United States v. Vigol, 2 U.S. (2 Dall.) 346–348 (C.C. Pa. 1795).
Ex Parte Corbly; Lockery; Hamilton; Sedgwick, reconstructed in *The Documentary History of the Supreme Court of the United States, 1789–1800*, vol. 6, 514–518.

William Paterson Bench Notes

United States v. Robert Porter, May 18, 1795, Heinz History Center, Pittsburgh Regional History Center, in association with the Smithsonian Institution. MFF2739. 1795.
United States v. John Barnet, May 29, 1795, Gilder Lehrman Institute, GLC01114.
United States v. Miller, June 1, 1795, Paterson Papers, 1689–1841, 2.B. Federal Court Case, file 119. Sarah Byrd Askew Library, William Paterson College. See David and Lorraine Cheng Library, William Paterson University.
United States v. Philson and Husband, June 3, 1795, Paterson Papers, 1689–1841, 2.B. Federal Court Cases, file 120. Sarah Byrd Askew Library, William Paterson College. See David and Lorraine Cheng Library, William Paterson University.

Documentary History

Marcus, Maeva, ed. *The Documentary History of the Supreme Court of the United States, 1789–1800*. Vols. 1–6. New York: Columbia University Press, 1990–1994.

Pennsylvania Archives

Pennsylvania Archives, First Series. 1852–1856. Edited by Samuel Hazard. Vol. 10. Harrisburg, [Pa.]: Clarence M. Busch.
Pennsylvania Archives, Second Series. 1896. Edited by John B. Linn and William H. Egle. Vol. 4. Harrisburg, [Pa.]: Clarence M. Busch.

Library of Congress

Pennsylvania Whiskey Rebellion Collection, Manuscript Division, Library of Congress.

Microfilm

Criminal Case Files of the U.S. Circuit Court for the Eastern District of Pennsylvania, 1791–1840 (National Archives Microfilm Publication M986). National Archives Federal Records Center, Philadelphia.
Minutes of the U.S. Circuit Court for the Eastern District of Pennsylvania, 1790–1844 (National Archives Microfilm Publication M932). National Archives Federal Records Center, Philadelphia.
Misc. Letters of the Dep't of State 1784–1825 (National Archives Microfilm Publication M179). National Archives Federal Records Center, Philadelphia.

Collections

Adams Administration. Petitions for Pardon, 1789–1860. Records Group 59. National Archives.
Alexander Addison Papers. Darlington Collection. Special Collections Department. University of Pittsburgh.
Bradford Family Papers. Historical Society of Pennsylvania.
David Bradford Letters. Louisiana and Lower Mississippi Valley Collection. Louisiana State University.
Bradford Family Papers. Louisiana State University.
Arthur Campbell Papers. Filson Historical Society. Louisville, Kentucky.
Craig Papers. Carnegie Library, Pittsburgh.
George M. Dallas Papers. Historical Society of Pennsylvania.
Founders Online. National Archives. https://founders.archive.gov.
Albert Gallatin Papers. New York Historical Society, NHi.
Simon Gratz Collection. Historical Society of Pennsylvania.
John Heinz History Center. Pittsburgh Regional History Center, in association with the Smithsonian Institution.
Irvine Papers. Historical Society of Pennsylvania.
Gilder Lehrman Institute of American History. The Gilder Lehrman Collection, 1493–1859. Documents Relating to 1794.
Neville Papers. Carnegie Library, Pittsburgh.
William Paterson Papers. 1689–1841. Sarah Byrd Askew Library. William Paterson College. See David and Lorraine Cheng Library, William Paterson University.

William Paterson Papers. 1766–1898. Special Collections, University Archives. Rutgers University Library.
Richard Peters Papers. Historical Society of Pennsylvania.
Petitions for Pardons, 1789–1860, Box 1. Misc. Files—Washington's Term. General Records of the Department of State (Record Group 59). National Archives.
Timothy Pickering Papers. Massachusetts Historical Society.
Rawle Family Papers, 1697–1845. Historical Society of Pennsylvania.
Sargent Papers. Massachusetts Historical Society.
John William Wallace Papers. Historical Society of Pennsylvania.
Oliver Wolcott Manuscripts. Connecticut Historical Society.

APPENDIX B

Circuit Court Trial Records

Prisoners
    20 marched from the western country
    64 jailed or faced charges in Philadelphia
52 indictments issued
    Indictments
        24 indictments for treason
        2 indictments for felony (robbing the mail)
        26 indictments for speech-related misdemeanors
            1 for writing a seditious letter
            6 for seditious speech
            19 for liberty pole raising
    Failed Indictments
        4 not indicted for misprision of treason
        5 not indicted for speech-related misdemeanors
        12 not indicted for treason
    Disposition of Cases
        12 indictments brought to trial
            8 in seven trials (April and May 1795)
            4 in two trials (October 1795)
    Treason
        2 indicted for treason pardoned during trial
        1 indicted for treason amnestied
        12 indicted for treason not prosecuted as fled
        22 charged with treason but not yet indicted released
        10 indicted and tried for treason
            8 indicted and tried for treason found innocent
            2 indicted and tried for treason convicted and pardoned
    Felony
        1 indicted for felony (robbing the mail) not prosecuted as fled
        1 indicted for felony (robbing the mail) prosecuted instead for treason (and convicted, see above)

Misdemeanors
> 24 indicted for misdemeanors released
> 2 speech-related misdemeanors tried and found innocent

SUM: 2 convictions for 52 indictments

Note: Based on Wythe Holt's review of trial records. Holt, "Federal Whiskey," chapter 5: 4–8; Holt, "Whiskey Rebellion," 75–76.

NOTES

Introduction

1. Lin-Manuel Miranda, track 35, *Hamilton: An American Musical* (2014 Workshop), as performed off-Broadway, New York, Public Theater, May 2014. The earlier version was the second half of "One Last Ride," which was cut when the musical transitioned to Broadway. The final version appears as track 32 in the 2015 Broadway cast recording; it reflects Washington's career ending quietly; in the original, he leaves in triumph having led federal troops into battle. https://genius.com/Lin-manuel-miranda-one-last-ride-lyrics.

2. Washington, Address to Congress, November 19, 1794, https://founders.archives.gov; Engels, *Enemyship*, 3, 7–11, 30, 125–126; Fletcher, *Comic*, 3–10; White, *Backcountry*, 131–133; Marshall, *Life*, 185; Larson, *Trials*.

3. Owen, *Political*, 138–142.

4. Tachau, "New," 99–104.

5. Sharp, *American*, 93, 107–111; Bouton, *Taming*, 217–219; Newman, *Fries's*, 146–164; Connor, "Politics," 259–281.

6. Robertson, "'Look,'" 1268.

7. Spero, *Frontier*.

8. Spero, *Frontier*, 4, 8, 245–246.

9. Gallo, "Improving," 136, 139, 146–147; Griffin, *American*; Hogeland, *Autumn*; Silver, *Our*.

10. Washington to John Witherspoon, March 10, 1784, https://founders.archives.gov; Cook, *Washington's*, 121–122, 139.

11. Crumrine and Ellis, *History*, 856–860; Konkle, *Life*, 173–189; Rowe, *Embattled*, 189–191; Rowe, *Thomas*, 193–194; Hulbert, *Washington*, 143–159; Egle, *Notes*, 38–41.

12. Porter, "Washington," 7–14.

13. Loudon, *Selection*, 1:49–63; 2:349–355; French, *Native*; Hermes, "Justice"; Kawashima, "Forced"; Kawashima, *Puritan*; Knowles, *Reading*; Reid, *Law*; Williams Jr., "Algebra"; Yazzie, "Life."

14. Wilf, "Invention," 503, 507; see 496–507.

15. Rao, "Federal"; Brackenridge, *Incidents*.

16. A similar oppositionality appears between friends of order and friends of liberty,

and court and country, as they were adapted to the backcountry and city in the American republic of the 1790s. Watts, "If," 86; 81–102; Slaughter *Whiskey*, 127; Elkins and McKitrick, *Age*, 13–21.

17. Watts, "If," 81–86, 89–90; Elkins and McKitrick, *Age*; Cornell, *Other*.
18. White, *Backcountry*, xiv–xv, 3, 8, 10–11, 112.
19. White, *Backcountry*, 35, 48, 53, 87.
20. White, *Backcountry*, xiii–xv, 112.
21. White, *Backcountry*, 60–61, 64, 66, 68.
22. Elkins and McKitrick, *Age*; Reed, "Between"; Connor, "Politics."
23. Gould, "Political"; Gould, "Patron-Client"; Slaughter, "Crowds"; Wilf, *Law's*.
24. Reed, "Between."
25. Bouton, *Taming*.
26. Blinka, "'This'"; Ifft, "Treason."
27. Slaughter, "King"; Myrsiades, "Tale."
28. Holt, "Federal Whiskey"; Holt, "Whiskey Rebellion."
29. Boyd, "Whiskey Rebellion, Popular Rights," 81–82.
30. Harper, "Rebellion," 45.
31. Reed, "Between," 43–45; Gould, "Patron-Client"; Gould, "Political."
32. Owen, *Political*, 115–117.
33. Mittal and Weingast, "Self-Enforcing."
34. Billings and Tarter, *"Esteemed"*; Crow, *Thomas*; Pearson, *Remaking*; Fernandez and Dubber, *Law*; Hoffer and Hoffer, *Clamor*; Konefsky, "Legal"; Kessler, *Inventing*; Watson, "Changes."
35. Brewer, *By*; Tomlins and Mann, *Many*; Twitty, *Before*; Harris, *Hanging*; Piker, *Four*; Chamberlain, "Execution"; Grandjean, "'Our'"; Gallay, *Indian*; Kittredge, *Lewd*; Hall, *Rape*; Ben-Atar and Brown, *Taming*; Dayton, *Women*.
36. Silbey, "Making," 45; Mezey, "Law," 46; Nelken, "Using"; Bourdieu, *Outline*; Geertz, "Thick."
37. Fitzpatrick, "'Damned,'" 2–3.
38. Capoccia and Kelemen, "Study," 357; Myrsiades, "Constituting," 102, 107; Reed, "Between," 38.
39. Mezey, "Law," 57.
40. Fitzpatrick, "'Damned,'" 2, 11–13; Amsterdam and Bruner, "Dialectics," 226–230; Sarat and Kearns, "Cultural," 7–8; Cotterrell, "Concept"; Friedman, "Concept"; Nelken, "Disclosing/Invoking."
41. Lyotard, *Peregrinations*, 38; Myrsiades, "Language," 201–208; Gramsci, *Selections*, 33, 389; Myrsiades, "Constituting," 111; Cheal, "Hegemony," 110.
42. Cornell, *Other*, 41–43; Cornell, "American," 332–333, 341.
43. Cornell, *Other*, 41–43.
44. Webster, "Examination," 56–57.
45. Washington, Address to Congress, November 19, 1794, https://founders.archives.gov/.
46. Jefferson to James Madison, January 30, 1787, https://founders.archives.gov/.
47. Slaughter, "Friends."
48. Hamilton used the term "Whiskey Insurrection" in a letter to his sister-in-law af-

ter the insurgency had been quelled. Hamilton to Angelica Church, December 8, 1794, https://founders.archives.gov/; Hamilton to Angelica Church, December 8, 1794, in Syrett, *Papers of Alexander Hamilton* 17:428–429. Isaac Ariail Reed argues that whiskey was "a form of currency and a powerful actant" as well as a symbol that stood for "a particular understanding of 'liberty', in particular independence and anti-tax sentiment"; Imagination Collectif, "From," 201; Reed, "Between"; Bouton, *Taming*, 218–219.

Chapter 1. The Government Narrative and Its Western "Experiment"

1. Harper, *Transformation*, 98; Ferguson, *Early*, 64, 92–96, 116, 161–163; Newlin, *Life*, 71, 74.
2. Loughran, *Republic*, 57, 110, 112; 240–241; Anderson, *Imagined*.
3. Elkins and McKitrick, *Age*, 463–483.
4. Reed, "Between."
5. Hamilton to John Jay, September 3, 1792, Syrett, *Papers*, 12:316–317; George Washington to Alexander Hamilton, September 7, 1792, Syrett, *Papers*, 12:331–333; John Jay to Alexander Hamilton, September 8, 1792, Syrett, *Papers*, 12:334–335; Edmund Randolph to Alexander Hamilton, September 8, 1792, Syrett, *Papers*, 12:336–340; Alexander Hamilton to George Washington, September 9, 1792, Syrett, *Papers*, 12:344–347; 316, 332, 334, 336.
6. Neville to George Clymer, November 17, 1791, Wolcott Papers, folder IX.10, vol. 19, no. 11.
7. Brackenridge, *History*, 31–36.
8. Neville to George Clymer, November 7, 1792, Wolcott Papers, folder IX.10, vol. 19, no. 14.
9. A note to that effect in Hamilton's handwriting was appended to John Neville's letter to George Clymer on August 23, 1792, ALS, Connecticut Historical Society; Alexander Hamilton to Tench Coxe, September 1, 1792, n2, https://founders.archives.gov/.
10. Syrett, *Papers*, 12:306n3; Alexander Hamilton to Tench Coxe, September 1, 1792, n3, https://founders.archives.gov/ for the text of the August 23 letter.
11. Syrett, *Papers*, 12:307–309n5, Alexander Hamilton to Tench Coxe, September 1, 1792, n5, https://founders.archives.gov/, and "Minutes of the Meeting at Pittsburgh—1792," *Pennsylvania Archives*, 2nd ser., 25–26, for the text of the meeting minutes.
12. Hamilton to Tench Coxe, September 1, 1792, https://founders.archives.gov/; Syrett, *Papers*, 12:305–310.
13. Coxe to Alexander Hamilton, October 19, 1792, https://founders.archives.gov/.
14. Clymer to Alexander Hamilton, September 28, 1792, https //founders.archives.gov/; George Clymer to Alexander Hamilton, October 4, 1792, https://founders.archives.gov/; George Clymer to Alexander Hamilton, October 10, 1792, https://founders.archives.gov/. Clymer was an influential source, though his cowardice in collecting evidence resulted in piecemeal information and unreliable reports. His identification of rebel leaders and his overview of rebel activity was poorly informed and misleading; Elkins and McKitrick, *Age*, 467.
15. Clymer to Alexander Hamilton, October 10, 1792, https://founders.archives.gov/; Baldwin, *Whiskey*, 87–90.
16. Ferguson, *Early*, 119–120.

17. Clymer to Alexander Hamilton, October 10, 1792, https://founders.archives.gov/.
18. Clymer to Alexander Hamilton, October 4, 1792, https://founders.archives.gov/.
19. Findley, *History*, 42; George Clymer to Alexander Hamilton, September 28, 1792, https://founders.archives.gov/.
20. Clymer to Alexander Hamilton, September 28, 1792, October 10, 1792, https://founders.archives.gov/; Alexander Addison to Clymer, September 29, 1792, Clymer to Addison, Oct 1, 1792, Oliver Wolcott Papers; Grundfest, George, 399–306, 412–419.
21. The account appeared initially in the *Pittsburgh Gazette* on October 22, 1792, and was reprinted in Philadelphia to Clymer's chagrin.
22. October 20, 1792; October 29, 1792; November 17, 1792, in *The Mail; or Claypoole's Daily Advertiser*.
23. Hamilton to George Washington, September 1, 1792, Syrett, *Papers*, 12:312.
24. Hamilton to George Washington, September 9, 1792, Syrett, *Papers*, 12:345–346; Slaughter, *Whiskey*, 122; "Proclamation," September 15, 1792, *Pennsylvania Archives*, 2nd ser., 27–28. The proclamation appeared as a broadside and was then published in newspapers. The draft included Edmund Randolph's comments, which Hamilton advised Washington undermined the text as they were not well founded; Slaughter, *Whiskey*, 122–123. Hamilton, it was speculated, also authored the proclamation of August 7, 1794, though there is no conclusive evidence that he did so; notes for "Proclamation," August 7, 1794, and Hamilton's letter to Washington, August 5, 1794, https://founders.archives.gov/.
25. Hamilton to John Jay, September 3, 1792, Syrett, *Papers*, 12:316–317.
26. Findley, *History*, 44.
27. Washington to Alexander Hamilton, September 7, 1792, Syrett, *Papers*, 12:331–333.
28. Randolph to Alexander Hamilton, September 8, 1792, https://founders.archives.gov/.
29. Randolph to Alexander Hamilton, September 8, 1792, Syrett, *Papers*, 12:338.
30. Tachau, "George," 21.
31. Hamilton to George Washington, September 9, 1792, Syrett, *Papers*, 12:344–347.
32. Foner, *Democratic-Republican*, 4–5; Link, *Democratic-Republican*.
33. Hamilton to George Washington, August 5, 1794, Syrett, *Papers*, 17:24–58.
34. "Minutes of the Meeting at Pittsburgh—1792," *Pennsylvania Archives*, 2nd ser., 26.
35. "Proclamation," September 15, 1792, *Pennsylvania Archives*, 2nd ser., 27.
36. Hamilton to George Washington, September 1, 1792, Syrett, *Papers*, 12:311–313; see Alexander Hamilton to George Washington, September 9, 1792, Syrett, *Papers*, 12:344–347.
37. Hamilton to Tench Coxe, September 1, 1792, https://founders.archives.gov/; Syrett, *Papers*, 12:305–310.
38. Slaughter, *Whiskey*, 119–120.
39. Hamilton to George Washington, August 5, 1794, Syrett, *Papers*, 17:51.
40. Hamilton to George Washington, August 5, 1794, Syrett, *Papers*, 17:52.
41. Randolph to George Washington, August 5, 1794, Wharton, *State*, 158.
42. Randolph's obstruction of Hamilton's efforts to send a militia would contribute to his downfall in the Fauchet affair in 1795, which would discourage others who challenged the government narrative; Tachau, "George," 34.

43. Hamilton to Angelica Church, October 23, 1794, Syrett, *Papers*, 17:340.
44. Hamilton to Angelica Church, December 8, 1794, Syrett, *Papers*, 17:428–429.
45. Randolph to George Washington, August 18, 1794, https://founders.archives.gov/.
46. Hamilton to George Washington, August 6, 1794, https://founders.archives.gov/; Alexander Hamilton to George Washington, August 16, 1794, https://founders.archives.gov/; "Treasury Department, August 5th, 1794," *Dunlap and Claypoole's American Daily Advertiser*, August 21, 1794.
47. A postscript in the newspaper included the Hamilton letter to Washington of August 16 and a reply from B. Dandridge on behalf of the president on August 19. The president's reply read that he "perceives no objection" with the qualification that he was "relying that the facts contained in the report, have been stated with due care, and from authentic sources"; *Dunlap and Claypoole's American Daily Advertiser*, August 21, 1794 (reply dated August 18, 1794).
48. The following meetings were cited: 1791 in Brownsville, referred to as Redstone Old Fort; 1791 in Washington County; 1791 and 1792 in Pittsburgh; and 1794 in Mingo Creek and at Parkinson's Ferry. The resolutions were taken at the 1791 Brownsville and 1792 Pittsburgh meetings.
49. Randolph supported the report anonymously in the public press under the pen name "Germanicus," clarifying that withdrawal from the common burden afflicted not merely bandits or rebels but the western country more generally.
50. Hamilton to George Washington, September 2, 1794, Syrett, *Papers*, 17:180–190.
51. *Pennsylvania Archive*, 1st ser., 10:757; McClure, *Ends*, 570.
52. Brackenridge, *Incidents*, 3:6–7; Findley, *History*, 32–33.
53. *Pennsylvania Gazette*, March 4, 1789; Griffin, *American*, 224, 241, 340n64; Arthur Campbell Papers, January 2, February 17, 1792.
54. Findley, *History*, 59; Cornell, *Other*, 203.
55. Hamilton to George Washington, August 5, 1794, Syrett *Papers*, 17:35–36.
56. "Proclamation," August 7, 1794, Wharton, *State*, 118.
57. Hamilton to George Washington, August 5, 1794, Syrett, *Papers*, 17:40–41.
58. Gallatin was a representative to the Pennsylvania Assembly, 1790–1793, a participant in rebel assemblies from 1791 on, a U.S. senator from 1793–1794, and a member of Congress from 1795–1801.
59. Gallatin, *Speech*, 30, 32.
60. [Findley], *Review*, 102, 125. Findley was a member of Congress from 1791–1799 and from 1803–1817; he attended rebel assemblies late in the conflict.
61. Findley, *History*, 224.
62. Findley, *History*, 164–165.
63. Findley, *History*, 164, 226, 291–292, 295–297.
64. Findley, *History*, 226, 295.
65. Findley, *History*, 165, 297, 311–312.
66. Findley, *History*, 227–228.
67. Randolph, *Vindication*, 94; Elkins and McKitrick, *Age*, 425–431.
68. Randolph, *Vindication*, 47–48; Tachau, "George," 24–34.
69. Randolph, *Vindication*, 45.
70. Findley, *History*, 306, 312.

262   NOTES TO CHAPTER ONE

71. Knox to George Washington, August 4, 1794, https://founders.archives.gov/.
72. "Proclamation," August 7, 1794, Wharton, *State*, 119.
73. "Proclamation," August 7, 1794, Wharton, *State*, 118–119.
74. "Proclamation," August 7, 1794, Wharton, *State*, 118.
75. Lee to Alexander Hamilton, September 13, 1794, https://founders.archives.gov/; Fennell, "From," 262n7.
76. Findley, *History*, 303.
77. Findley, *History*, 304, 306.
78. Randolph, "Appointment," August 8, 1794, *Pennsylvania Archives*, 2nd ser., 116.
79. "Proclamation," September 25, 1794, Wharton, *State*, 141.
80. August 7, 1794, Proclamation and Randolph's letter to Washington, August 5, 1794; Slaughter, *Whiskey*, 196.
81. Washington's Proclamation (August 7) to ready the federal militia was read at the rebel assembly at Parkinson's Ferry (August 14); the reaction was reported to the commission on the same day. The commission's first meeting with the rebels on August 21 was conducted in the full knowledge the militia was forming. The commission's report to the president was provided on September 24. The president's second proclamation on September 25 revealed that the militia was already on the march. The commission was thus shadowed by the threat of military force. The commission reinforced the predilection for military force by its refusal to fashion a realistic timetable and process for rebel submission, its insistence on complete submission, even by those who claimed they had no part in the rebellion, and its perceived unwillingness to embrace civil authority absent the aid of a military force.
82. "Report of the United States Commissioners," September 24, 1794, *Pennsylvania Archives*, 2nd ser., 293–302; Proclamation, September 25, 1794, Wharton, *State*, 141. Elkins and McKitrick, *Age*, 481–482; 1 Stat. 403; Alexander Hamilton to Rufus King, October 30, 1794, https://founders.archives.gov/. A cabinet meeting on August 24 authorized the militia to begin assembling, but the orders were not made public until September 1. On September 9, Washington ordered the units to rendezvous. On September 25, he ordered them to march west and he set off on September 30. The statute calling out a federal militia for the four western counties was not authorized by the president until November 29, ten days after his address to Congress and more than a month after the militia actually entered the western country.
83. Hamilton to George Washington, August 2, 1794, Syrett, *Papers*, 17:15–19; Edmund Randolph to George Washington, August 5, 1794, Wharton, *State*, 156–159; Henry Knox to George Washington, August 4, 1794, https://founders.archives.gov/; William Bradford to George Washington, August, n.d., 1794, *Washington Papers*, 33:284–291.
84. "Conference at the President's," *Pennsylvania Archives*, 2nd ser., 122; "Conference," August 2, 1794, Syrett, *Papers*, 17:12–13.
85. Lindsay Chervinsky makes the argument that Washington's cabinet acted to sideline not only state government but also Congress in its handling of the Whiskey Rebellion and that Hamilton, Knox, and Randolph "helped ensure that the cabinet supported and promoted presidential leadership." She contends Washington took his cabinet's advice to shape policy and sought its counsel, indicating that he preferred to work with its agreement. While much of what she suggests has merit, her conclusion that the cabi-

net "worked toward a shared goal" and that Washington "convened cabinet meetings to build consensus and provide political cover for his controversial and precedent-setting decisions" seems to go further than the evidence indicates. Chervinsky, *Cabinet*, 263.

86. Chesney, "Democratic-Republican," 1525–1579; Davis, "Guarding," 43–62; Sioli, "Democratic," 288–304; Foner, *Democratic-Republican*, 3–51.

87. Neem, "Freedom," 270–271.

88. Martin, *Government*, 85–90; Wood, *Empire*, 162–164, 203–204.

89. Neem, "Freedom," 263, 271.

90. Cobbett, *Bone*, 33–35.

91. Martin, *Government*, 87; Wood, *Empire*, 163.

92. *Pittsburgh Gazette*, April 5, 1794.

93. "Remonstrance to the President and Congress on Opening Navigation of the Mississippi River," Foner, *Democratic-Republican*, 127–128; dated March 24, 1794; *Pittsburgh Gazette*, April 5, 1794.

94. Washington to Edmund Randolph, April 11, 1794, *Washington Papers*, 33:475; George Washington to Burges Ball, September 25, 1794, *Writings of George Washington*, 505–507; George Washington to Henry Lee, August 26, 1794, htps//founders.archives .gov/; Carroll and Ashworth, *George*, 182, 182n48.

95. Washington to Daniel Morgan, October 8, 1794, https://founders.archives.gov/.

96. Martin, *Government*, 88; Wood, *Empire*, 162, 164. It was not until national political parties appeared in the 1830s that American democracy as "a fully legitimate cultural value" emerged. Until then democracy was in a state of struggle and at risk of collapse. The critical issue of the role of voluntary associations as intermediaries between the people and their government was complicated because neither the Constitution nor Bill of Rights nor a "general rule of law" provided for freedom related to forming associations. Political parties would become the "intermediate entity" between the people and their government. Elkins and McKitrick, *Age*, 451, 455–456, 460, 485, 488.

97. Madison to James Monroe, December 4, 1794, in Hunt, 221–223; Wood, *Empire*, 204; Fritz, *American*, 185.

98. Randolph to Alexander Hamilton, September 8, 1792, Syrett, *Papers*, 12:336–340.

99. Madison, "House Address to the President," November 27, 1794; Madison, *Papers*, 390; James Madison to James Monroe, December 4, 1794, https://founders.archives.gov/.

100. Hamilton to John Jay, September 3, 1792, Syrett, *Papers*, 12:316–317.

101. "Minutes of the Meeting at Pittsburgh—1792," *Pennsylvania Archives*, 2nd ser., 25–26.

102. Hamilton to George Washington, September 2, 1794, Syrett, *Papers*, 17:180–190.

103. Hamilton to George Washington, September 2, 1794, Syrett, *Papers*, 17:180–190.

104. Ferguson, *Early*, 115.

105. Addison to Thomas Mifflin, March 31, 1794, *Pennsylvania Archives*, 2nd ser., 50–51.

106. Hamilton to George Washington, September 2, 1794, Syrett, *Papers*, 17:180–190.

107. Martin, *Government*, 58–59.

108. [Hamilton], "Tully," letter 3, August 28, 1794, Syrett, *Papers*, 17:159–161; originally published in *The Philadelphia Gazette and Universal Daily Advertiser*, August 28, 1794.

109. Hamilton to George Washington, September 2, 1794, Syrett, *Papers*, 17:180–190; Reed, "Between," 48.

110. Hamilton to George Washington, August 5, September 2, 1794, Syrett, *Papers*, 17:24–58, 180–190.
111. September 29, 1792, *Gazette of the United States*.
112. Sizemore, "George," 46, 49, 54.
113. "Proclamation," August 7, 1794, Wharton, *State*, 118–119.
114. Randolph to Alexander Hamilton, September 8, 1792, Syrett, *Papers*, 12:337; "Proclamation," September 25, 1794, Wharton, *State*, 141.
115. [Hamilton], "Tully," letter 1, August 23, 1794, Syrett, *Papers*, 17:132–138; *Philadelphia Gazette and Universal Daily Advertiser*, August 23, 1794.
116. [Hamilton], "Tully," letter 2, August 26, 1794, Syrett, *Papers*, 17:148–150; *Philadelphia Gazette and Universal Daily Advertiser*, August 26, 1794. [Hamilton], "Tully," letter 3, August 28, 1794, Syrett, *Papers*, 17:159–161; *Philadelphia Gazette and Universal Daily Advertiser*, August 28, 1794.
117. [Hamilton], "Tully," letter 4, September 2, 1794, Syrett, *Papers*, 17:175–180; *Philadelphia Gazette and Universal Daily Advertiser*, September 2, 1794.
118. "Proclamation," September 25, 1794, Wharton, *State*, 141.
119. August 12, 1794, *General Advertiser*.
120. "Proclamation," September 25, 1794, Wharton, *State*, 141.
121. Washington to John Jay, November 1–4, 1794; https://founders.archives.gov/.
122. Washington to John Jay, November 1–4, 1794; https://founders.archives.gov/.
123. [Randolph], *Germanicus*, letter 1, 4. Randolph wrote under the pen name "Germanicus" in a series of thirteen public letters explaining the president's address.
124. Washington to Thomas Jefferson, July 6, 1796, https://founders.archives.gov/.
125. "Jefferson's Conversation with Washington," July 10, 1792, https://founders.archives.gov/; Elkins and McKitrick, *Age*, 289–290.
126. Bartoloni-Tuazon, *For*; Wills, *Cincinnatus*; Ellis, *His*; Ellis, *American*; Shogan, "George"; Hein, "George"; Schwartz, "Social"; McDonald, "Presidential"; Harris, "'George"; Wood, "Greatness."
127. Washington to John Jay, November 1–4, 1794; https://founders.archives.gov/.
128. Albert Gallatin, a leading voice in the rebellion, recognized that Washington's objective in calling out the federal militia was to send the message that republican government would enforce its law and that its citizens would sacrifice for the sake of "that fundamental principle of government." He had no doubt that Washington believed the democratic experiment had fulfilled itself and that republican government, however extensive its territory, could support itself, "even in the case of a disobedience of any part of the body politic." Gallatin, *Speech*, 23.
129. Washington to John Jay, November 1–4, 1794; https://founders.archives.gov/.
130. Washington to Henry Lee, August 26, 1794; https://founders.archives.gov/.
131. "Sixth Annual Address to Congress," November 19, 1794, *Writings of George Washington*, 28.
132. [Randolph], *Germanicus*, letter 3, 12. Randolph felt he had defended Washington's conduct during the Whiskey Rebellion with his public letters; Edmund Randolph to James Madison, November 1, 1795; https://founders.archives.gov/.
133. [Randolph], *Germanicus*, letter 5, 19.
134. [Randolph], *Germanicus*, letter 2, 9–10; letter 8, 69–70.

135. Randolph to George Washington, October 11, 1794, *Writings of George Washington*, 474; Fritz, *American*, 180, 366n72.

136. [Randolph], *Germanicus*, Letter 4, 16–18.

137. Jefferson to James Madison, December 28, 1794, https://founders.archives.gov/; Slaughter, *Whiskey*, 221.

138. Fritz, *American*, 185–188.

139. Elkins and McKitrick, *Age*, 492–494; George Washington, "Farewell Address," September 19, 1796, https://founders.archives.gov/; Markowitz, "Washington's," 173–191.

140. Fornieri, "Washington's," 370.

141. Fornieri, "Washington's," 367, 369–371.

142. Washington's September 19, 1796, farewell address expressed his hopes for the nation. It was a warning of the danger to the Union from divisions from within and external threats from foreign powers and has been construed as "a declaration of sovereignty" and against foreign influence; it combined the special status of the nation (its idealism) and its interests (its realism); and it was preoccupied with western expansion and empire. Elkins and McKitrick, *Age*, 490–493; George Washington to Thomas Jefferson, July 6, 1796, https://founders.archives.gov/.

143. Addison, *Reports*, 105, 108; Neville to George Clymer, November 7, 1792, https://founders.archives.gov/.

144. Owen, *Political*, 125–127; Randolph, *Vindication*, 82.

145. Coxe to Alexander Hamilton, October 19, 1792, https://founders.archives.gov/.

146. Hulsebosch, "Fulfillment," 234–235.

147. Hulsebosch, "Fulfillment," 210–213, 215–216.

148. Hulsebosch, "Fulfillment," 225, 228.

149. Hulsebosch, "Fulfillment," 221, 224. The Jay Treaty was signed on November 19, 1794, the same day as President Washington's address to Congress, and was ratified on June 24, 1795.

150. Fisher Ames, in *Debates and Proceedings in the Congress*, 947.

151. Wilson, "Introduction," 34–35; Cobbett, in Wilson, *William*, 208.

152. Cobbett, *Bone*, 40–41.

153. Randolph's reference appeared in a letter to John Jay, August 18, 1794, explaining what he had told William Bradford; Randolph, *Vindication*, 73–74, 83, 86.

154. *Philadelphia Gazette*, September 10, 1794.

155. *Gazette of the United States*, October 4, 1794.

156. Madison to James Monroe, December 4, 1794, https://founders.archives.gov/; *U.S. Constitution*, Art. 1, Sec. 8.

157. 1 Stat. 424–425; Hogeland, *Autumn*, 375–376; Urwin, "'Army."

158. Reed, "Between."

159. Washington was involved in a prominent western land case before the Pennsylvania Supreme Court in 1786; Rowe, *Embattled*, 189–191. By the time he became president, his personal wealth was tied up in land on the frontier, which he had begun aggregating as early as 1752. He was especially interested in the land around Pittsburgh, where the rebellion was to take place. His expansive holdings led to questions about the "opportunity" offered in western Pennsylvania to test execution of the excise law or to mount a federal militia and whether either was motivated by personal benefit. As Thomas

Slaughter contends, Washington was open to the accusation that his "private experiences influenced his public decisions" in the western uprising. Slaughter, *Whiskey*, 75–89; Elkins and McKitrick, *Age*, 35–36.

160. Sizemore, "George," 47.

161. While he was still a Supreme Court justice, James Wilson was bankrupted by his land schemes and jailed for his debts; he died in disgrace. Washington found that his own western landholdings never garnered him the income he had hoped for.

162. Elkins and McKitrick, *Age*, 112–113, 126, 211, 217–218, 220, 251–252, 401–402.

163. Reed, "Between," 27–64.

164. Brackenridge, *History*, 227; Slaughter, *Whiskey*, 196–203.

165. Carroll and Ashworth, *George*, 181.

166. Sizemore, "George," 45, 56–57.

167. Robertson, "'Look,'" 1264–1265, 1277–1278; Wood, *Radicalism*, 147, 169, 245, 365; Huston, "Rethinking," 46–71; Owen, "Legitimacy"; Selinger, "Rethinking," 270.

Chapter 2. Federal, State, and Popular Law in the Western Country

1. Martin, *Government*, 25.

2. Bouton, *Taming*, 218–219; Maier, *From*, 277; Martin, *Government*, 27–28; Gilje, *Road*, 44–49, 58.

3. Maier, *From*, 275, 279–282; Curott and Fink, "Bandit"; Gilje, *Road*; Maier, "Popular"; Wood, "Note."

4. Slaughter, *Whiskey*, 32–33, 39–40, 53.

5. McConville, "Rise," 89; Bouton, *Taming*, 160.

6. McConville, "Rise," 97, 100; Pencak, "Introduction," 7, 16; Abrahams, "White."

7. Harper, *Transformation*, 17–57; Gould, "Political"; Gould, "Patron-Client."

8. Klein, "Ordering," 662, 668–669, 675; Fennell, "From," 147–148, 151, 176.

9. Pencak, "Introduction," 8; Walsham, "Rough," 243–245; Thompson, "Moral," 78–79; Abrahams, "Introduction," 30, 34.

10. Klein, "Ordering," 66in1, 662, 678–679.

11. Abrahams, "Introduction," 30, 34.

12. Bouton, "Tying," 423; Dinsmore, "Courts."

13. Bouton, *Taming*, 151–157, 205; Bouton, "Road," 859, 870–883.

14. Only two of fifty-four cases of county officers set for prosecution in the 1780s and 1790s were tried; Bouton, *Taming*, 154; Bouton, "Road," 870–871; Marietta and Rowe, *Troubled*.

15. Slaughter, "Crowds," 26–28.

16. Slaughter, *Whiskey*, 84–89, 118, 121, 177; Griffin, *American*; Harper, *Transformation*; Hogeland, *Autumn*; Abernathy, *Western*; Friedenberg, *Life*; Silver, *Our*; Taylor, "Land"; Wilkinson, *Land*.

17. Jensen et al., *Documentary*, 101–103; Ferguson, *Early*, 98–99; Owen, *Political*, 101–103.

18. With the first change of government, from 1801 to 1810, the problem of the judiciary would be resolved, particularly the conflict between state and federal courts over their authority and jurisdiction, the Alien and Sedition Acts of 1798, and a rash of judicial impeachments; Ellis, *Jeffersonian*, 4–5, 12.

19. The insurgency was a more violent combination of social classes that mixed a political elite with common laborers; Sharp, *American*, 93–100; Sharp, "Whiskey," 119–120.

20. Ferguson, *Early*, 62, 64, 73–74, 92; Sharp, *American*, 97–98.

21. Cornell, "Aristocracy," 1172.

22. Jensen, "Dissent," 626–630.

23. "Brutus," Borden, *Anti-Federalist*, no. 84.

24. Jensen, "Dissent," 632–634, 637–638.

25. Brackenridge campaigned to represent Alleghany County in the convention and was the only western member of the Pennsylvania Assembly to favor the convention. [Brackenridge], "Cursory Remarks on the Federal Constitution," *Pittsburgh Gazette*, March 1, 1788; Ferguson, *Early*, 94–95; Newlin, *Life*, 92–106.

26. Ellis, *Jeffersonian*, 4–5, 12.

27. Centinel [Samuel Bryan], October 5, 1787, *Independent Gazetteer*; Ireland, *Religion*, 39–45, 109–143; Holt, "'To,'" 1491.

28. Holt, "Federal Courts as the Asylum"; Holt, "'To,'" 1463, 1473, 1505.

29. Robreno, "Learning," 559, 562, 564, 572–574.

30. Holt, "Federal Courts Have Enemies," 319–321, 324–325, 325n95.

31. "Citizen," *American Daily Advertiser*, December 20, 1791; Storing, *Complete*; Ketcham, *Anti-Federalist*; Borden, *Anti-Federalist*.

32. "Martin," Borden, *Anti-Federalist*, no. 83.

33. "Brutus," "Power of the Judiciary," *New York Journal*, February 28, 1788; "Brutus," Borden, *Anti-Federalist*, no. 81.

34. Holt, "'To,'" 1458, 1465–1468; Holt, "Federal Courts as Asylum," 346, 348, 356, 368, 371.

35. Holt, "'To,'" 1485.

36. McClure, *Ends*, 566.

37. Dinsmore, "Courts," 69–70, 90, 106, 108.

38. Dinsmore, "Courts, 58, 142, 191–192, 194.

39. Rowe, *Embattled*, 204, 221–222.

40. 1789 Judiciary Act, chap. 20, sec. 29, 1 Stat. 73; 1793 Judiciary Act, chap. 22, sec. 3, 1 Stat. 333.

41. Brackenridge, *Incidents*, 266n; Rowe, *Embattled*, 221–223, 232.

42. Addison to Thomas Mifflin, November 4, 1792, *Pennsylvania Archives*, 2nd ser., 30–33.

43. Addison to George Clymer, September 29, 1792, Syrett, *Papers*, 12:518–519.

44. Addison to Thomas Mifflin, November 4, 1792, *Pennsylvania Archives*, 2nd ser., 32.

45. The federal court system—established by the Judiciary Act of 1789—was tasked with dealing with the fundamental problem of economic order, particularly when state courts were unable to control riots; Holt, "'To,'" 1425–1426, 1458.

46. Addison, *Reports*, 47–48, 53.

47. Slaughter, *Whiskey*, 114–115; Addison, *Reports*, 49.

48. Addison, *Reports*, 49.

49. Addison to Thomas Mifflin, November 4, 1792, *Pennsylvania Archives*, 2nd ser., 32; Thomas Mifflin to George Washington, October 5, 1792, *Pennsylvania Archives*, 2nd ser., 28–29; Thomas Mifflin to Judges of the Pennsylvania Supreme Court, October 5, 1792, *Pennsylvania Archives*, 2nd ser., 29.

50. Slaughter, *Whiskey*, 125–127.

51. Addison to George Clymer, September 29, 1792, Syrett, *Papers*, 12:519n5; George Clymer to Alexander Hamilton, October 4, 1792, Syrett, *Papers*, 12:517–522.

52. Addison to Thomas Mifflin, March 31, 1794, *Pennsylvania Archives*, 2nd ser., 51.

53. Addison to Thomas Mifflin, May 12, 1794, *Pennsylvania Archives*, 2nd ser., 53. Secretary of the Commonwealth Alexander Dallas apologized for the governor who, he claimed, never expected that Addison's letter to him would have been shared by the president; Alexander Dallas to Alexander Addison, May 24, 1794, *Pennsylvania Archives*, 2nd ser., 55.

54. Addison to Alexander Dallas, July 14, 1794, *Pennsylvania Archives*, 2nd ser., 62.

55. Broadside, July 25, 1794, Gilder Lehrman Institute.

56. "Conference at the President's," August [2], 1794, *Pennsylvania Archives*, 2nd ser., 123–124.

57. Mifflin to George Washington, August 5, 1794, Wharton, *State*, 1442–1444.

58. Randolph to Thomas Mifflin, August 7, 1794, https://founders.archives.gov/; Thomas Mifflin to Edmund Randolph, August 12, 1794, https://founders.archives.gov/.

59. Brackenridge, *Incidents*, 3:6–8, 13; Newlin, *Life*, 64; Slaughter, *Whiskey*, 11–12, for a 1786 assault in Washington County involving Graham that went unprosecuted.

60. Brackenridge, *Incidents*, 3:13.

61. Addison, *Reports*, 312, 313.

62. In the end, though the United States may have asked for all past duties, it waived doing so in 1794.

63. Addison, *Reports*, 191.

64. Brackenridge, *Incidents*, 1:24–5; Slaughter, *Whiskey*, 177.

65. Brackenridge, *Incidents*, 1:24.

66. Brackenridge, *Incidents*, 1:24.

67. Addison, *Reports*, 274–276.

68. An acolyte of the federal militia, Woods pushed mercilessly to prosecute Brackenridge.

69. Addison, *Reports*, 126.

70. Addison, *Reports*, 277.

71. Ifft, "Treason," 176.

72. *Independent Gazetteer*, September 17, 1794; [Unsigned] "Letter to the Governor on the Feeling at Carlisle," September 15, 1794, *Pennsylvania Archives*, 2nd ser., 253–254; Findley, *History*, 160–161; Griffin, *American*, 227, 341n80; William Lyon to Thomas Mifflin, September 12, 1794, Wolcott Papers, no. 31; Rowe, *Thomas*, 281–282.

73. Owen, *Political*, 98–102; Cornell, "Aristocracy," 1152–1155.

74. Ifft, "Treason," 169, 175.

75. Ifft, "Treason," 168–169, 172, 175.

76. Brackenridge, *Incidents*, 2:9.

77. Brackenridge, *Incidents*, 1:86.

78. Brackenridge, *Incidents*, 1:76, 123.

79. Chief Justice McKean (a member of the Pennsylvania Commission) and Justice Yeates (a member of the U.S. Commission) were the ones who questioned opening the court. The Pennsylvania Commission was appointed by Governor Mifflin and included McKean and General William Irvine.

80. Brackenridge, *Incidents*, 1:124.

81. Hamilton to George Washington, September 2, 1794, *Pennsylvania Archives*, 2nd ser., 246.

82. Addison to David Redick, March 25, 1794, Gilder Lehrman Institute.

83. Rowe, *Embattled*, 135. Whereas Westmoreland County had a county court in 1773, Washington County in 1781, and Fayette County in 1783, Alleghany County did not have one until 1793; Slaughter, *Whiskey*, 32–33, 38–40, 117, 118, 256.

84. Brackenridge, *Modern* (White's edition), 359.

85. Brackenridge, *Law*, 570; Parker, "Time," 101.

86. Reid, *Constitutional*, 212–213

87. Parker, "Time," 68, 70; Reid, *Constitutional*, 237; Ellis, *Jeffersonian*, 112, 114–115, 161–162.

88. Ellis, *Jeffersonian*, 4–5.

89. Ellis, *Jeffersonian*, 11; Tachau *Federal*.

90. Offut, "'Of,'" 87, 225.

91. Stimson, *American*, 3.

92. Stimson, *American*, 4–6, 8–9 Horwitz, *Transformation*, 142–143.

93. Steinberg, "Spirit," 236–239; Bessler, *Private*, xxiv–xxvii.

94. Steinberg, "Spirit," 244; Steinberg, *Transformation*, 2; Bessler, "Public;" Bessler, *Private*.

95. Steinberg, "Spirit," 244; Steinberg, *Transformation*, 2.

96. Steinberg, *Transformation*, 1–2; Steinberg, "Spirit," 232–233.

97. Offut, "'Of,'" 259–265.

98. Mann, "Formalization," 463–466, 480.

99. Dinsmore, "Courts," 142, 198.

100. McKean, *Pennsylvania Archives*, 2nd ser., 496–500; *Williams v. Craig*, 1 U.S. 313, 314–315 (Pa. 1788); Oldham and Kim, "Arbitration," 254.

101. *Primer v. Kuhn*, 1 U.S. 452, 456 (Pa. 1789); Oldham and Kim, "Arbitration," 252.

102. Brackenridge, *Law*, 434.

103. Dallas, *Reports*, 1:vi.

104. *Lessee of Samuel Dixon v. Samuel Morehead* (1794), Addison, *Reports*, 216–231.

105. Addison, *Reports*, 224–225.

106. Addison, *Reports*, 219–221.

107. Addison, *Reports*, 226.

108. Addison, *Reports*, 222, 230.

109. *Carlisle Gazette*, April 4, 1788.

110. Bouton, *Taming*, 205, 307n22.

111. Brackenridge, *Incidents*, 3:25, 149; Findley, *History*, 56. Hogeland claims that the Mingo Creek Society operated as early as 1792 in relation to an attack on an excise collector, Robert Johnson, but only formally constituted itself with "charters and resolutions […] officially signed" in 1794; Hogeland, *Whiskey*, 263.

112. Brackenridge, *Incidents*, 1:86.

113. Brackenridge, *Incidents*, 3:25.

114. Hogeland argues that by supplying an extralegal alternative to the official court system, Mingo Creek spearheaded popular democracy, deploying attacks as a militia-based society against excisemen and coercing "would-be litigants to appeal to its own, extralegally elected judges"; Hogeland, *Whiskey*, 263–264.

115. Brackenridge, *Incidents*, 3:26.
116. Brackenridge, *Incidents*, 3:25, 25n, 26; Bouton, "Road," 881. A third western democratic society instituted in April in the town of Washington was organized along the lines of eastern societies and had no known platform regarding the excise law or extralegal courts.
117. The Mingo Creek Constitution document appears in summary in Brackenridge, *Incidents*, 3:148–149 and is discussed in Brackenridge, *Incidents*, 1:25–26; a copy of the original is deposited in the Rawle Family Papers, 1:18, under the title "Constitution for the District of Hamiltons"; Slaughter, *Whiskey*, 163–165, 264n12; Bouton references it as "Constitution of the Society of United Freemen"; Bouton, *Taming*, 205, 307n22.
118. Findley, *History*, 56.
119. Hogeland, *Whiskey*, 118–119.
120. *Pittsburgh Gazette*, June 28, 1794.
121. Brackenridge, *Incidents*, 3:25–26.
122. Findley, *History*, 56–57.
123. Findley, *History*, 56.
124. Fennell, "From," 101, 103.
125. Fennell, "From," 102–103.
126. *Pittsburgh Gazette*, June 21, 1794; Fennell, "From," 98, 101.
127. Albert Gallatin performed a leadership role in the tax resistance from July 1791 to September 1794. He served as clerk or secretary at six antitax meetings, including two (Parkinson's Ferry and Brownsville) of the four most consequential joint-county assemblies during the rebellion. He was a conferee at the meeting of rebels with the U.S. Commissioners.

James Edgar played a central role in the Brownsville Assembly in delivering a moral message that countered the effect of the radical leader David Bradford. Edgar attended meetings in 1791 and 1792 (though he does not appear in the minutes of critical meetings). He attended the Parkinson's Ferry assembly and was a member of the committee of twelve conferees who met with the U.S. Commissioners.

Hugh Henry Brackenridge floor-managed debates, negotiated the resolutions the assembly agreed to, and helped institute a system of committees to structure the assembly process at the Parkinson's Ferry assembly. He delivered speeches in each of four critical rebel assemblies at the height of the rebellion and, as a conferee at the meeting of rebels with the U.S. Commissioners, wrote the rebel report that was debated at the Brownsville assembly.

128. Baldwin, *Whiskey*, 39; William Findley was in the U.S. Congress from 1791 through the rebellion and for some time thereafter. He can be located at only one early meeting in 1791, at Brownsville; of the major assemblies at the height of the rebellion, he only appeared at Parkinson's Ferry. At an October meeting at Parkinson's Ferry after the hostilities, the rebels appointed him and David Redick to meet as emissaries to President Washington in Carlisle. Eicholz, "Closer."
129. Bouton, "William," 235–240; Cornell, *Other*, 203–207, 225–226.
130. James Marshall was involved in the assemblies from as early as the 1787 Patriotic Convention. He served as a delegate to the Pittsburgh and the Brownsville meetings of 1791, the Pittsburgh meeting of 1792, and the Canonsburgh meeting in 1793. Marshall of-

fered critical resolutions at Parkinson's Ferry that shifted the balance of influence to the moderates.

David Bradford appeared at the 1787 Washington County Patriotic Convention and in the multicounty meetings in Pittsburgh in 1791 and 1792; he drew up, with James Marshall, the contentious remonstrances for the 1792 meeting that so infuriated Hamilton. He spoke at the Mingo Creek assembly, Braddock's Field, Parkinson's Ferry, and Brownsville and was one of the twelve conferees at the meeting with the U.S. Commissioners. McClure, "Let Us."

131. McClure, "Let Us," 72–81; Bouton, "William," 237–243; Brackenridge, *Incidents*, 2:29; Albert Gallatin to Jean Bacollet, March 9, 1793; Gallatin to Thomas Clare, March 9, 1793, Gallatin Papers.

132. Baker, "James"; McClure, "Let Us"

133. Baker, "James"; Brackenridge, *Incidents*, 3:17–18; Crumrine and Ellis, *History*, 102, 277, 728; Harper, *Transformation*, 103. Support for resisting within the terms of what was constitutionally allowable was a hallmark of depositions and testimony in the rebel trials.

134. Political alliances in western Pennsylvania were fluid. Constitutionalists (representing an affection for the liberal state constitution of 1776) were opposed to Republicans (who were then a federalist political group) in the 1780s. Federalists (who correlated with Republicans) opposed Anti-Federalists (who correlated with Constitutionalists) in the late 1780s' ratification fight. Anti-Federalists became identified with democratic-republicans, which became the origins of the Jeffersonian Republican party at the turn of the century. Owen, *Political*, 113, 162–164; Ireland, *Religion*, xvi–xvii, 191, 211, 213, 216.

135. Owen, *Political*, 113, 116–117, 162–164; Ireland, *Religion*, xvi–xvii, 191, 211, 213, 216.

136. Brackenridge, *History*, 25–26.

137. Herman Husband expressed the common class-inspirational aspect of the rebellion that advocated revolution and "leveling, millennial, or radical critiques of equality." Holt, "Federal Whiskey," chap. 3: 10, 25–30; Fennell, "From,' 54, 192–226; Hogeland, *Whiskey*, 71–95.

138. Fennell traces four hundred rebels; half that number were simply anonymous figures unlisted by tax collectors rather than prominent men. Of the remaining two hundred, less than one-third owned taxable whiskey stills; only 15 percent of the total sample had even that much property. Sixty-three were militia officers, of which twenty-one were ordinary men. Of those who were distillers, twenty-four were elected or appointed officials. Fennell, "From," 147–148, 151, 176.

139. Fennell, "From," 152; Findley, *History*, 145.

140. Reed, "Between," 43–45.

141. Harper's survey of Fayette County finds that 90 percent of the population were settlers; Harper, "Rebellion," 41.

142. Harper identifies one hundred men as elite leaders in Washington and Fayette counties, 72 percent of whom were in the top 10 percent of taxable wealth. Harper, *Transformation*, 141–174; Harper, "Rebellion," 39–56.

143. Harper, "Rebellion," 49–50.

144. Brackenridge, *History*, 31–36.

145. Gould determines who were leaders based on the number and type of political offices held in civilian life, eliminating all but those who supported radical events; he ex-

272   NOTES TO CHAPTER TWO

cludes critical organizational and persuasive activities at rebel assemblies and narrows the time frame for the rebellion to the two-month period that constituted the most violent arc of the rebellion. Government and assembly documents, by contrast, show that many of the leaders Gould selects had significantly less participation and performed less influential roles in meetings and assemblies than many he eliminates. Gould's list features the following figures: James Marshall, Edward Cook, David Bradford, Craig Ritchie, John McDowell, James Allison, and John Cannon. Gould, "Political"; Gould, "Patron-Client."

146. Information for the present study is collated from government documents, participant histories, newspapers, meeting minutes, trial records, letters, and reports from 1791–1795.

147. Cornell, *Other*, 179–181, 201–204.

148. Gallatin, *Writings*, 3–4. The petition argued that given the scarcity of cash and the disproportionate impact on the petitioners' real wealth, the tax would prove more onerous in the West than in the East.

149. Gallatin, *Writings*, 3; Currie, "Constitution," 786.

150. Gallatin, *Speech*, 5–7.

151. Brackenridge, *Incidents*, 1:110–113.

152. Carnahan, "Pennsylvania," 39; Findley, *History*, 125–126.

153. Carnahan, "Pennsylvania," 134, 139; Brackenridge, *Incidents*, 1:111.

154. Brackenridge, *Incidents*, 1:113–114.

155. Gallatin, *Speech*, 19.

156. Gallatin, *Writings*, 8–9.

157. Sharp, "Whiskey," 119–120, 129.

158. "The Watchman," *Aurora General Advertiser*, February 28, 1795.

159. President of the German Republican Society, Henry Kammerer, *Aurora General Advertiser*, December 27, 1794.

160. Brod, "Rethinking," 162–171, 166, 184–185; Currie, "Constitution," 855; Bhagwat, "Associational," 982–983, 990–992; Inazu, *Liberty's*.

161. Cornell, *Other*, 200–210.

162. Adams to Abigail Adams, December 14, 1794, https://founders.archives.gov/; Chesney, "Democratic-Republican," 1578; Davis, "Whiskey."

163. Ames, in *Debates*, 927–929. Sharp argues that Washington exaggerated the connection of the Democratic societies to the Whiskey Rebellion, though he holds that their members "had a common purpose." Sharp, "Whiskey," 124, 126.

164. U.S. Commission to Edmund Randolph, August 17, 1794, *Pennsylvania Archives*, 2nd ser., 138–139. Washington to Burges Ball, September 25, 1794, https://founders.archives.gov/.

165. Charles, "Originalism," 531–535; Rosenberg, "Alexander," 399–407, 415–417; Rowe, "Alexander," 248. Addison's views, and the judicial conduct that flowed from them (several times he prevented his fellow judge, a Republican, from addressing a grand jury in response to Addison's partisan charges), would eventually drive him from the bench; he was impeached and convicted for his politics on the bench along party lines in 1803.

166. Addison, *Reports*, 156–157, 159–160.

167. Addison, *Reports*, 160.

168. Gallatin to John Badollet, May 20, 1795; Gallatin to Thomas Clare, May 30, 1795.

169. Martin, *Government*, 39–44; Cornell, *Other*, 201–207.

170. Findley, *History*, 48–49.
171. Findley, *History*, 49–50.
172. Findley, *History*, 42; Randolph to George Washington, August 5, 1794, Wharton, *State*, 156–158; Alexander Hamilton to George Washington, August 5, 1794, https://founders.archives.gov/.
173. Gallatin, *Speech*, 5, 13–14; Martin, *Government*, 114; Cornell, *Other*, 203.
174. Gallatin, *Speech*, 5.
175. Gallatin and Findley seemed to have diverged on one point. Findley held that a permanent group identity would have rendered the assemblies an illegitimate alternative to the established government. Gallatin relied on the fact that "the meetings did not call themselves delegates of the people." Gallatin, *Speech*, 5–7. Brod, "Rethinking," 162–171, 166, 184–185; Currie, "Constitution," 355; Inazu, "Forgotten"; Inazu, *Liberty's*, 982–983, 990–992. Brod's rationale is based on his analysis of Art. 1, Sec. 2, the Tenth Amendment, and the First Amendment, which provided combined support for "the value of popular sovereignty and self-government."
176. Cornell, "Mobs," 73–74, 76, 82, 85; Cornell, "Beyond," 256–257. Influential eighteenth-century legal commentator St. George Tucker argued the constitutional case for the right to resist, relying on Art. 1, Sec. 8 and the Second and Tenth Amendments. The 1786 Shays Rebellion in Massachusetts and the 1787 Carlisle riot in Pennsylvania relied on a natural law right to revolution. Cornell, *Well-Regulated*, 73–74, 102–104
177. The Mingo Creek, Couch's Fort, and Braddock's Field assemblies were tied to militia musters. The militia under the command of James McFarland led the attack on Bower Hill that famously incited the most violent part of the rebellion. John Hamilton's Mingo Creek militia, responsible for the destruction at Bower Hill, was engaged in the formation of the Mingo Creek democratic society, one of three such societies in the West (Washington and the Mouth of Yough were the other two), which, institutionally, kept themselves apart from the assemblies while many of their members participated in both. Bouton, *Taming*, 232, 235; Brackenridge, *History*, 47, 82; Hogeland, *Whiskey*, 117–123, 152; Baldwin, *Whiskey*, 118, 154; Slaughter, *Whiskey*, 178–179.
178. Coxe later served as Hamilton's revenue commissioner during the rebellion.
179. "A Pennsylvanian," *Pennsylvania Gazette*, February 20, 1788; Halbrook and Kopel, "Tench," 363; Cornell, "Beyond," 261; Konig, "Arms," 180–181, 183.
180. Konig, "Arms," 181, 183.
181. Cornell, "Beyond," 259, 262.
182. Cornell, "Beyond," 256–257.
183. Cornell, "Mobs," 890, 894; Cornell, *Well-Regulated*, 74, 76.
184. Cornell, "Mobs," 896; Cornell, *Well-Regulated*, 76. The radical aspect of the militia broke out in a 1787 riot in Carlisle in which local militia freed from jail Anti-Federalists who had rioted over a Federalist celebration of Pennsylvania's ratification of the Constitution; Cornell, *Other*, 108, 115; Cornell, *Well-Regulated*, 55–58, 64, 80–81; Cornell, "Aristocracy." Owen, *Political*, 98n65, argues with Cornell's treatment of the riot as rooted in "'plebeian' class-consciousness."
185. Cornell, "Beyond," 263–265.
186. Cornell, *Well-Regulated*, 66; Currie, "Constitution," 813–816. In 1790, Secretary of War Henry Knox proposed military reform that would have organized a national militia under the control of the federal government.

187. Mifflin to George Washington, August 5, 1794, https://founders.archives.gov/; Edmund Randolph to George Washington, August 7, 1794, https://founders.archives.gov/. The federal militia in the Whiskey Rebellion was eventually recruited from Virginia, Pennsylvania, New Jersey, and Maryland.

188. U.S. Constitution, Article 1, Sec. 8; Cornell, *Well-Regulated*, 89; "The Late Insurrection in the Western Counties," *Washington Spy*, December 26, 1794; Cornell, "Mobs," 898, 901–902.

189. Cornell, *Well-Regulated*, 84.

190. Cornell, *Well-Regulated*, 70; Cornell, "Mobs," 897–898.

191. Findley, *History*, 145.

192. Brackenridge, *Incidents*, 1:40–41; Brackenridge, *History*, 109–112.

193. Brackenridge, *Incidents*, 1:59, 64.

194. Brackenridge, *Incidents*, 1:59; Brackenridge, *History*, 87; Slaughter, *Whiskey*, 185.

195. Brackenridge, *Incidents*, 1:58, 61.

196. Brackenridge, *Incidents*, 1:60–61.

197. Hogeland, *Whiskey*, 240; Baldwin, *Whiskey*, 120–123.

198. Brackenridge, *Incidents*, 1:62–63.

199. Brackenridge, *Incidents*, 1:64–65.

200. Brackenridge, *Incidents*, 1:79–84.

201. Brackenridge, *Incidents*, 1:83–84; Slaughter, *Whiskey*, 179–181.

202. Carnahan, "Pennsylvania," 136.

203. Findley, *History*, 122.

204. Brackenridge, *Incidents*, 1:108.

205. Carnahan, "Pennsylvania," 136–137; Brackenridge, *Incidents*, 1:108–109.

206. Carnahan, "Pennsylvania," 136–137.

207. Brackenridge, *Incidents*, 1:108–109.

208. Findley, *History*, 122.

209. Fennell, "From," 288.

210. De Josselin de Jong, "Customary," 111–117; Simpson, "Common," 119–138; Woodman, "Some," 83–110; Van den Bergh, "Concept," 5–32.

211. Simpson, "Common," 119, 36–137; Woodman, "Some," 95–99, 102.

212. Sarat and Kearns, *Law in Everyday*; Myrsiades, "Narratives," 250–264.

213. Van den Bergh, "Concept," 12.

214. Wilf, *Law's*, 194, 196; Geertz, "Thick"; Sarat and Kearns, *Law in the Domain*; Amsterdam and Bruner, "Dialectics," 20–53.

Chapter 3. The Culture of Resistance and Its Agitation-Propaganda

1. Wilf, *Law's*, 1–3.

2. Koenigs, "'Nothing'"; Geertz, "Thick", 239–240; Amsterdam and Bruner, "Dialectics," 229–230.

3. Scott, *Domination*; Hobsbawm and Ranger, *Invention*.

4. Hobsbawm and Ranger, *Invention*, 1–5, 10.

5. White, *Content*.

6. Hobsbawm and Ranger, *Invention*, 1–14.

7. "Indian Conference at Philadelphia."
8. Brackenridge, *Incidents*, 1:34.
9. Brackenridge, "Indian," 38–46; Brackenridge, "Letter," 36–37; *Thompson v. Johnson* 6 Binn. 68 (Pa. 1813) 68–82; *Lessee of Cox against Cromwell* 3 Binn. 114 (Pa. 1810), 114–121; Ridner, " Archibald," 549–554; Silver, *Our*, 282–285.
10. Slaughter, *Whiskey*, 93–94.
11. Brackenridge, "Thoughts on the Excise," 50–51.
12. Grandjean, "'Our," 925–950; Griffin, *American*, 176–180, 192–195, 262–267.
13. Grandjean, "'Our," 927, 940.
14. Griffin, *American*, 266.
15. Thompson, *Whigs*.
16. Bouton, *Taming*, 160; Hogeland, *Whiskey*, 34.
17. Griffin, *American*, 47–49, 74–78, 80, 83; Fennell "Rebelliousness," 6, 10–11.
18. Griffin, *American*, 231. The Shays's Rebellion of 1787 used comparable practices; Taylor, "Regulators," 146–148.
19. Fennell, "From," 5–16, 51, 58, 60, 64, 83, 99–100, 107, 114–115, 129, 150,161, 260; *Pennsylvania Archives*, 1st ser., 10:594–595; Hogeland, *Whiskey*, 20–21; Bouton, *Taming*, 44; Findley, *History*, 32.
20. Crumrine and Ellis, *History*, 263.
21. Griffin, *American*, 176–177, 192, 262.
22. Slaughter, "Crowds," 20.
23. Slaughter, *Whiskey*, 188; Brackenridge, *Incidents*, 1:54.
24. August 8, 1794, "Instructions," 116–118; August 20–22, "Proceedings," 155–158; "Pennsylvania Commission," 158–159; "U.S. Commission," 159–161, 163–164; "Rebel Committee," 161–162. *Pennsylvania Archives*, 2nd ser., vol. 4.
25. Clymer to Alexander Hamilton, October 10, 1794; https://founders.archives.gov/.
26. "Proceedings," August 20, 1794, *Pennsylvania Archives*, 2nd ser., 156–157.
27. "Proceedings," August 20, 1794, *Pennsylvania Archives*, 2nd ser., 156.
28. "Proceedings," August 20, 1794, *Pennsylvania Archives*, 2nd ser., 158.
29. Carnahan, "Pennsylvania," 135–136.
30. Brackenridge, *Incidents*, 2:7; Brackenridge, *Gazette*; Brackenridge, "Trial," 25–35.
31. *Pittsburgh Gazette*, August 23, 1794; Brackenridge, *Incidents*, 2:6–8, 46; "Indian Treaty"; Findley, *History*, 119, 121, 163–164; Brackenridge, *History*, 206–207; Newlin, *Life*, 166–167; Slaughter, *Whiskey*, 272–1.
32. Brackenridge, *Incidents*, 2:6; *Pennsylvania v. Jacob Cribs, Daniel Harold, and eleven others*, 1795.
33. Brackenridge, *Incidents*, 2:6; "Indian Treaty," 460–461.
34. Slaughter, *Whiskey*, 206.
35. Baldwin, *Whiskey*, 192; Brackenridge, *Incidents*, 2:6.
36. "Indian Conference at Philadelphia," 528.
37. Curran, "Examining."
38. "Indian Treaty," 459.
39. "Indian Treaty," 460–461.
40. "Indian Treaty," 460.
41. "Indian Treaty," 460–461.
42. Findley, *History*, 163–164; "Indian Treaty," 459.

43. Newlin, *Life*, 166–167; Carnahan, "Pennsylvania," 135–136; Findley, *History*, 119–120, 163–164.

44. Brackenridge, *History*, 206–207.

45. Slaughter, *Whiskey*, 208; Griffin, *American*, 226–227; Shaw, *American*, 59, 181, 183, 192–193; Gilje, *Road*, 49. 56.

46. Bouton, *Taming*, 236.

47. Baldwin, Whiskey, 103; Hogeland, *Whiskey*, 132.

48. Brackenridge, *Incidents*, 2:99; 3:137; *Philadelphia Gazette and Universal Daily Advertiser*, October 4, 1794.

49. Fennell, "From," 98.

50. Albert Gallatin, in William Rawle's notes taken for the trial, mentions "[a] small flag with six stripes"; "Extract from the Notes of Mr. Rawle," Brackenridge, *Incidents*, 3:137. Bouton, *Taming*, 235; Slaughter, *Whiskey*, 188; Hogeland, *Whiskey*, 182; Gideon, "Whiskey." The Scenery Hill flag can be found at the Century Inn, Scenery Hill, Pennsylvania. William Paterson's bench notes for the Robert Porter trial cite three witnesses who testify to a flag sent with a message on paper to General Neville at the Bower Hill attack on his home, but none specifies the type of flag or a design on the flag; William Paterson bench notes, *United States v. Robert Porter*, May 18, 1795, Heinz History Center, MFF2739. 1795.

51. Griffin, *American*, 227–228, 341n90; deposition, Rawle Papers, 1:101.

52. Griffin, *American*, 227, 341n82, 341n83; Rawle Papers, 1:61, 119.

53. Eddy to Thomas Mifflin, October 10, 1794; *Gazette of the United States and Daily Evening Advertiser*, October 18, 1794; Fennell, "From," 260, 262.

54. Bouton, *Taming*, 238, 312n54.

55. Slaughter, *Whiskey*, 208–209, 273; Griffin, *American*, 227–228, 273n8, 341n88; Rawle Papers, 1:51–57, 74–101, 110, 123, 126–127, 135.

56. Findley, *History*, 312.

57. *General Gazette*, September 20, 1794; Bouton, *Taming*, 237.

58. Washington, Address to Congress, November 19, 1794.

59. Hamilton to Thomas Lee, September 13, 1794, https://founders.archives.gov/.

60. Slaughter, *Whiskey*, 209.

61. As quoted, Bedford County dockets, Bouton, *Taming*, 236, 312n49; William Bradford to the Secretary of State, September 5, 1794, Whiskey Rebellion Collection, Library of Congress; William Bradford to the President of the United States, August 17, 1794, https://founders.archives.gov/.

62. Findley, *History*, 322–323.

63. Holt, "Federal Whiskey," chap. 5: 4, 9; Holt refers to federal attempts by prosecutor Rawle against "sedition-related speech activity," including making "liberty poles criminal," as an abject failure; Holt, "Federal Whiskey," chap. 5: 8.

64. Holt, "Federal Whiskey," chap. 5: 4–5.

65. As quoted, Brackenridge, *History*, 319.

66. Extract from Robert Porter's memoir, Brackenridge, *History*, 332.

67. *United States v. Robt. Philson and Herman Husband*, True Bill, misdemeanor, for May 11, 1795; Paterson Papers, Court Cases, 1765–1802, 2.B, Federal Court Cases.

68. Gallatin to John Badollet, May 20, 1795; Albert Gallatin to Thomas Clare, May 30, 1795; Gallatin Papers.

69. Addison, *Reports*, 274–276.
70. John Holcroft had earlier been involved in Shays's Rebellion; Hogeland, *Whiskey*, 131.
71. Brackenridge, *Incidents*, 2:13.
72. Brackenridge, *Incidents*, 3:148; Baldwin, *Whiskey*, 103.
73. *Pittsburgh Gazette*, July 23, 1794.
74. Findley, *History*, 63.
75. Slaughter, *Whiskey*, 179; Baldwin *Whiskey*, 114–115.
76. "Extracts from the Notes of Mr. Rawle," Brackenridge, *Incidents*, 3:133–134, 136; William Rawle to Alexander Addison, July 17, 1795, December 24, 1794, *Pennsylvania Archives*, 2nd ser., 420–421, 448; Albert Gallatin to John Badollet, May 20, 1795, Gallatin Papers; Albert Gallatin to Hanna Gallatin, May 12, 1795, Gallatin Papers.
77. *United States v. John Barnet*, May 29, 1795, Gilder Lehrman Institute, GLC01114.
78. Hamilton to George Washington, November 17, 1794, Syrett, *Papers*, 17:381–382; Alexander Hamilton to George Washington, August 5, 1794, Syrett, *Papers*, 17:24–58; Alexander Hamilton to William Rawle, November 17–19, 1794, Syrett, *Papers*, 17:378–381.
79. "Proclamation of Gen. Henry Lee, November 29, 1794," *Pennsylvania Archives*, 2nd ser., 402–403; Holt, "Federal Whiskey," chap. 4: n32; chap. 5: n29.
80. Brackenridge, *Incidents*, 1:79; Alexander Hamilton to George Washington, August 5, 1794, Syrett, *Papers*, 17:49.
81. Brackenridge, *Incidents*, 1:79.
82. Carnahan, "Pennsylvania," 130.
83. Brackenridge, *Incidents*, 1:79; Findley, *History*, 121.
84. Carnahan, "Pennsylvania," 130, 140.
85. Carnahan, "Pennsylvania," 140.
86. *Pittsburgh Gazette*, July 5, 1794.
87. "Advertisement," *Pittsburgh Gazette*, July 23, 1794; Syrett, *Papers*, 12:381–382n1.
88. Hamilton to George Washington, November 17, 1794, Syrett, *Papers*, 12:381n1, for the text of the advertisement.
89. *Pittsburgh Gazette*, June 28, 1794.
90. *Pittsburgh Gazette*, July 5, 1794.
91. *Pittsburgh Gazette*, June 21, 1794; *Pittsburgh Gazette*, May 10, 1794.
92. Findley, *History*, 121, 128.
93. Crumrine and Ellis, *History*, 263–271.
94. Crumrine and Ellis, *History*, 271n.
95. Cobbett, *Bone*, 36.
96. Cobbett, *Bone*, 38–40.
97. Brackenridge, *Incidents*, 2:8–9; *Pittsburgh Gazette*, September 13, 1794; Alexander Hamilton to George Washington, November 17, 1794, Syrett, *Papers*, 12:381n1. John Gaston shows up among prisoners in confinement; Alexander Hamilton to George Washington, November 17, 1794, Syrett, *Papers*, 12:373.
98. Brackenridge, *Incidents*, 2:8–9.
99. Brackenridge, *Incidents*, 2:72.
100. Carnahan, "Pennsylvania," 124–125; Brackenridge, *Incidents*, 1:33–34.
101. Brackenridge, *Incidents*, 1:37.
102. Carnahan, "Pennsylvania," 124.
103. Findley, *History*, 92.

104. Brackenridge, *Incidents*, 1:60–61.
105. Brackenridge, *Incidents*, 1:71–72.
106. Brackenridge, *Incidents*, 1:70–71.
107. Brackenridge, *Incidents*, 1:87–88.
108. Brackenridge, *Incidents*, 1:95.
109. Brackenridge, *Incidents*, 1:29, 32.
110. Jay, "Intention," 38–39.
111. Shaffer, "Making"; Silver, *Our*, 232–238.
112. Ridner, "Archibald," 548–551; Silver, *Our*, 281–285.
113. Vol. 4 appears in the White edition; Brackenridge, *Modern*, 178–229.
114. Quotations from *Modern Chivalry* are from Ed White's edition; Patterson, "Hugh," 35, 54, 59–60; Koenigs, "'Nothing,'" 313.
115. Chaden, "Dress," 55–72; Schultz, "Uncovering," 306–311.
116. Brackenridge, *Modern*, 204–206, 216.
117. Brackenridge, *Modern*, 221–222.
118. Brackenridge, *Modern*, 206, 212, 215.
119. Brackenridge, *Modern*, 315.
120. Brackenridge, *Modern*, 215.
121. Brackenridge, *Modern*, 340.
122. Brackenridge, *Modern*, 375.
123. Brackenridge, *Modern*, 504.
124. Brackenridge, *Modern*, 504.
125. Brackenridge, *Modern*, 466.
126. Brackenridge, *Modern*, 210.
127. Brackenridge, *Modern*, 191, 210–211.
128. Brackenridge, *Modern*, 190.
129. Brackenridge, *Modern*, 193.
130. Brackenridge, *Modern*, 206.
131. Brackenridge, *Modern*, 193.
132. Brackenridge, *Modern*, 383.
133. Brackenridge, *Modern*, 381, 393.
134. Brackenridge, *Modern*, 384.
135. Brackenridge, *Modern*, 463.
136. Brackenridge, *Modern*, 456–462.
137. Brackenridge, *Modern*, 272–274.
138. Ferguson, *Law*, 125.
139. Curtis and Resnick, "Images," 1727–1772.
140. Brackenridge, *Modern*, 359.
141. Brackenridge, *Modern*, 273.
142. Brackenridge, *Modern*, 341; Curtis and Resnick, "Images," 1770–1771.
143. Scott, *Domination*.
144. *Gazette of the United States and Daily Evening Advertiser*, October 18, 1794.
145. Carnahan, "Pennsylvania," 127.
146. Gramsci, *Selections*.

Chapter 4. Judges and Grand Jury Charges

1. Holt, "Whiskey Rebellion," 74–81; Holt, "Federal Whiskey"; Ifft, "Treason," 171–177; Slaughter, "King," 58, 89–95, 102–104; Hurst, "Treason, III," 818, 818n236, 829n263; Blinka, "This," 167–170.
2. Brackenridge, *Incidents*, 3:63.
3. Shapiro, "*Beyond*," 112.
4. The charges studied here were delivered in state (three), county (one), and federal courts (two in district courts, ten in circuit courts); ten were delivered in Pennsylvania (one in Philadelphia criminal court, three in the western courts, two in district court, and four in circuit court). Other circuit court charges were delivered in Virginia (two) and one each in New Jersey, Delaware, Georgia, and New Hampshire. Courts included the Pennsylvania Supreme Court, the western courts of Pennsylvania, the U.S. Supreme Court, the U.S. Circuit Court, and the U.S. District Court. Two charges were delivered in 1792, one by Pennsylvania Supreme Court chief justice Thomas McKean and one by president judge of the Pennsylvania Western Courts Alexander Addison. Three charges were delivered in 1794 as President Washington considered and ordered a federalized militia: one by Addison, and two by federal judge Richard Peters, of the United States District Court for the District of Pennsylvania; Addison delivered another charge after the militia arrived. In April 1795, just before the trials began, Supreme Court justice John Blair delivered a charge in the Circuit Court of Georgia. Justice Paterson provided three grand jury charges in 1795 (in April, May, and June) in the circuit courts of New Jersey, Pennsylvania, and Delaware. The Pennsylvania charge was read to the grand jury that indicted the rebels brought for trial to Philadelphia. In the aftermath of the trials, six additional grand jury charges addressed the rebellion: three in the Circuit Court of Pennsylvania (Supreme Court justice James Iredell, in April 1796 and April 1799; and Supreme Court justice Samuel Chase, in April 1800). Two appeared in the Circuit Court of Virginia (Justice Iredell in November 1795; and Justice William Cushing in November 1798), and one in the Circuit Court of New Hampshire in October 1795, by Cushing.
5. Wilf, "First," 1675–1698.
6. Brackenridge, *Law*, 538–539.
7. Wilf, "First," 1685–1686.
8. James Kent, as quoted in Wilf, "First," 1686n60.
9. Wilf, "First," 1686.
10. Benjamin Austin, as quoted in Wilf, "First," 1687n66.
11. Judges who published their grand jury charges did so to influence popular and legal culture in the public sphere.
12. Wilf, "First," 1695–1697.
13. Myrsiades, "Grand," 158–178; Friedman, *History*, 102.
14. Blackstone, *Commentaries*, 4:343, 349; Schwartz, "Demythologizing," 701–703; Thomas, "Blackstone's," 1211. The grand jury was preserved in the Constitution's Fifth Amendment as a right in felony cases and in the Bill of Rights as a check on federal and legislative power; Washburn, "Restoring," 2346.
15. Washburn, "Restoring," 2343; Younger, "Grand Juries," 265, 268. By the end of the eighteenth century, the grand jury's powers had declined and its legitimacy was questioned; Thomas, "Blackstone's Curse," 1239. Schwartz, "Demythologizing," 731–732.

16. Langbein, *Origins*, 45; Thomas, "Blackstone's," 1214; Shapiro, "*Beyond*," 86–92, 111–112; Schwartz, "Demythologizing," 701–703; Younger, "Grand Juries," 265, 268. In 1783, as a prosecutor, Thomas McKean sued Eleazer Oswald while refusing to recuse himself as a judge in the case; the grand jury received witnesses not admitted by the court and refused to indict Oswald or reconsider its decision when McKean directed them to do so. Myrsiades, "Grand," 165–172; Rowe, *Embattled*, 170–172; Roeber, *Faithful*.

17. Younger, "Grand Juries,", 257–258, 265–268; Younger, "Grand Jury," 26–49.

18. Washburn, "Restoring," 2344; Thomas, "Blackstone's," 1203.

19. Lynch, *Role*, 2–3, 20–21, 42–46, 49.

20. Myrsiades, "Grand," 165–172; Shapiro, "*Beyond*," 87–90.

21. Schwartz, "Demythologizing," 759–760; Younger, "Grand Jury," 28. Western juries, unlike urban grand juries in the East, were not routinely packed by members of the upper classes.

22. Younger, "Grand Juries," 259; Rowe, *Thomas*, 187; Washburn, "Restoring," 2341–2342; Thomas, "Blackstone's," 1213; Shapiro, "*Beyond*," 87–93, 111–113.

23. Established in Bushel's case, 1670; Constable, *Law*; Anand, "Origins"; Myrsiades, "Grand," 159–160; Shapiro, "*Beyond*," 87.

24. Republicans believed in the wisdom of a government of popular participation; Federalists were suspicious of common man juries. Where Federalists controlled the judiciary by their appointment of judges and prosecutors, they used the grand jury to control political opposition to the government; local grand juries and state courts were supplanted by changes of vicinage. Schwartz, "Demythologizing," 701–703, 721–726.

25. Larson, "Revolutionary," 1457–1462, 1511–1512; The Judiciary Act of 1789, sec. 29, 1 Stat. 73. The Pennsylvania Act of 1785 for the Better Regulation of Juries controlled jury selection for Pennsylvania and was applied in *United States v. Insurgents*; Dallas, *Reports*, 2:335, 341.

26. Famously, Federalist marshals packed grand juries that proceeded to indict Republican printers Thomas Cooper, Matthew Lyon, and John Thomson Callender in sedition cases in 1800; Schwartz, "Demythologizing," 723–724, 726, 732.

27. *Statutes at Large of Pennsylvania*, 487, 492–494.

28. Defense counsel made a great deal of representation from the western country in trial juries, making liberal use of jury challenges to give them considerable leeway in the composition of juries; Holt, "Whiskey," 74–81; Albert Gallatin's letters, May 12, 1795; May 15, 1795; May 18–19, 1795; May 20, 1795; May 30, 1795, Gallatin Papers.

29. Holt, "Whiskey Rebellion," 75–76. For trial figures, see appendix B; Wythe Holt argues that Federalist judges' reluctance to allow grand jurors from the western counties explained the grand jury's fifty-two indictments (for treason, misprision of treason—a misdemeanor—felony, and other misdemeanors); Holt, "Federal Whiskey," chap. 5: 4–7.

30. Albert Gallatin to Hannah Gallatin, May 12, 1795, Gallatin Papers. Jury composition as it related to Whiskey Rebellion trial juries is discussed in chap. 5.

31. Ellis, *Jeffersonian*, 12; Marcus, *Documentary*, 3:457.

32. O'Connor, *William*, 230; White, *Law*, 204, 206.

33. Snyder, "Charges," 291.

34. O'Connor, *William*, 258, 275.

35. Schwartz, "Demythologizing," 727–732, 750–751, 755–756; Charles, "Originalism," 533–534; Younger, "Grand Juries," 263.

36. Judiciary Act of 1789, chap. 20, sec. 4, 1 Stat. 73. Two Supreme Court justices were originally scheduled to sit at the Philadelphia trials because of the importance of the trials; the format was changed in 1793 to one Supreme Court justice and one district court judge; 1793 Judiciary Act, chap. 22, sec. 1, 1 Stat. 333.

37. "A Militia Man," *Aurora*, January 14, 1795.

38. Ifft, "Treason," 175–176.

39. Slaughter, *Whiskey*, 114–115.

40. Addison, *Reports*, 47–49, 53.

41. Addison, *Reports*, 50–52.

42. Ifft, "Treason," 175.

43. Addison, *Reports*, 100; *New Jersey Journal*, September 24, 1794.

44. Sec. 2 of the Militia Act of 1792 required legal authorization from an associate justice or district judge to activate a federal militia; An Act for Calling Forth the Militia, 1792, chap. 28, sec. 2, 1 Stat. 264; August 4, 1794, *Pennsylvania Archives*, 2nd ser., 70.

45. Addison, *Reports*, 101.

46. Addison, *Reports*, 111.

47. Addison, *Reports*, 104–105.

48. Addison, *Reports*, 113.

49. Addison, *Reports*, 126–127.

50. Addison, *Reports*, 113.

51. Addison, *Reports*, 115.

52. Addison, *Reports*, 118, 120.

53. Addison, *Reports*, 124–125.

54. *Aurora*, July 25, 1799; Marcus, *Documentary*, 3:375; Rosenberg, "Alexander."

55. *Aurora*, January 14, 1795.

56. Addison to Thomas Mifflin, March 31, 1794; Alexander Hamilton to George Washington, September 2, 1794, *Pennsylvania Archives*, 2nd ser., 51, 246; Findley, *History*, 291–293.

57. Brackenridge, *Incidents*, 2:10, 14, 30; possibly Addison's September 6, 1794, or September 22, 1794, charge; Addison, *Reports*, 100–112; *The Philadelphia Gazette and Universal Daily Advertiser*, October 10, 1794.

58. Sometimes reported as "Husbands," Ifft, "Treason," 182n54; Husband was at the meeting in Bedford, Redstone (Brownsville), and Parkinson's Ferry assemblies.

59. Paterson's manuscript notes for *United States v. Philson and Husband*, Gilder Lehrman Institute, GLC01114.

60. Presser, "Tale," 34–40.

61. "Charge of Judge Peters of the U.S. Courts," [August 19, 1794], *Pennsylvania Archives*, 2nd ser., 150, 153.

62. "Charge of Chief Justice McKean," November 8, 1792, *Pennsylvania Archives*, 2nd ser., 36.

63. Charge of Judge Peters, District Court of Pennsylvania, *Gazette of the United States*, September 30, 1794. Novak, *People's*, 12–14; Hall, *Magic*, 168–169.

64. Hamilton to Henry Lee, October 20, 1794, Syrett, *Papers*, 12:331–336; Wharton, *State*, 159–161.

65. Robreno, "Learning," 560–561.
66. Gallatin to Hannah Gallatin, June 1, 1795, Gallatin Papers; Marcus, *Documentary History*, 3:53.
67. Presser, "Tale," 38, 40, 104–106, 109.
68. *United States v. Insurgents*, Dallas, *Reports*, 2:341.
69. *United States v. Mitchell*, Dallas, *Reports*, 2:348–357; Peters presided in the first *Fries* trial with Supreme Court justice James Iredell and in the second one with Supreme Court justice Samuel Chase.
70. *Case of Fries* (1799), 207.
71. Presser, "Tale," 38, 40, 104–106, 109.
72. Hurst provides a floor for the discussion on English law in America; Hurst, "Treason, I,", 226–272; Hurst, *Law*, 68–125.
73. Slaughter, "King," 72–74.
74. Slaughter, "King," 57–58 on Chapin and Hurst. Chapin, *American*.
75. Hurst, "Treason, I," 229, 235–249, 258, 263; Hurst, "Treason, II," 396; Hurst, *Law*, 71, 75–79, 80–81, 84–85, 93, 97–98, 127.
76. Hale, *History*, 80; Blackstone, *Commentaries*, 4:75.
77. Hale, *History*, 84, 151. Hurst, *Law*, 34–38. Hurst contends that the English commentators Matthew Hale and Michael Foster seemed convinced that an overt act was required for all aspects of 25 Edw. III's definition of treason.
78. Hale, *History*, 135, 148, 152; Foster, *Report*, 213, 219; Blackstone, *Commentaries*, 4:82.
79. Hurst, *Law*, 33, 38–39.
80. Hurst, *Law*, 26, 20–28.
81. Hurst, "Treason, III," 818; Hurst, *Law*, 195–196; Dallas, *Reports*, 2:355.
82. Blackstone, *Commentaries*, 4:82.
83. Steilen, "Bills," 767–897.
84. Langbein, *Origins*, 97–102; Steilen, "Bills," 824, 827–830.
85. Steilen, "Bills," 830, 860.
86. Steilen, "Bills," 827.
87. With the re-establishment of rules, procedures, and jury trials to be conducted by the Pennsylvania Supreme Court in Philadelphia, there were 118 prosecutions and 2 hangings. Hurst, "Treason, I," 254–256; Hurst, *Law*, 89–92; Steilen, "Bills," 872–874, 880–888; Young, "Treason," 293–295, 300, 302, 306–307; *Respublica v. Abraham Carlisle*, Dallas, *Reports*, 1:35–38; *Respublica v. John Roberts*, Dallas, *Reports*, 1:39–40; Larson, "Revolutionary," 1449–1457, 1495–1497; Messer, "Species," 303–332. The 1777 Pennsylvania law remained on the books until 1840.
88. Young, "Treason," 296, 298.
89. Hurst, "Treason, I," 254, 256.
90. Dallas, *Reports*, 1:38.
91. Dallas, *Reports*, 1:38.
92. Hurst, "Treason, I," 237–238; Hurst, *Law*, 76–77.
93. Hurst, "Treason, I," 240–242, 251–252, 258; Hurst, "Treason, III," 816; Hurst, *Law*, 78–80, 86–88, 93–94, 194.
94. Hurst, "Treason, II," 403–414; Hurst, *Law*, 133–142; Wilson, Collected *Works*, 2:666.
95. Larson, *Trials*.
96. 25 Edw. III, stat. 5, 351, chap. 2.

97. Wilson, *Collected Works*, 2:664–665. A U.S. Supreme Court justice from 1789 to 1798 and author of influential lectures on the law in 1790–1791, Wilson presided in the circuit court Whiskey Rebellion trial *United States v. Hamilton*. Hall, *Political*, 1, 16, 21, 27–28; Seed, *James*, 150; Hurst, "Treason, II," 404–405; Hurst, *Law*, 134–135.

98. Wilson and M'Kean, *Commentaries*, 75.

99. Wilson, *Collected Works*, 2:664–665; Hurst, "Treason, II," 409; Hurst, *Law*, 138–139.

100. Wilson, *Collected Works*, 2:664. So long as the Constitution was in force, treason would be "correctly and permanently ascertained" and its citizens "covered from the fury even of legislative tempests"; Wilson, "Charge of the Hon.," appendix 2, 40; Wilson, *Charge Delivered*, 9; Wilson, *Collected Works*.

101. Hamilton, Madison, and Jay [Publius], *Federalist*, 59; Madison, no. 43.

102. Tucker, referring to James Madison, no. 43, *Federalist Papers*; Tucker, *Blackstone's*, vol. 5, n. B.

103. Slaughter, "King," 59–60

104. Slaughter, "King," 60–61, 72–73.

105. Hurst, "Treason, III," 811; Hurst, *Law*, 190–191.

106. Hurst, "Treason, I," 245, 258; Hurst, *Law*, 82, 93.

107. Hurst, "Treason, II," 404; Hurst, *Law*, 134–135.

108. O'Connor, *William*, 181, 183.

109. O'Connor, *William*, 140–143.

110. Washington to John Jay, October 5, 1789; George Washington to John Rutledge, September 29, September 30, 1789; Marcus, *Documentary*, 1:1, :1, 20–21; Simpson, "President's," 64–66; Hickox and Liviano, "William," 57–58; Bernstein, "William."

111. Paterson was the last appointee to receive bipartisan support as Washington's judgment was criticized by the politics surrounding the 1795 Jay Treaty; Simpson, "President," 68–69, 72.

112. O'Connor, *William*, 224–225, 249, 252–253, 255. The failed New Jersey plan originated as a result of Shays's Rebellion, 1786, which exemplified the need to authorize drastic measures to suppress popular rebellions; O'Connor, *William*, 147–148.

113. O'Connor, *William*, 282; Hickox and Liviano, "William."

114. Marcus, *Documentary*, 2:368.

115. Paterson to Euphemia Paterson, February 20, 1795, Marcus, *Documentary*, 3:6 and 1n5.

116. Slaughter, "King," 90–91; Slaughter, *Whiskey*, 220; Ifft, "Treason," 173–174; Blinka, "'This,'" 169n200; O'Connor, *William*, 234–236, 249, 258, 270, 284; Brackenridge, *Incidents*, 2:63.

117. Unlike Justice Iredell in the *Fries* case, Paterson failed to advise the jury that its task was to consider only whether the defendant was guilty of the crime charged and not to consider that the safety of the nation required the prisoner be punished; O'Connor, *William*, 328n35, 249; Blinka, "'This,'" n221. Slaughter considered the trials "political theater"; that from pressure to convict and fear the rebels would go free the judges decided which were the best cases to get convictions; that "political exigencies" were served by acting decisively to convict and then mercifully pardon; Slaughter, *Whiskey*, 219–220; Slaughter, "King," 90–91. Blinka cites Justice Paterson for referring in court to the defense's "crafty" argument; the reference was actually to "crafty leaders" of the rebellion; Blinka, "'This,'" 169; in *United States v. Vigol* (1795), in Dallas, *Reports*, 2:347. Holt, "Whis-

key Rebellion," 74, contends that the judiciary gave "specious reasons" for changing venue to Philadelphia; he does so despite Justice James Wilson's procedurally sound and well-argued opinion in *United States v. Hamilton* (1795); Dallas, *Reports*, 3:18. Justice Paterson's opinion in *United States v. Insurgents* favored the defendants on the technicalities, consistent with what Paterson called the defense's "reasonable and just" argument; Dallas, *Reports*, 2:342. Holt notes that none of the rebels was discharged in Philadelphia because of lack of evidence despite the Porter case where Justice Paterson charged and the jury agreed that no evidence was presented that had to be answered and that Porter was not guilty; Holt, "Whiskey Rebellion," 74–75; Brackenridge, *History*, 331; Albert Gallatin to Hannah Gallatin, May 18–19, 1795, Gallatin Papers.

118. In cases that carried a possible death penalty, such as treason, English law traditionally required proof so manifest that it could not be contradicted. Colonial law in Massachusetts used a standard of beyond reasonable doubt for the first time in the 1770 Boston Massacre trials; it appears likely that distorted and suppressed evidence and testimony in the criminal adversary system (like that in the Whiskey Rebellion trials) provided an incentive to elevate the standard of proof to beyond a reasonable doubt. The term itself was not used in U.S. law until the 1798 trial of Matthew Lyon for seditious libel ("beyond all reasonable substantial doubt") in the Circuit Court of Vermont, though it was already becoming the standard for trial juries; Langbein, *Origins*, 33, 262, 265–266; Morano, "Reexamination," 516–519; Shapiro, *"Beyond,"* 22, 24, 140. Justice James Wilson in the Whiskey Rebellion case *United States v. Hamilton* held that the highest standard of proof, moral certainty (which formed the basis for the beyond reasonable doubt standard), and not probability, should hold for both grand juries and petite juries; Dallas, *Reports*, 3:17–18.

119. Paterson, grand jury charge, April 2, 1795, Marcus, *Documentary*, 3:11–13.

120. Paterson, grand jury charge, May 4, 1795, Marcus, *Documentary*, 3:41–42; *Genius of Liberty & New-Jersey Advertiser*, October 26, 1795. The last two trials were held in October after which the government gave up its efforts to punish the whiskey rebels.

121. Paterson, undated grand jury charge, Marcus, *Documentary*, 3:459; written between 1793 and 1800.

122. Paterson, undated grand jury charge, Marcus, *Documentary*, 3:463–464.

123. Wilson, *Collected Works*, 2:663–668; Hurst, "Treason, II," 404–405; Seed, *James*, 150.

124. Wilson, *Collected Works*, 2:663, 667.

125. Paterson to Edmund Randolph, June 6, 1795, *Washington Papers*, file 33.

126. *Vanhorne's Lessee v. Dorrance*, 2 U.S. 304, Dallas, *Reports*, 2:304–320.

127. *Vanhorne*, Dallas, *Reports*, 2:304. Paterson had served as a U.S. senator and co-authored the 1789 Judiciary Act creating the federal court system. As a governor of New Jersey (1791–1793), he resisted English common law in his reform of New Jersey law.

128. *Vanhorne*, Dallas, *Reports*, 2:304.

129. *Vanhorne*, Dallas, *Reports*, 2:307.

130. Dallas was secretary of the commonwealth of Pennsylvania (1791–1801) at the time of the Whiskey Rebellion and a member of the Pennsylvania Commission appointed by Governor Mifflin to meet with the rebels.

131. Marcus, *Documentary*, 3:2; O'Connor, *William*, 234–235; Gallatin to Hannah Gallatin, June 1, 1795, Gallatin Papers. Whether Paterson charged juries based on English

common law precedents, read the treason law constructively, or directed verdicts, the defense did not complain it was mistreated or denied an opportunity to argue its case. While he exercised his judicial discretion fully, the legal analysis in his jury charges was neither slipshod nor disregardful of the law as it stood. Nor was he brought up for impeachment for his judicial work, as were Addison and Peters. Brackenridge remarked that the trials provided an abundance of evidence to provide a proper defense; where it did not do so, as Gallatin found, there were numerous acquittals and discharged cases; Brackenridge, *Incidents*, 3:151. Albert Gallatin to John Badollet, May 20, 1795, Gallatin Papers. Findley indicated that interested witnesses were "expressly contradicted by unexceptionable testimony"; Findley *History*, 216–217; 318.

132. *Vanhorne*, Dallas, *Reports*, 2:308.

133. *Vanhorne*, Dallas, *Reports*, 2:311–312.

134. Holt, "Whiskey Rebellion," 77, 77n162; William Rawle seemed ready to terminate the trials after he lost two trials in the October term. Just before the circuit court met in April 1796, he dropped the remaining charges.

135. Paterson, grand jury charge, Circuit Court of Delaware, June 8, 1795, Marcus, *Documentary*, 3:57.

136. Vermont (1791) and Kentucky (1792) had joined the Union by 1795; Paterson, grand jury charge, June 8, 1795, Marcus, *Documentary*, 3:59.

137. Paterson, grand jury charge, June 8, 1795, Marcus, *Documentary*, 3:60.

138. During the April 1795 term of the Georgia Circuit Court, three admiralty cases were decided and subsequently appealed to the Supreme Court, which affirmed two and reversed the third; Marcus, *Documentary*, 3:62n3.

139. Blair, grand jury charge, Circuit Court of Georgia, April 27, 1795, Marcus, *Documentary*, 3:32.

140. Blair, grand jury charge, April 27, 1795, Marcus, *Documentary*, 3:32.

141. Blair, grand jury charge, April 27, 1795, Marcus, *Documentary*, 3:33.

142. Blair, grand jury charge, April 27, 1795, Marcus, *Documentary*, 3:34–35.

143. Iredell, grand jury charge, Circuit Court of Virginia, November 23, 1795, Marcus, *Documentary*, 3:74–79; Circuit Court of Pennsylvania, April 12, 1796, Marcus, *Documentary*, 3:106–114; Circuit Court of Pennsylvania, April 11, 1799, Marcus, *Documentary*, 3:332–345; Carpenter, *Two*, 1–16.

144. Iredell, grand jury charges, April 12, 1796, November 23, 1795, Marcus, *Documentary*, 3:75, 107.

145. Iredell, grand jury charge, April 12, 1796, November 23, 1795, Marcus, *Documentary*, 3:75–76, 107.

146. Iredell, grand jury charge, November 23, 1795, Marcus, *Documentary*, 3:76–77.

147. Iredell, grand jury charge, November 23, 1795, Marcus, *Documentary*, 3:78.

148. Peters's comments appear in a postscript to a letter he sent to Justice Paterson (April 24, 1799) begging for Paterson's presence in Philadelphia for the *Fries* trial; Marcus, *Documentary*, 3:352–353.

149. Iredell, response to grand jury, Circuit Court of Pennsylvania, May 15, 1799, Carpenter, *Two*, 15.

150. Cushing, grand jury charge, Circuit Court of Virginia, November 23, 1798, Marcus, *Documentary*, 3:313.

151. Ellis, *Jeffersonian*, 79.

152. Chase, grand jury charge, Circuit Court of Pennsylvania, April 12, 1800, Marcus, *Documentary*, 3:413–414.

153. The sample presented here represents eight jury statements responding to grand jury charges by six judges who specifically addressed rebellion against the government and the Whiskey Rebellion from 1792 to 1799.

154. June 9, 1795, Marcus, *Documentary*, 3:61, in response to William Paterson, Circuit Court of Delaware; April 11, 1799, Carpenter, *Two*, 15–16, in response to James Iredell, Circuit Court of Pennsylvania; April 29, 1795, Marcus, *Documentary*, 3:39, in response to John Blair, Circuit Court of Georgia.

155. November 8, 1792, *Pennsylvania Archives*, 2nd ser., 37, in response to Chief Justice Thomas McKean, Pennsylvania Supreme Court.

156. November 8, 1792, *Pennsylvania Archives*, 2nd ser., 37; April 2, 1796, Marcus, *Documentary*, 3:102, in response to James Iredell, Circuit Court of New Jersey.

157. October 24, 1795, Marcus, *Documentary*, 3:71, in response to William Cushing, Circuit Court of New Hampshire; April 29, 1795, Marcus, *Documentary*, 3:39; April 12, 1796, Marcus, *Documentary*, 3:113–114, in response to James Iredell, Circuit Court of Pennsylvania; April 2, 1796, Marcus, *Documentary*, 3:102.

158. April 11, 1799, Carpenter, *Two*, 15–16; April 12, 1796, Marcus, *Documentary*, 3:113–114.

159. Jury statement, August 19, 1794, Circuit Court of Pennsylvania, *Gazette of the United States*, August 22, 1794.

160. Jury statement, Circuit Court of Georgia, April 29, 1795, Marcus, *Documentary*, 3:39

161. Jury statement, Circuit Court New Jersey, April 2, 1796, Marcus, *Documentary*, 3:102.

162. Jury statement, Circuit Court of Pennsylvania, April 12, 1796, Marcus, *Documentary*, 3:113.

163. Jury statement, Circuit Court of Pennsylvania, May 15, 1799, Carpenter, *Two*, 15.

164. Rao, "Federal."

165. Paterson, grand jury charge, May 4, 1795, Marcus, *Documentary*, 3:41–42.

166. Lienesch, "Reinterpreting," 161.

167. Lienesch, "Reinterpreting," 177, 179–181.

168. Pencak, "Fine," 122–123; Patterson, "Federalist," 117.

169. Pencak, "Fine," 123.

170. Washington to Henry Lee, October 31, 1786, https://founders.archives.gov/.

171. Washington to James Madison, March 31, 1787, https://founders.archives.gov/; James Madison to George Washington, March 18, 1787, https://founders.archives.gov/.

172. Publius, Federalist, no 2; *Independent Journal*, October 31, 1787; Burd, "Revolutionary," 5–8.

Chapter 5. The Trials, 1795

1. *Ex parte Corbly; Lockery; Hamilton; Sedgewick*, in Marcus, *Documentary* 6:514–518; Larson, *Trials*, 236–239; Holt, "Federal Whiskey," chap. 5.

2. Slaughter, *Whiskey*, 216–218. Washington found "the army could be put in motion" by the 23rd of October; he provided instructions on October 20, and General Lee sent

NOTES TO CHAPTER FIVE 287

out general orders on October 21; the army reached the western counties in early November; Washington, *Diaries*, 195.

3. Washington, *Diaries*, 195; Rich, "Washington," 344–348; George Washington to Henry Lee, October 20, 1794, https://founders.archives.gov/.
4. Washington to Henry Lee, October 20, 1794, https://founders.archives.gov/.
5. Findley, *History*, 143, 160.
6. Washington to Henry Lee, October 20, 1794, https://founders.archives.gov/; Alexander Hamilton to Henry Lee, October 20, 1794, https://founders.archives.gov/; Brackenridge, *Incidents*, 2:65–67.
7. Brackenridge, *Incidents*, 2:70.
8. Stephen Fordham to his wife, October 19, 1794, Gilder Lehrman Institute.
9. Findley, *History*, 219.
10. Findley, *History*, 222.
11. Findley, *History*, 222, 227.
12. Brackenridge, *Incidents*, 1:62; "Examination," Syrett, *Papers*, 12:382–387.
13. [Findley], *Review*; Findley, *History*, 240–241, 246, 249–250.
14. Findley, *History*, 279–280.
15. Hamilton to William Rawle, July 10, 1795, Rawle Family Papers.
16. Brackenridge, *Incidents*, 1:61.
17. Brackenridge, *Incidents*, 2:78.
18. Brackenridge, *Incidents*, 3:32, 35.
19. Brackenridge, *Incidents*, 2:78–80.
20. Brackenridge, *Incidents*, 2:71.
21. Hamilton to George Washington, September 2, 1794, *Pennsylvania Archives*, 2nd ser., 248.
22. Hamilton to George Washington, September 2, 1794, *Pennsylvania Archives*, 2nd ser., 242–243.
23. Hamilton to George Washington, September 2, 1794, *Pennsylvania Archives*, 2nd ser., 242.
24. Hamilton seems to have realized how much conditions had been misrepresented after he arrived in the West; Slaughter, *Whiskey*, 271n25.
25. Findley, *History*, 295.
26. Findley, *History*, 305.
27. Wilson to George Washington, August 4, 1794, *Pennsylvania Archives*, 2nd ser., 70; Findley, *History*, 318.
28. Hamilton to Tench Coxe, [August 1, 1794], n. ::, https://founders.archives.gov/.
29. Wilson to George Washington, August 4, 1794, *Pennsylvania Archives*, 2nd ser., 70.
30. Bradford to George Washington, August 5, 1794, https://founders.archives.gov/.
31. Bradford to George Washington, August, n.d., 1794, *Washington Papers*, 33:284–291.
32. Randolph to George Washington, August 5, 1794, Wharton, *State*, 156. Randolph was secretary of state 1794–1795 and attorney general 1789–1794.
33. Randolph to George Washington, August 5, 1794, Wharton, *State*, 158.
34. Mifflin to George Washington, August 12, 1794, *Pennsylvania Archives*, 2nd ser., 129.
35. Mifflin to George Washington, August 5, 1794, Wharton, *State*, 142, 144, 148–151; Thomas Mifflin to George Washington, August 12, 1794, *Pennsylvania Archives*, 2nd ser., 130.

36. Randolph to Thomas Mifflin, August 30, 1794, Wharton, *State*, 154–155; Edmund Randolph to Thomas Mifflin, August 7, 1794, Syrett, *Papers*, 17:61–72; Edmund Randolph to Thomas Mifflin, August 7, 1794, *Pennsylvania Archives*, 2nd ser., 96–104.

37. Randolph suggested that Mifflin had disregarded certain critical evidence himself, which must have "escaped your excellency's attention: else they are too material to have omitted in your review of the evidence, and too conclusive not to have set aside the supposition which you entertained"; Wharton, *State*, 154. The version of the letter included in Syrett, *Papers*, 17:163–167, is not complete; Wharton, *State*, 152–156.

38. Swiss-born Gallatin's 1794 election to the Senate was invalidated on the grounds of citizenship requirements.

39. Gallatin to Hannah Gallatin, May 12, 1795; Gallatin to John Badollet, May 20, 1795, Gallatin Papers.

40. Gallatin to Hannah Gallatin, May 18–19, 1795, Gallatin Papers.

41. Charles Nisbet corresponded regularly on the rebellion with Judge Addison. Charles Nisbet to Alexander Addison, January 13, 1795, February 20, 1795, Addison Papers, 1786–1803, DAR. 1925.06.

42. Brackenridge, *Incidents*, 2:63.

43. Slaughter, *Whiskey*, 170–171, 177, 182.

44. Bradford to his father-in-law Elias Boudinot, August 1, 1794, Wallace Papers, vol. 2; Slaughter, *Whiskey*, 267n15.

45. 1794 Excise Act, chap. 49, sec. 9, 1 Stat. 378.

46. Rawle to Edmund Randolph, July 30, 1794, Rawle Family Papers.

47. Rawle to Alexander Addison, July 3, 1794, Rawle Family Papers; William Rawle to Edmund Randolph July 30, 1794, Rawle Family Papers.

48. U.S. Commission Report, September 24, 1794, *Pennsylvania Archives*, 2nd ser., 296; Slaughter, *Whiskey*, 198.

49. Brackenridge, *Incidents*, 1:95.

50. Brackenridge, *Incidents*, 1:89. Art. 2, Sec. 2 of the Constitution holds that "[t]rials shall be held in the state where the crime was committed."

51. Brackenridge, *Incidents*, 3:34.

52. Hamilton to Henry Lee, October 20, 1794, https://founders.archives.gov/.

53. Brackenridge, *Incidents*, 2:80.

54. Holt, "'To,'" 1461n146.

55. Farrand, *Records*, 46.

56. Holt, "'To,'" 1463n156.

57. Farrand, *Records*, 46, 133; Holt, "'To,'" 1464n160; Robreno, "Learning," 560, 571–572.

58. Wilmarth Jr., "Elusive," 178–179, 183.

59. 1791 Excise Act, chap. 15, sec. 42, 1 Stat. 199; Ifft, "Treason," 166.

60. 1794 Excise Act, chap. 49, sec. 9, 1 Stat. 378; Slaughter, *Whiskey*, 170, 198.

61. 1789 Judiciary Act, chap. 20, sec. 29, 1 Stat. 73; Marcus, *Documentary*, 6:515n6.

62. 1793 Judiciary Act, chap. 22, sec. 3, 1 Stat. 333. The 1793 Act was referenced by the defense in the *Fries* trial in 1799 but not invoked in the Whiskey Rebellion trials, which relied on the stronger, more specific 1789 Judiciary Act (sec. 29).

63. Slaughter, *Whiskey*, 170, 182, 198, 270n21.

64. "Charge of Judge Peters of the U.S. Courts," August 19, 1794., U.S. District Court of Pennsylvania, *Pennsylvania Archives*, 2nd ser., 149.

65. *Gazette of the United States,* September 30, 1794, *Pennsylvania Archives,* 2nd ser., 153; Novak, *People's,* 12–14; Hall, *Magic,* 168–169.

66. Robreno, "Learning," 555, 571.

67. Dallas, *Reports,* 2:343

68. 1789 Judiciary Act, chap. 22, sec. 29, 1 Stat. 73.

69. Baird, *Copies,* 73; Marcus *Documentary,* 6:6, 521.

70. Dallas, *Reports,* 2:335–345.

71. Dallas, *Reports,* 2:344

72. 3 U.S. 17, 1795.

73. 1793 Judiciary Act, chap. 22, sec. 3, 1 Stat. 333.

74. Marcus, *Documentary,* 6:514–517; Holt, "Federal Whiskey," chap. 5: 1–2, 5.

75. *Case of Fries,* 876, 908, 912; *Case of Fries,* Circuit Court, District of Pennsylvania. 9 F. Cas. 826; 1799 U.S. App. Lexis 35; 3 Dall. 515; Carpenter, *Two*; Presser, "Tale," 86–89; Elsmere, "Trials," 437–439; Newman, *Fries's,* 166–167, 171–172. Although he sat on the bench, Peters also testified as a witness for the prosecution in the trial. Justice James Iredell was the second justice on the bench.

76. *Case of Fries,* 842.

77. *Case of Fries,* 845.

78. Iredell offered that his doubts had been stated by Justice Wilson and that he was "inclined to think this was a great reason which guided the decision; otherwise a doubt would not have been intimated." The court ought not, therefore, allow "a doubt on point of law" and risk an appeal on the decision of the court, thereby "defeating the prosecution of a case so important." *Case of Fries,* 846.

79. Farrand, *Records,* 46–47.

80. Ten cases for treason, misdemeanor, and procedural issues provide material for the present study: four transcripts in manuscript from Justice Paterson's notes (John Barnet; Robert Porter; Thomas Miller; Robert Philson and Herman Husband); five law reports from Dallas's law reports (John Mitchell; Philip Vigol; John Hamilton; James Stewart and Edward Wright; *The Insurgents of Pennsylvania*); and the ex parte hearings (John Corbly; John Loughery; John Hamilton; Thomas Sedgwick) taken from U.S. Supreme Court minutes and Marcus, *Documentary,* vol. 6.

81. Wharton, *State,* 106; Friedman, *History,* 65–115, 207–251; White, *Law,* 109–192.

82. An Act for the Gradual Abolition of Slavery, 1780; Amendment to the 1780 Gradual Abolition Act, 1788; Newman, *Transformation*; Melish, *Disowning.*

83. Bradford to Elias Boudinot, August 1, 1794, Wallace Papers, vol. 2; Brackenridge, Findley, and Gallatin documented Rawle's shortcomings.

84. Dallas, *Reports,* 3:17. Findley held that Secretary Hamilton was directly responsible for a potential injustice in John Hamilton's case that could easily have convicted the accused despite the secretary's own doubt that proving it would have been difficult. Findley, *History,* 230.

85. Marcus, *Documentary,* 6:515–517; Holt, "Federal Whiskey," chap. 5: 2–4.

86. Dallas, *Reports,* 2:343–345.

87. Dallas, *Reports,* 2:335, 341–342.

88. Gallatin to Hannah Gallatin, May 15, 1795, Gallatin Papers.

89. Dallas, *Reports,* 2:342.

90. Holt, "Federal Whiskey," chap. 5: 6.

91. Blinka, "'This,'" 169–170; Albert Gallatin to John Badollet, May 20, 1795, Gallatin Papers; Albert Gallatin to Hannah Gallatin, May 15, 1795, Gallatin Papers. In his letter to Badollet, Gallatin reported the following: "The petty jury consist of 108, to wit 60 of the city and neighborhood, *12* from Fayette, *12* from Washington, *12* from Alleghany, and *12* from Northumbd—— on every trial the 60 from the city and neighborhood & the *12* from that County where the offence was committed compose the venire & their names put in a box, out of which *12* are drawn by lot to try the issue; but in cases of treason the accused has a right to challenge *35* without assigning any reason." In his letter of May 15 to his wife, he reported that with the 35 challenges out of the 72 to draw from "the chance of the accused person is, of course to have one third of the county where the fact was committed." Trial records show that from the western counties only 12 out of 72— 36 from Philadelphia County; 15 from Delaware County; and 9 from Chester County— were called to form a pool for each of the 10 cases tried, from which trial jurors would be chosen; Holt, "Federal Whiskey," chap. 5: 5–6; *United States v. Insurgents*, in Dallas, *Reports*, 2:339, 342.

92. Rawle to Alexander Addison, August 15, 1795, October 29, 1795, *Pennsylvania Archives*, 2nd ser., 450, 535.

93. Gallatin to Hannah Gallatin, May 12, 1795, Gallatin Papers. Gallatin remained in Philadelphia throughout the trials to report on them in detail, largely in letters to his wife that reveal a detailed attention to the trials as well as familiarity with witnesses, jury members from the West, and defense counsel; Gallatin was a witness in *United States v. Vigol* and *United States v. Philson and Husband*. Extracts from Rawle's notes include statements by Gallatin; Brackenridge, *Incidents*, 3:136–137.

94. Gallatin to John Badollet, May 20, 1795, Gallatin Papers.

95. Porter's narrative, Brackenridge, *History*, 331.

96. Gallatin to Hannah Gallatin, June 1, 1795, Marcus, *Documentary*, 6:53.

97. Gallatin to Hannah Gallatin, May 18–19, 1795, Gallatin Papers.

98. Gallatin to Hannah Gallatin, June 1, 1795, Marcus, *Documentary*, 6:53.

99. See here Holt's unpublished work based on trial records, generously made available to the author.

100. Holt, "Federal Whiskey," chap. 5: 15n20.

101. Gallatin to Thomas Clare, May 30, 1795, Gallatin Papers; William Rawle to Alexander Addison, August 15, 1795, *Pennsylvania Archives*, 2nd ser., 449; Holt, "Federal Whiskey," chap. 5, 5; "General Lee's Proclamation of Pardon," *Pennsylvania Archives*, 2nd ser., 403.

102. Holt, "Federal Whiskey," chap. 5: 6–7, 11–12.

103. Gallatin to Hannah Gallatin, June 1, 1795, Marcus, *Documentary*, 6:53.

104. Gallatin to Hannah Gallatin, June 1, 1795, Marcus, *Documentary*, 6:53.

105. Passed by the Pennsylvania Assembly on May 14, 1776, and superseded in 1777 by a second act, Pennsylvania's Treason Act was in effect until 1860. Larson, *Trials*, 70–73; Young, "Treason," 294.

106. *United States v. Insurgents*, 335–342.

107. *United States v. Insurgents*, 341.

108. Larson, *Trials*, 70–76, 96–106, 189–190, 226–227; Young, "Treason," 294; Ousterhout, "Controlling," 3–16.

109. Baldwin, *Whiskey*, 165; Hogeland, *Whiskey*, 238. Gallatin to Hannah Gallatin, May 25, 1795; Gallatin to John Badollet, May 20, 1795; Slaughter, *Whiskey*, 219.

110. Dallas, *Reports*, 2:346.

111. Marcus, *Documentary*, 3:12; O'Connor, *William*, 234.

112. Gallatin to Hannah Gallatin, May 25, 1795; Brackenridge, *Incidents*, Appendix, 3:66.

113. Findley, *History*, 211: Gallatin, to John Badollet, May 20, 1795; Slaughter, *Whiskey*, 219; Baldwin, *Whiskey*, 257.

114. Dallas, *Reports*, 2:349. Under common law, suppressing the excise office was a particular rather than a general act, so that it did not rise to levying war against the state. Further, lawless conduct by other persons was riot in legal terms, not treason. Mitchell himself did not commit an overt act, much less one with intent.

115. Dallas, *Reports*, 2:350; Hurst, "Treason, I," 243; Hurst, *Law*, 80–81.

116. Dallas, *Reports*, 2:349.

117. Chapin, *American*, 3, 86; William Bradford to George Washington, August, [5], 1794, https://founders.archives.gov/.

118. Dallas, *Reports*, 2:353–354.

119. Dallas, *Reports*, 2:354–355.

120. Foster, *Report*, 218.

121. Dallas, *Reports*, 2:350, 353.

122. Dallas, *Reports*, 2:350–351

123. Dallas, *Reports*, 2:351.

124. Dallas, *Reports*, 2:350.

125. Dallas, *Reports*, 2:353.

126. Dallas, *Reports*, 2:352.

127. Dallas, *Reports*, 2:349–352, 353.

128. Dallas, *Reports*, 2:355.

129. Blackstone, *Commentaries*, 4:75, 82; Hale, *History*, 80, 84, 151.

130. Dallas, *Reports*, 2:355–356; Slaughter, "King," 94.

131. Paterson's sole legal citation in *Mitchell* was to Foster, *Report*, 213, which he used to link marching to Neville's with a treasonable intention, claiming that "[t]he very act of marching is considered as carrying the traitorous intention into effect." But Foster, 213, said that a bare conspiracy is "not an overt act [. . .] *unless the rising be effected*." Paterson might better have cited Foster, *Report*, 218 (as Bradford did in prosecuting *Mitchell*) to the effect that "[l]isting and marching are sufficient overt acts without coming to a battle or action," that is, "*bellum levatum* [where battle has not taken place], though not *bellum percussum* [where battle has taken place]"; Dallas, *Reports*, 2:354. It is possible that Paterson, or Dallas in reporting it, mistook the citation.

132. Dallas, *Reports*, 2:356.

133. Dallas, *Reports*, 2:350–352.

134. Dallas, *Reports*, 2:355–356; Rawle, in Dallas, *Reports*, 2:349–350.

135. The defense called attention to Bradford's admission, which they had "laid down in all the books, which have been cited," that conspiracy was not treason; Dallas, *Reports*, 2:351.

136. Gallatin to John Badollet, May 20, 1795, Gallatin Papers; William Paterson, bench

notes, *United States v. Philson and Husband*, June 3, 1795, Paterson Papers, 1689–1841, file 120.

137. *United States v. Mitchell*, Dallas, *Reports*, 2:348–357; *United States v. John Barnet*, 1795, Gilder Lehrman Institute, GLC01114; William Paterson, bench notes, *United States v. Miller*, June 1, 1795, Paterson Papers, 1689–1841, file 119.

138. Dallas, *Reports*, 2:350.

139. Slaughter, *Whiskey*, 178–179; Bouton, *Taming*, 232–235; Brackenridge, *History*, 44–47; Hogeland, *Whiskey*, 117–123, 152; Baldwin, *Whiskey*, 118, 154.

140. Konig, "Arms," 181, 183.

141. Dallas, *Reports*, 2:349; *United States v. Robert Porter*, May 18, 1795, Heinz History Center, MFF2739. 1795.

142. Paterson's bench notes: *United States v. Robert Porter*, May 18, 1795, Heinz History Center, MFF2739. 1795; *United States v. John Barnet*, May 29, 1795, Gilder Lehrman Institute, GLC01114; *United States v. Miller*, June 1, 1795, Paterson Papers, 1689–1841, 2.B. Federal Court Cases, file 119; *United States v. Philson and Husband*, June 3, 1795, Paterson Papers, 1689–1841, 2.B. Federal Court Cases, file 120.

143. The *Vigol* treason trial involved an attack against excise collector Benjamin Well's house; Dallas, *Reports*, 2:346–348.

144. The number of pages devoted to prosecution witnesses in Paterson's *Porter* version (fifteen and a half) were comparable to the number in *Barnet* (seventeen and a half) and *Miller* (fifteen and a half), with the other two presenting minimal pages for defense witnesses (two pages in *Barnet* and one in *Miller*). In *Miller*, one prosecution witness (Col. David Phillips) was given five manuscript pages, one was given three (James Barlow), and one was given two and a half (David Hamilton); the other witnesses received less than a page, four of them a paragraph or less. Defense witnesses received a paragraph or less. A similar pattern appeared with prosecution witnesses in *Barnet*: Arthur Gardener took up five manuscript pages and two other prosecution witnesses (James McAllister and Baldwin) took four; James Wherry took two; the rest ranged from a page to a few lines. The defense witnesses ranged from one and a half pages (Hugh Henry Brackenridge) to a paragraph.

145. Brackenridge, *History* 328–329.

146. Gallatin to Hannah Gallatin, May 18–19, 1795, Gallatin Papers; Absalom Baird to Susy Baird, May 23, 1795, Baird, *Copies*, 80.

147. The extracts were provided by J. M. Porter in response to a request from Henry Marie Brackenridge, Hugh Henry Brackenridge's son; Brackenridge, *History*, 328–332. Porter's trial appears in a brief law report in Dallas, *Reports*, 2:345. Of the two versions of bench notes for *Porter* that appear in the Heinz History Center, one is less than half as long as the other: 208 lines compared with 501 lines.

148. Based on the length of Paterson's notes for each witness in *Porter*, four of the twelve witnesses were of particular interest to the judge: David Lewis, Col. David Phillips, John Baldwin, and John McDonald. Three witnesses appeared both in the Porter and the Miller trials (Phillips, David Hamilton, and Arthur Gardner, who also testified in the Barnet trial) and five were turncoat witnesses (McDonald, Phillips, Hamilton, Gardner, and George Parker). Of the twelve prosecution witnesses in *Porter*, the most prolific were Lewis (171 lines in Paterson's version as opposed to forty-five in the reduced

version), Baldwin (sixty-five cut to thirty-two), and the turncoats Philips (seventy-five lines cut to twenty-three) and McDonald (thirty lines cut to thirteen).

149. Holcroft did testify in the Whiskey Rebellion trials, but not in *Porter*; Holt, "Federal Whiskey," chap. 4, n32; chap. 5, n29.

150. Brackenridge, *History*, 329.

151. Brackenridge, *History*, 329, 332.

152. Brackenridge, *History*, 331.

153. Dallas, *Reports*, 2:345.

154. Gallatin to Hannah Gallatin, June 1, 1795.

155. Paterson's bench notes on Lewis cite Foster, *Report*, 213, 217–218, 190, and Hale, *History*, 111–130.

156. Dallas, *Reports*, 2:346–347; Paterson, grand jury charge, May 4, 1795, Marcus, *Documentary*, 3:41–42. Not only is Paterson's use of induction no more than a generalization without an underlying principle or negatives accounted for, and thereby a vulnerable process in the law, but a process that enumerates fact situations that cannot deliver constant, unchanging rules; Hunter, "No," 369–383.

157. Dallas, *Reports*, 2:356.

158. Hale, *History*, 144–146; Foster, *Report*, 218.

159. Hale, *History*, 150.

160. Garner, *Black's*, 1014, 1507.

161. Foster, *Report*, 208. If the assembly was by intent arrayed for war without any act of war being attempted, it would, according to Hale, *History*, 151, not have constituted an act of war (*bellum percussum*) but an act in the manner of levying war (*bellum levatum*). Foster, *Report*, 218, considered *bellum levatum* a sufficient overt action to constitute treason without coming to battle.

162. Holt, "New," 256–260, 268, 270; Hogeland, *Whiskey*, 259–261; Fennell, "From," 190–225.

163. Blackstone, *Commentaries*, 4:80, found that a high misdemeanor that amounted only to spoken words was no treason, for spoken words could be taken as an "equivocal and ambiguous" utterance expressed in heat or mistakenly remembered by hearers. If written down, by contrast, Blackstone said, "it argues more deliberate intention," the words themselves not being the treason "but the deliberate act of writing them."

164. Horatius, nos. 1–4, *Genius of Liberty*, October 5, 1795, October 12, 1795, October 19, 1795, October 26, 1795; O'Connor, *William*, 237–238.

165. Jay's experience gave Paterson the perfect excuse to stay on the court and refuse Washington's request to take over Randolph's position of secretary of state when Randolph was accused of colluding with the French. O'Connor, *William*, 238.

166. Horatius, no. 2, *Genius of Liberty*, October 12, 1795; O'Connor, *William*, 239.

167. While students of the insurrection have found fault with many of the extreme claims made by the Washington administration, Bouton's claims of continuing popular movements from 1754 to 1799 make Paterson's fears of a systemic threat appear less like paranoia and more like a realistic assessment; Bouton, *Taming*, 28–29, 145–167, 204, 208, 218, 226, 244.

168. O'Connor, *William*, 275, 329n39; William Paterson to Edmund Randolph, June 6, 1795, Marcus, *Documentary*, 3:56.

169. O'Connor, *William*, 270, 275, 329n39; Blinka offers that the whole process in the Whiskey Rebellion trials mirrored the way that offenders were tried, convicted, pardoned, and brought back into the community during the Revolution; Blinka, "'This,'" n200; Slaughter, "King," 91.

170. O'Connor, *William*, 275, 329n39.

171. White, *Content*, 15–16.

172. Hunter, "No," 373–377.

173. "Incog."To George Washington, June 10, 1795, https://founders.archives.gov/.

174. Helmuth and Hendel to George Washington, June 12, 1795, https://founders.archives.gov/; Bradford, *Enquiry*; Holt, "Whiskey Rebellion," 78n164.

175. Helmuth and Hendel to George Washington, June 12, 1795, https://founders.archives.gov/, n1. The *Vigol* jury "induced" William Lewis as counsel for Vigol to present their petitions to the president. Six members signed each petition, one of which included the foreman of the jury.

176. Philadelphia Citizens to George Washington, June 15, 1795, https://founders.archives.gov/.

177. Helmuth and Hendel to Bartholomew Dandridge Jr., June 16, 1795, https://founders.archives.gov/, n1.

178. "Draft of George Washington's Seventh Annual Address to Congress," November 28–December 7, 1795, https://founders.archives.gov/, n18.

Chapter 6. A Rebel Defense

1. Friedman, *History*, 81–104, 226–252; Konefsky, "Legal," 68–105; Hall, *Magic*, 211–225; White, *Law*, 47, 245–246, 279–291.
2. Pearson, *Remaking*, 49–72; Friedman, *History*; Konefsky, "Legal"; White, *Law*.
3. Hall, *Magic*, 214; Friedman, *History*, 235–236; White, *Law*, 286.
4. Friedman, *History*, 242.
5. Hall, *Political*, 27–29; *Pennsylvania Packet and Daily Advertiser*, December 25, 1790.
6. Kirby, *Reports*.
7. Regular, official law reports that could provide a distinctively American body of law would have to wait until well into the next century. Lawyers in the Whiskey Rebellion trials in 1795 would have had available to them selected cases from "before and since the Revolution" (from 1754 on) reported from the Pennsylvania Supreme Court; reports of cases from the U.S. Circuit Courts and the U.S. Supreme Court were not published until 1798, and then only selectively; Dallas, *Reports*. Alexander Dallas's reports were approved for publication and subscribed to by five Pennsylvania Supreme Court justices: Thomas McKean, William A. Atlee, Jacob Rush, George Bryan, and Edward Shippen. Cohen and O'Connor, *Guide*, 17–22, 117–124; Surrency, "Law," 48–66, 53–55, 58; Joyce, "Rise," 1292–1293, 1296. On law reports, Briceland, "Ephraim"; Coquillette, "First"; Coquillette, "Legal"; Dunn, "Proprietors"; *North American Review* (1824), 371–382.
8. Friedman, *History*, 242; Surrency, "Law," 50.
9. Coquillette, "Legal," 340–342; Briceland, "Ephraim," 306; Friedman, *History*, 81–83.
10. Brackenridge, *Law*, 88–89; 538–540.
11. Cohen and O'Connor, *Guide*, 2; Kirby, *Reports*, iii–iv.

12. Dallas to Jonathan Dayton, October 18, 1802, Dallas Papers; Joyce, "Rise," 1306.

13. Joyce, "Rise," 1298.

14. Briceland, "Ephraim," 302n17, 304; Connecticut Supreme Court of Errors, *Fitch v. Brainerd, 1805*.

15. Presser, "Tale," 181. Besides summarizing law reports and court records of the rebel trials, studies have touched on the changing relation of judges and jury from old-style (represented by the rebel trials) to new-style trials or treated the trials as an expression of class conflict and partisanship; other have depicted the "aristocratic feudalism" of the government and the "highly charged political atmosphere" that characterized the conduct of the trials. Holt, "Whiskey Rebellion," 74–81; Holt, "Federal Whiskey"; Ifft, "Treason," 171–177; Slaughter, "King," 58, 89–95, 102–104; Blinka, "'This,'" 167–170; Tauchau, "Treason," 34–36; Myrsiades, "Tale"; Hurst, "Treason, III," 818, 818n236, 829n263. For legal historiography, Gerber, "Bringing"; Ross, "Legal"; Konig, "Summary."

16. Brown, *Forum*, 455–456; McFarland, *William*, ii–iv.

17. Young, "Treason," 302.

18. Brackenridge, "Thoughts on the Present" and "Thoughts on the Excise," Marder, *Incidents*, 38–46, 47–51.

19. Dallas, *Reports*, 2:335–357. Dallas, *Reports*, 3:17–18.

20. Brackenridge's treason notes first appeared in 1795 in his "Dissertation on the Treason Laws of the United States," an appendix to *Incidents of the Insurrection*. Brackenridge added comments to his earlier treason notes in *Law Miscellanies*, 1814, a legal project that he called a "Pennsylvania Blackstone" and his biographer referred to as an "Americanization of Blackstone." Brackenridge, *Law*, i; Newlin, *Life*, 292.

21. Brackenridge, "On," 475; 474–502.

22. Brackenridge, "On," 475.

23. Brackenridge, *Incidents*, 3:132–139.

24. Brackenridge, *Incidents*, 3:151.

25. Brackenridge, *Incidents*, 3:151.

26. Brown, *Forum*, 255. Paterson's papers remain unavailable to the public; McFarland, *William*, iii–iv; personal correspondence with the estate. Dallas did not publish his extended report of *Mitchell* and an abbreviated report of *Vigol* until 1798, three years after Brackenridge published his treason notes.

27. Brackenridge, Appendix *Incidents*, 3:62.

28. *Case of Fries*. 1799. Circuit Court, District of Pennsylvania. 9 F. Cas. 826; 1799 U.S. App. Lexis 35; 3 Dall. 515; *United States v. Burr*, Case No. 14,693, Circuit Court, District of Virginia, 25 F. Cas. 55 August 31, 1807. Targets of the sedition trials included William Duane, Benjamin Franklin Bache, James Thomson Callender, and Thomas Cooper; *United States v. Callender, 1800, no. 14, 709 Circuit Court, D. Virginia*; Cooper, *Account*; Smith, "*Aurora*, I"; Smith, "*Aurora*, II"; Hoffer, *Free*.

29. Kessler, *Inventing*; Billings and Tarter, "*Esteemed*"; Crow, *Thomas*; Pearson, "Work"; Amsterdam and Bruner, "Dialectics"; Geertz, "Thick."

30. Brackenridge, *Incidents*, 3:65.

31. Addison's law reports included fifty-four of Brackenridge's cases over the period from 1791 to 1799. They included a range of cases from murder (five), ejectment (twelve), land disputes (eight), and debts (six) to a miscellany of trespass, forgery, theft, riot, tax,

trouver (payment for delivery), assault, penalty for marriage, taking as a slave, indenture, will, dower, and payment for services. The cases were tried in the four western counties involved in the rebellion: Alleghany (twenty-seven), Washington (twelve), Westmoreland (fourteen), and Fayette (one). Brackenridge was for the plaintiff in twenty-one cases (of which he won seven, lost eleven, and split two) and for the defense in thirty-two (of which he won fourteen, lost eighteen, and split two). He had co-counsel 17 times, in some cases more than one co-counsel: Ross (five times), Young (five times), Campbell (three times), Carson (three), Galbraith (two), Collins, Woods, M'Keehan, and Pentecost. Addison, *Reports*; Eakin, "Hugh"; Williams, "Hugh."

32. Newlin, *Life*, 2, 57–59.

33. Brackenridge, *Incidents*, 3:35; Brackenridge, *Incidents*, 2:75, 78; Slaughter, *Whiskey*, 218–219; Findley, *History*, 222, 227.

34. Brackenridge, *Incidents*, 2:71.

35. Brackenridge, *Incidents*, 3:65.

36. Brackenridge, *Incidents*, 3:65–66.

37. Brackenridge, *Incidents*, 3:35.

38. Brackenridge, *Incidents*, 1:115. At an earlier point, 1792, Brackenridge did not think the outrages were treason, but felt that "legal cognizance should be taken" and offenders brought to justice; Brackenridge, *Incidents*, 3:20, 23; Fritz, *American*, 173.

39. Brackenridge, *Incidents*, 3:151.

40. Brackenridge, *Incidents*, 1:29.

41. Brackenridge, *Incidents*, 1:42.

42. Brackenridge, *Incidents*, 1:33, 39, 50, 115.

43. Brackenridge, *Incidents*, 3:151.

44. On July 16, when thirty-seven rebels initially gathered at Neville's house, Neville killed one of their number, Oliver Miller. William Lewis prosecuted John Neville for homicide in that unprovoked killing; Slaughter, *Whiskey*, 179–181; Brackenridge, *Incidents*, 1:73; 3:151.

45. Lewis continued to defend in treason cases: *Fries* (1799) and *Burr* (1807); Henry J. Young said of Lewis and James Wilson that they defended "in nearly every treason case" in Pennsylvania till the end of the century; McFarland, *William*, 10–11, 76–77; Young, "Treason," 302.

46. Brackenridge, *Incidents*, 3:36.

47. Brackenridge, *Incidents*, 3:36–37.

48. Brackenridge, *Incidents*, 3:37.

49. In *Washington v. Scott et al.* (1786), a celebrated case, Brackenridge defended settlers against George Washington. In a second trial, which Rowe claims was the most "closely watched early western trial," Brackenridge defended the Delaware Indian Mamachtaga (1785). Both cases were before the Pennsylvania Supreme Court. Brackenridge, "Trial"; Rowe, *Thomas*, 190–194; Rowe, *Embattled*, 188–191; Newlin, *Life*, 62–63; Slaughter, *Whiskey*, 78–89. Brackenridge was familiar with the Philadelphia scene and desired its attention; Brackenridge, *Modern*, 176. He spent 1786–1787 in Philadelphia as the representative from Alleghany County to the state assembly and would often travel to Philadelphia between 1792 and 1795 for business having to do with publishing the first two parts of his novel *Modern Chivalry*. He maintained contact there with fellow Princeton alumni Wil-

liam Bradford (his roommate), Henry Lee (whom he tutored), Philip Freneau (fellow author and classmate), and James Madison (member along with Bradford and Freneau, of Brackenridge's Whig literary club at Princeton University); Newlin, *Life*, 11, 126, 155, 170; Marder, *Hugh*, 26.

50. At the cusp of the trials, Brackenridge had convinced himself he would be welcomed as a brother by those "who had a warm side to the insurrection"; instead, he found "[o]n all sides I stood in the most odious predicament." Brackenridge, *Incidents*, 3:35.

51. William Lewis defended in *Hamilton, Stewart*, and *Insurgents*; Lewis and Moses Levy in *Vigol*; Lewis and Joseph Thomas in *Porter*; Thomas and Edward Tilghman in *Mitchell*; McFarland, *William*, 10–11, 76–77; Young, "Treason," 294, 302.

52. Gallatin, letter to Hannah Gallatin, June 1, 1795, Marcus, *Documentary*, 3:53; Rowe, *Embattled*, 276. Tilghman's reputation was such that he was nominated for chief justice of the Pennsylvania Supreme Court in 1806 but declined the appointment.

53. Binney, "Leaders," 5, 7; Primrose, "Biography," 30–40; McFarland, *William*; Brown, *Forum*; Hansen, "William." Rawle was appointed Pennsylvania's first U.S. attorney in 1791 and served in that capacity until 1800.

54. Brackenridge, *Incidents*, 3:37; Brackenridge, *History*, 326.

55. Brackenridge's son Henry Marie reasserted his father's claim that he "prepared himself to appear in the defense" and that he withdrew in the face of the prejudice his clients would face if he persisted in their defense. Henry Marie claimed that Hugh Henry's published "notes of his intended argument" could be read as a "good outline on the law of constructive treason," the same doctrine that Chief Justice Marshall "recognized" in *Burr*; thereafter, according to Henry Marie, the Whiskey Rebellion would be known as a riot and not treason; Brackenridge, *History*, 326. Hogeland credits Henry Marie's history with being an intelligent restatement of his father's role based on "important primary material"; Hogeland, *Whiskey*, 246.

56. Blackstone, *Commentaries*, 4:75.

57. Brackenridge, "On," 474, 494, 501.

58. Brackenridge, "On," 491, 496.

59. Brackenridge, "On," 491.

60. Brackenridge, "On," 492.

61. When the whiskey rebels came to trial, a clearer break from English constructivism and abuse of individual rights was becoming apparent, but American judges continued to enhance state power at the expense of individual rights, favor the prosecution, conflate riot and treason, and utilize constructive treason in linking intent to "ambiguous actions"; Slaughter, "King," 60–62, 70–71, 74–75, 81.

62. Myrsiades, "Tale," 142–145.

63. Myrsiades, "Tale," 144.

64. Myrsiades, "Tale," 146.

65. Myrsiades, "Tale," 147–148, 151–152.

66. Myrsiades, "Tale," 152.

67. Blackstone, *Commentaries*, 4:75.

68. Brackenridge, *Law*, 196.

69. Brackenridge, "On," 497–498.

70. Blackstone, *Commentaries*, 4:75.

71. Brackenridge, "On," 475n.

72. Wilson, *Collected Works*, 2:663.

73. Brackenridge, "On," 494. Wilson had argued similarly that assembling in a warlike manner (with commanders, banners, in great numbers in "continuance together") was a levying of war but only so long as it was "an actual insurrection or rebellion." Otherwise, the conduct was no more than a great riot. If distinguishing between a riot and treason was too fine a line, he would resolve "on the side of the inferiour crime"; Wilson, *Collected Works*, 2:667–668.

74. Brackenridge, "On," 494. As Wilson would hold, as to a private quarrel as a motive, a particular party as an object, or a specific nuisance that affected "in point of interest, the parties who assemble," none of these was a levying of war but a felony or trespass. Insurrection had to accomplish an end that was general, to have a public nature, and "to alter the established law, or to render it ineffectual." Wilson, *Collected Works*, 2:668.

75. Brackenridge, "On," 494–495.

76. Brackenridge, "On," 495.

77. Brackenridge, "On," 494; Hunter, "No," 373, 375, 379–380.

78. Brackenridge, *Modern*, 382.

79. Newlin, *Life*, 268.

80. Brackenridge, "On," 477–478, 495.

81. Foster, *Report*, 218; Hale, *History*, 144–146; Brackenridge, "On," 495.

82. Brackenridge, "On," 476.

83. *Morris' Lessee v. Vanderen*, 1 Dall. 64 (PA 1782); Brackenridge, *Law*, 37, 39, 41. Common law was justified in Pennsylvania in the Act of 1777, which declared it in force and binding. Brackenridge resisted efforts to abolish it, convinced that those "who raised this hue and cry" had little idea what common law was; Brackenridge, *Law*, 33–34, 47; Pound, *Spirit*, 115–117, 119; Blackstone, *Commentaries*, 1:102–103.

84. Brackenridge, *Law*, 53.

85. Brackenridge's views were elaborated in the 1797 volume of his multivolume *Modern Chivalry* (1792–1815), a work described as "the only sustained record of [...] Federalist, republican America['s] unruly, inclusive, democratic vision." Devoted to a satire of the Whiskey Rebellion, that volume discussed allegiance from a popular perspective, while the 1804 and 1805 volumes provided "Observations" on common law. Brackenridge's novel appeared in three editions: Lewis Leary (1965 edition), Claude M. Newlin (1937 edition), and Ed White (2009 edition). All citations in this study are from the White edition. Battistini, "Federalist," 149–150; Elliott, *Revolutionary*, 174; Gilmore, "Eighteenth-Century," 181; Martin, "On," 241; Myrsiades, *Law*, 217–228.

86. Brackenridge, Modern, 358–359, 394, 400.

87. Brackenridge, *Modern*, 258, 260, 261n34.

88. Brackenridge, *Modern*, 260.

89. Brackenridge, *Modern*, 261n34. The differentiated acceptance of common law by state constitutions supported Wilson's idea of the selective continuity of the unwritten past (English common law) and the written present law (American text), confounding the clean break that many supposed had occurred. For Wilson, the long experience of common law coupled with "opinion" (the basis of American law) gave a stronger foundation to consent and was a good fit as an "experiment." Parker, "Time," 71, 76–77, 84–86, 91–95, 100.

90. Brackenridge, *Modern*, 260.
91. Sapienza, *Modern*, xiv.
92. Brackenridge, *Modern*, 255, 200. Brackenridge's view exemplifies Roscoe Pound's idea of the proper use of common law: "for the greatest part law must always be found through application of reason to causes as they arise and the testing of principles in their actual operation"; Pound, *Spirit*, 265.
93. Brackenridge, *Modern*, in the 1805 volume, 391. Sir John Holt (1642–1710) was the lord chief justice of England from 1689 to 1710; Justice Bushrod Washington (1762–1829) sat on the U.S. Supreme Court from 1798 to 1829; Justice William Paterson (1745–1806) sat on the U.S. Supreme Court from 1793 to 1806; John Marshall (1755–1835) was chief justice of the U.S. Supreme Court from 1801 to 1835.
94. Blackstone, *Commentaries*, 2:450; Brackenridge, *Law*, 57, 63.
95. Brackenridge, *Law*, 52, 63. The process was similar to reasoning by analogy from particular cases to "discover" a principle of law that evolved from a "shared experience of what works," its authority relying on collective rather than individual reason and on what worked in practice rather than trusting one's reason; see David Strauss as discussed in Steilen, "Reason," 286, 288; Steilen, "Democratic."
96. Brackenridge, *Law*, 64, 72.
97. Matthew Steilen explains that "artificial reason" was already inherent within the classical view of common law expounded by Edward Coke and Matthew Hale. Long study would reveal how custom had resolved disputes and lawyers could then "identify, evaluate, and apply the rule of law," emphasizing the use of reason; Steilen, "Reason," 297.
98. Brackenridge, "On," 496, 501. In the treason trials of 1778, Wilson argued mightily, if unsuccessfully, for the two-witness standard Brackenridge supported; he made sure it was included in the Constitution; Hall, *Political*, 16.
99. Blackstone, *Commentaries*, 4:356.
100. Hurst, "Treason, I," 244–245, 244n28; Hurst, *Law*, 81–82. Colonial Connecticut law allowed that the proof offered by two witnesses was sufficient though they did not witness the same act. Foster, *Report*, 22, adds that the proof might be general and the particulars of the act "need not be set forth"; both approaches allowed leeway in using judicial interpretation.
101. Brackenridge, "On," 494–495.
102. Brackenridge, "On," 495.
103. Brackenridge, "On," 496.
104. Brackenridge, "On," 497.
105. Brackenridge, "On," 498.
106. Brackenridge, "On," 498–499. Brackenridge addressed as well the Federalists' instrumental claim that calling out a federal militia against the insurgents by itself justified calling the rebels' acts treasonous, for "unless such outrages as these were construed treason [the government] could not move to suppress them." Brackenridge submitted that the Militia Act referred to "an insurrection of an inferior nature," an unlawful combination or an opposing of the laws; it did not reach to high treason, that is, to "traitorously conspiring to overthrow the government."
107. Brackenridge, "On," 495, 497, 498.
108. Wilson had offered that levying war was evinced more clearly from its purpose than from the manner of its execution, so that intention was the best means to assess

whether war was being levied against the United States and its authority; Wilson, *Collected Works*, 2:667.

109. As a Pennsylvania Supreme Court justice, Brackenridge contributed to the 1807 review required by the Pennsylvania Assembly that asked how much of English statutory law ought to be regarded as state law; Brackenridge, *Law*, 49, 57; Newlin, *Life*, 282–285; Rowe, *Embattled*, 282.

110. Newlin, *Life*, 295; Brackenridge, *Law*, 296.

111. Brackenridge, *Modern*, 456–462; Ferguson, *Law*, 122–128.

112. Brackenridge, *Modern*, 218–222; see as well, "In the Manner of Montaigne" (in the 1804 volume, added in 1815) in Brackenridge, *Modern* (1937), 616–620. Brackenridge was a Scottish émigré (born in Scotland in 1748, he lived there until 1753) who became acquainted with the marquis in 1791 in the West; the marquis had left America by the time of the Whiskey Rebellion; Newlin, *Life*, 1, 186–187n20.

113. Brackenridge, *Modern*, 219.

114. Farrago represents one of several voices that reflect aspects of Brackenridge's experiences and views, among them the blind lawyer, the marquis, and, preeminently, the narrator of the novel; Newlin, *Life*, 186–189, 255–256, 260, 262. Much of his political philosophy is introduced through these characters, which offers the author an opportunity to explore his thoughts and conflicts.

115. Brackenridge brought Thomas Paine, Montaigne, Rousseau, and the Scottish realists into his consideration of allegiance and rebellion; Schultz, "Uncovering."

116. Brackenridge, *Modern*, 218–219.

117. Brackenridge, *Modern*, 219.

118. Brackenridge, *Modern*, 220.

119. Brackenridge, *Modern*, 220.

120. Brackenridge, *Modern*, 220–221.

121. Cranston, "Ideas," 11–12; Foisneau, "Governing," 94n3, 96.

122. Foisneau, "Governing," 99–100, 104.

123. *Henfield*, Wharton, *State*, 49–89.

124. Stephens, "Federalism," 494–495; Roche, "Loss," 270; Marcus, *Wilson*, 162; Elkins and McKitrick, *Age*, 345, 353.

125. *Henfield*, Wharton, *State*, 49–51, 58, 63, 65.

126. *Henfield*, Wharton, *State*, 57–58; Jay, "Origins," 1003–1116, 1046–1047.

127. Justice Wilson sat with Justice James Iredell and District Judge Richard Peters on a Special Circuit Court for the Middle Circuit and the Pennsylvania District, held in Philadelphia on July 22, 1793.

128. Jefferson to Gouverneur Morris, August 16, 1793, https://founders.archives.gov/; *Henfield*, Wharton, *State*, 85–89.

129. *Henfield*, Wharton, *State*, 58.

130. Blackstone, *Commentaries*, 1:366.

131. Hale, *History*, 1:59; a subject who received protection from his sovereign was "bound by his allegiance to be true and faithful" to him and his laws; Larson, "Forgotten," 876.

132. Blackstone, *Commentaries*, 1:368.

133. Blackstone, *Commentaries*, 1:369.

134. Brackenridge, *Law*, 295, 406–408; Fletcher, "Ambivalence," 1619; Blackstone, *Commentaries*, 1:369, 453.
135. Brackenridge, *Law*, 295, 407, 416.
136. Brackenridge, "On," 295, 412–414, 480, 483.
137. Brackenridge, *Law*, 47, 424; Blackstone, *Commentaries*, 1:102–103.
138. Brackenridge, "On," 489.
139. Brackenridge, *Law*, 412–413.
140. Brackenridge, *Law*, 414; Brackenridge, "On," 500; Blackstone, *Commentaries*, 1:369.
141. Brackenridge, "On," 485, 500.
142. Brackenridge, "On," 476.
143. Brackenridge, *Incidents*, 141–42, 93–94, 112–115; Newlin, *Life*, 145, 151, 153–154, 158.
144. Du Ponceau in Brackenridge, *Law*, 416; Tucker, "Expatriation," in Tucker, *Blackstone's*, vol. 2, note K.
145. Brackenridge, *Law*, 427; he refers in a note to Peter Stephen Du Ponceau.
146. Talbot v. Janson, 3 Dall. 133; in Brackenridge, *Law*, 416–418; Jay, "Origins," 1088n411.
147. Tucker, "Expatriation," in Tucker, *Blackstone's*, vol. 2, note K.
148. Brackenridge, *Law*, 404, 424; Brackenridge, *Modern*, 504.
149. Newlin, *Life*, 302.
150. Ferguson, *Trial*, 82.
151. Adams to Benjamin Rush, September 1, 1807, https://founders.archives.gov/.
152. Paterson had mentored Burr in the law, and there was some speculation that if Paterson left the court Burr would replace him; Kennedy, *Burr*, 350.
153. Kennedy, *Burr*, 351–353.
154. Jefferson to James Madison, January 30, 1787, https://founders.archives.gov/; Ferguson, *Trial*, 97.
155. Ketter, "Chief."
156. *Ex Parte Bollman and Ex Parte Swartwout*, 8 U.S. 75 (1807).
157. Faulkner, "John," 247–248, 254; Stimson, *American*, 138–139; Chapin, *American*, 98–113.
158. Hurst, "Treason, II," 427–431; Hurst, "Treason, III," 836.
159. *United States v. Burr*, 11.
160. *United States v. Burr*, 12.
161. *United States v. Burr*, 14.
162. *United States v. Burr*, 25.
163. *United States v. Burr*, 26.
164. *United States v. Burr*, 25.
165. *United States v. Burr*, 26; Judge George Jeffreys (1645–1689), the notorious English hanging judge, presided over the infamous "Bloody Assizes" of 1685; Newmyer, *Treason*, 109, 158–159.
166. Paterson died September 8, 1806.
167. The consensus is that Marshall left constructive treason alive and levying war broadly defined. The line between riot and treason was still undefined and opposition to one "general" law still stood; the inconsistency between the *Bollman* and *Burr* opinions left the necessity for force imprecise. Yet Marshall's definition of levying war "was more

302   NOTES TO CHAPTER SIX AND CONCLUSION

comprehensive than any previously articulated from a federal bench." Slaughter, "King," 111, 116, 118.

168. *United States v. Burr*, 27.
169. Brackenridge, "On," 501–502.
170. Slaughter, "King," 118.
171. Gerber, "Bringing," 363.
172. Konig, "Summary," 49.
173. Ross, "Legal," 32–34; Gerber, "Bringing," 364–365.
174. Hall, *Magic*, 6.
175. Davidson, *Revolution*, 173–178; Nelson, "'Indications"; Gilmore, "Republican"; Battistini, "Federalist"; Schultz, "Uncovering"; Gilmore, "Eighteenth-Century"; Hirsch, "Brackenridge."
176. Sapienza, *Modern*, xiv, 110.
177. Sapienza, *Modern*, 52, 74n45.
178. Newlin, *Life*, 294–299.
179. Brackenridge, *Law*, 424, 427.
180. Brackenridge, *Law*, 576.
181. Newlin, *Life*, 284; Brackenridge, *Law*, 49.
182. Slaughter, "King," 74.
183. Slaughter, "King," 62.
184. Bouton, *Taming*, 42, 51, 105, 219; Martin, *Government*; Kramer, *People*; Cornell, *Other*; Wilf, *Law's*; Fritz, *American*.

Conclusion. An Afterword

1. "Camp Near Carlisle," *Gazette of the United States and Daily Advertiser*, October 4, 1794; *Gazette of the United States and Daily Advertiser*, October 11, 1794; *New Jersey State Gazette*, October 29, 1794; *Rising Sun*, November 7, 1794; *Medley or Newbedford Marine Journal*, June 5, 1795; "Extract of a letter from a gentleman in Hagerstown," *Carlisle Gazette*, September 24, 1794; "A letter from Bedford County," *New Jersey Journal*, September 10, 1794.
2. Melish, *Disowning*, 161.
3. On narrative construction that engages culture, politics, and law: Gooding-Williams, *Reading*, particularly Crenshaw and Peller; Butler; and Baker, "Scene." Also, Morrison, *Race-ing*, particularly Crenshaw; Morrison; Lacour; Bhabha; and Lubiano.
4. Melish, *Disowning*, 251.
5. Ferguson, *Law*, 11.
6. White, *Law*, 4–5, 10.
7. Ferguson, *Law*, 12, 16; Paine, "Thoughts," 103.
8. Ferguson, *Law*, 22.
9. Ferguson, *Law*, 13; New York Public Library, Astor, Lenox, and Tilden foundations.
10. Hamilton to Angelica Church, December 8, 1794, Syrett, *Papers*, 17:428–429.
11. Clymer to Alexander Hamilton, October 10, 1792, https//founders.archives.gov/.
12. Bouton, *Taming*, 217–218.
13. Henriques, "George," 34–41.

14. McInnus, "George," 131, 149, 152–153; Osman, "Cincinnatus," 421–446; Sizemore, "George," 43–74; Bartoloni-Tuazon, *For*; Elkins and McKitrick, *Age*, 48–49; Wills, *Cincinnatus*.

15. Randolph, *Vindication*, 47–48.

16. Elkins and McKitrick, *Age*, 46–49; Bartoloni-Tuazon, *For*, 13–29; Wood, *Empire*, 74–85; Wills, *Cincinnatus*. In an ironic early nineteenth-century footnote, Washington Irving's Rip Van Winkle, having awoken from a twenty-year sleep begun before the Revolution, would to his bewilderment find that a sign on the village inn had replaced the face of George III with that of George Washington. Everything, including the language of liberty and political governance, in his view, had changed beyond recognition; Wood, *Empire*, 1.

17. Clymer to Alexander Hamilton, September 28, 1792, October 4, 1792, October 10, 1792, https://founders.archives.gov/.

18. Griffin, *American*, 48, 74; *Pennsylvania Archives*, 1st ser., 10:757; McClure, *Ends*, 570; Brackenridge, *Incidents*, 3:6–7; Findley, *History*, 32–33.

19. 1792 Militia Act, chap. 28, sec. 2, 1 Stat. 264.

20. White, *Backcountry*, 210.

21. Linebaugh and Rediker, *Many-Headed*, 225–252.

22. Cobbett, *Works*, 37; Cobbett, *Rush-Light*, 1:48, 28; Wilson, "Introduction," 34.

23. *New York Daily Advertiser*, February 26, 1795; Martin, *Government*, 92, 222n42.

24. "Citizens," *New York Journal & Patriotic Register*, July 6, 1793; "American Occurrences," *New York Journal & Patriotic Register*, December 25, 1793.

25. Findley, *History*, 303; Findley, *History*, 226, 292–292, 295–296.

26. Randolph, *Vindication*, 45.

27. Lieberman et al., "Trump"; Levitsky and Way, "Myth"; Capoccia and Ziblatt, "Historical"; Fukuyama, "Why"; Diamond, "Facing."

28. Capoccia and Ziblatt, "Historical," 933–934; Capoccia and Kelemen, "Study."

29. Mettler and Lieberman, *Recurring*; Casey, "Making"; Elkins and McKitrick, *Age*.

30. Mettler and Lieberman, *Recurring*, 26, 58.

31. Brooke, "Consent"; Huston, "Rethinking"; Wood, "Conspiracy"; Wood, *Radicalism*; Carter, "Denouncing"; Cornell, *Other*; Martin, *Government*; Owen, "Legitimacy," Peart and Smith, "Afterword"; Taylor, "Art"; Maier, *From*; Gilje, *Road*.

32. Brooke, "Consent," 238.

33. Imagination Collectif, "Whiskey," 104.

34. Wood, "Conspiracy," 403–405, 429; Hofstadter, *Paranoid*.

35. Hofstadter, *Paranoid*.

36. Van der Linden et al. "Paranoid," 24–25.

BIBLIOGRAPHY

Collections

Addison, Alexander. *Reports of Cases in the County Courts of the Fifth Circuit, and in the High Court of Errors and Appeals of the State of Pennsylvania, and Charges to Grand Juries of Those Courts.* Washington John Colerick, 1800.

Boorstin, Daniel A., Bennet Frankel, and Irving J. Helman, eds. *Delaware Cases, 1792–1830.* 3 vols. St Paul: West Publishing, 1943.

Dallas, Alexander. *Reports of Cases Ruled and Adjudged in the Several Courts of the United States, and of Pennsylvania, Held at the Seat of the Federal Government.* 4 vols. Philadelphia: Aurora Office, 1790, 1798, 1799, 1807.

The Debates and Proceedings in the Congress of the United States. 4 Annals of Congress; Third Congress; Second Session, November 1794. Vol. 4. Washington, [D.C.]: Gales and Seaton, 1855.

George Washington Papers at the Library of Congress, 1741–1799. 4th ser., General Correspondence, 1697–1799.

Hamilton, Alexander. *The Papers of Alexander Hamilton,* edited by Harold C. Syrett. 27 vols. New York: Columbia University Press, 1961–1987.

Hunt, Gaillard, ed. Transcription: The Writings of James Madison Vol. 6. New York: G. P. Putnam's Sons, 1909–1910.

Madison, James. *The Papers of James Madison,* edited by J. C. A. Stagg. Charlottesville: University of Virginia Press, 2010.

Statutes at Large of Pennsylvania for 1682–1801, edited by James Tyndale Mitchell and Henry Flanders. Harrisburg, [Pa]: Clarence M. Busch, 1887.

Wharton, Francis. *State Trials of the United States during the Administrations of Washington and Adams, with References Historical and Professional.* New York: B. Franklin, 1849.

Washington, George. *The Papers of George Washington.* Vol. 6, *The Diaries of George Washington,* edited by Donald Jackson and Dorothy Tworig. Charlottesville: University Press of Virginia, 1979.

———. *The Writings of George Washington from the Original Manuscript Sources, 1745–1799,* edited by John C. Fitzpatrick. Vols. 34–35. Washington, D.C.: United States Government Printing Office, 1940.

Wilson, James. *Collected Works of James Wilson*, edited by Kermit L. Hall and Mark David Hall. Indianapolis: Liberty Fund, 2007.

———. *The Works of James Wilson*, edited by R. G. McCloskey. Vol. 3. Cambridge, Mass.: Belknap Press, 1967.

Sources

Abernathy, Thomas Perkins. *Western Lands and the American Revolution*. New York: Russell & Russell, 1937.

Abrahams, Roger D. "Introduction: A Folklore Perspective." In *Riot and Revelry in Early America*, edited by William Pencak, Matthew Dennis, and Simon P. Newman, 21–40. University Park: Pennsylvania State University Press, 2002.

———. "White Indians in Penn's City: The Loyal Sons of St. Tammany." In *Riot and Revelry in Early America*, edited by William Pencak, Matthew Dennis, and Simon P. Newman, 179–205. University Park: Pennsylvania State University Press, 2002.

Amsterdam, Anthony G., and Jerome Bruner. "The Dialectics of Culture." In *Minding the Law*, 226–230. Cambridge, Mass.: Harvard University Press, 2000.

Anand, Sanjeez. "The Origins, Early History and Evolution of the English Criminal Trial Jury." *Alberta Law Review* 40, no. 2 (2005): 407–432.

Anderson, Benedict. *Imagined Communities: Reflections on the Origin and Spread of Nationalism*. New York: Verso Books, 1971.

Baird, Absalom. *Copies of Authentic Letters and Papers Throwing Some Light on the History of Doctor Absalom Baird of the Army of the Revolution*. Historical Society of Western Pennsylvania: Northern Micrographics, 1999.

Baker, Houston. "Scene . . . Not Heard." In *Reading Rodney King, Reading Urban Uprising*, edited by Robert Gooding-Williams, 38–50. New York: Routledge, 1993.

Baker, Meg. "James Marshel & Western Pennsylvania." 2007. https://freepages.rootsweb.com/~mabgenealogy/genealogy/jmarshel.html.

Baldwin, Leland D. *Whiskey Rebels: The Story of a Frontier Uprising*. Pittsburgh: University of Pittsburgh Press, 1939.

Barber, William D. "'Among the Most Techy Articles of Civil Police': Federal Taxation and the Adoption of the Whiskey Excise." William and Mary Quarterly 3rd ser., 25, no. 1 (1968): 58–84.

Bartoloni-Tuazon, Kathleen. *For Fear of an Elective King: George Washington and the Presidential Title Controversy of 1789*. Ithaca, N.Y.: Cornell University Press, 2014.

Battistini, Robert. "Federalist Decline and Despair on the Pennsylvania Frontier: Hugh Henry Brackenridge's *Modern Chivalry*." *Pennsylvania Magazine of History and Biography* 133, no. 2 (2009): 149–166.

Ben-Atar, Doron S., and Richard D. Brown. *Taming Lust: Crimes against Nature in the Early Republic*. Philadelphia: University of Pennsylvania Press, 2014.

Bercovitch, Sacvan. *The American Jeremiad*. Madison: University of Wisconsin Press, 1978.

Bernstein, R. B. "William Paterson: Conservative Revolutionary in an Age of Crisis." Paper presented on December 6, 2002, at William Paterson University. David and Lorraine Cheng Library, William Paterson University. https://www.wpunj.edu/library/pdf/bernstein-WP-2.pdf.

Bessler, John D. *Private Prosecution in America: Its Origins, History, and Unconstitutionality in the Twenty-First Century*. Durham, N.C.: Carolina Academic Press, 2022.

———. "The Public Interest and the Unconstitutionality of Private Prosecutors." *Arkansas Law Review* 47, no. 3 (1994): 511–602.

Bhabha, Homi K. "A Good Judge of Character: Men, Metaphors, and the Common Culture." In *Race-ing Justice, En-gendering Power: Essays on Anita Hill, Clarence Thomas, and the Construction of Social Reality*, edited by Toni Morrison, 232–250. New York: Pantheon Books, 1992.

Bhagwat, Ashutosh. "Associational Speech." *Yale Law Journal* 120, no. 5 (2011): 978–1030.

Billings, Warren M., and Brent Tarter. *"Esteemed Bookes of Law" and the Legal Culture of Early Virginia*. Charlottesville: University of Virginia Press, 2017.

Binney, Horace. "The Leaders of the Old Bar of Philadelphia." *Pennsylvania Magazine of History and Biography* 14, no. 1 (1890): 1–27.

Blackstone, William. *Commentaries on the Laws of England*. 13th ed. 4 vols. London: A Strahan, 1800.

Blinka, Daniel D. "'This Germ of Rottenness': Federal Trials in the New Republic, 1789–1807." *Creighton Law Review* 36, no. 2 (2003): 135–189.

Borden, Morton, ed. *The Anti-Federalist Papers*. East Lansing: Michigan State University Press, 1965.

Bourdieu, Pierre. *Outline of a Theory of Practice*. Translated by Richard Nice. Cambridge: Cambridge University Press, 1977.

Bouton, Terry. "A Road Closed: Rural Insurgency in Post-Independence Pennsylvania." *Journal of American History* 87, no. 3 (2000): 855–887.

———. *Taming Democracy: "The People," the Founders, and the Troubled Ending of the American Revolution*. Oxford: Oxford University Press, 2007.

———. "Tying up the Revolution: Money, Power, and the Regulation in Pennsylvania, 1765–1800." PhD. diss., Duke University, 1996.

———. "Was the 'Whiskey Rebellion' *Really* about Whiskey?" *Westmoreland History* 19, no. 3 (2014): 4–12.

———. "William Findley, David Bradford, and the Pennsylvania Regulation of 1794." In *Revolutionary Founders: Rebels, Radicals, and Reformers in the Making of the Nation*, edited by Alfred F. Young, Gary B. Nash, and Ray Raphael, 233–252. New York: Vintage, 2012.

Boyd, Steven. "The Whiskey Rebellion, Popular Rights, and the Meaning of the First Amendment." *Topic: A Journal of the Liberal Arts* 45 (1994): 73–84.

———, ed. *The Whiskey Rebellion: Past and Present Perspectives*. Westport, Conn.: Greenwood Press, 1985.

Brackenridge, Hugh Henry. *Gazette Publications*. Carlisle, [Pa.]: Alexander and Phillips, 1806.

———. *Incidents of the Insurrection in the Western Parts of Pennsylvania, in the Year 1794*. Philadelphia: John M'Culloch, 1795.

———. *Law Miscellanies: Containing an Introduction to the Study of the Law, Notes on Blackstone's Commentaries, Shewing the Law of Pennsylvania from the Law of England and What Acts of Assembly Might Require to be Repealed or Modified*. Philadelphia: P. Sterne, 1814.

---. "Letter from Angus MacMore." In *Incidents of the Insurrection*, edited by Daniel Marder, 36–37. New Haven, Conn.: College and University Press, 1972.

---. *Modern Chivalry, Containing the Adventures of Captain John Farrago and Teague O'Regan, His Servant*, edited by Lewis Leary. 1792, 1793, 1797. Reprint, Albany, N.Y.: New College and University Press, 1965.

---. *Modern Chivalry*. Edited by Claude M. Newlin. New York: American Book, 1937.

---. *Modern Chivalry*. Edited by Ed White. Indianapolis: Hackett Publishing, 2009.

---. "On the Treason Laws of the United States." In *Law Miscellanies: Containing an Introduction to the Study of the Law, Notes on Blackstone's Commentaries, Shewing the Law of Pennsylvania from the Law of England and What Acts of Assembly Might Require to be Repealed or Modified*, 474–502. Philadelphia: P. Sterne, 1814.

---. "Thoughts on the Excise Law." In *Incidents of the Insurrection*, edited by Daniel Marder, 47–51. New Haven, Conn.: College and University Press, 1972.

---. "Thoughts on the Present Indian War." In *Incidents of the Insurrection*, edited by Daniel Marder, 38–46. New Haven, Conn.: College and University Press, 1972.

---. "The Trial of Mamachtaga." In *Incidents of the Insurrection*, edited by Daniel Marder, 25–35. New Haven, Conn.: College and University Press, 1972.

Brackenridge, Henry Marie. *History of the Western Insurrection in Western Pennsylvania, Commonly Called the Whiskey Insurrection, 1794*. Pittsburgh, 1859.

Bradford, William. *An Enquiry How Far the Punishment of Death Is Necessary in Pennsylvania*. Philadelphia: T. Dobson, 1793.

Brewer, Holly. *By Birth or Consent: Children, Law, and the Anglo-American Revolution in Authority*. Chapel Hill: University of North Carolina Press, 2005.

Briceland, Alan V. "Ephraim Kirby: Pioneer of American Law Reporting, 1789." *American Journal of Legal History* 16, no. 4 (1972): 297–319.

Brod, Nicholas S. "Rethinking a Reinvigorated Right to Assemble." *Duke Law Journal* 63, no. 1 (2013): 155–197.

Brooke, John L. "Consent, Civil Society, and the Public Sphere in the Age of Revolution and the Early American Republic." In *Beyond the Founders: New Approaches to the Political History of the Early American Republic*, edited by Jeffrey L. Pasley, Andrew W. Robertson, and David Waldstreicher, 207–250. Chapel Hill: University of North Carolina Press, 2004.

Brown, David Paul. *The Forum; or Forty Years Full Practice at the Philadelphia Bar*. Vol. 1. Philadelphia: Robert H. Small, 1856.

Brutus [Samuel Bryan]. "Bill of Rights." In *The Anti-Federalist Papers*, edited by Morton Borden, no. 84. East Lansing: Michigan State University Press, 1965.

---. "Power of the Judiciary." In *The Anti-Federalist Papers*, edited by Morton Borden, no. 81. East Lansing: Michigan State University Press, 1965.

Burd, Kyler. "The Revolutionary Language and Behavior of the Whiskey Rebels." *Journal of the American Revolution*, December 10, 2020, https://allthingsliberty.com.

Butler, Judith. "Endangered/Endangering: Schematic Racism and White Paranoia." In *Reading Rodney King, Reading Urban Uprising*, edited by Robert Gooding-Williams, 15–22. New York: Routledge, 1993.

Capoccia, Giovanni, and R. Daniel Kelemen. "The Study of Critical Junctures: Theory,

Narrative, and Counterfactuals in Historical Institutionalism." *World Politics* 59, no. 3 (2007): 341–369.

Capoccia, Giovanni, and Daniel Ziblatt. "The Historical Turn in Democratization Studies: A New Research Agenda for Europe and Beyond." *Comparative Political Studies* 43, nos. 8–9 (2010): 931–968.

Carnahan, James. "The Pennsylvania Insurrection of 1794, Commonly Called the Whiskey Insurrection." In *Proceedings of the New Jersey Historical Society*, 115–152. 1st ser. Vol. 7. Edison: New Jersey Historical Society, 1851–1852.

Carpenter, Thomas. *The Two Trials of John Fries, on an Indictment for Treason; Together with a Brief Report of the Trials of Several Other Persons, for Treason and Insurrection, in the Counties of Bucks, Northampton and Montgomery, in the Circuit Court of the United States*. Philadelphia: William W. Woodward, 1800.

Carroll, John Alexander, and Mary Wells Ashworth. *George Washington: First in Peace*. Vol. 7. New York: Charles Scribner's Sons, 1957.

Carter, Katlyn Marie. "Denouncing Secrecy and Defining Democracy in the Early American Republic." *Journal of the Early Republic* 40, no. 3 (2020): 409–433.

Casey, Nicholas. "Making Political Forecasts, and Wincing All the While." *New York Times*, Sunday, November 17, 2019, A23.

Castronovo, Russ. *Propaganda 1776: Secrets, Leaks, and Revolutionary Communications in Early America*. New York: Oxford University Press, 2014.

Chaden, Caryn. "Dress and Undress in Brackenridge's *Modern Chivalry*." *Early American Literature* 26, no. 1 (1991): 55–72.

Chafee, Zechariah, Jr. "Delaware Cases, 1792–1800." In *Essays in the History of Early American Law*, edited by David H. Flaherty, 489–513. Chapel Hill: University of North Carolina Press, 1969.

Chamberlain, Ava. "The Execution of Moses Paul: A Story of Crime and Contact in Eighteenth-Century Connecticut." *New England Quarterly* 77, no. 3 (2004): 414–450.

Chapin, Bradley. *The American Law of Treason: Revolutionary and Early National Origins*. Seattle: University of Washington Press, 1964.

Charles, Patrick J. "Originalism, John Marshall, and the Necessary and Proper Clause: Resurrecting the Jurisprudence of Alexander Addison." *Cleveland State Law Review* 58, no. 3 (2010): 529–574.

Cheal, David J. "Hegemony, Ideology and Contradictory Consciousness." *Sociological Quarterly* 20, no. 1 (1979): 109–117.

Chervinsky, Lindsay. *The Cabinet: George Washington and the Creation of an American Institution*. Cambridge, Mass.: Harvard University Press, 2020.

Chesney, Robert M. "Democratic-Republican Societies, Subversion, and the Limits of Legitimate Political Dissent in the Early Republic." *North Carolina Law Review* 82, no. 5 (2004): 1525–1579.

Clouse, Jerry A. *The Whiskey Rebellion: Southwestern Pennsylvania's Frontier People Test the American Constitution*. Harrisburg: Pennsylvania History and Museum Commission, 1994.

Cobbett, William. *A Bone to Gnaw for the Democrats, to Which is Prefixed a Rod, for the Backs of Critics*. London: J. Wright, 1797.

———. "History of the American Jacobins, Commonly Denominated Democrats." In

William Cobbett, Peter Porcupine in America: Pamphlets on Republicanism and Revolution, edited by David Wilson, 182–216. Ithaca, N.Y.: Cornell University Press, 1994.

———. *Porcupine's Works: Containing Various Writings and Selections.* Vol. 1. London: William Cobbett, 1801.

———. "The *Rush-Light,*" no. 4. In *Porcupine's Works.* Vol. 2. London: Cobbett and Morgan, 1801.

———. *The Works of Peter Porcupine.* Philadelphia: Thomas Bradford, 1796.

Cohen, Morris L., and Sharon H. O'Connor. *A Guide to the Early Reports of the Supreme Court of the United States.* Littleton, Colo.: Fred B. Rothman, 1995.

Connor, G. E. "The Politics of Insurrection: A Comparative Analysis of the Shays', Whiskey, and Fries' Rebellions." *Social Science Journal* 29, no. 3 (1992): 259–281.

Constable, Marianne. *The Law of the Other: The Mixed Jury and Changing Conceptions of Citizenship, Law, and Knowledge.* Chicago: University of Chicago Press, 1994.

Cook, Roy Bird. *Washington's Western Lands.* Strasburg, Va.: Shenandoah Publishing, 1930.

Cooke, Jacob E. "The Whiskey Insurrection: A Re-evaluation." *Pennsylvania History: A Journal of Mid-Atlantic Studies* 30, no. 3 (1963): 316–346.

Coombe, Rosemary J. "Contingent Articulations: A Critical Cultural Studies of Law." In *Law in the Domains of Culture,* edited by Austin Sarat and Thomas R. Kearns, 21–64. Ann Arbor: University of Michigan Press, 1998.

Cooper, Thomas. *An Account of the Trial of Thomas Cooper, of Northumberland; on a Charge of Libel against the President of the United States.* Philadelphia: John Bioren, 1800.

Cooper, Grace Rogers. "Thirteen-Star Flags: Keys to Identification." *Smithsonian Studies in History and Technology* 21 (Washington, D.C.: Smithsonian Institution Press, 1973). Available in pdf and other formats at Smithsonian Research Online, https://doi.org/10.5479/si.00810258.21.1.

Coquillette, Daniel R. "First Flower—The Earliest American Law Reports and the Extraordinary Josiah Quincy Jr. (1744–1775)." *Suffolk University Law Review* 30, no. 1 (1996): 1–34.

———. "The Legal Education of a Patriot: Josiah Quincy Jr.'s Law Commonplace (1763)." *Arizona State Law Journal* 39, no. 2 (2007): 317–375.

Cornell, Saul. "American History in a Postmodern Age." *William and Mary Quarterly* 50, no. 2 (1993): 329–341.

———. "Aristocracy Assailed: The Ideology of Backcountry Anti-Federalism." *Journal of American History* 76, no. 4 (1990): 1148–1172.

———. "Beyond the Myth of Consensus: The Struggle to Define the Right to Bear Arms in the Early Republic." In *Beyond the Founders: New Approaches to the Political History of the Early American Republic,* edited by Jeffrey L. Pasley, Andrew W. Robertson, and David Waldstreicher, 251–273. Chapel Hill: University of North Carolina Press, 2004.

———. "Mobs, Militias, and Magistrates: Popular Constitutionalism and the Whiskey Rebellion." *Chicago-Kent Law Review* 81, no. 3 (2006): 883–903.

———. *The Other Founders: Anti-Federalism and the Dissenting Tradition in America, 1788–1828.* Chapel Hill: University of North Carolina Press, 1999.

———. "'To Assemble Together for their Common Good': History, Ethnography, and the Original Meanings of the Rights of Assembly and Speech." *Fordham Law Review* 84, no. 3 (2015): 915–934.

———. *A Well-Regulated Militia: The Founding Fathers and the Origins of Gun Control in America*. New York: Oxford University Press, 2006.

Cotterrell, Roger. "The Concept of Legal Culture." In *Comparing Legal Cultures*, edited by David Nelken, 13–22. Aldershot, UK: Dartmouth, 1997.

Countryman, Edward. "The Problem of the Early American Crowds." *Journal of American Studies* 7, no. 1 (1973): 77–90.

Coxe, Brinton. *An Essay on Judicial Power and Unconstitutional Legislation, Being a Commentary on Parts of the Constitution of the United States*. Philadelphia: Kay and Brother, 1893.

Craig, Neville B. *Exposure of the Many Misstatements in H. M. Brackenridge's History of the Whiskey Rebellion*. Pittsburgh: John S. Davison, 1859.

———. *The History of Pittsburgh, with a Brief Notice of its Facilities of Communication and Other Advantages for Commercial and Manufacturing Purposes*. 1851. Reprint. 225–249. Pittsburgh: J. R. Weldin, 1917.

Cranston, Maurice. "Ideas and Ideologies: The Intellectual Origins and Development of the French Revolution." *History Today* 39, no. 5 (1989): 10–14.

Crenshaw, Kimberle. "Whose Story Is It Anyway? Feminist and Antiracist Appropriations of Anita Hill." In *Race-ing Justice, En-gendering Power: Essays on Anita Hill, Clarence Thomas, and the Construction of Social Reality*, edited by Toni Morrison, 402–440. New York: Pantheon Books, 1992.

Crenshaw, Kimberle, and Gary Peller. "Reel Time/Real Justice." In *Reading Rodney King, Reading Urban Uprising*, edited by Robert Gooding-Williams, 56–72. New York: Routledge, 1993.

Crow, Matthew. *Thomas Jefferson, Legal History, and the Art of Recollection*. Cambridge: Cambridge University Press, 2017.

Crumrine, Boyd, and Franklin Ellis. *History of Washington County, Pennsylvania, with Biographical Sketches of Many of Its Pioneers and Prominent Men*. Philadelphia: H. L. Everts, 1882.

Curott, Nicholas A., and Alexander Fink. "Bandit Heroes: Social, Mythical, or Rational?" *American Journal of Economics and Sociology* 72, no. 2 (2012): 470–497.

Curran, Jonathan. "Examining Public Opinion during the Whiskey Rebellion." *Journal of the American Revolution*, September 7, 2021, https://allthingsliberty.com.

Currie, David P. "The Constitution in Congress: Substantive Issues in the First Congress, 1789–1791." *University of Chicago Law Review* 61, no. 3 (1994): 775–866.

Curtis, Dennis E., and Judith Resnick. "Images of Justice." *Yale Law Journal* 96, no. 8 (1987): 1727–1772.

Dalton, Susan. *Engendering the Republic of Letters: Reconnecting Public and Private Spheres in Eighteenth-Century Europe*. Montreal: McGill-Queen's University Press, 2003.

Davidson, Cathy. *Revolution and the Word: The Rise of the Novel in America*. Oxford: Oxford University Press, 1986.

Davis, Jeffrey A. "Guarding the Republican Interest: The Western Pennsylvania Democratic Societies and the Excise Tax." *Pennsylvania History: A Journal of Mid-Atlantic Studies* 67, no. 1 (2000): 43–62.

———. "The Whiskey Rebellion and the Demise of the Democratic-Republican Societies of Pennsylvania." *Topic: A Journal of the Liberal Arts* 45 (1994): 22–38.

Dayton, Cornelia Hughes. *Women before the Bar: Gender, Law, and Society in Connecticut, 1639–1789*. Chapel Hill: University of North Carolina Press, 1995.

De Josselin de Jong, J. P. B. "Customary Law: A Confusing Fiction." In *Folk Law: Essays in the Theory and Practice of "Lex Non Scripta,"* edited by Alison Dundes Renteln and Alan Dundes, 111–117. Vol. 1. Madison: University of Wisconsin Press, 1994.

Diamond, Larry. "Facing Up to Democratic Recession." In *Democracy in Decline?*, edited by Larry Diamond and Marc F. Plattner, 98–118. Baltimore: Johns Hopkins University Press, 2015.

Dinsmore, James. "Courts and Western Pennsylvania Lands: The Origins of the Attack on Pennsylvania Courts, 1790–1810." PhD. diss., Temple University, 1990.

Dunn, Gerald T. "Proprietors—Sometimes Predators: Early Court Reporters." *Yearbook, Supreme Court Historical Society* (1976): 61–72.

Eakin, Myrl. "Hugh Henry Brackenridge—Lawyer." *Western Pennsylvania Historical Magazine* 10, no. 3 (1927): 164–170.

Egle, William Henry, ed. *Notes and Queries: Historical, Biographical and Genealogical: Relating Chiefly to Interior Pennsylvania*. Harrisburg, [Pa.]: Harrisburg Publishing, 1893.

Eicholz, Hans L. "A Closer Look at 'Modernity': The Case of William Finley and Trans-Appalachian Political Thought." *Topic: A Journal of the Liberal Arts* 45 (1994): 57–72.

Elkins, Stanley, and Eric McKitrick. *The Age of Federalism: The Early American Republic, 1788–1800*. New York: Oxford University Press, 1993.

Elliott, Emory, *Revolutionary Writers: Literature and Authority in the New Republic, 1725–1810*. Oxford: Oxford University Press, 1986.

Ellis, Joseph J. *American Dialogue: The Founders and Us*. New York: Vintage, 2018.

———. *His Excellency, George Washington*. New York: Vintage, 2004.

Ellis, Richard E. *The Jeffersonian Crisis: Courts and Politics in the Young Republic*. New York: Oxford University Press, 1971.

Elsmere, Jane Shaffer. "The Trials of John Fries." *Pennsylvania Magazine of History and Biography* 103, no. 4 (1979): 437–439.

Engels, Jeremy. *Enemyship: Democracy and Counter-Revolution in the Early Republic*. East Lansing: Michigan State University Press, 2010.

"Examination of Hugh Henry Brackenridge." In *The Papers of Alexander Hamilton*, edited by Harold C. Syrett, 382–387. Vol. 12. New York: Columbia University Press, 1961–1987.

Farrand, Max, ed. *The Records of the Federal Convention of 1787*. Vol. 2. New Haven, Conn.: Yale University Press, 1911.

Faulkner, Robert K. "John Marshall and the Burr Trial." *Journal of American History* 53, no. 2 (1966): 247–258.

Fennell, Dorothy Elaine. "From Rebelliousness to Insurrection: A Social History of the Whiskey Rebellion, 1765–1802." PhD. diss., University of Pittsburgh, 1981.

Ferguson, Robert A. *Law and Letters in American Culture*. Cambridge, Mass.: Harvard University Press, 1984.

———. *The Trial in American Life*. Chicago: University of Chicago Press, 2007.

Ferguson, Russell. *Early Western Pennsylvania Politics*. Pittsburgh: University of Pittsburgh Press, 1938.
Fernandez, Angela, and Markus D. Dubber, eds. *Law Books in Action: Essays on the Anglo-American Legal Treatise*. Oxford: Hart Publishing, 2012.
Findley, William. *History of the Insurrection in the Four Western Counties of Pennsylvania: In the Year 1794; and an Historical Review of the Previous Situation of the Country*. Philadelphia: Samuel Harrison Smith, 1796.
[Findley, William]. *A Review of the Revenue System Adopted by the First Congress under the Constitution*. Philadelphia: T. Dobson, 1794.
Fitzpatrick, Peter. "'The damned word': Culture and Its (In)compatibility with Law." *Yale Journal of Law and the Humanities* 13, no. 1 (2001): 2–13.
Fletcher, Angus. *Comic Democracies from Ancient Athens to the American Republic*. Baltimore: Johns Hopkins University Press, 2016.
Fletcher, George P. "Ambivalence about Treason (Law, Loyalty, and Treason: How Can the Law Regulate Loyalty without Imperiling It?)." *North Carolina Law Review* 82, no. 5 (2004): 1611–1627.
Foisneau, Luc. "Governing a Republic: Rousseau's General Will and the Problem of Government." *Republics of Letters: A Journal for the Study of Knowledge, Politics, and the Arts* 2, no. 1 (2010): 93–104.
Foner, Philip S., ed. *The Democratic-Republican Societies, 1790–1800*. Westport, Conn.: Greenwood Press, 1976.
Fornieri, Joseph R. "Washington's Farewell Address and Lincoln's Lyceum Address." *White House Studies* 5, no. 3 (2005): 365–382.
Foster, Michael. *A Report of Some Proceedings on the Commission for the Trial of the Rebels in the Year 1746, in the County of Surry, and of Other Crown Cases*. London: E. and R. Brooke, 1792.
French, Laurence Armand. *Native American Justice*. Chicago: Burnham, 2003.
Friedenberg, David M. *Life, Liberty and the Pursuit of Land: The Plunder of Early America*. New York: Prometheus, 1992.
Friedman, Lawrence M. "The Concept of Legal Culture: A Reply." In *Comparing Legal Cultures*, edited by David Nelken, 33–40. Aldershot, UK: Dartmouth, 1997.
———. *A History of American Law*. 3rd ed. New York: Touchstone, 2005.
Fritz, Christian G. *American Sovereigns: The People and America's Constitutional Tradition before the Civil War*. Cambridge: Cambridge University Press, 2008.
Fukuyama, Francis. "Why Is Democracy Performing So Poorly?" *Journal of Democracy* 26, no. 1 (2015): 11–20.
Gallatin, Albert. *The Speech of Albert Gallatin a Representative from the County of Fayette in the House of Representatives of the General Assembly of Pennsylvania on the Important Question Touching the Validity of the Elections Held in the Four Western Counties of the State, on the 14th Day of October, 1794*. Philadelphia: William W. Woodward, 1795.
———. *The Writings of Albert Gallatin*, edited by Henry Adams. Vol. 1. Philadelphia: L. P. Lippincott, [1879].
Gallay, Allan, ed. *Indian Slavery in Colonial America*. Lincoln: University of Nebraska Press, 2009.

Gallo, Marcus. "Improving Independence: The Struggle over Land Surveys in Northwestern Pennsylvania in 1794." *Pennsylvania Magazine of History and Biography* 142, no. 2 (2018): 131–161.

Garner, Bryan A., ed. *Black's Law Dictionary*. 7th ed. St. Paul: West Group, 1999.

Geertz, Clifford. "Thick Description: Toward an Interpretive Theory of Culture." In *The Interpretation of Cultures: Selected Essays*, 3–36. New York: Basic Books, 1973

Gerber, Scott D. "Bringing Ideas Back In—A Brief Historiography of American Colonial Law." *American Journal of Legal History* 51, no. 2 (2011): 359–374.

Gideon, Richard R. "The Whiskey Flags." *Nava News* 33, nos. 3–4 (2000): 6–9.

Gilje, Paul A. *The Road to Mobocracy: Popular Disorder in New York City, 1763–1834*. Chapel Hill: University of North Carolina Press, 1987.

Gilmore, Michael T. "Eighteenth-Century Oppositional Ideology and Hugh Henry Brackenridge's *Modern Chivalry*." *Early American Literature* 13, no. 2 (1978): 181–192.

Gilmore, Paul. "Republican Machines and Brackenridge's Cave: Aesthetics and Models of Machinery in the Early Republic." *Early American Literature* 39 no. 2 (2004): 299–322.

Gould, Roger V. "Patron-Client Ties, State Centralization, and the Whiskey Rebellion." *American Journal of Sociology* 102, no. 2 (1996): 400–429.

———. "Political Networks and the Local/National Boundary in the Whiskey Rebellion." In *Challenging Authority: The Historical Study of Contentious Politics*, edited by Michael P. Hanagan, Leslie Page Moch, and Wayne te Brake, 36–53. Minneapolis: University of Minnesota Press, 1998.

Gramsci, Antonio. *Selections from Cultural Writings*. Translated by William Boelhower. Cambridge, Mass.: Harvard University Press, 1985.

Grandjean, Katharine. "'Our Fellow-Creatures & Our Fellow-Christians': Race and Religion in Eighteenth-Century Narratives of Indian Crime." *American Quarterly* 62, no. 4 (2010): 925–950.

Griffin, Patrick. *American Leviathan: Empire, Nation, and Revolutionary Frontier*. New York: Hill and Wang, 2007.

Grundfest, Jerry. *George Clymer, Philadelphia Revolutionary*. New York: Arno Press, 1982.

Hagen, Carrie. "The First Presidential Pardon Pitted Alexander Hamilton against George Washington." *Smithsonian Magazine*, August 29, 2017, https://www.smithsonianmag.com/history/firstpresidential-pardon-pitted-hamilton-against-george-washington-180964659/#tJdiw6M8AT8SwUBR.99.

Halbrook, Stephen P., and David P. Kopel. "Tench Coxe and the Right to Keep and Bear Arms." *William and Mary Bill of Rights Journal* 7, no. 2 (1999): 347–399.

Hall, Kermit L. *The Magic Mirror: Law in American History*. New York: Oxford University Press, 1989.

Hall, Mark David. *The Political and Legal Philosophy of James Wilson, 1742–1798*. Columbia: University of Missouri Press, 1997.

Hale, Matthew. *The History of the Pleas of the Crown*. London: E. and R. Nutt and R. Gosling, 1736.

Hall, Randall L., ed. *A Rape in the Early Republic: Gender and Legal Culture in an 1806 Virginia Trial*. Lexington: University of Kentucky Press, 2017.

Hamilton, Alexander, James Madison, and John Jay [Publius]. *The Federalist: A Collection* of Essays, Written in Favour of the New Constitution, as Agreed upon by the Federal Convention, September 17, 1787. New York: J. & A. McLean, 1788.

Hansen, J. H. "William Lewis: His Influences on Early American Law." MA thesis, University of North Colorado, 1999.

Harper, R. Eugene. "Rebellion Contained: A Socioeconomic Approach to the Whiskey Rebellion and the Role of the Local Elite." *Topic: A Journal of the Liberal Arts* 45 (1994): 39–56.

———. *The Transformation of Western Pennsylvania, 1770–1800*. Pittsburgh: University of Pittsburgh Press, 1991.

Harris, J. William. *The Hanging of Thomas Jeremiah: A Free Man's Encounter with Liberty*. New Haven, Conn.: Yale University Press, 2009.

Harris, Todd C. "'George Washington': A Revolutionary Approach to Leadership." *Leadership & Organization Development Journal* 39, no. 8 (2018): 995–1009.

Hein, David. "George Washington and the Patience of Power." *Modern Age* 57, no. 4 (2015): 35–43.

Henriques Peter R. "George Washington: America's Atlas." *American History* (November–December 2016): 34–41.

Hermes, Katherine. "'Justice Will Be Done Us': Algonquin Demands for Reciprocity in the Courts of European Settlers." In *The Many Legalities of Early America*, edited by Christopher Tomlins and Bruce H. Mann, 123–149. Chapel Hill: University of North Carolina Press, 2001.

Hickox, Charles F., and Andrew C. Liviano. "William Paterson." *Journal of Supreme Court History* 17, no. 1 (1992): 57–58.

Hirsch, David H. "Brackenridge Ideas and the Man of Reason." In *Reality and Idea in the Early American Novel*, 49–73. The Hague: Mouton, 1971.

Hobsbawm, Eric, and Terence Ranger, eds. *The Invention of Tradition*. Cambridge: Cambridge University Press, 1983.

Hoffer, Peter Charles. *The Free Press Crisis of 1800: Thomas Cooper's Trial for Seditious Libel*. Lawrence: University Press of Kansas, 2011.

———. *The Treason Trials of Aaron Burr*. Lawrence: University of Kansas Press, 2008.

Hoffer, Peter Charles, and Williamjames Hull Hoffer. *The Clamor of Lawyers: The American Revolution and Crisis in the Legal Profession*. Ithaca, N.Y.: Cornell University Press, 2018.

Hoffman, Ronald, and Peter Albert, eds. *Launching the "Extended Republic": The Federalist Era*. Charlottesville: University of Virginia Press, 1996.

Hofstadter, Richard. "The Paranoid Style in American Politics." *Harper's Magazine*, November 19, 1964.

———. *The Paranoid Style in American Politics and Other Essays*. New York: Vintage, 1964.

Hogeland, William. *Autumn of the Black Snake: George Washington, Mad Anthony Wayne, and the Invasion that Opened the West*. New York: Farrar, Straus and Giroux, 2017.

———. *The Whiskey Rebellion: George Washington, Alexander Hamilton, and the Frontier Rebels Who Challenged America's Newfound Sovereignty*. New York: Simon and Schuster, 2006.

Holt, Wythe. "'Federal Courts as the Asylum to Federal Interests': Randolph's Report, the Benson Amendment, and the 'Original Understanding' of the Federal Judiciary." *Buffalo Law Review* 36, no. 2 (1987): 341–372.

———. "Federal Courts Have Enemies in All Who Fear Their Influence on State Objects: The Failure to Abolish Supreme Court Circuit-Riding in the Judiciary Acts of 1792 and 1793." *Buffalo Law Review* 36, no. 2 (1987): 301–340.

———. "The Federal Whiskey Rebellion Cases of 1795 and the Rise of the National Security State." Unpublished manuscript, 2010. Kindly furnished by the author in typescript.

———. "'To Establish Justice': Politics, the Judiciary Act of 1789, and the Invention of the Federal Courts." *Duke Law Journal* 1989, no. 6 (1989): 1421–1531.

———. "The New Jerusalem: Herman Husband's Egalitarian Alternative to the United States Constitution." In *Revolutionary Founders: Rebels, Radicals, and Reformers in the Making of the Nation*, edited by Alfred F. Young, Gary B. Nash, and Ray Raphael, 253–272. New York: Vintage, 2012.

———. "The Whiskey Rebellion of 1794: A Democratic Working-Class Insurrection." Paper presented at the Georgia Workshop in Early American History, Athens, Georgia, January 23, 2004. 83 pp. https://docplayer.net/40350460-The-whiskey-rebellion-of-1794-a-democratic-working-class-insurrection-wythe-holt-1.html.

Horwitz, Morton J. *The Transformation of American Law, 1780–1860*. Cambridge, Mass.: Harvard University Press, 1977.

Hulbert, Archer Butler. *Washington and the West, Being George Washington's Diary of September, 1784, Kept During his Journey into the Ohio Basin in the Interest of a Commercial Union Between the Great Lakes and the Potomac River*. New York: Century, 1905.

Hulsebosch, Daniel J. "The Fulfillment Revisited: Political Experience, Enlightenment Ideas, and the International Constitution." *The New England Quarterly* 91, no. 1 (2018): 209–239.

Hunter, Dan. "No Wilderness of Single Instances: Inductive Inference in Law." *Journal of Legal Education* 48, no. 3 (1998): 365–401.

Hurst, James Willard. *The Law of Treason in the United States: Collected Essays*. Westport, Conn.: Greenwood Publishing, 1971.

———. "Treason in the United States: I. Down to the Constitution." *Harvard Law Review* 58, no. 2 (1944): 226–272.

———. "Treason in the United States: II. The Constitution." *Harvard Law Review* 58, no. 3 (1945): 395–444.

———. "Treason in the United States: III. Under the Constitution." *Harvard Law Review* 58 no. 6 (1945): 806–857.

Huston, Reeve. "Rethinking the Origins of Partisan Democracy in the United States, 1795–1840." In *Practicing Democracy: Popular Politics in the United States from the Constitution to the Civil War*, edited by Daniel Peart and Adam I. P. Smith, 46–71. Charlottesville: University of Virginia Press, 2015.

Ifft, Richard A. "Treason in the Early Republic: The Federal Courts, Popular Protest, and Federalism during the Whiskey Rebellion." In *The Whiskey Rebellion: Past and Present Perspectives*, edited by Steven R. Boyd, 165–182. Westport, Conn.: Greenwood Press, 1985.

Imagination Collectif, The. "From Whiskey Rebellion to Donald Trump and the Question of Power: An Interview with Isaac Ariail Reed." *Sociaini Studia* 13, no. 4 (2017): 99–104.

Inazu, John D. "The Forgotten Freedom of Assembly." *Tulane Law Review* 84, no. 3 (2010): 565–612.

———. *Liberty's Refuge: The Forgotten Freedom of Assembly*. New Haven, Conn.: Yale University Press, 2012.

"Indian Conference at Philadelphia," December 1, 1790, January 10, 1791, February 7, 1791. *Pennsylvania Archives*, 2nd ser., vol. 4. Edited by John B. Linn and William H. Egle, 527–537. Harrisburg, [Pa.]: Clarence M. Busch, 1896.

"An Indian Treaty." *Pennsylvania Archives*, 2nd ser., vol. 4. Edited by John B. Linn and William H. Egle, 458–463. Harrisburg, [Pa.]: Clarence M. Busch, 1896.

Iredell, James. "Grand Jury Charge." In *The Two Trials of John Fries, on an Indictment for Treason; Together with a Brief Report of the Trials of Several Other Persons, for Treason and Insurrection, in the Counties of Bucks, Northampton and Montgomery, in the Circuit Court of the United States*, transcribed by Thomas Carpenter, 1–16. Philadelphia: William W. Woodward, 1800.

Ireland, Owen. *Religion, Ethnicity, and Politics: Ratifying the Constitution in Pennsylvania*. University Park: Penn State University Press, 1995.

Jay, Martin. "Intention and Irony: The Missed Encounter Between Hayden White and Quentin Skinner." *History and Theory* 52, no. 1 (2013): 32–48.

Jay, Stewart. "Origins of Federal Common Law: Part One." *University of Pennsylvania Law Review* 133, no. 5 (1985): 1003–1116.

Jensen, Merrill. "The Dissent of the Minority of the Convention." In *The Documentary History of the Ratification of the Constitution*, vol. 2, *Ratification of the Constitution by the States: Pennsylvania*, edited by Merrill Jensen, John P. Kaminski, and Gaspare J. Saladino, 626–630. Madison: State Historical Society of Wisconsin, 1976.

Jensen, Merrill, John P. Kaminski, and Gaspare J. Saladino, ed. *The Documentary History of the Ratification of the Constitution*. Vol. 2, *Ratification of the Constitution by the States: Pennsylvania*. Madison: State Historical Society of Wisconsin, 1976.

Joyce, Craig. "The Rise of the Supreme Court: An Institutional Perspective on Marshall Court Ascendency." *Michigan Law Review* 83, no. 5 (1985): 1291–1391.

Kawashima, Yasuhide. "Forced Conformity: Puritan Criminal Justice and Indians." *University of Kansas Law Review* 25, no. 3 (1977): 361–374.

———. *Puritan Justice and the Indian: White Man's Law in Massachusetts, 1630–1763*. Middletown, Conn.: Wesleyan University Press, 1986.

Kennedy, Roger G. *Burr, Hamilton, and Jefferson: A Study in Character*. New York: Oxford University Press, 2000.

Kessler, Amalia D. *Inventing American Exceptionalism: The Origins of American Adversarial Legal Culture*. New Haven, Conn.: Yale University Press, 2017.

Ketcham, Ralph, ed. *The Anti-Federalist Papers and the Constitutional Convention Debates*. 1986. Reprint. New York: Signet Classics, 2003.

Ketter, Christian. "Chief Justice Marshall's Judicial Statesmanship amid *In Re Burr*: A Pragmatic Political Balancing against President Jefferson Over Treason." *University of Illinois Chicago John Marshall Law Review* 53, no. 4 (2021): 789–908.

Kirby, Ephraim. *Reports of Cases Adjudged in the Superior Court of the State of Connecticut, from the Year 1785, to May 1798 with Some Determinations of the Supreme Court of Errors*. Litchfield, Conn.: Collier and Adam, 1789.

Kittredge, Katharine, ed. *Lewd and Notorious: Female Transgression in the Eighteenth Century*. Ann Arbor: University of Michigan Press, 2003.

Klein, Rachel N. "Ordering the Backcountry: The South Carolina Regulation." *William and Mary Quarterly* 38, no. 4 (1981): 661–680.

Knowles, F. E. *Reading American Indian Law: Foundational Principles*. Cambridge: Cambridge University Press, 2020.

Koenigs, Thomas. "'Nothing but Fiction': *Modern Chivalry*, Fictionality, and the Political Public Sphere in the Early Republic." *Early American Literature* 50, no. 2 (2015): 301–330.

Kohn, Richard H. *Eagle and Sword: The Federalists and the Creation of the Military Establishment in America, 1783–1802*. New York: Free Press, 1975.

Kohn, Richard H. "The Washington Administration's Decision to Crush the Whiskey Rebellion." *Journal of American History* 59, no. 3 (1972): 567–584.

Konefsky, Alfred. "The Legal Profession from the Revolution to the Civil War." In *The Cambridge History of Law in America*, edited by Michael Grossberg and Christopher Tomlins, 68–105. Vol. 2. New York: Cambridge University Press, 2008.

Konig, David Thomas. "Arms and the Man: What Did the Right to Keep Arms Mean in the Early Republic." *Law and History Review* 25, no. 1 (2007): 177–185.

———. "A Summary View of the Law of British America." *William and Mary Quarterly* 50, no. 1 (1993): 42–50.

Konkle, Burton Alva, *The Life and Times of Thomas Smith, 1745–1809*. Philadelphia: Campion, 1904.

Kramer, Larry D. *The People Themselves: Popular Constitutionalism and Judicial Review*. Oxford: Oxford University Press, 2004.

Krappe, Alexander H. "Observations on the Origin and Development of the Idea of Justice." *University of Chicago Law Review* 12, no. 2 (1945): 179–197.

Lacour, Claudia Brodsky. "Doing Things With Words: 'Racism' as Speech Act and the Undoing of Justice." In *Race-ing Justice, En-gendering Power: Essays on Anita Hill, Clarence Thomas, and the Construction of Social Reality*, edited by Toni Morrison, 127–158. New York: Pantheon Books, 1992.

Langbein, John H. *The Origins of Adversary Criminal Law*. Oxford: Oxford University Press, 2003.

Larson, Carlton F. W. "The Forgotten Constitutional Law of Treason and the Enemy Combatant Problem." *University of Pennsylvania Law Review* 154, no. 4 (2006): 863–926.

———. "The Revolutionary American Jury: A Case Study of the 1778–1779 Philadelphia Treason Trials." *Southern Methodist University Law Review* 61, no. 4 (2008): 1441–1524.

———. *The Trials of Allegiance: Treason, Juries, and the American Revolution*. New York: Oxford University Press, 2019.

Levitsky, Steven, and Lucan Way. "The Myth of Democratic Recession." *Journal of Democracy* 26, no. 1 (2015): 45–58.

Lewis, William. *Memoirs of the Life and Religious Experience of William Lewis, Late of Bristol: To Which are Added, Extracts of Letters, Addressed by Him to Individuals, on Different Occasions*. Philadelphia: B. & T. Kite, 1821.

Lieberman, Robert C., Suzanne Mettler, Thomas B. Pepinsky, Kenneth M. Roberts, and Richard Valelly. "The Trump Presidency and American Democracy: A Historical and Comparative Analysis." *Perspectives on Politics* 17, no. 2 (2019): 470–479.

Lienesch, Michael. "Reinterpreting Rebellion: The Influence of Shays's Rebellion on American Political Thought." In *In Debt to Shays: The Bicentennial of an Agrarian Rebellion*, edited by Robert A. Gross, 161–182. Charlottesville: University Press of Virginia, 1993.

Linebaugh, Peter, and Marcus Rediker. "The Many-Headed Hydra: Sailors, Slaves, and the Atlantic Working Class in the Eighteenth Century." *Journal of Historical Sociology* 3, no. 3 (1990): 225–252.

Link, Eugene P. *Democratic-Republican Societies: 1790–1800*. New York: Columbia University Press, 1942.

Lofquist, William S. "Justice on the Western Frontier: The Death Penalty in Pre-Industrial Pittsburgh, 1754–1820." *Pennsylvania History: A Journal of Mid-Atlantic Studies* 85, no. 4 (2018): 556–593.

Loudon, Archibald, ed. *A Selection of Some of the Most Interesting Narratives, or Outrages, Committed by the Indians in Their War with the White People*. 2 vols. Carlisle, [Pa.]: A. Loudon, 1808.

Loughran, Trish. *The Republic in Print: Print Culture in the Age of U.S. Nation Building, 1770–1870*. New York: Columbia University Press, 2007.

Lubiano, Wahneema. "Black Ladies, Welfare Queens, and State Minstrels: Ideological War by Narrative Means." In *Race-ing Justice, En-gendering Power: Essays on Anita Hill, Clarence Thomas, and the Construction of Social Reality*, edited by Toni Morrison, 323–363. New York: Pantheon Books, 1992.

Lynch, David. *The Role of Circuit Courts in the Formation of United States Law in the Early Republic: Following Supreme Court Justices Washington, Livingston, Story and Thompson*. Portland: Hart Publishing, 2018.

Lyotard, Jean-François. *Peregrinations: Law, Form, Event*. New York: Columbia University Press, 1988.

Maier, Pauline. *From Resistance to Revolution: Colonial Radicals and the Development of American Opposition to Britain, 1765–1776*. New York: Norton, 1972.

———. "Popular Uprisings and Civil Authority in Eighteenth-Century America." *William and Mary Quarterly* 27, no. 1 (1970): 3–35.

Mann, Bruce H. "The Formalization of Informal Law: Arbitration Before the American Revolution." *New York University Law Review* 59, no. 3 (1984): 443–481.

Marcus, Maeva, ed. *The Documentary History of the Supreme Court of the United States, 1789–1800*. 6 vols. New York: Columbia University Press, 1990–1994.

———. "Wilson as a Justice." *Georgetown Journal of Law and Public Policy*. 17, no. 1 (2019): 147–166.

Marder, Daniel. *Hugh Henry Brackenridge*. New York: Twayne Publishers, 1967.

———, ed. *Incidents of the Insurrection*. New Haven, Conn.: College and University Press, 1972.

Marietta, Jack D., and G. S. Rowe. *Troubled Experiment: Crime and Justice in Pennsylvania, 1682–1800*. Philadelphia: University of Pennsylvania Press, 2006.

Markowitz, Arthur A. "Washington's Farewell and the Historians: A Critical Review." *Pennsylvania Magazine of History and Biography* 94, no. 2 (1970): 173–191.

Marshall, John. *Life of George Washington, Commander in Chief of the American Forces, during the War Which Established the Independence of His Country, and First President of the United States.* Vol. 5. Fredericksburg, [Va.]: Citizen's Guild of Washington's Boyhood Home, 1926.

Martin, Luther. "Trial by Jury." In *The Anti-Federalist Papers*, edited by Morton Borden, no. 83. East Lansing: Michigan State University Press, 1965.

Martin, Robert W. T. *Government by Dissent: Protest, Resistance, and Radical Democratic Thought in the Early American Republic.* New York: New York University Press, 2013.

Martin, Wendy. "On the Road with the Philosopher and the Profiteer: A Study of Hugh Henry Brackenridge's *Modern Chivalry*." *Eighteenth Century Studies* 4, no. 3 (1971): 241–256.

McClure, James Patrick. "The Ends of the American Earth: Pittsburgh and the Upper Ohio Valley to 1795." PhD. diss., University of Michigan, 1983.

———. "'Let Us Be Independent': David Bradford and the Whiskey Insurrection." *Pittsburgh History* 74, no. 2 (1991): 72–86.

McConville, Brendan. "The Rise of Rough Music: Reflections on an Ancient New Custom in Eighteenth-Century New Jersey." In *Riot and Revelry in Early America*, edited by William Pencak, Matthew Dennis, and Simon P. Newman, 87–102. University Park: Pennsylvania State University Press, 2002.

McDonald, Forrest. "Presidential Character: The Example of George Washington." *Perspectives on Political Science* 26, no. 3 (1997): 134–139.

McFarland, Esther Ann. *William Lewis, Esquire: Enlightened Statesman, Profound Lawyer, and Useful Citizen.* Darby, Pa.: Diane Publishing, 2012.

McInnus, Maurie D. "George Washington: Cincinnatus or Marcus Aurelius?" In *Thomas Jefferson, the Classical World, and Early America*, edited by Peter S. Onuf and Nicholas P. Cole, 128–168. Charlottesville: University of Virginia Press, 2011.

Melikan, R. A. "Introduction." In *Domestic and International Trials, 1700–2000*, vol. 3, *The Trial in History*, edited by R. A. Melikan, 1–11. Manchester: Manchester University Press, 2003.

Melish, Joanne Pope. *Disowning Slavery: Gradual Emancipation and "Race" in New England, 1780–1860.* Ithaca, N.Y.: Cornell University Press, 1998.

Messer, Peter C. "'A Species of Treason & Not the Least Dangerous Kind': The Treason Trials of Abraham Carlisle and John Roberts." *Pennsylvania Magazine of History and Biography* 123, no. 4 (1999): 303–332.

Mettler, Suzanne, and Robert C. Lieberman. *The Recurring Crises of American Democracy: Four Threats.* New York: St. Martin's Griffin, 2020.

Mezey, Naomi. "Law as Culture." In *Cultural Analysis: Cultural Studies and the Law: Moving Beyond Legal Realism*, edited by Austin Sarat and Jonathan Simon, 37–72. Durham, N.C.: Duke University Press, 2003.

Mittal, Sonia, and Barry R. Weingast. "Self-Enforcing Constitutions: With an Application to Democratic Stability in America's First Century." *Journal of Law, Economics, and Organization* 29, no. 2 (2013): 278–302.

Morano, Anthony A. "A Reexamination of the Development of the Reasonable Doubt Rule." *Boston University Law Review* 55, no. 3 (1975): 507–529.

Morrison, Toni, ed. *Race-ing Justice, En-gendering Power: Essays on Anita Hill, Clarence Thomas, and the Construction of Social Reality.* New York: Pantheon Books, 1992.

———. "Friday on the Potomac." In *Race-ing Justice, En-gendering Power: Essays on Anita Hill, Clarence Thomas, and the Construction of Social Reality*, edited by Toni Morrison, vii–xxx. New York: Pantheon Books, 1992.
Myrsiades, Linda. "Constituting Resistance: Narrative Construction and the Social Theory of Resistance." *Symploke* 1, no. 2 (1993): 101–120.
———. "Grand Juries, Legal Machines, and the Common Man Jury." *College Literature* 35 no. 3 (2008): 158–178.
———. "A Language Game Approach to Narrative Analysis of Sexual Harassment Law in *Meritor v. Vinson*." *College Literature* 25, no. 1 (1998): 200–230.
———. *Law and Medicine in Revolutionary America: Dissecting the Rush v. Cobbett Trial, 1799*. Bethlehem: Lehigh University Press, 2012.
———. "Narratives of Law and Disorder." In *Cultural Representation in Historical Resistance: Complexity and Construction in Greek Guerilla Theater*, 250–264. Lewisburg, Pa.: Bucknell University Press, 1999.
———. "A Tale of a Whiskey Rebellion Judge: William Paterson, Grand Jury Charges, and the Trials of the Whiskey Rebels." *Pennsylvania Magazine of History and Biography* 140, no. 2 (2016): 129–165.
Neem, Johann N. "Freedom of Association in the Early Republic: The Republican Party, the Whiskey Rebellion, and the Philadelphia and New York Cordwainers' Case." *Pennsylvania Magazine of History and Biography* 128, no. 3 (2003): 259–290.
Nelken, David. "Disclosing/Invoking Legal Culture: An Introduction." *Social and Legal Studies* 4, no. 4 (1995): 435–452.
———. "Using the Concept of Legal Culture." *Australian Journal of Legal Philosophy* 29 (2004): 1–26.
Nelson, Dana D. "'Indications of the Public Will': *Modern Chivalry*'s Theory of Democratic Representation." *ANQ* 15, no. 1 (2002): 223–40.
———. "Between Savagery and Civilization: The Whiskey Rebellion and a Democratic Middle Way." In *Commons Democracy: Reading the Politics of Participation in the Early United States*, edited by Dana D. Nelson, 53–83. New York: Fordham University Press, 2016.
Nelson, William E. *Americanization of the Common Law: The Impact of Legal Change on Massachusetts Society, 1760–1830*. Cambridge, Mass.: Harvard University Press, 1975.
———. *Common Law in Colonial America*. Vol. 1, *The Chesapeake and New England, 1607–1660*. New York: Oxford University Press, 2008.
———. *Common Law in Colonial America*. Vol. 2, *The Middle Colonies and the Carolinas, 1660–1730*. New York: Oxford University Press, 2013.
———. *Common Law in Colonial America*. Vol. 3, *The Chesapeake and New England, 1660–1750*. New York: Oxford University Press, 2016.
———. *Common Law in Colonial America*. Vol. 4, *Law and the Constitution on the Eve of Independence, 1735–1776*. New York: Oxford University Press, 2018.
———. *E Pluribus Unum: How the Common Law Helped Unify and Liberate Colonial America, 1607–1776*. New York: Oxford University Press, 2019.
Newlin, Claude M. *The Life and Writings of Hugh Henry Brackenridge*. Princeton, N.J.: Princeton University Press, 1932.
Newman, Paul Douglas. *Fries's Rebellion: The Enduring Struggle for the American Revolution*. Philadelphia: University of Pennsylvania Press, 2004.

Newman, Richard S. *The Transformation of American Abolitionism: Fighting Slavery in the Early Republic*. Chapel Hill: University of North Carolina Press, 2001.

Newmyer, R. Kent. *The Treason Trial of Aaron Burr: Law, Politics, and the Character Wars of the New Nation*. Cambridge: Cambridge University Press, 2012.

Novak, William J. *People's Welfare: Law and Regulation in Nineteenth-Century America*. Chapel Hill: University of North Carolina Press, 1996.

O'Connor, John E. *William Paterson: Lawyer and Statesman, 1745–1806*. New Brunswick, N.J.: Rutgers University Press, 1979.

Offut, William M., Jr. *"Of Good Laws" & "Good Men": Law and Society in the Delaware Valley, 1680–1710*. Urbana: University of Illinois Press, 1995.

———. "The Limits of Authority: Courts, Ethnicity, and Gender in the Middle Colonies, 1670–1710." In *The Many Legalities of Early America*, edited by Christopher L. Tomlins and Bruce H. Mann, 357–387. Chapel Hill: University of North Carolina Press, 2001.

Oldham, James, and Su Jin Kim. "Arbitration in America: The Early History." *Law and History Review* 31, no. 1 (2013): 241–266.

Osman, Julia. "Cincinnatus Reborn: The George Washington Myth and French Renewal During the Old Regime." *French Historical Studies* 38, no. 3 (2015): 421–446.

Ousterhout, Anne M. "Controlling the Opposition in Pennsylvania during the American Revolution." *Pennsylvania Magazine of History and Biography* 105, no. 1 (1981): 3–34.

Owen, Kenneth. "Legitimacy, Localism, and the First Party System." In *Practicing Democracy: Popular Politics in the United States from the Constitution to the Civil War*, edited by Daniel Peart and Adam I. P. Smith, 173–195. Charlottesville: University of Virginia Press, 2015.

———. *Political Community in Revolutionary Pennsylvania, 1774–1800*. New York: Oxford University Press, 2018.

Paine, Thomas. "Thoughts on the Present State of American Affairs." In *Common Sense*. Philadelphia: W. and T. Bradford, 1776.

Parker, Kunal M. "Time as Consent: Common Law Thought after the Revolution." *Common Law, History, and Democracy in America, 1790–1900: Legal Thought before Modernism*, 67–116. New York: Cambridge University Press, 2011.

Patterson, Marc R. "Hugh Henry Brackenridge and Representation." In *Authority, Autonomy, and Representation in American Literature, 1776–1865*, 34–60. Princeton, N.J.: Princeton University Press, 2014.

Patterson, Stephen E. "The Federalist Reaction to Shays's Rebellion." In *In Debt to Shays: The Bicentennial of an Agrarian Rebellion*, edited by Robert A. Gross, 101–118. Charlottesville: University Press of Virginia, 1993.

Pearson, Ellen Holmes. *Remaking Custom: Law and Identity in the Early American Republic*. Charlottesville: University of Virginia Press, 2011.

———. "A Work in Progress: Perspectives on the Evolution of American Legal Culture." *Early American Literature* 54. no. 1 (2019): 217–235.

Peart, Daniel Peart, and Adam I. P. Smith. "Afterword." In *Practicing Democracy: Popular Politics in the United States from the Constitution to the Civil War*, edited by Daniel Peart and Adam I. P. Smith, 281–285. Charlottesville: University of Virginia Press, 2015.

Pencak, William. "'The Fine Theoretic Government of Massachusetts Is Prostrated to the Earth': The Response to Shays's Rebellion Reconsidered." In *In Debt to Shays: The Bicentennial of an Agrarian Rebellion*, edited by Robert A. Gross, 121–143. Charlottesville: University Press of Virginia, 1993.

———. "Introduction: A Historical Perspective." In *Riot and Revelry in Early America*, edited by William Pencak, Matthew Dennis, and Simon P. Newman, 3–20. University Park: Pennsylvania State University Press, 2002.

Piker, Joshua. *The Four Deaths of Acorn Whistler: Telling Stories in Colonial America*. Cambridge, Mass.: Harvard University Press, 2013.

Porter, David. "Washington v. Anarchy: A Prelude to the Whiskey Rebellion." *Topic: A Journal of the Liberal Arts* 45 (1994): 7–14.

Pound, Roscoe. *The Spirit of Common Law*. Francestown, N.H.: Marshall Jones, 1921.

Presser, Stephen B. "Original Misunderstanding: The English, the Americans, and the Dialectic of Federalist Constitutional Jurisprudence." *Northwestern University Law Review* 84, no. 1 (1989–1990): 106–185.

———. "A Tale of Two Judges: Richard Peters, Samuel Chase, and the Broken Promise of Federalist Jurisprudence.' *Northwestern University Law Review* 73, no. 1 (1978): 26–111.

Primrose, William. "Biography of William Lewis." *Pennsylvania Magazine of History and Biography* 20, no. 1 (1896): 30–40.

[Randolph, Edmund.] *Germanicus*. Philadelphia, [1794]. Microfiche. Early American Imprints. 1st ser., no. 27597.

Randolph, Edmund. *A Vindication of Mr. Randolph's Resignation*. Philadelphia: Samuel H. Smith, 1795.

Rao, Gautham. "The Federal Posse Comitatus Doctrine: Slavery, Compulsion, and Statecraft in Mid-Nineteenth-Century America." *Law and History Review* 26, no. 1 (2008): 1–56.

Reed, Isaac Ariail. "Between Structural Breakdown and Crisis Action: Interpretation in the Whiskey Rebellion and the Salem Witch Trials." *Critical Historical Studies* 3, no. 1 (2016): 27–64.

Reid, John Phillip. *Constitutional History of the American Revolution*. Vol. 1. Madison: University of Wisconsin Press, 1986.

———. *A Law of Blood: The Primitive Law of the Cherokee Nation*. New York: New York University Press, 1970.

Rich, Bennett M. "Washington and the Whiskey Insurrection." *Pennsylvania Magazine of History and Biography* 65, no. 3 (1941): 334–352.

Ridner, Judith. "Archibald Loudon and the Politics of Print and Indian-Hating in the Early Republic." *Early American Studies* 19, no. 3 (2021): 528–567.

Robertson, Andrew W. "'Look on This Picture . . . And on This!': Nationalism, Localism, and Partisan Images of Otherness in the United States, 1787–1820." *American Historical Review* 106, no. 4 (2001), 1263–1280.

Robreno, Eduardo C. "Learning to do Justice: An Essay on the Development of the Lower Federal Courts in the Early Years of the Republic." *Rutgers Law Journal* 29, no. 3 (1998): 555–578.

Roche, John P. "Loss of American Nationality: The Years of Confusion." *Western Political Quarterly* 4, no. 2 (1951): 268–294.

Roeber, A. G. *Faithful Magistrates and Republican Lawyers: Creators of Virginia Legal Culture, 1680–1810*. Chapel Hill: University of North Carolina Press, 1981.
Rosenberg, Norman L. "Alexander Addison and the Pennsylvania Origins of Federalist First-Amendment Thought." *Pennsylvania Magazine of History and Biography* 108, no. 4 (1984): 399–417.
Ross, Richard J. "The Legal Past of Early New England: Notes for the Study of Law, Legal Culture, and Intellectual History," *William and Mary Quarterly* 50, no. 1 (1993): 28–41.
Rowe, G. S. "Alexander Addison: The Disillusionment of a 'Republican Schoolmaster.'" *Western Pennsylvania Historical Magazine* 62, no. 3 (1979): 221–250.
———. *Embattled Bench: The Pennsylvania Supreme Court and the Forging of a Democratic Society, 1684–1809*. Newark: University of Delaware Press, 1994.
———. *Thomas McKean: The Shaping of an American Republicanism*. Boulder: Colorado University Press, 1978.
Sanderson, James. "Agrarianism in Hugh Henry Brackenridge's Articles for *The Pittsburgh Gazette*." *Early American Literature* 22, no. 3 (1987): 306–319.
Sapienza, Madeline. *Modern Chivalry in Early American Law: H.H. Brackenridge's Legal Thought*. Lanham, Md.: University Press of America, 1992.
Sarat, Austin, and Thomas S. Kearns. "The Cultural Lives of Law." In *Law in the Domains of Culture*, edited by Austin Sarat and Thomas S. Kearns, 1–20. Ann Arbor: University of Michigan Press, 2000.
———, eds. *Law in the Domain of Culture*. Ann Arbor: University of Michigan Press, 1998.
———, eds. *Law in Everyday Life*. Ann Arbor: University of Michigan Press, 1995.
Schoenbachler, Matthew. "Republicanism in the Age of Democratic Revolution: The Democratic-Republican Societies of the 1790s." *Journal of the Early Republic* 18, no. 2 (1998): 237–261.
Schultz, Lucille M. "Uncovering the Significance of the Animal Imagery in *Modern Chivalry*: An Application of Scottish Common Sense Realism." *Early American Literature* 14, no. 3 (1979–1980): 306–311.
Schwartz, Barry. "Social Change and Collective Memory: The Democratization of George Washington." *American Sociological Review* 56, no. 2 (1991): 221–236.
Schwartz, Helene E. "Demythologizing the Historic Role of the Grand Jury." *American Criminal Law Review* 10, no. 4 (1971–1972): 701–770.
Scott, James C. *Domination and the Arts of Resistance: Hidden Transcripts*. New Haven, Conn.: Yale University Press, 1990.
Seed, Geoffrey. *James Wilson*. Millwood, N.Y.: KTO Press, 1978.
Selinger, Jeffrey S. "Rethinking the Development of Legitimate Party Opposition in the United States, 1793–1828." *Political Science Quarterly* 127, no. 2 (2012): 263–287.
Shaffer, Jason. "Making 'an Excellent Die': Death, Mourning, and Patriotism in the Propaganda Plays of the American Revolution." *Early American Literature* 41, no. 1 (2006): 1–27.
Shankman, Andrew. *Crucible of American Democracy: The Struggle to Fuse Egalitarianism and Capitalism in Jeffersonian Pennsylvania*. Lawrence: University Press of Kansas, 2004.

Shapiro, Barbara. *"Beyond Reasonable Doubt" and "Probable Cause": Historical Perspectives on the Anglo-American Law of Evidence.* Berkeley: University of California Press, 1991.

Sharp, James Roger. *American Politics in the Early Republic: The New Nation in Crisis.* New Haven, Conn.: Yale University Press, 1993.

———. "The Whiskey Rebellion and the Question of Representation." In *The Whiskey Rebellion: Past and Present Perspectives,* edited by Steven R. Boyd, 119–143. Westport, Conn.: Greenwood Press, 1985.

Shaw, Peter. *American Patriots and the Rituals of Revolution.* Cambridge, Mass.: Harvard University Press, 1981.

Shogan, Colleen J. "George Washington: Can Aristotle Recapture What His Countrymen Have Forgotten?" In *George Washington: Foundation of Presidential Leadership and Character,* edited by Ethan Fishman, William D. Pederson, and Mark J. Rozell, 53–69. Westport, Conn.: Praeger, 2001.

Silbey, Susan S. "Making a Place for Cultural Analyses of Law." *Law & Social Inquiry* 17, no. 1 (1992): 39–48.

Silver, Peter. *Our Savage Neighbors: How Indian War Transformed Early America.* New York: Norton, 2009.

Simpson, A. W. B. "The Common Law and Legal Theory." In *Folk Law: Essays in the Theory and Practice of "Lex Non Scripta,"* edited by Alison Dundes Renteln and Alan Dundes, 119–138. Vol. 1. Madison: University of Wisconsin Press, 1994.

Simpson, Brooks D. "President Washington's Appointments to the Supreme Court." *Journal of Supreme Court History* 17, no. 7 (1992): 63–74.

Sioli, Marco M. "The Democratic Republican Societies at the End of the Eighteenth Century: The Western Pennsylvania Experience." *Pennsylvania History: A Journal of Mid-Atlantic Studies* 60, no. 3 (1993): 288–304.

Sizemore, Michelle. "George Washington vs. the Phantom: Rival Sovereigns and Long Eighteenth-Century Insurrection." In *American Enchantment: Rituals of the People in the Post-Revolutionary World,* 43–74. Oxford: Oxford University Press, 2018.

Slaughter, Thomas P. "Crowds in Eighteenth-Century America: Reflections and New Directions." *Pennsylvania Magazine of History and Biography* 115, no. 1 (1991): 3–34.

———. "The Friends of Liberty, the Friends of Order, and the Whiskey Rebellion." In *The Whiskey Rebellion: Past and Present Perspectives,* edited by Steven R. Boyd, 9–30. Westport, Conn.: Greenwood Press, 1985.

———. "'The King of Crimes': Early American Treason Law, 1787–1860." In *Launching the "Extended Republic": The Federalist Era,* edited by Ronald Hoffman and Peter Albert, 54–135. Charlottesville: University of Virginia Press, 1996.

———. "The Tax Man Cometh: Ideological Opposition to Internal Taxes, 1760–1790." *William and Mary Quarterly* 41, no. 4 (1984): 566–591.

———. *The Whiskey Rebellion: Frontier Epilogue to the American Revolution.* New York: Oxford University Press, 1986.

Smith, James Morton. "The *Aurora* and the Alien and Sedition Laws, Part I: The Editorship of Benjamin Franklin Bache." *Pennsylvania Magazine of History and Biography* 77, no. 1 (1953): 3–23.

———. "The *Aurora* and the Alien and Sedition Laws, Part II: The Editorship of William Duane." *Pennsylvania Magazine of History and Biography* 77, no. 2 (1953): 123–155.

Snyder, Henry L. "Charges to Grand Juries: The Evidence of the Eighteenth-Century Short-Title Catalogue." *Historical Research* 67, no. 164 (1994): 286–300.
Spero, Patrick. *Frontier Country: The Politics of War in Early Pennsylvania*. Philadelphia: University of Pennsylvania Press, 2016.
Steilen, Matthew. "Bills of Attainder." *Houston Law Review* 53, no. 3 (2016): 767–897.
———. "The Democratic Common Law." *Journal Jurisprudence* 10 (July 2011): 437–486.
———. "Reason, the Common Law, and the Living Constitution." *Legal Theory* 17, no. 4 (2011): 279–300.
Steinberg, Allen. "'The Spirit of Litigation': Private Prosecution and Criminal Justice in Nineteenth Century Philadelphia." *Journal of Social History*, 20, no. 2 (1986): 231–249.
———. *The Transformation of Criminal Justice: Philadelphia, 1800–1880*. Chapel Hill: University of North Carolina Press, 1989.
Stephens, Beth. "Federalism and Foreign Affairs: Congress's Power to 'Define and Punish ... Offenses against the Law of Nations.'" *William and Mary Law Review* 42, no. 2 (2000): 447–558.
Stephens, Bret. "This Is the Other Way That History Ends." *New York Times*, 31 August 2022, A-19. Op-ed.
Stimson, Shannon C. *The American Revolution in the Law: Anglo-American Jurisprudence before John Marshall*. Princeton, N.J: Princeton University Press, 1990.
Storing, Herbert J., ed. *The Complete Anti-Federalist*. Vol. 3. Chicago: University of Chicago Press, 1981.
Surrency, Erwin C. "Law Reports in the United States." *The American Journal of Legal History* 25, no. 1 (1981): 48–66.
Sweet, James H. "Is History History? Identity Politics and Teleologies of the Present." *Perspectives on History*, 60, no. 5A (August 19, 2022).
Sword, Wiley. *President Washington's Indian War: The Struggle for the Old Northwest, 1790–1795*. Norman: University of Oklahoma Press, 1985.
Tachau, Mary K. Bonsteel. *Federal Courts in the Early Republic: Kentucky, 1789–1816*. Princeton, N.J.: Princeton University Press, 1978.
———. "George Washington and the Reputation of Edmund Randolph." *Journal of American History* 73, no. 1 (1986): 15–34.
———. "A New Look at the Whiskey Rebellion." In *The Whiskey Rebellion: Past and Present Perspectives*, edited by Steven R. Boyd, 97–118. Westport, Conn.: Greenwood Press, 1985.
———. "Treason and the 'Whiskey Insurrection.'" *Historic U.S. Court Cases: An Encyclopedia*. London: Routledge, 2001.
Taylor, Alan. "'The Art of Hook & Snivey': Political Culture in Upstate New York during the 1790s." *Journal of American History* 79, no. 4 (1993): 1371–1396.
———. "Land and Liberty on the Post-Revolutionary Frontier." In *Devising Liberty: Preserving and Creating Freedom in the New American Republic*, edited by David Thomas Konig, 81–108. Stanford, Calif.: Stanford University Press, 1995.
———. "Regulators and White Indians: Forms of Agrarian Resistance in Post-Revolutionary New England." In *In Debt to Shays: The Bicentennial of an Agrarian Rebellion*, edited by Robert A. Gross, 145–160. Charlottesville: University Press of Virginia, 1993.

Thomas, Suja A. "Blackstone's Curse: The Fall of the Criminal, Civil, and Grand Juries and the Rise of the Executive, the Legislature, the Judiciary, and the States." *William and Mary Law Review* 55, no. 3 (2014): 1195–1239.

Thompson, E. P. "The Moral Economy of the English Crowd in the Eighteenth Century." *Past and Present* 50, nc. 1 (1971): 76–136.

———. *Whigs and Hunters: The Origin of the Black Act*. New York: Pantheon Books, 1975.

Tomlins, Christopher L., and Bruce H. Mann, eds. *The Many Legalities of Early America*. Chapel Hill: University of North Carolina Press, 2020.

Tucker, St. George. *Blackstone's Commentaries: with Notes of Reference, to the Constitution and Laws, of the Federal Government of the United States*. 5 vols. Philadelphia: W. Y. Birch and A. Small, R. Carr, 1803.

Twitty, Anne. *Before Dred Scott: Slavery and Legal Culture in the American Confluence, 1787–1857*. New York: Cambridge University Press, 2016.

Urwin, Gregory J. A. "'The Army of the Constitution': The Military, American Values, and the Early Republic." *Foreign Policy Institute Footnotes* (March 9, 2012): 1–5.

Van den Bergh, G. C. J. J. "The Concept of Folk Law in Historical Context: A Brief Outline." In *Folk Law: Essays in the Theory and Practice of "Lex Non Scripta,"* edited by Alison Dundes Renteln and Alan Dundes, 5–32. Vol. 1. Madison: University of Wisconsin Press, 1994.

Van der Linden, Saunder, Costas Panagopoulos, Flavio Azevedo, and John T. Jost. "The Paranoid Style in American Politics Revisited: An Ideological Asymmetry in Conspiratorial Thinking." *Political Psychology* 42, no. 1 (2021): 23–51.

Walsham, Alexandra. "Rough Music and Charivari: Letters Between Natalie Zemon Davis and Edward Thompson, 1970–1972. Essay." *Past and Present* 235, no. 1 (2017): 243–248.

Washburn, Kevin K. "Restoring the Grand Jury." *Fordham Law Review* 76, no. 5 (2008): 2333–2346.

Waterman, Julius S. "Thomas Jefferson and Blackstone's Commentaries." In *Essays in the History of Early American Law*, edited by David H. Flaherty, 451–488. Chapel Hill: University of North Carolina Press, 1969.

Watson, Alan. "An Approach to Customary Law." In *Folk Law: Essays in the Theory and Practice of "Lex Non Scripta,"* edited by Alison Dundes Renteln and Alan Dundes, 141–157. Vol. I. Madison: University of Wisconsin Press, 1994.

Watson, Andrew. "Changes in American Court Advocacy during the Long Nineteenth Century: Classical Influences, their Decline, Similarities and Comparisons with England and Wales." *Journal of European History of Law* 2, no. 1 (2020): 14–21.

Watts, Edward. "'If Indians Can Have Treaties, Why Cannot We Have One Too?'" In *Messy Beginnings: Postcoloniality and Early American Studies*, edited by Malini Johar Schueller and Edward Watts, 31–102. New Brunswick, N.J.: Rutgers University Press, 2003.

Webster, Noah. "An Examination into the Leading Principles of the Federal." In *Pamphlets on the Constitution of the United States*, edited by Paul Leicester Ford, 25–65. Philadelphia: Prichard & Hall, 1888.

Webster, Richard. *Philadelphia Preserved: Catalog of the Historic American Buildings Survey*. Philadelphia: Temple University Press. 1976.

White, Ed. *The Backcountry and the City: Colonization and Conflict in America*. Minneapolis: University of Minnesota Press, 2005.
White, G. Edward. *Law in American History: From the Colonial Years through the Civil War*. Oxford: Oxford University Press, 2012.
White, Hayden. *The Content of the Form: Narrative Discourse and Historical Representation*. Baltimore: Johns Hopkins University Press, 1987.
White, James Boyd. *Justice as Translation: An Essay in Cultural and Legal Criticism*. Chicago: University of Chicago Press, 1990.
White, Kenneth A. "'Such Disorders Can Only be Cured by Copious Bleedings': The Correspondence of Isaac Craig during the Whiskey Rebellion." *Western Pennsylvania Historical Magazine* 67, no. 3 (1984): 213–242.
Wilf, Steven. "The First Republican Revival: Virtue, Judging, and Rhetoric in the Early Republic." *Connecticut Law Review* 32, no. 5 (2000): 1675–1698.
———. *Law's Imagined Republic: Popular Politics and Criminal Justice in Revolutionary America*. Cambridge: Cambridge University Press, 2010.
———. "The Invention of Legal Primitivism." *Theoretical Inquiries in Law* 10, no. 2 (2009): 485–510.
Wilkinson, Norman. *Land Policy and Speculation in Pennsylvania, 1779–1800: A Test of the New Democracy*. 1958. Reprint. New York: Arno Press, 1979.
Williams, Mildred. "Hugh Henry Brackenridge as a Judge of the Supreme Court of Pennsylvania, 1799–1816." *Western Pennsylvania Historical Magazine* 10, no. 4 (1927): 210–223.
Williams, Robert A., Jr. "The Algebra of Federal Indian Law: The Hard Trail of Decolonizing and Americanizing the White Man's Jurisprudence." In *Reading American Indian Law: Foundational Principles*, edited by Grant Christensen and Melissa L. Tatum, 47–71. Cambridge: Cambridge University Press, 2020.
Wills, Garry. *Cincinnatus: George Washington and the Enlightenment*. Garden City: Doubleday, 1984.
Wilmarth, Arthur E., Jr. "Elusive Foundation: John Marshall, James Wilson, and the Problem of Reconciling Popular Sovereignty and Natural Law Jurisprudence in the New Federal Republic." *George Washington Law Review* 72, nos. 1–2 (2003): 113–193.
Wilson, David A. "Introduction." *William Cobbett, Peter Porcupine in America: Pamphlets on Republicanism and Revolution*, 1–49. Ithaca, N.Y.: Cornell University Press, 1994.
Wilson, James. *A Charge Delivered by that Hon. James Wilson, Esq. to the Grand Jury, Impannelled for the Circuit Court of the United States, Holden for the Middle Circuit at the Capital in the City of Richmond, and District of Virginia*. Richmond: Augustine Davis, 1791.
———. "Charge of the Hon. James Wilson, esq. Judge of the Federal Circuit Court for the District of Pennsylvania, to the Grand Jury of Said Court, delivered April 12, 1790." *American Museum, or Universal Magazine* 7 (1790), Appendix 2, 35–42.
———. "Of Crimes, Immediately against the Community." In *The Works of James Wilson*, edited by R. G. McCloskey, 663–668. Vol. 2. Cambridge, Mass.: Belknap Press, 1967.
Wilson, James, and Thomas M'Kean. *Commentaries on the Constitution of the United States of America, with that Constitution Prefixed, in Which are Unfolded, the Principles*

of Free Government, and the Superior Advantage of Republicanism Demonstrated. London: J. Debrett, J. Johnson, and J. S. Jordan, 1792.

Wood, Gordon S. "Conspiracy and the Paranoid Style: Causality and Deceit in the Eighteenth Century." *William and Mary Quarterly* 39, no. 3 (1982): 401–441.

———. *Empire of Liberty: A History of the Early Republic, 1789–1815.* Oxford: Oxford University Press, 2009.

———. "The Greatness of George Washington." *Virginia Quarterly Review* 68, no. 2 (1992): 189–207.

———. "A Note on Mobs in the American Revolution." *William and Mary Quarterly* 23, no. 4 (1966): 635–642.

———. *The Radicalism of the American Revolution.* New York: Vintage, 1991.

Woodman, Gordon R. "Some Realism about Customary Law—The West African Experience." In *Folk Law: Essays in the Theory and Practice of "Lex Non Scripta,"* edited by Alison Dundes Renteln and Alan Dundes, 83–110. Vol. 1. Madison: University of Wisconsin Press, 1994.

Yazzie, Robert. "'Life Comes from It': Navajo Justice Concepts." In *Reading American Indian Law,* edited by Grant Christensen and Melissa L. Tatum, 121–139. Cambridge: Cambridge University Press, 2020.

Young, Henry J. "Treason and Punishment in Revolutionary Pennsylvania." *Pennsylvania Magazine of History and Biography* 90, no. 3 (1966): 287–313.

Younger, Richard D. "Grand Juries and the American Revolution." *Virginia Magazine of History and Biography* 63, no. 3 (1955): 257–268.

———. "The Grand Jury Under Attack." *Journal of Criminal Law, Criminology, and Police Science* 46, no. 1 (1955): 26–49.

INDEX

Adams, John: on assemblies, 86; grants pardon, 81
Addison, Alexander, 27, 41; on arbitration, 75–76; attacked by Hamilton, 32, 41, 71, 138; biography, 86; compared to Husband, 139; conflicted, 71–72; on "constitutional resistance," 41–42, 138; conversion to Federalist, 86, 136, 138; on democratic rights, 86–87; grand jury charges, 136–139; impeachment, 272n165; indicts rebellion, 137–138; Jay Treaty, 50; as judge, 86; judicial activities, 65–72; law reports and Brackenridge, 295–296n31; on liberty poles as crime, 111, 137; resentment against, 71; supervising western courts, 137
agitation-propaganda, 8, 15, 21; as legal culture, 125; in popular culture, 98–99; Tom the Tinker, 114
Alien and Sedition Acts, 151–152, 266n18
allegiance, 17, 222–224; legitimacy of, 207
American Revolution, 4, 7–8, 15, 39–40; bills of attainder, 95; committees of safety, 106; compared to Whiskey Rebellion, 294n169; culture and, 99; debts, 53; distinguished from rebellion, 84; grand juries in, 133; inversion of, 245; legacy of, 158, 207, 234, 240 as precedent, 131, 151; representation, 85; secession and, 207; shift from, 139; themes, 108; trials, 282n87; vindication, 50
Ames, Fisher, 50, 86
Anti-Federalism, 9, 15; minority ratification report, 62–63
Anti-Federalists, 3, 8, 58, 60–65; in assemblies, 80–81; on political meetings, 87–88; western, 62, 70, 81
arbitration, 74–76
assemblies, rebel, 3–6, 16; Anti-Federalists in, 62; assembling with arms, 88–90; associational rights, 85–86; Braddock's Field, 5, 87, 91–93; Brownsville (Old Redstone Fort), 6, 29, 87, 93–95; Committee of Safety, 94; compared to militia, 90; constituencies, 79–80, 271n138; Couch's, 5; courts in, 90–96; customary liberties, 79; defined, 79–80; discourse, 8; elite participation, 83; factions, 79, 83; First Amendment rights, 90; government perspective on, 90–91; history of, 80; leadership, 79, 82; link to democratic societies, 77–78; meetings, 4–5, 80; middling class influence, 82–83; Mingo Creek, 5; organizational structure, 80; Parkinson's, 5, 87, 92–93; peoples' rights, 79, 85–86; popular agency, 58; popular sovereignty, 240; radical mob influence, 5, 80, 82; representation, 85; role in rebellion, 90; value of, 240
"Atticus," 51

backcountry, 7–8, 12, 16, 59, 62; Brackenridge on, 119; democracy in, 206; instability of courts, 72, 77; militia units, 89; oppositionality, 257–258n16
banditry, 32–33, 36, 52–53; "banditti," 32–33, 36, 102
bill of attainder, 95, 142
bill of rights, 63, 179

"Black Boys," 101, 245
Blackstone, William, 3; adopting English law, 219; applying English law, 219; common law, 142; constructive treason, 216–217; expatriation, 225–226; on grand juries, 133; influence of, 243; on words, 293n163
Blair, John: heated rhetoric, 150–151; grand jury charge, 150–151
Brackenridge, Hugh Henry, 22; in Addison's law reports, 295–296n31; allegiance, 222–224; Anti-Federalist burlesque, 63; on arbitration, 75–76; as author of "The Indian Treaty," 104, 107; biography, 213–214, 296–297n49, 300n112; on Bradford, 91; on *Burr*, 227–230; common law, 298n83; constitutional definition, 220–222; as defense counsel, 211, 213–216, 297n55; defense of Presley Neville, 93; defense of Samuel Jackson, 93–95; democracy, 223; on democratic societies, 77–78; expatriation, 224–227; Federalist, 84; French Revolution, 223; humor, 115–118; on Indian treaties, 100; judicial construction, 216–219; on law reports, 132; on Marshall, 227–230; on Neville and Woods, 166; organizing assemblies, 80; precedent, 219–220, 299n95, 299n97; *quo animo*, 222; rebel leader, 84, 270n127; satirizing law, 121–123; secession, 223, 226–227; treason notes, 210–213, 297n55; on West, 100–101; western lawyer, 68–69, 71
—works: "Death of General Montgomery," 118; "Dissertation on Treason Law," 295n20; "Expediency of a Pardon," 212, 214; *Law Miscellanies*, 72, 219–220; *Modern Chivalry*, 72, 118–123, 219–220, 222–224, 227, 298n85; "Thoughts on the Excise Law," 100–101
Braddock's Field, 87; courts in, 91–93
Bradford, David, 5; on assembly court, 92; biography, 81; on evidence, 167; as rebel leader, 26, 270–271n130; "Robespiere," 91; secession, 106; stealing U.S. mail, 91
Bradford, William, 38–39, 91; on death penalty, 205; on liberty poles as crime, 110; prosecutor, 136
Brownsville, 87; courts in, 93–95
"Brutus," 63
Butler, trial in assembly court, 91–92

"Centinel," 64
Chase, Samuel, grand jury charge, 153
"Citizen, A," 64

Clymer, George, 23–27, 29; cowardice, 259n14; instructions to Addison, 66; supervising collections in West, 25–27
Cobbett, William: on democratic societies, 39, 50–51; Hydra, 245–246; *Porcupine's Gazette*, 50–51; on Tom the Tinker, 115; on western rebellion, 39, 51
colonialization, 7–8
"combinations," 36–37, 52–53, 245
Commission, Pennsylvania, 5, 71, 268n79
Commission, U.S., 5–6, 30, 71; "The Indian treaty" and, 104; instructions, 37; report, 6, 35, 37; military force and, 262n81; protests against, 69–70, 104; rebels as Indians, 102–104
communication, 21–23; audience, 33–34; Hamilton's rhetoric, 34; Washington's information campaign, 47–48
conference, presidential, 30, 37–39; cabinet reports, 30; resistance by Pennsylvania officials, 67
"constitutional resistance," 4, 5, 39, 41–43, 52, 55; Addison on, 41–42; Hamilton on, 39, 41–43
Cornplanter, Chief, 100, 104, 116
"Correspondents," 51
courts, 58; arbitration, 15, 60, 74–76; assembly courts, 59, 90–96; colonial courts, 60; confidence in, 72–73; county courts, 15, 60, 71–72; debt courts, 76; democratic society courts, 59, 76–78; establishment western courts, 269n83; extralegal courts, 15, 60; federal courts, 11, 71; federal-state court conflicts, 64, 66, 70–71, 266n18; militia courts, 15, 78–79; Pennsylvania courts, 65–71; popular courts, 59; popular participation, 58, 60, 73–79; private prosecution, 15, 60; rebel courts, 15; state courts, 60, 70–71; western courts, 60, 76
Coxe, Tench, 25, 50; on right to bear arms, 88
Craig, Isaac, 92; biography of, 92; in Neville's circle, 92; trial in assembly court, 92, 117
culture: complementing cultures, 98; conflicting cultures, 11–12, 14, 125–126; cultural activity, 99; cultural language, 125; cultural resistance, 123–126; inventions, 123; legal, 9–10, 12–14, 98, 123–124, 238, 242–243; official, formal, 10, 14; popular, 7–8, 11, 79; shaping effect, 243; traditions, 98, 123; unofficial, informal, 10, 14, 125; vernacular, 22, 98
Cushing, William, grand jury charges, 152–153

INDEX 333

Dallas, Alexander, 46, 67; on arbitration, 75; law reports, 75; on Paterson, 148–149, political offices, 284n130
"Death of General Montgomery" (Brackenridge), 118
Defalcation Statute (1705), 75
defense, rebel, 207–213; allegiance, 222–224; argument, 210; Brackenridge as counsel, 213–216; *Burr*, 227–230; Constitution, 220–222; expatriation, 224–227; judicial construction, 216–219; Marshall, 227–230; precedent, 219–220; 216; treason law, 216–219
democracy, 2, 11–12, 49, 51–53, 58, 59; Anti-Federalism and, 62, 81; backcountry, 246; Brackenridge on, 119; contemporary democracy, 246–249; cultural value of, 263n96; democratic constitutionalism, 85; democratic populism, 158; democratic vision, 234; intermediaries, 263n96; local, 75; participation, 4, 17, 206, 207; rebel democracy, 126; representation, 16, 79; test of, 44; threat to, 40, 246–249
democratic societies, 3, 36, 39–40, 47–48, 50– 51; connected to Whiskey Rebellion, 40, 152; Democratic Society of Washington, 40, 270n116; German Republican Society, 85; linked to assemblies, 77–78; Mingo Creek Society, 76–78, 269n110, 269n113; Mouth of the Yough Society, 77–78; reviled by Washington, 28, 40, 48–49; similar to American Revolution, 28; society constitutions, 77–78; society courts, 59, 76–78
"Democritus," 78
"Dissertation on Treason Law" (Brackenridge), 295n20
Dixon v. Morehead (1794), 75

Eastern Pennsylvania Circuit Court, Philadelphia, 16, 152–153, 156, 172
Edgar, John, 62; Anti-Federalist, 84; organizing assemblies, 80; rebel leader, 84, 270n127
elite, 9, 16, 21, 24–26, 39, 54–57, 61; in assemblies, 82, 271n138; leaders, 271n142, 271–272n145; in population, 271nn141–142
Erie, Lake, 7, 105
evidence: army's judicial arm and, 162; problems of, 161–168
Ex Parte Bollman (1807), 228
Ex Parte Corbly; Lockery; Hamilton; Sedgewick (1795), 289n80

Ex Parte Swartwout (1807), 228
exceptionalism, 140, 156–157, 207
Excise Act (1791), 170, 288n59; amendment (1794), 170, 288n60
"Expediency of a Pardon" (Brackenridge), 212, 214
"experiment," 15, 54; as test, 24–25, 29–31, 33

Fauchet, Jean Antoine Joseph, 34–35, 51
Faulkner, William, 24, 66, 136
federal army: federal militia, 4–6, 15, 31, 35–37, 44; standing army, 50–51, 54, 88–89; timeline, 262nn81–82, 286–287n2
federalism, 2, 9, 39
Federalists, 2, 8, 40, 54, 58; on dissenting meetings, 86; fear of state courts, 64–65; Federalist judges, 130, 132–133, 135, 153
Ferguson, Robert A., 223, 243
Findley, William, 22, 62; on assemblies, 273n175; biography, 80–81; conflict with Hamilton, 33–34, 165; countering Hamilton's narrative, 33–35, 37; on democratic societies, 77–78; on evidence, 166; on "The Indian Treaty," 104; on judicial arm of army, 164–165; on liberty poles as crime, 110; on militia, 89; as "Nestor," 80; nickname "Monongahela,' 27; on political meetings, 87; political representative, 261n60; as rebel leader, 26, 270n128
First Amendment, 2, 9, 62; distinguishing riot, 70; legal case, 69–70
French Revolution, 3, 39, 151, 246; Brackenridge on, 119; grand juries on, 156; Paterson on, 202
Fries, Case of (1799), 141, 153; Fries's Rebellion, 6, 152; vicinage in, 172
frontier, 8, 21, 53; frontier justice, 11, 61; "frontier theory," 230; instability, 72, 100; liminality, 102; order, 75

Gallatin, Albert, 62, Anti-Federalism, 83; on assemblies, 273n175; on democracy and Washington, 264n128; on juries, 134–135; on liberty poles as crime, 110; on militia and Washington, 264n128; opinion of Bradford, 81; organizing assemblies, 80; on political meetings, 87–88; political office, 288n38; political representative, 261n58; rebel leader, 26, 83–85, 270n127; source for rebel trials, 290n93; speech to Pennsylvania Assembly, 33
Gaston, John, 115
George Washington v. James Scott, et al. (1786), 7

Graham, William, 32, 68, 114
grand jury, 16; Addison's charges, 136–139; authority of judges, 132–135; Blair's charges, 150–151; charges of, 16, 135, 279n4, 279n11, 280nn14–15; Chase's charges, 153; compared to assemblies, 158; Cushing's charges, 152–153; effect on government, 133; Federalists and, 280n24; independence of jury, 133–134; Iredell's charges, 152; jury composition, 134; jury statements, 16; legal sources, 131–132; makeup of, 134–135; McKean and Oswald, 280n16; packing, 280n21, 280n26; Paterson's charges, 144–150; Peters's charges, 136, 139–141; power of, 133–134; precursor to trials, 157, 160; Republicans and, 280n24; role of, 133

Hamilton (Miranda), 1–2, 257n1
Hamilton, Alexander: agitating for use of force, 27, 29, 33, 42; ambition, 2, 35; author of proclamations, 260n24; discourse of, 33–34, 43; on gathering evidence, 166, 287n24; influence on Washington, 38, 45–46; instructions to General Lee, 163–164; judicial narrative and, 153; liberty poles and, 110; narrative of, 35, 39, 41–43; provoking rebellion, 34–35; report to Washington (August 5, 1794), 14–15, 22, 30–33, 261n48; report to Washington (September 2, 1794), 32, 39, 41; role in accompanying militia, 30–31, 34, 164–165; stratagems, 35; on Tom the Tinker, 112; "Tully," 42–43, 53; use of "Whiskey Insurrection," 259n48
Henfield's case (1793), 224–225
Holcroft, John: as Tom the Tinker, 111–112; witness in rebel trials, 293n149
humor: in assemblies, 115–118; *Modern Chivalry*, 118–123
Husband, Herman: antipathy toward, 199; attends assemblies, 281n58; biography, 199; compared to Addison, 139; trial of, 87; utopian preacher, 271n137
Hydra, 8, 245–246

"Indian Treaty, The," 104–107; New Jersey in, 106–107
Indians, 7, 8, 61; blackening, 101–102; Delaware, 7; in disguise, 101–102; going native, 56, 102; identity of, 99–104; Indian conferences, 104–105; "The Indian Treaty" satire, 104–107; inferiority of, 101; Iroquois Confederation, 7; the "other," 101; rebels as, 102–104; Shawnee, 7; wars, 54; western, 99–101; white Indians, 15–16, 61, 101–102, 104–105
Iredell, James: grand jury charge, 151–152; on rebellion, 152; Wilson's influence, 289n78

Jackson, Samuel, assembly trial, 93–95
Jay, John, 23, 27
Jay Treaty, 50–51
Jefferson, Thomas, 17, 43; on *Burr*, 227–228
judges, 74; authority of, 132; in circuit court, 281n36; in debt courts, 76; in early republic, 132, 297n61; Federalist, 11, 16, 130, 132–133, 135; grand jury judges, 153–154; mixed functions with jury, 201; prominence of, 161; role of, 154
Judiciary Act (1789), 62; federal jurisdiction, 65; judicial reform, 65; reliance on, 288n62; state jurisdiction, 65
juries, 73–74; challenges, 280n28; Gallatin on, 134–135; jury composition, 134; jury of neighbors, 134, 162; jury statements, 138–139, 153–156, 286n153; on rebellion, 155, 157; relationship with judges, 154–155; role of, 154–155; western jurors, 280n29
justice: alternate forms of, 74–76; popular, 15, 60, 73, 76, 96; rough, 16, 60, 101; vernacular, 95

Kent, James, 132
Kentucky, 6, 30, 61, 106
Kirby, Ephraim, 209
Kirkpatrick, James, 91; expulsion, 93; in Neville's circle, 91
Knox, Henry, 35, 38, 92; military reform, 273n186

Lake Erie, 7, 105
law: common law, 16; constructions, 161; debtors, 61; English law, 16; evolution of, 157; extralegal, 15; federal-state conflict, 68, 160–161, 178; as frame, 243; history of, 16, 141–144; jurisdiction, 59; legal mechanisms, 97; legal practices, 60; legal primitivism, 7–8; legal profession, 207–210; official law, 96; officials, 61, 63; participation in, 59–60, 74–75, 79; popular acceptance, 59, 61, 71–73, 96; popular law, 73, 96; private prosecution, 74; reasonable doubt, 284n118; representation, 207; sources, 139; statutory law, 16; in transition, 130–131; treatises, 209; unofficial law, 79, 95–96

Law Miscellanies (Brackenridge), 72, 219–220
law reports, 68, 132, 173, 186, 189–190, 200; Brackenridge on, 209; Dallas on, 209; Kent and, 132; Kirby on, 209; publication of, 294n7; state of, 208–209
Lenox, David, 5, 69
Lessee of Samuel Dixon v. Samuel Morehead (1794), 75–76, 269n104
Lewis, William: on evidence, 168; on inconvenience, 171, 172; as rebel lawyer, 161–162; in treason trials, 296n45, 297n51
liberty poles, 107–111; as crime, 110–111 failure to criminalize, 276n63; flags, 108, 276n50; legal case, 69–70; liberty tree, 51; as message, 109; origin of, 108; slogans, 108; traditions, 108–109; ubiquity, 109
localism, 2, 8, 11, 15, 21–22, 54; extreme, 75, 95–96; jurisdictional conflicts, 59; local conditions, 65–66

Madison, James, 40; on vicinage, 170
Marshall, James, 62; Anti-Federalist, 81; biography, 81; as rebel leader, 26, 81, 270–271n130
Marshall, John, 16; in *Burr*, 16, 227–230, 301–302n167; on Paterson, 228–230; on treason law, 229–230
McKean, Thomas, 46, 67, 70; on arbitration, 75; on extrajudicial practices, 75; trampling on laws, 139
Mifflin, Thomas, 46; chastised by Randolph, 67–68, 288n37; directives to state judiciary, 66–67; on evidence, 167–168; on military power, 67; Presqu'Isle, 50
militia, 5, 16, 38–39; Anti-Federalist fear of, 63; authorization, 52, 68; community regulators, 8, 88–89; compared to assembly, 90 courts, 78–79; justification, 51; link to assemblies, 78; link to democratic societies, 77–78; musters and assemblies, 273n177; New Jersey, 104, 106–107, 146; nullification, 89; radical aspect, 273n184; relation to rebellion, 88, 93; right to insurrection, 88; second amendment right, 2, 9, 88; state recruitment, 274n187; trial argument on, 88–89. *See* federal army
Militia Act (1792), 52, 89, 245; Brackenridge on, 299n106
"Militia Man, A," 138
Miranda, Lin-Manuel, 1–2
Mitchell, John, opinions on character of, 181

mobs, 5, 11, 32, 39–40; in assemblies, 80, 93; Brackenridge on, 119–120; crowds, 61; culture and, 98; mentality, 54
Modern Chivalry (Brackenridge), 72, 118–123, 219–220, 222–224, 227, 298n85
Morris' Lessee v. Vanderen (1782), 298n83

narratives, 3, 10, 14–15; abstraction, 53, 57; appeal of, 53; assessing, 52, 57; backstory, 53; competing, 11–16, 245; compositional process, 54–55; on French Revolution, 156; government, 11, 22–29, 36–43, 52–53, 159–160, 204, 241–242; government discourse, 9, 23, 46–47; government "story," 46–47, 54–55; inversion, 56; judicial, 16, 150–161, 203–204, 241–242; lessons, 47; motivation, 53–54; official legitimacy, 55; oppositionality, 55, 57; rebel, 96, 240–242; rebel perspective, 2–4, 9, 16–17, 58–59; rebel self-presentation, 126; rebel status, 244–245; simplification, 56; Washington's construction, 51
nation: national authority, 60–61, 173; national government, 52, 54, 58; nationalizing, 22, 60, 207; nation-building, 50; nationhood, 16
"Nestor," 44
Neville, John, 5, 22–25, 29, 114; attack on Bower Hill home, 5, 78, 296n45; biography, 23–24; "connection," 24, 82–83; serving writs, 69; threat to allegiance, 50
Neville, Presley: assembly court trial, 92–93; biography, 92; militia and, 79, 92
North Carolina, 6, 30

Ohio Valley, 61, 106

pardons, 147, 164
Parkinson's Ferry, 87; assembly court at, 92–93
Paterson, William: appointment as justice, 145, 283n111; bench notes, 186–190, 200–201; biography, 144–145; as conservative, 157–158; on Constitution, 149; constructivist tendencies, 147, 149; example as judge, 140; fear of systemic threat, 293n167; as Federalist, 202; on Foster, 291n131; on French Revolution, 202; grand jury charges, 135, 144–150; Horatius essays, 201–202; judicial approach, 147–148, 293n156; message of, 157; notes on *Barnet*, 193–197; notes on *Miller*, 197–198; notes on *Philson and Husband*, 198–200; notes on

Paterson, William (*continued*)
  Porter, 190–193, 292n147; partisan conduct, 201–202; performance in rebel trials, 145, 147, 157, 187, 283–284n117, 284–285n131; political offices, 284n127, 293n165; political theory of, 158; report to Washington, 203; reputation, 145; restraint, 150; on Tom the Tinker, 112; *U.S. v. Mitchell*, 147; *Vanhorne's Lessee*, 148–149, 157; views on insurrection, 146–147, 149–150; witnesses in bench notes, 292n144, 292–293n148
Penn, William: Penn's peace, 7; proprietorship, 7, 74
Pennsylvania v. Charles Craig, Adam Craig, and four others (1794), 68
Pennsylvania v. Jacob Cribs, Daniel Harold, and eleven others (1795), 70
Pennsylvania v. Norris Morrison et al. (1795), 69; on liberty poles, 111
Peters, Richard, 11; accompanying militia, 140; on *Fries's* bench, 282n69; grand jury charges, 136, 139–141; on jurisdiction, 140, 171; performance in treason trials, 140–141; prosecutorial justice, 140; on rebellion, 152; use of district court, 140; Washington's "Instructions," 163–164; as witness, 289n75
Philson, Robert, trial of, 87
Pittsburgh meeting, 25–29, 41–42
political parties, 271n134
Porter, Robert: on liberty poles as crime, 110; trial of, 190–193
Primer v. Kuhn (1789), 75
procedural issues, 173–177; habeas corpus, 174–175; indictment caption, 175; jury disclosures, 175; jury selection, 175–177; makeup of juries, 175–177; venire, 177; voir dire, 177
proclamations: September 15, 1792, 27, 29; August 7, 1794, 33, 35–37, 39; September 15, 1794, 43–44, 47; September 25, 1794, 37

Randolph, Edmund, 23, 37–39; advice to Washington, 45; conflict with Hamilton, 27–28, 30–31, 34; on evidence, 167–168; "Germanicus," 48–49, 53, 264n123, 264n132; on Hamilton's report, 261n49; legal advice, 27–28, 55, 87; political offices, 287n32; scandal with Fauchet, 51, 260n42; on vicinage, 170
ratification, 6, 9, 61–62, 267n25
Rawle, William: political office, 297n53; prosecutor, 136; shortcomings, 289n83; on Tom the Tinker, 112

rebellion, 4–6; despotic democracy and, 158–159; interactive with Constitution, 158
Republicans, 2, 58, 64; Republican judges, 132
Respublica v. Abraham Carlisle (1778), 142–143, 282n87
Respublica v. John Roberts (1778), 142–143, 282n87
Rousseau, Jean-Jacques, 224

secession, 15, 24, 51, 245
Second Amendment, 2, 9
Sedition Act, 40, 86, 152; targets of trials, 295n28
settlers, 53–54, 65
7 William III (1685), 221
Shays's Rebellion, 6; as archetype, 158; compared to Whiskey Rebellion, 159
Smilie, John, 62; rebel leader, 26
South Carolina, 6, 30
spies: Hamilton's, 23–27, 29–31; rebel, 114

taxation, 57; antitax movement, 58; Brackenridge on western, 100–101
"Thoughts on the Excise Law" (Brackenridge), 100–101
Tom the Tinker, 111–115; as author of "The Indian treaty," 104; in disguise, 102; identity of, 112–113; intimidation, 112–114; liberty poles and, 109; Reed on, 113; retires, 115; Scull on, 113; term "Tinker," 112; trial by press, 113
traditions, 15–16; invented, 98–99; prior traditions, 99
treason: common law, 141–142; constitutional definition, 143–144; history of, 141–143; law, 11, 141–143; Madison on, 144; 1777 Pennsylvania law, 142–143; Tucker on, 144; Wilson on, 143–144. *See also* Brackenridge, Hugh Henry; Paterson, William; trials, Whiskey Rebellion
Treason Act (1696), 142, 179
Treason Act, Pennsylvania (1777), 142–143, 177–179, 290n105
trials, Whiskey Rebellion, 177–203; on act of war, 293n161; audience of, 204; bench notes, 16, 186–190, 200–201; charges dropped, 285n134; compared to American Revolution, 294n169; defense counsel, 297n51; effect on judicial thinking, 131; equalizing playing field, 160; evidentiary issues, 16; importance of, 159; judicial framing, 131; juror's perspective, 204–205; jury selection, 290n91; law reports, 294n7; pardons, 147, 164, 204–205;

procedural issues, 16, 173–177; process of, 161–162; rebel defense, 205–206; sources, 289n80, 290n99; story of, 129; study of, 129–130; test of government, 130; for treason, 10–11; treatment of, 295n15; vicinage, 16, 169–173; writs, 168–169. *See also specific cases*

Tucker, St. George: on artificial treason, 144; right to resist, 273n176; on secession, 227

25 Edw. III, 1351: indeterminacy, 217–218; precursor on treason, 144, 179

Union, the: preservation of, 49–50, 56, 156–157
U.S. Post, robbery of, 91
U.S. v. Barnet (1795), 176–177, 193–197
U.S. v. Burr (1807), 16, 227–230
U.S. v. Callender (1800), 280n26, 295n28
U.S. v. Hamilton (1795), 172, 174, 202
U.S. v. Jacob Wolf (1796), 68
U.S. v. Miller (1795), 140–141, 177, 197–198
U.S. v. Mitchell (1795), 176–177, 181–186, 291n114
U.S. v. Philson and Husband (1795), 198–200; on liberty poles, 110–111
U.S. v. Porter (1795), 176, 190–193, 292n147
U.S. v. Stewart and Wright (1795), 171–172, 174–175
U.S. v. The Insurgents of Pennsylvania (1795), 140, 175, 178, 202
U.S. v. Vigol (1795), 176, 179–180, 292n143, 294n175

Vanhorne's Lessee v. Dorrance (1795), 248
Vicinage: Brackenridge on, 169–170; concessions, 169; decision to move trials, 168–173; federal versus state control, 64, 170–172; "inconvenience," 171–172; law on, 170–172; protests, 169; Wilson on, 170
Vigol, Philip, 180
Virginia, 6, 7, 61

Washington, George: Address to Congress, November 19, 1794, 15, 41, 43–48, 205; Atlas, 244; cabinet, 262n85; Cincinnatus, 244; curtailing constitutional liberties, 49; decisional authority, 38–39, 43–44; on democratic societies, 40, 78; on dissenting meetings, 86; domestic threat, 49–51; on evidence, 167–168; Farewell Address, September, 19, 1796, 43–44, 49, 265n142; independence of, 45–46; "Instructions" to General Lee, 162–164; international affairs, 49, 50–52; judicial narrative and, 153; "King George," 105, 244; landholder, 7, 265–266n159, 266n161; "last ride," 1–2; liberty poles and, 109–110; mythic figure, 244; owning the narrative, 45–46; pardons, 205; on rebellion, 48; reputation, 2; on Shays's Rebellion, 159; supporting Hamilton, 27, 29, 261n47; suppressing rebellion, 51–52; visit to western troops, 6, 53, 124; "Washington Giving the Laws to America," 243; writing historical record, 46

Washington v. Scott et al. (1786), 296–297n49
"Watchman, The," 85
Wayne, Anthony, 52, 106
Webster, Noah, 15, 153
Whiskey Rebellion: discursive culture of, 14; frontier, 7; outbreak, 7; as regulation, 6; tax rebellion, 2; test case, 7–9, 29–30; whiskey as symbol, 259n48
Williams v. Craig (1788), 75
Wilson, James: Addison's support, 137; authorizing 1792 Militia Act, 15, 33–34, 38, 53, 166–168; on common law, 298n89; disgraced, 266n161; on evidence, 166–168; judicial positions, 283n97; landholder, 53, 266n161; lectures, 208; on levying war, 298nn73–74, 299–300nn108; on treason, 143–144, 147; two-witness standard, 299n98; on vicinage, 170, 172

www.ingramcontent.com/pod-product-compliance
Lightning Source LLC
Chambersburg PA
CBHW030519230426
43665CB00010B/681